JOHN CONSTANTINE

HELLBLAZER

TAINTED LOVE

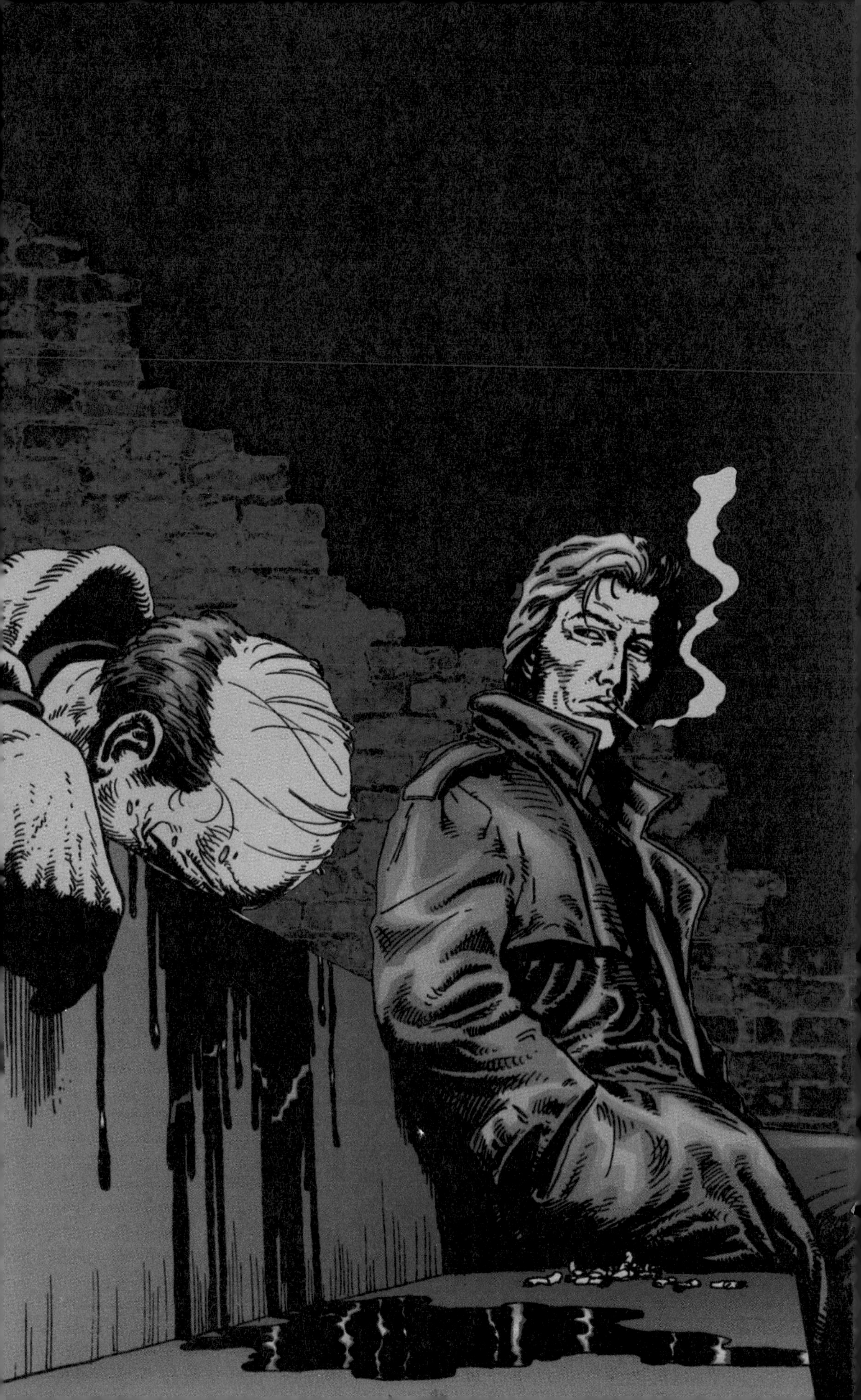

JOHN CONSTANTINE

HELLBLAZER

TAINTED LOVE

GARTH ENNIS
Writer

STEVE DILLON
Artist

TOM ZIUKO
STUART CHAIFETZ
Colorists

GASPAR SALADINO
Letterer

GLENN FABRY
Original covers

JOHN CONSTANTINE
HELLBLAZER
TAINTED LOVE

PUBLISHED BY DC COMICS. COVER,
INTRODUCTION AND COMPILATION
COPYRIGHT © 1998 DC COMICS.
ALL RIGHTS RESERVED.

ORIGINALLY PUBLISHED IN SINGLE
MAGAZINE FORM AS HELLBLAZER
68-71, VERTIGO JAM 1, HELLBLAZER
SPECIAL 1. COPYRIGHT © 1993 DC
COMICS. ALL RIGHTS RESERVED. ALL
CHARACTERS, THEIR DISTINCTIVE
LIKENESSES AND RELATED INDICIA
FEATURED IN THIS PUBLICATION ARE
TRADEMARKS OF DC COMICS.

THE STORIES, CHARACTERS,
AND INCIDENTS FEATURED IN
THIS PUBLICATION ARE ENTIRELY FICTIONAL.

DC COMICS, 1700 BROADWAY,
NEW YORK, NY 10019
A DIVISION OF WARNER BROS. -
A TIME WARNER ENTERTAINMENT
COMPANY

PRINTED IN CANADA. SECOND
PRINTING. ISBN: 1-56389-456-4
COVER ILLUSTRATION BY GLENN FABRY.

PUBLICATION DESIGN BY JASON LYONS.

TABLE OF CONTENTS

THE HELLBLAZER GALLERY

Man of mystery,
magus of great power—
these are two of
the facets of the man
called John Constantine.
Garbed in his familiar
trenchcoat, sporting
a trademark cigarette and
a cynical grin, Constantine
has practiced his unorthodox
brand of magic for years.
His recent love affair with
an old friend named Kit
seemed to lend him a new
stability, a fresh outlook
on life.

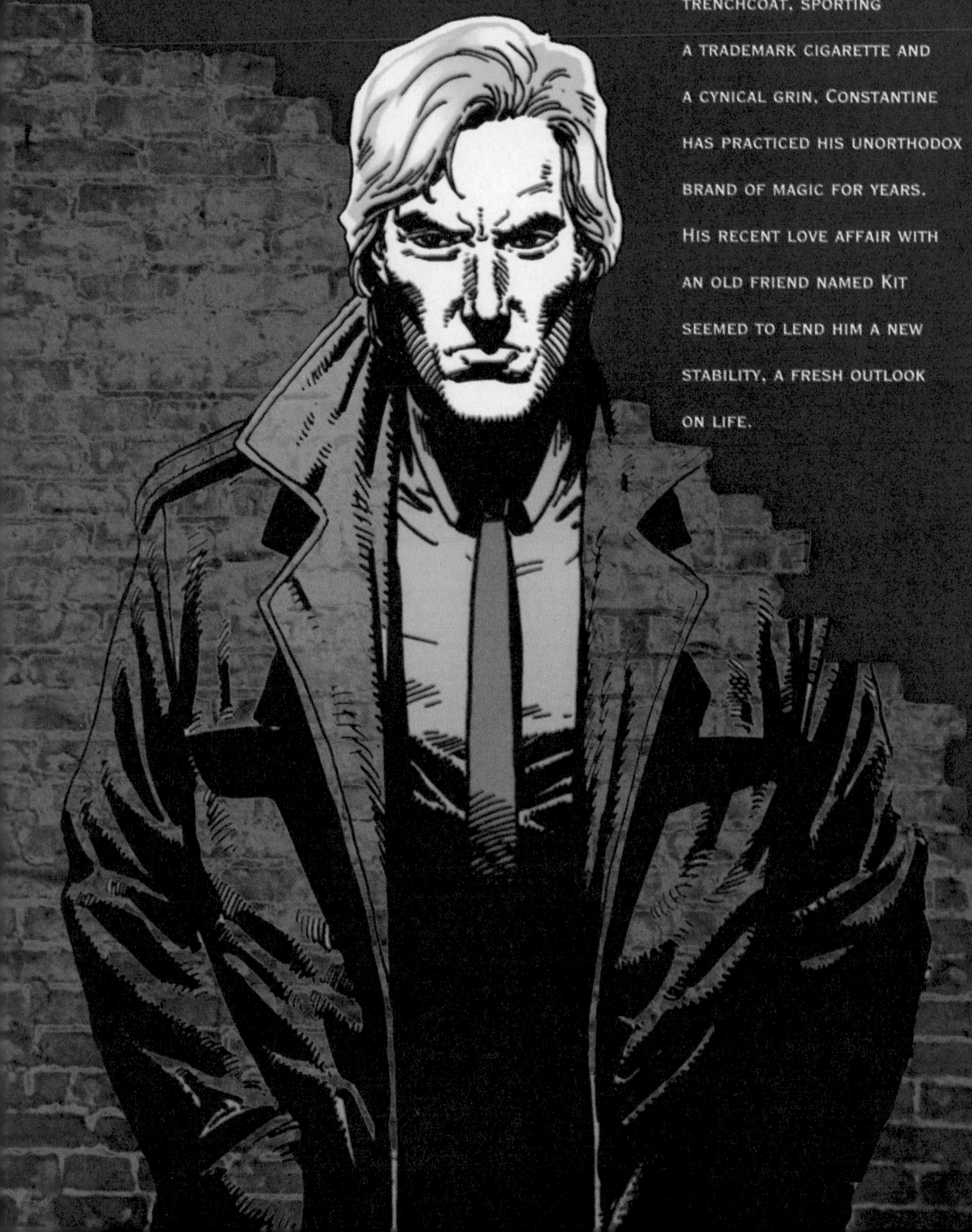

But magic always has its price, and there are other sides to John Constantine: the deceiver, the manipulator, the self-destructive victimizer. These aspects led Kit to leave him, sending him spiralling downward into despair.

Now he lives on the cold streets of London, finding what food and companionship he can among its forgotten denizens.

THE
LAST
NIGHT
OF THE
KING
OF THE
VAMPIRES

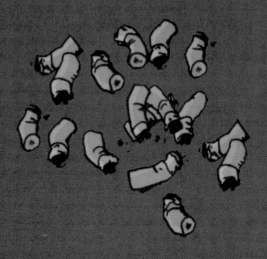

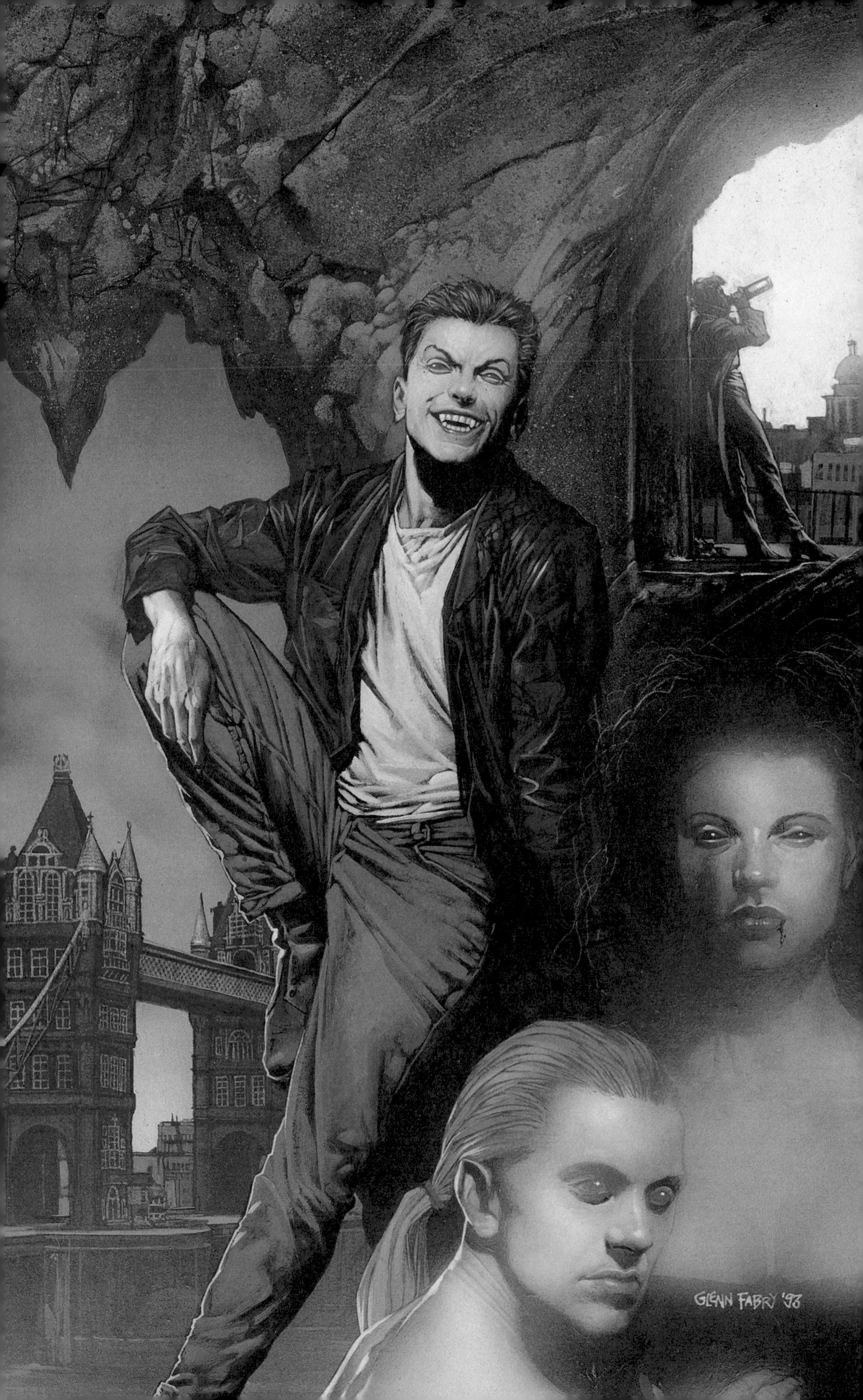
GLENN FABRY '93

HERE THEY ARE, THEN:

THERE'S KILLY FROM CORK, AND THE WEASEL WITH HIM. LIVING IN A KILBURN SQUAT 'TIL SOME TEAM OF BASTARDS KICKED THEM OUT. KILLY WAS STAMPIN' ON THE SECOND FELLA'S BALLS WHEN THE THIRD ONE SAPPED HIM.

HIS HEAD'S NOT BEEN RIGHT SINCE.

WEE SUE, WHO BIT A COPPER'S EAR HALF OFF HIM DOWN THE DILLY. FRIGGER DESERVED IT.

THE MILWALL CREW, WITH ANDY SEVERELY DOUBTIN' HE CAN KEEP THESE BASTARD TOMATOES DOWN FROM THE LOOK'VE THEM, AND KERNAHAN SPITTIN' THE TEETH AND BLOOD IT TOOK TO OPEN THE CAN...

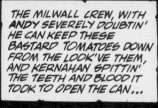

THOUSANDS MORE JUST LIKE THEM, BRITTLE LIVES OF COLD AND SICKNESS. LEANING ON IRON, LYING ON STONE, SOFT THINGS FORGOTTEN. PISS FROM THE SKY.

BRICK WALL ENDINGS.

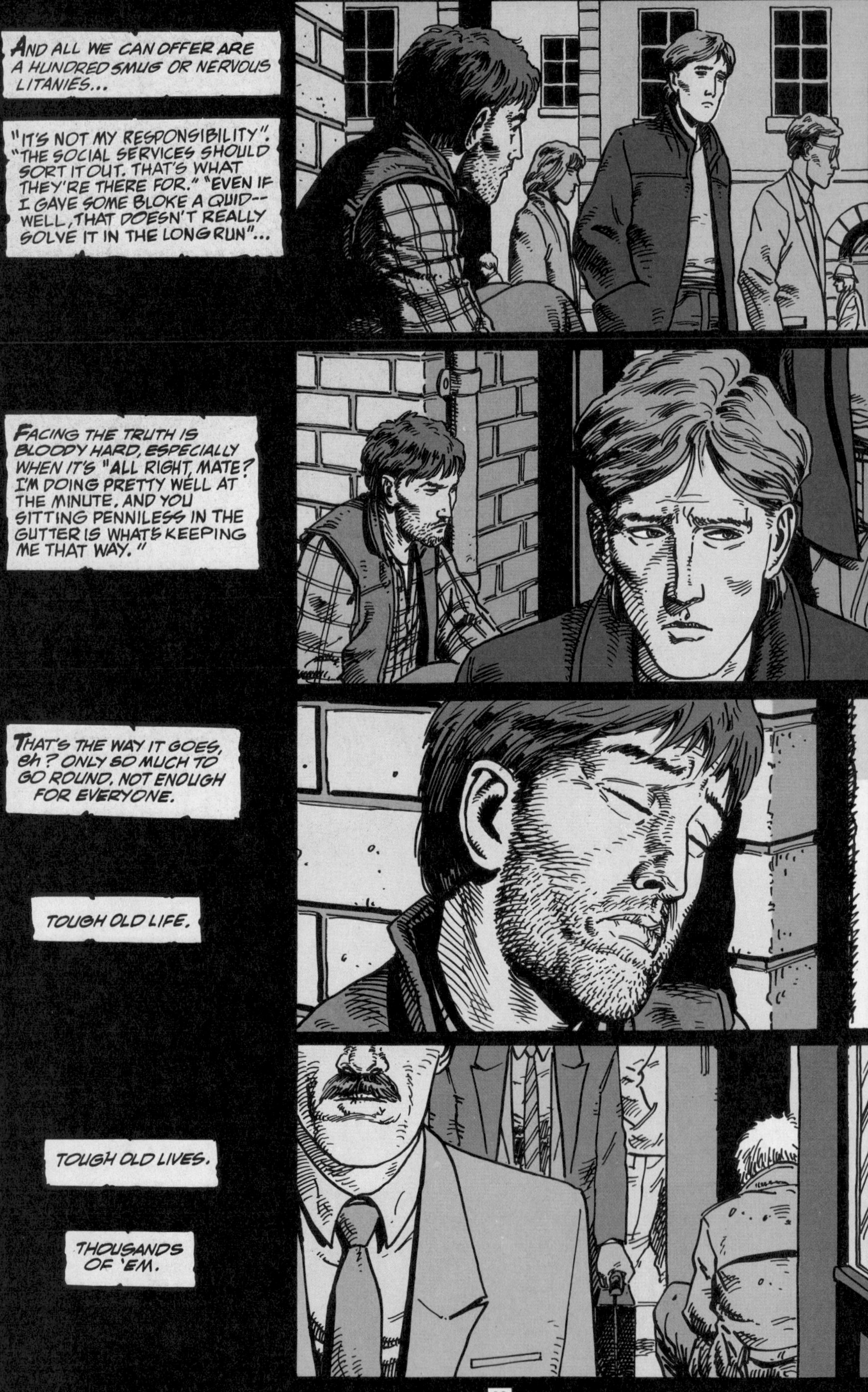
AND ALL WE CAN OFFER ARE A HUNDRED SMUG OR NERVOUS LITANIES...
"IT'S NOT MY RESPONSIBILITY". "THE SOCIAL SERVICES SHOULD SORT IT OUT. THAT'S WHAT THEY'RE THERE FOR." "EVEN IF I GAVE SOME BLOKE A QUID-- WELL, THAT DOESN'T REALLY SOLVE IT IN THE LONG RUN"...
FACING THE TRUTH IS BLOODY HARD, ESPECIALLY WHEN IT'S "ALL RIGHT, MATE? I'M DOING PRETTY WELL AT THE MINUTE, AND YOU SITTING PENNILESS IN THE GUTTER IS WHAT'S KEEPING ME THAT WAY."
THAT'S THE WAY IT GOES, eh? ONLY SO MUCH TO GO ROUND, NOT ENOUGH FOR EVERYONE.
TOUGH OLD LIFE.
TOUGH OLD LIVES.
THOUSANDS OF 'EM.

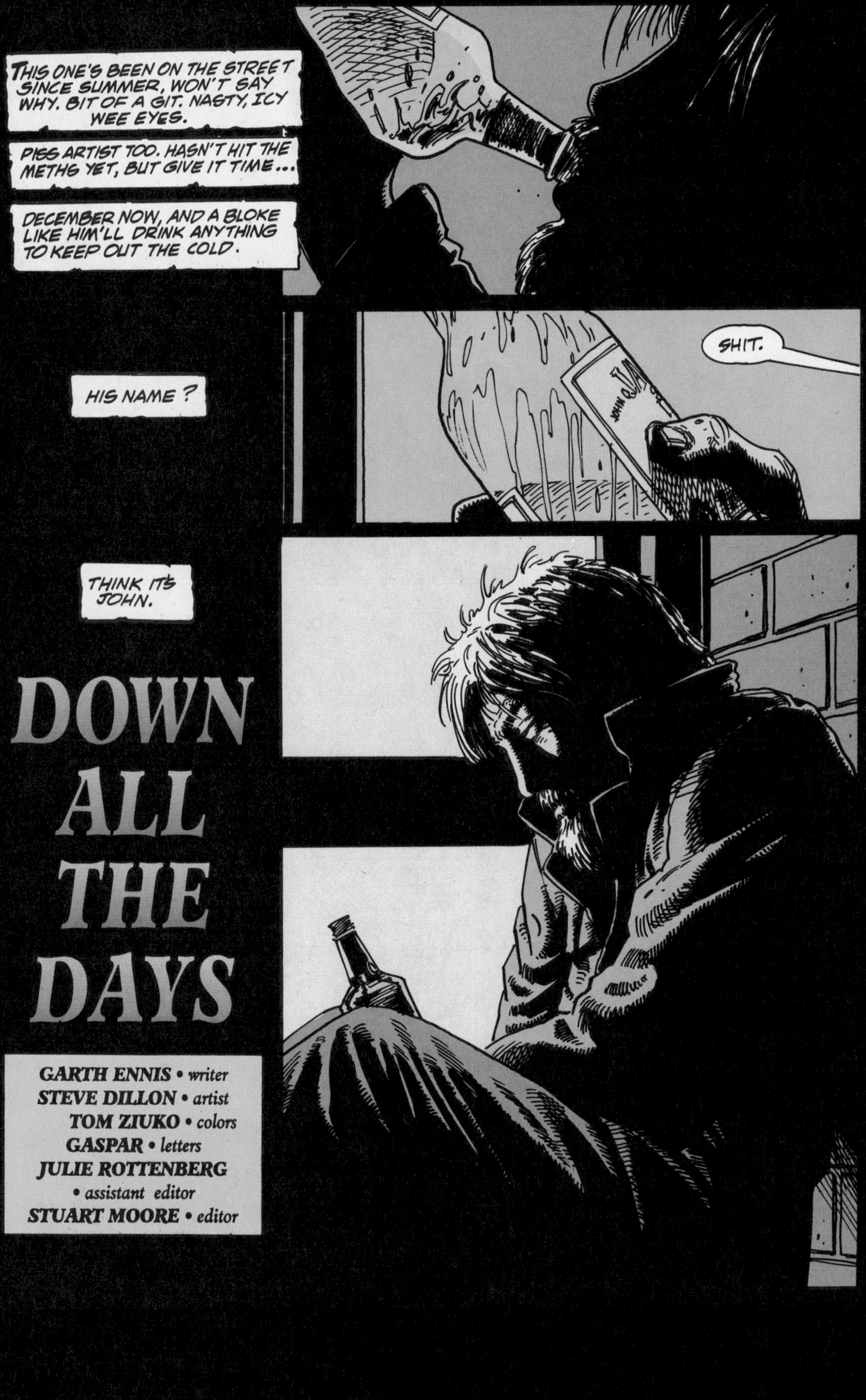
THIS ONE'S BEEN ON THE STREET SINCE SUMMER, WON'T SAY WHY. BIT OF A GIT. NASTY, ICY WEE EYES.
PISS ARTIST TOO. HASN'T HIT THE METHS YET, BUT GIVE IT TIME...
DECEMBER NOW, AND A BLOKE LIKE HIM'LL DRINK ANYTHING TO KEEP OUT THE COLD.
HIS NAME ?
SHIT.
THINK IT'S JOHN.
DOWN ALL THE DAYS
GARTH ENNIS • writer
STEVE DILLON • artist
TOM ZIUKO • colors
GASPAR • letters
JULIE ROTTENBERG • assistant editor
STUART MOORE • editor

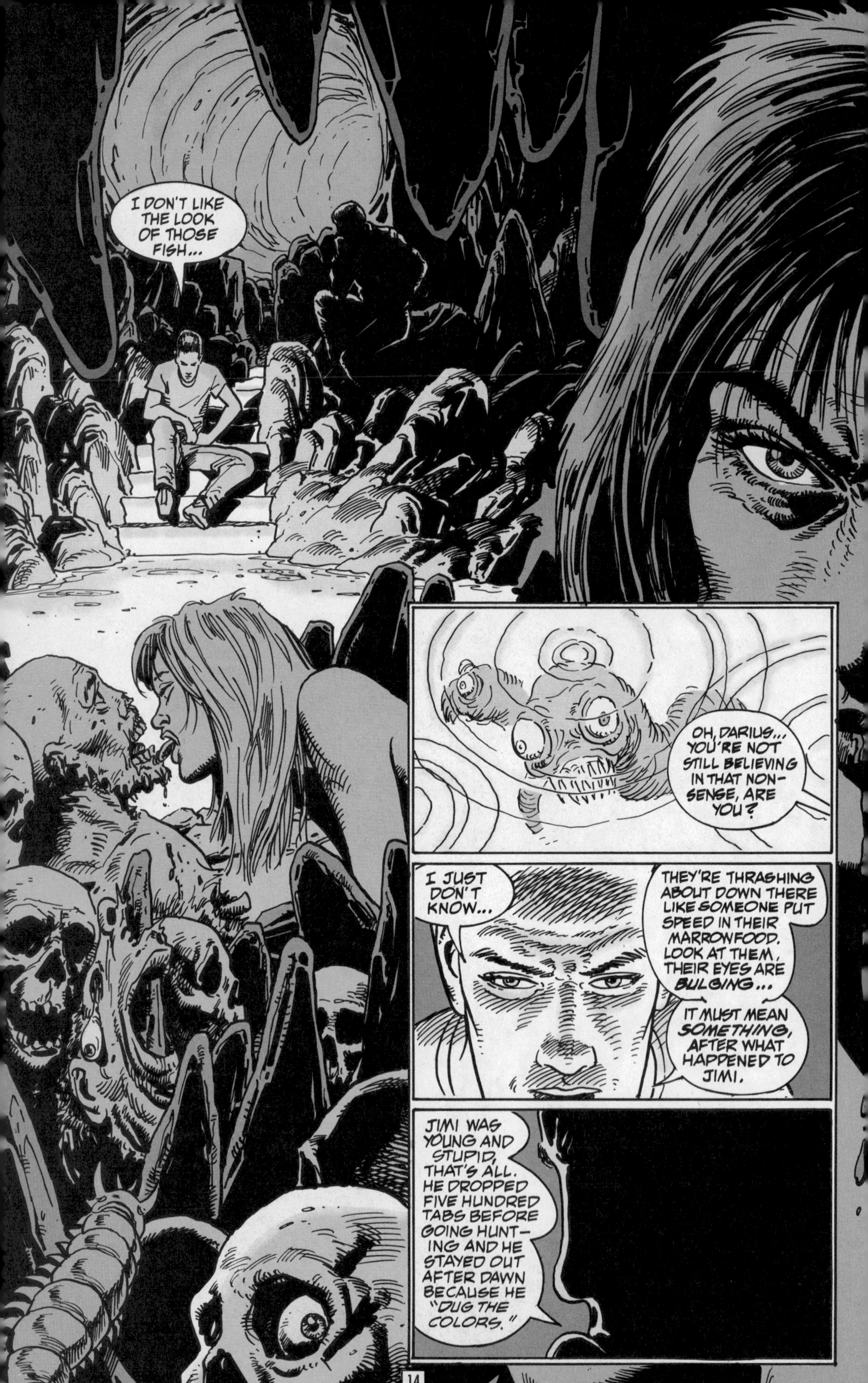
I DON'T LIKE THE LOOK OF THOSE FISH...
OH, DARIUS... YOU'RE NOT STILL BELIEVING IN THAT NON-SENSE, ARE YOU?
I JUST DON'T KNOW...
THEY'RE THRASHING ABOUT DOWN THERE LIKE SOMEONE PUT SPEED IN THEIR MARROWFOOD. LOOK AT THEM, THEIR EYES ARE *BULGING*...
IT MUST MEAN *SOMETHING*, AFTER WHAT HAPPENED TO JIMI.
JIMI WAS YOUNG AND STUPID, THAT'S ALL. HE DROPPED FIVE HUNDRED TABS BEFORE GOING HUNT-ING AND HE STAYED OUT AFTER DAWN BECAUSE HE "DUG THE COLORS."

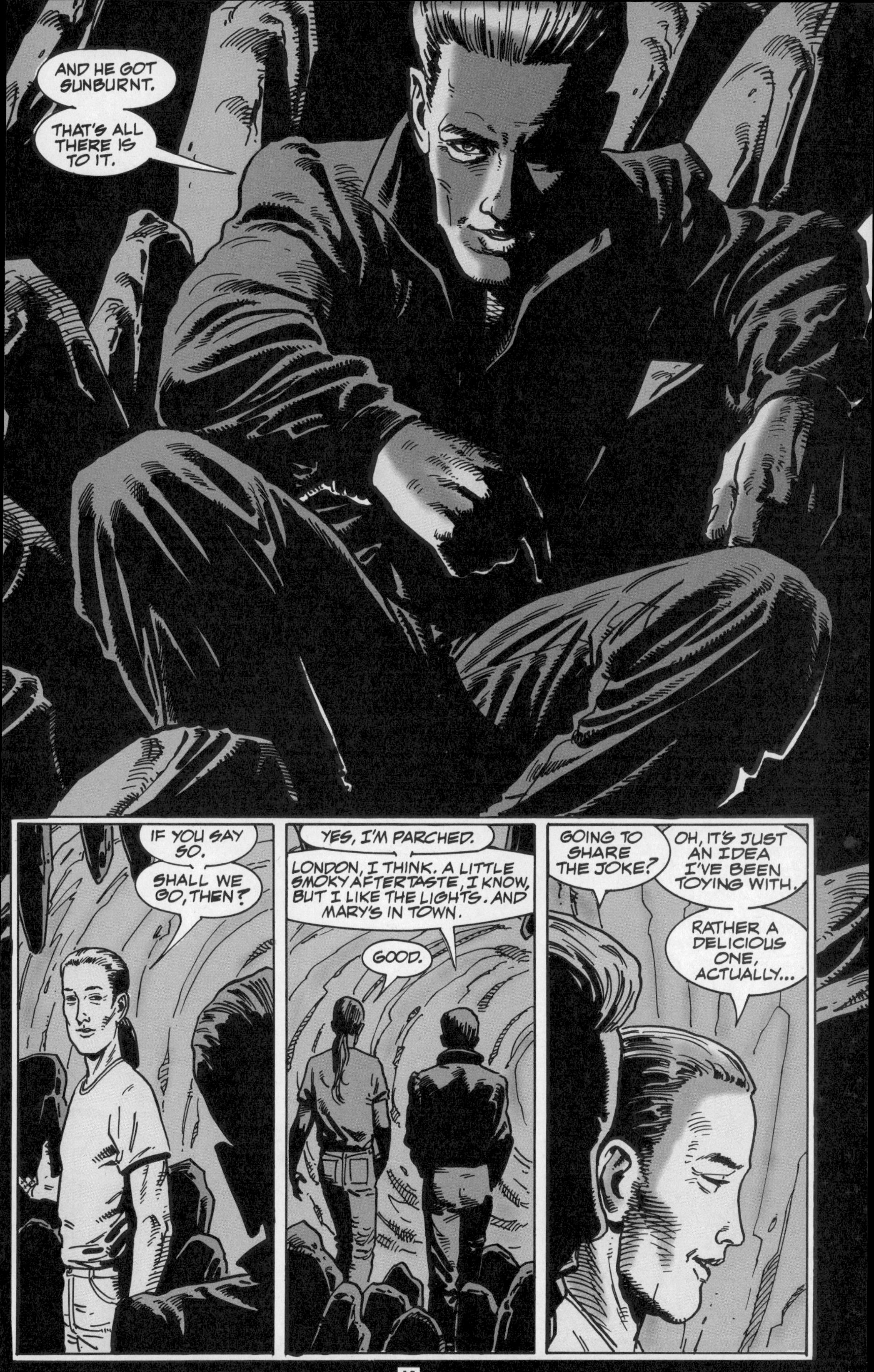
AND HE GOT SUNBURNT.
THAT'S ALL THERE IS TO IT.
IF YOU SAY SO.
SHALL WE GO, THEN?
YES, I'M PARCHED.
LONDON, I THINK. A LITTLE SMOKY AFTERTASTE, I KNOW, BUT I LIKE THE LIGHTS. AND MARY'S IN TOWN.
GOOD.
GOING TO SHARE THE JOKE?
OH, IT'S JUST AN IDEA I'VE BEEN TOYING WITH.
RATHER A DELICIOUS ONE, ACTUALLY...

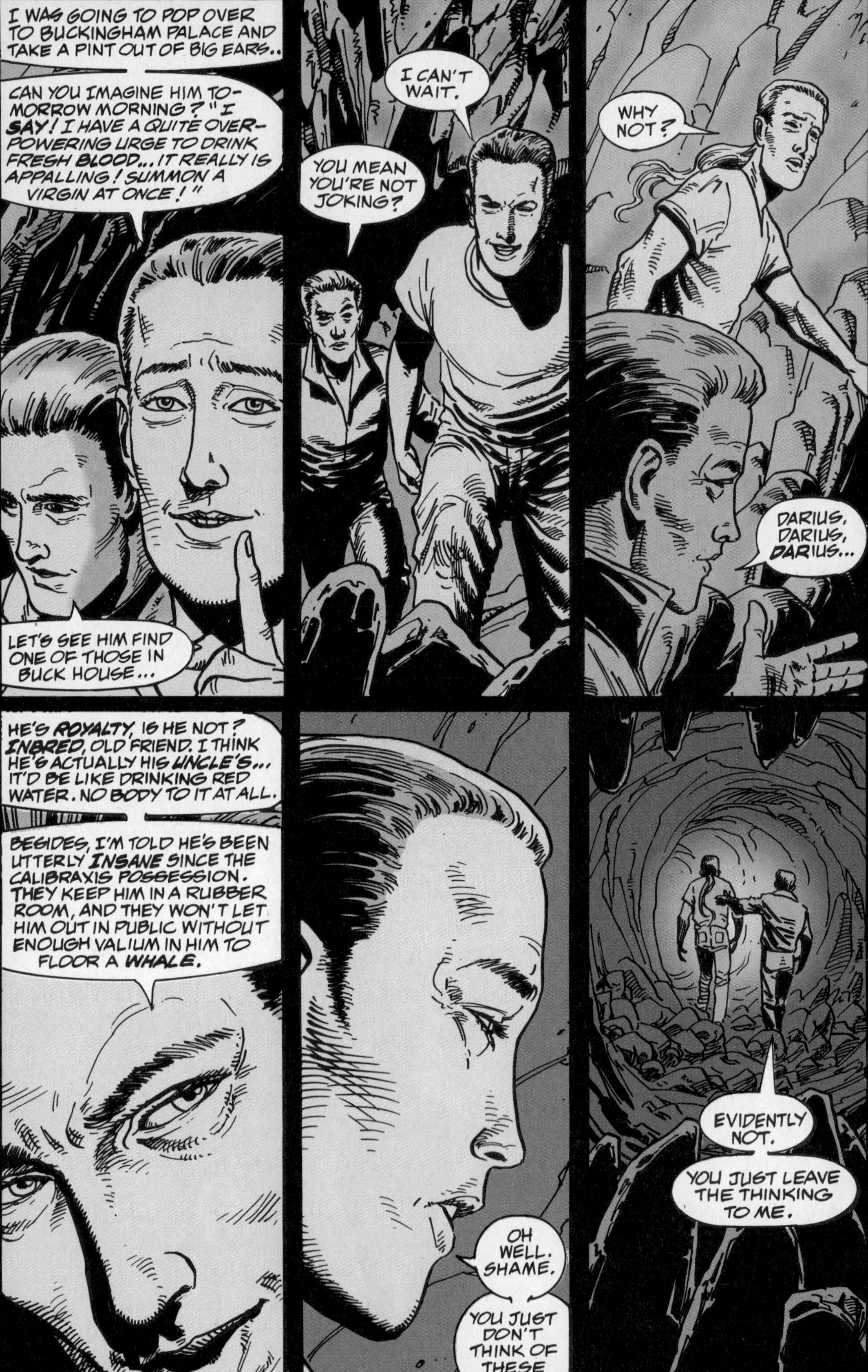

I WAS GOING TO POP OVER TO BUCKINGHAM PALACE AND TAKE A PINT OUT OF BIG EARS..
CAN YOU IMAGINE HIM TO-MORROW MORNING? "I SAY! I HAVE A QUITE OVER-POWERING URGE TO DRINK FRESH BLOOD... IT REALLY IS APPALLING! SUMMON A VIRGIN AT ONCE!"
LET'S SEE HIM FIND ONE OF THOSE IN BUCK HOUSE...
I CAN'T WAIT.
YOU MEAN YOU'RE NOT JOKING?
WHY NOT?
DARIUS, DARIUS, DARIUS...
HE'S ROYALTY, IS HE NOT? INBRED, OLD FRIEND. I THINK HE'S ACTUALLY HIS UNCLE'S... IT'D BE LIKE DRINKING RED WATER. NO BODY TO IT AT ALL.
BESIDES, I'M TOLD HE'S BEEN UTTERLY INSANE SINCE THE CALIBRAXIS POSSESSION. THEY KEEP HIM IN A RUBBER ROOM, AND THEY WON'T LET HIM OUT IN PUBLIC WITHOUT ENOUGH VALIUM IN HIM TO FLOOR A WHALE.
OH WELL. SHAME.
YOU JUST DON'T THINK OF THESE THINGS...
EVIDENTLY NOT.
YOU JUST LEAVE THE THINKING TO ME.

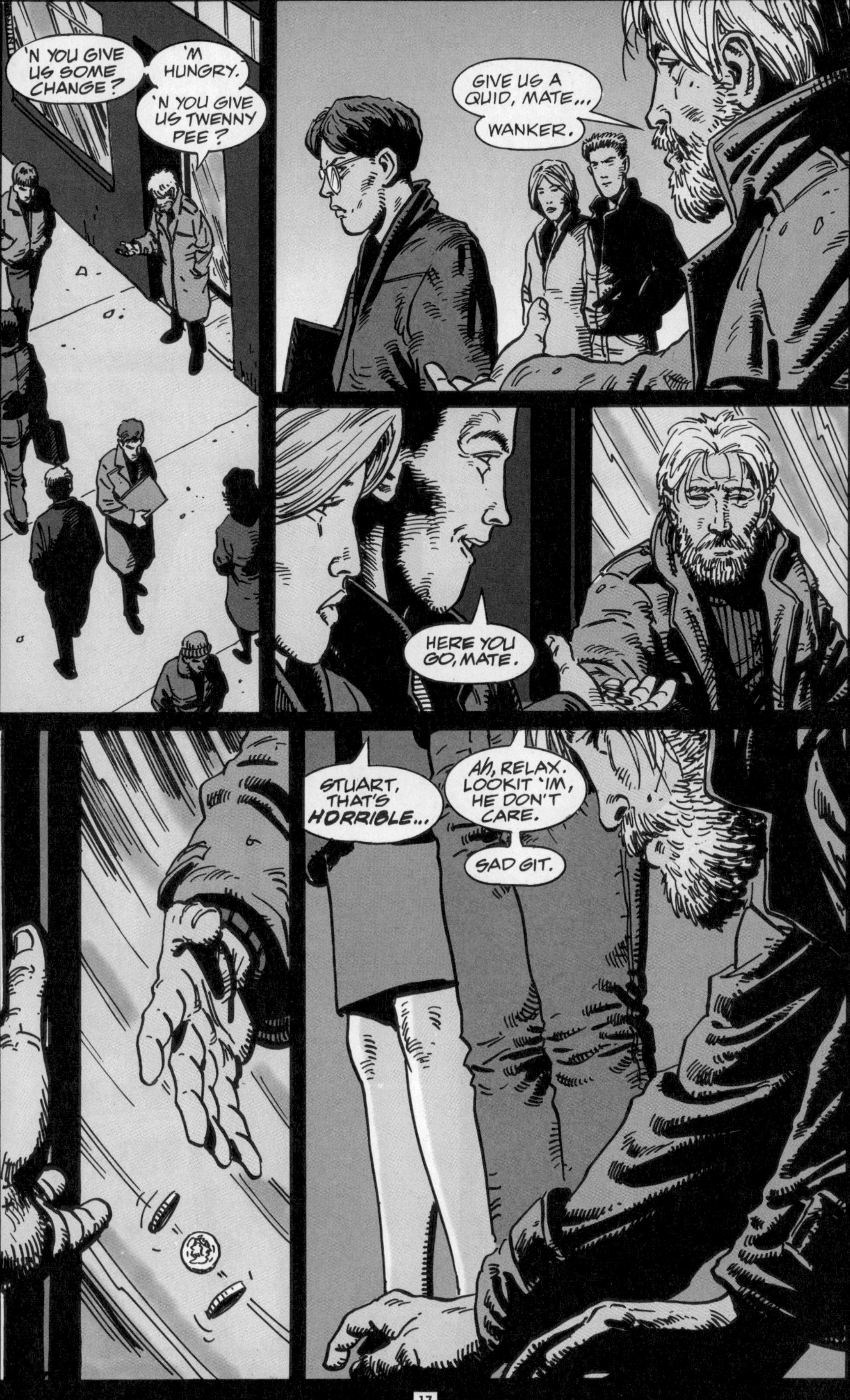
'N YOU GIVE US SOME CHANGE?
'M HUNGRY.
'N YOU GIVE US TWENNY PEE?
GIVE US A QUID, MATE...
WANKER.
HERE YOU GO, MATE.
STUART, THAT'S HORRIBLE...
AH, RELAX. LOOKIT 'IM, HE DON'T CARE.
SAD GIT.

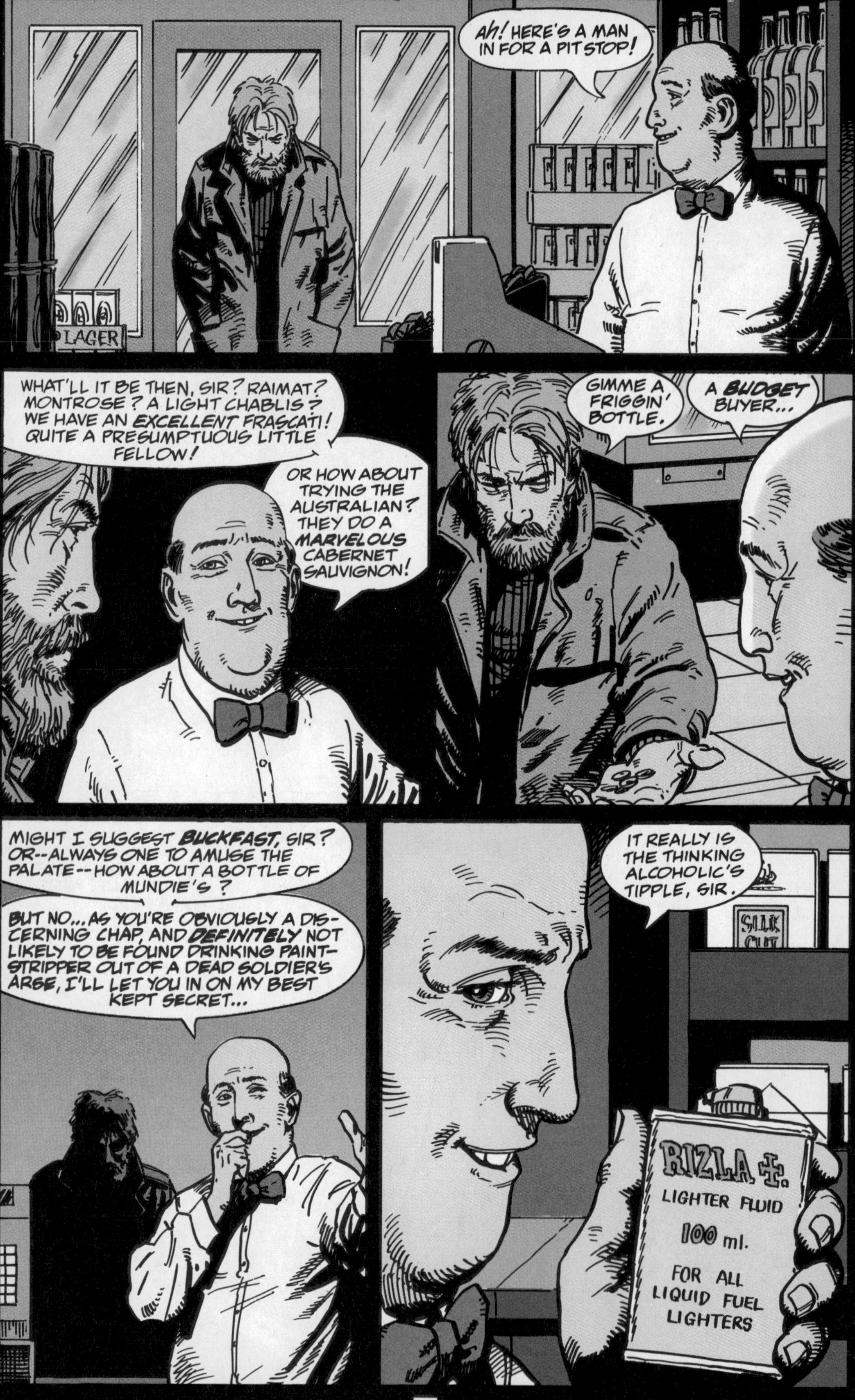
LAGER
AH! HERE'S A MAN IN FOR A PIT STOP!
WHAT'LL IT BE THEN, SIR? RAIMAT? MONTROSE? A LIGHT CHABLIS? WE HAVE AN EXCELLENT FRASCATI! QUITE A PRESUMPTUOUS LITTLE FELLOW!
OR HOW ABOUT TRYING THE AUSTRALIAN? THEY DO A MARVELOUS CABERNET SAUVIGNON!
GIMME A FRIGGIN' BOTTLE.
A BUDGET BUYER...
MIGHT I SUGGEST BUCKFAST, SIR? OR--ALWAYS ONE TO AMUSE THE PALATE--HOW ABOUT A BOTTLE OF MUNDIE'S?
BUT NO... AS YOU'RE OBVIOUSLY A DISCERNING CHAP, AND DEFINITELY NOT LIKELY TO BE FOUND DRINKING PAINT-STRIPPER OUT OF A DEAD SOLDIER'S ARSE, I'LL LET YOU IN ON MY BEST KEPT SECRET...
IT REALLY IS THE THINKING ALCOHOLIC'S TIPPLE, SIR.
SILK CUT
RIZLA +
LIGHTER FLUID
100 ml.
FOR ALL LIQUID FUEL LIGHTERS

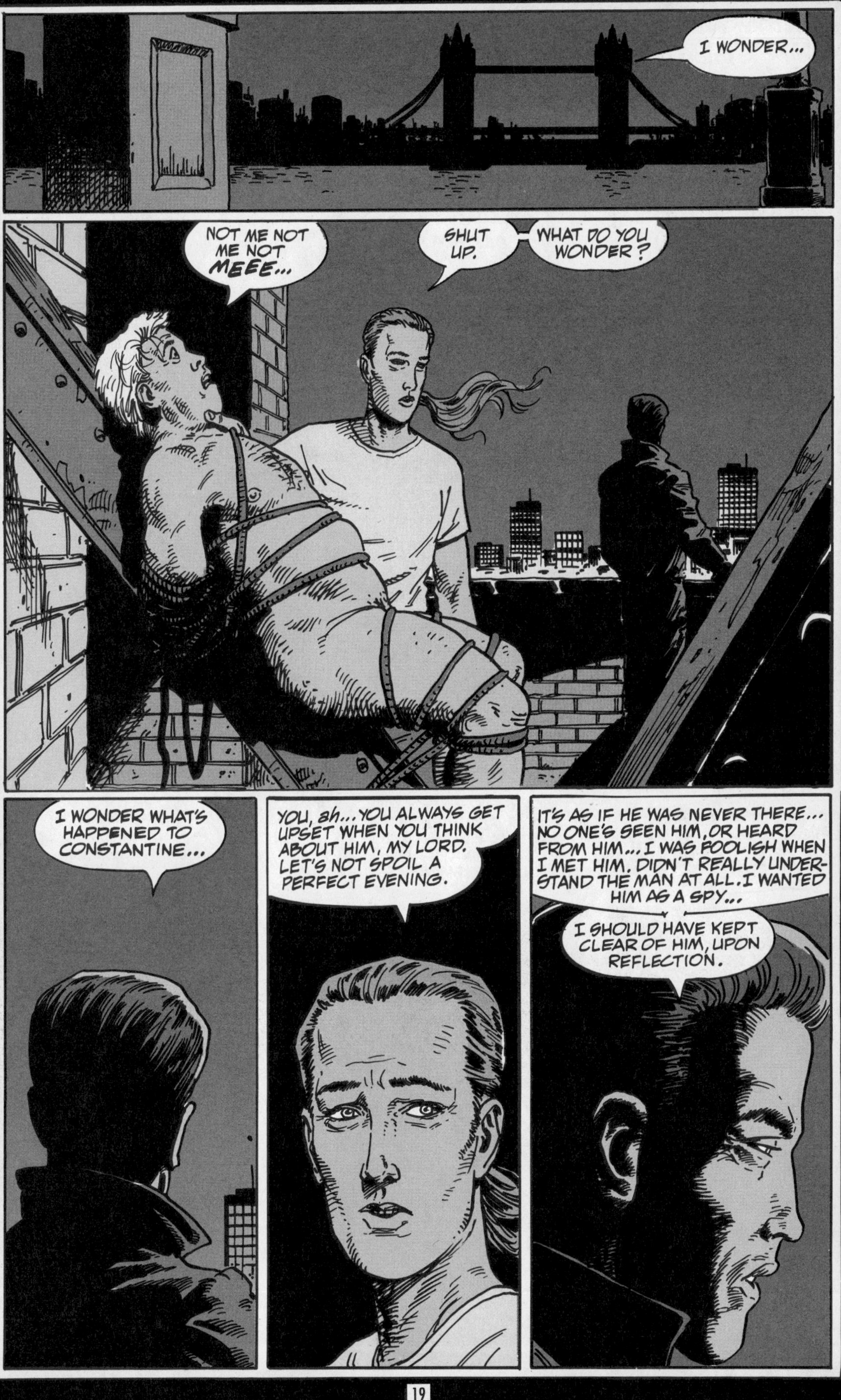
I WONDER...
NOT ME NOT ME NOT MEEE...
SHUT UP.
WHAT DO YOU WONDER?
I WONDER WHAT'S HAPPENED TO CONSTANTINE...
YOU, ah... YOU ALWAYS GET UPSET WHEN YOU THINK ABOUT HIM, MY LORD. LET'S NOT SPOIL A PERFECT EVENING.
IT'S AS IF HE WAS NEVER THERE... NO ONE'S SEEN HIM, OR HEARD FROM HIM... I WAS FOOLISH WHEN I MET HIM. DIDN'T REALLY UNDERSTAND THE MAN AT ALL. I WANTED HIM AS A SPY...
I SHOULD HAVE KEPT CLEAR OF HIM, UPON REFLECTION.

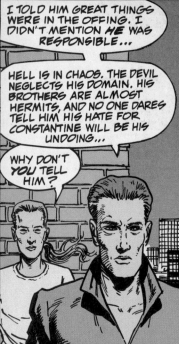

I TOLD HIM GREAT THINGS WERE IN THE OFFING. I DIDN'T MENTION *HE* WAS RESPONSIBLE...

HELL IS IN CHAOS. THE DEVIL NEGLECTS HIS DOMAIN. HIS BROTHERS ARE ALMOST HERMITS, AND NO ONE DARES TELL HIM HIS HATE FOR CONSTANTINE WILL BE HIS UNDOING...

WHY DON'T *YOU* TELL HIM?

BECAUSE I COULDN'T CARE LESS, ONE WAY OR THE OTHER.

WE'VE NEVER REALLY GOTTEN ON. HE SEES ME AS A USELESS HEDONIST, A DANDY WHO MEDDLES WITH THE WORLD FOR MY AMUSEMENT...

I SEE HIM AS A USELESS ANTIQUE.

PONDERING THE GRAND DESIGN AGAIN, MY LORD?

MARY...

AND WHAT HAVE YOU BEEN UP TO?

JUST THE USUAL DEPRAVITY.

CINDY SENDS HER LOVE, BUT IS OCCUPIED WITH THE ISRAELITES... A PITY. *I* THINK TONIGHT WILL BE WONDERFUL.

AND I SEE YOU'VE BROUGHT SOMETHING TO DRINK.

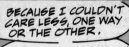

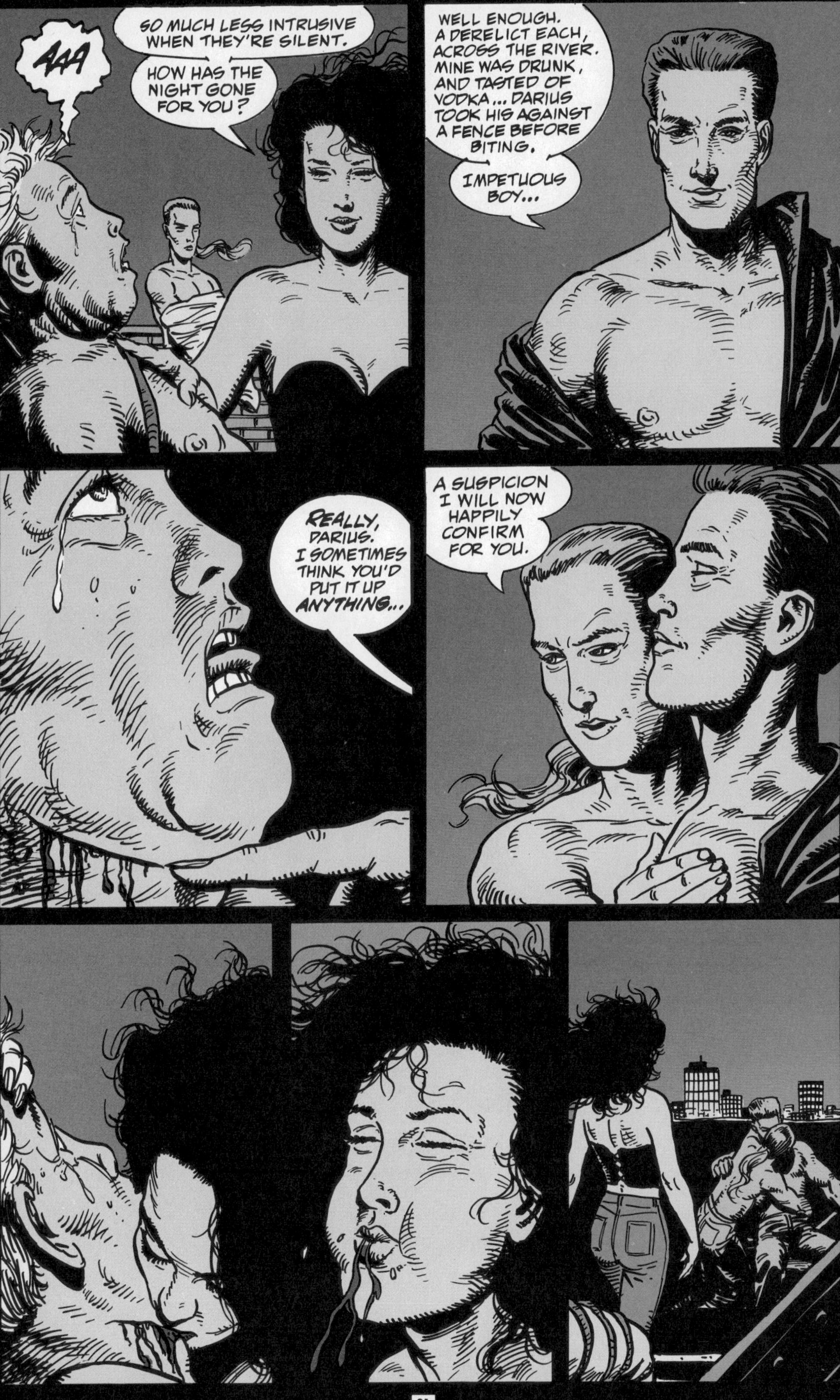
AAA
SO MUCH LESS INTRUSIVE WHEN THEY'RE SILENT.
HOW HAS THE NIGHT GONE FOR YOU?
WELL ENOUGH. A DERELICT EACH, ACROSS THE RIVER. MINE WAS DRUNK, AND TASTED OF VODKA... DARIUS TOOK HIS AGAINST A FENCE BEFORE BITING.
IMPETUOUS BOY...
REALLY, DARIUS. I SOMETIMES THINK YOU'D PUT IT UP ANYTHING...
A SUSPICION I WILL NOW HAPPILY CONFIRM FOR YOU.

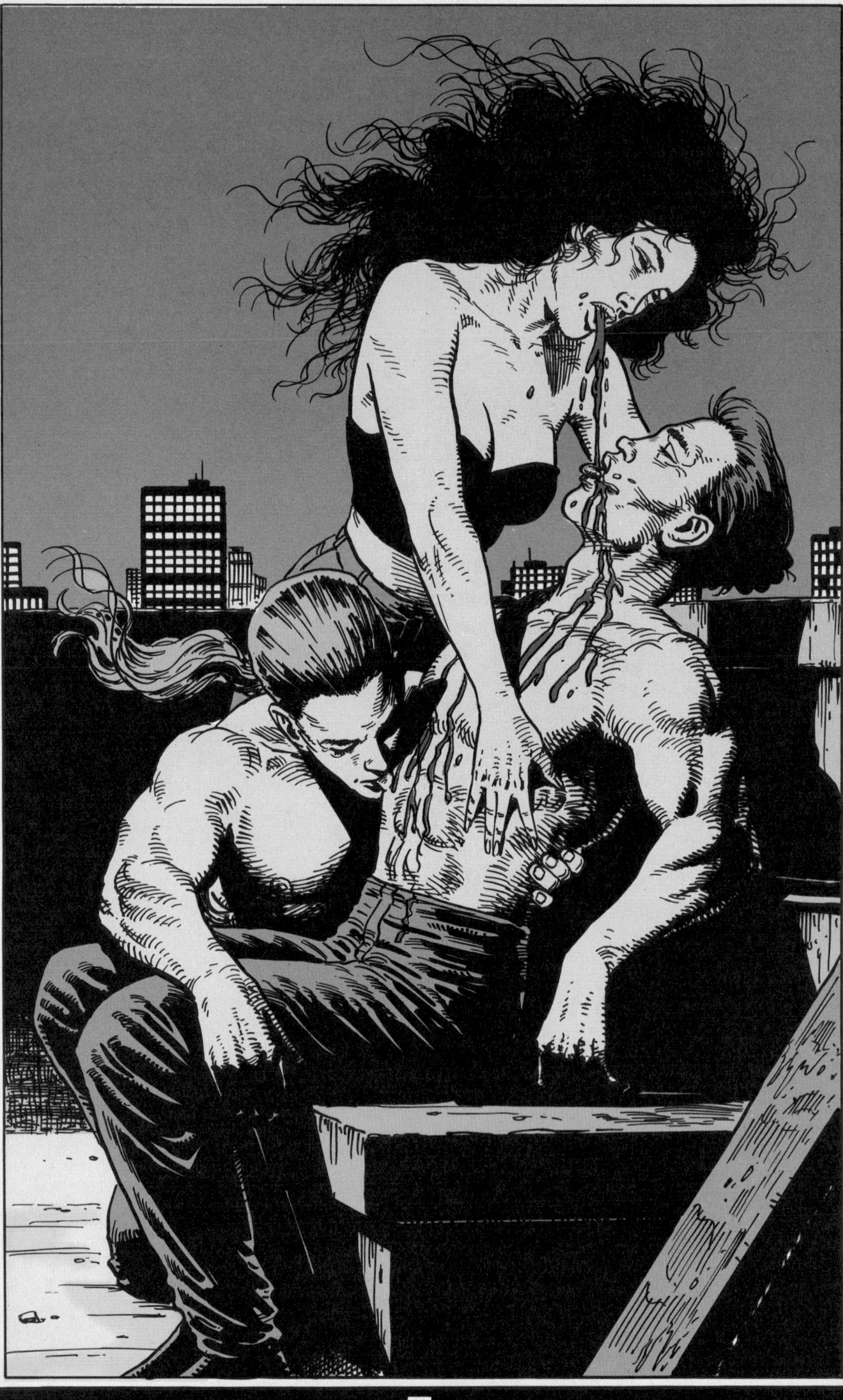

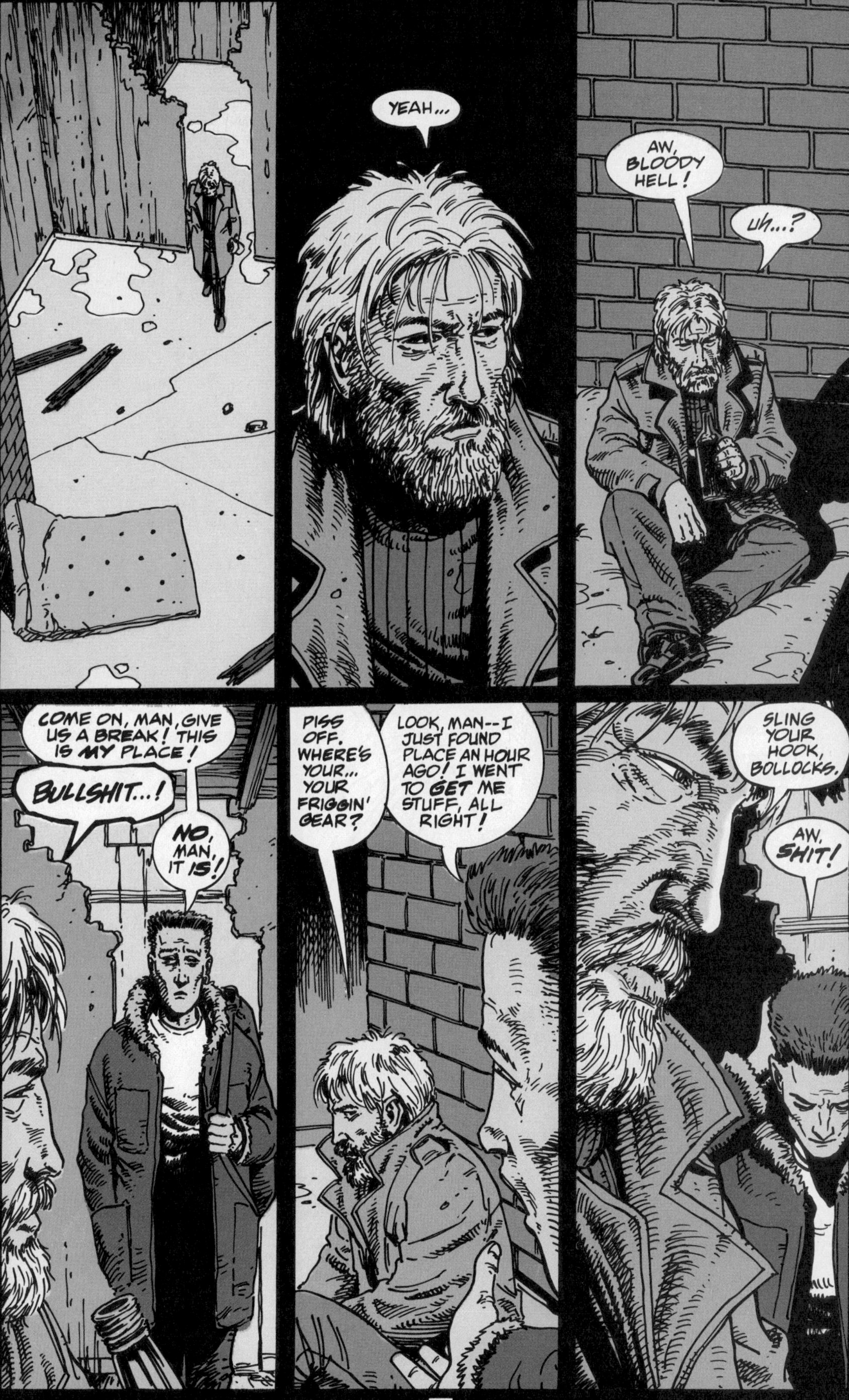
YEAH...
AW, BLOODY HELL!
uh...?
COME ON, MAN, GIVE US A BREAK! THIS IS MY PLACE!
BULLSHIT...!
NO, MAN, IT IS!
PISS OFF. WHERE'S YOUR... YOUR FRIGGIN' GEAR?
LOOK, MAN-- I JUST FOUND PLACE AN HOUR AGO! I WENT TO GET ME STUFF, ALL RIGHT!
SLING YOUR HOOK, BOLLOCKS.
AW, SHIT!

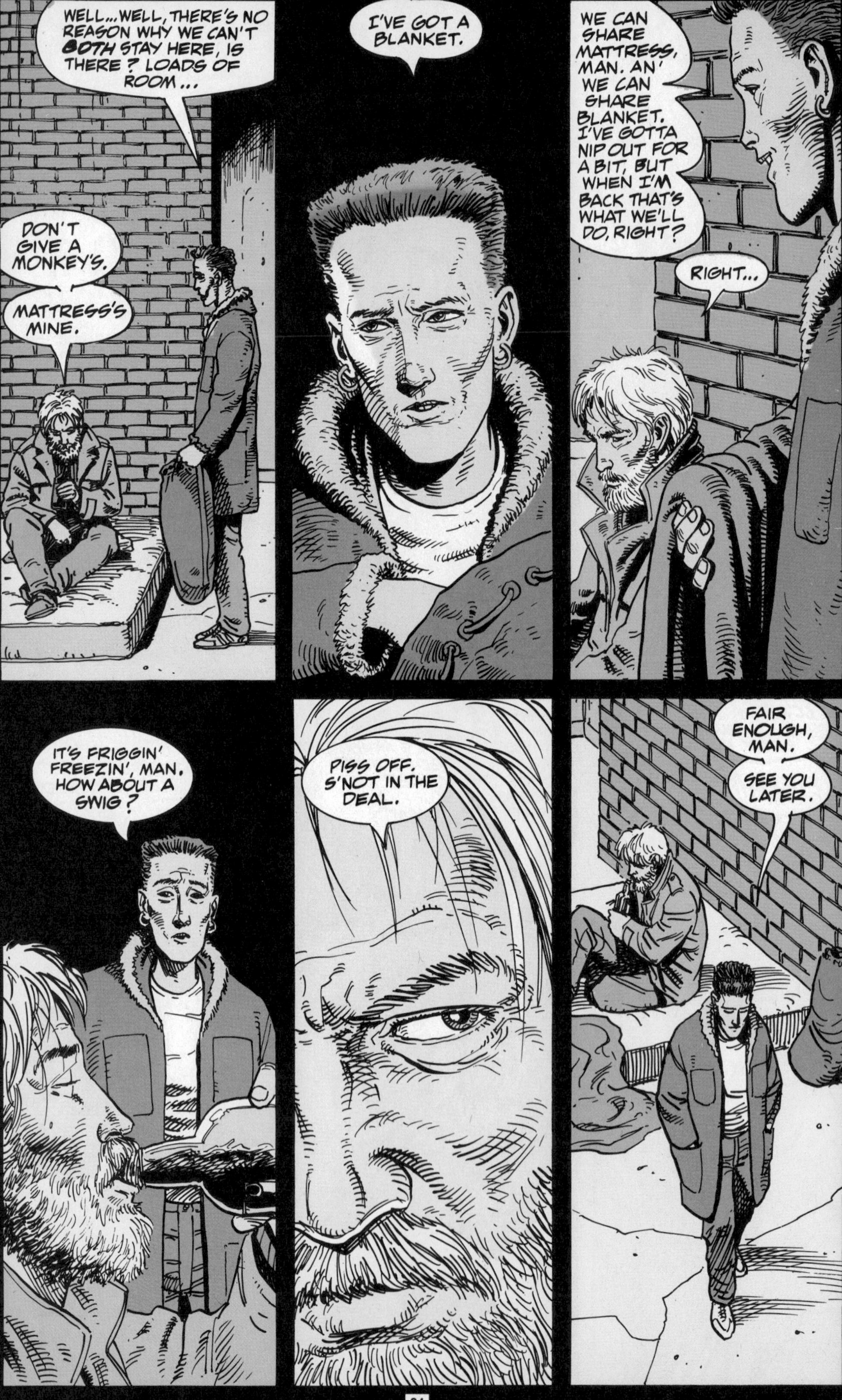
WELL...WELL, THERE'S NO REASON WHY WE CAN'T BOTH STAY HERE, IS THERE? LOADS OF ROOM...
DON'T GIVE A MONKEY'S.
MATTRESS'S MINE.
I'VE GOT A BLANKET.
WE CAN SHARE MATTRESS, MAN. AN' WE CAN SHARE BLANKET. I'VE GOTTA NIP OUT FOR A BIT, BUT WHEN I'M BACK THAT'S WHAT WE'LL DO, RIGHT?
RIGHT...
IT'S FRIGGIN' FREEZIN', MAN. HOW ABOUT A SWIG?
PISS OFF. S'NOT IN THE DEAL.
FAIR ENOUGH, MAN.
SEE YOU LATER.

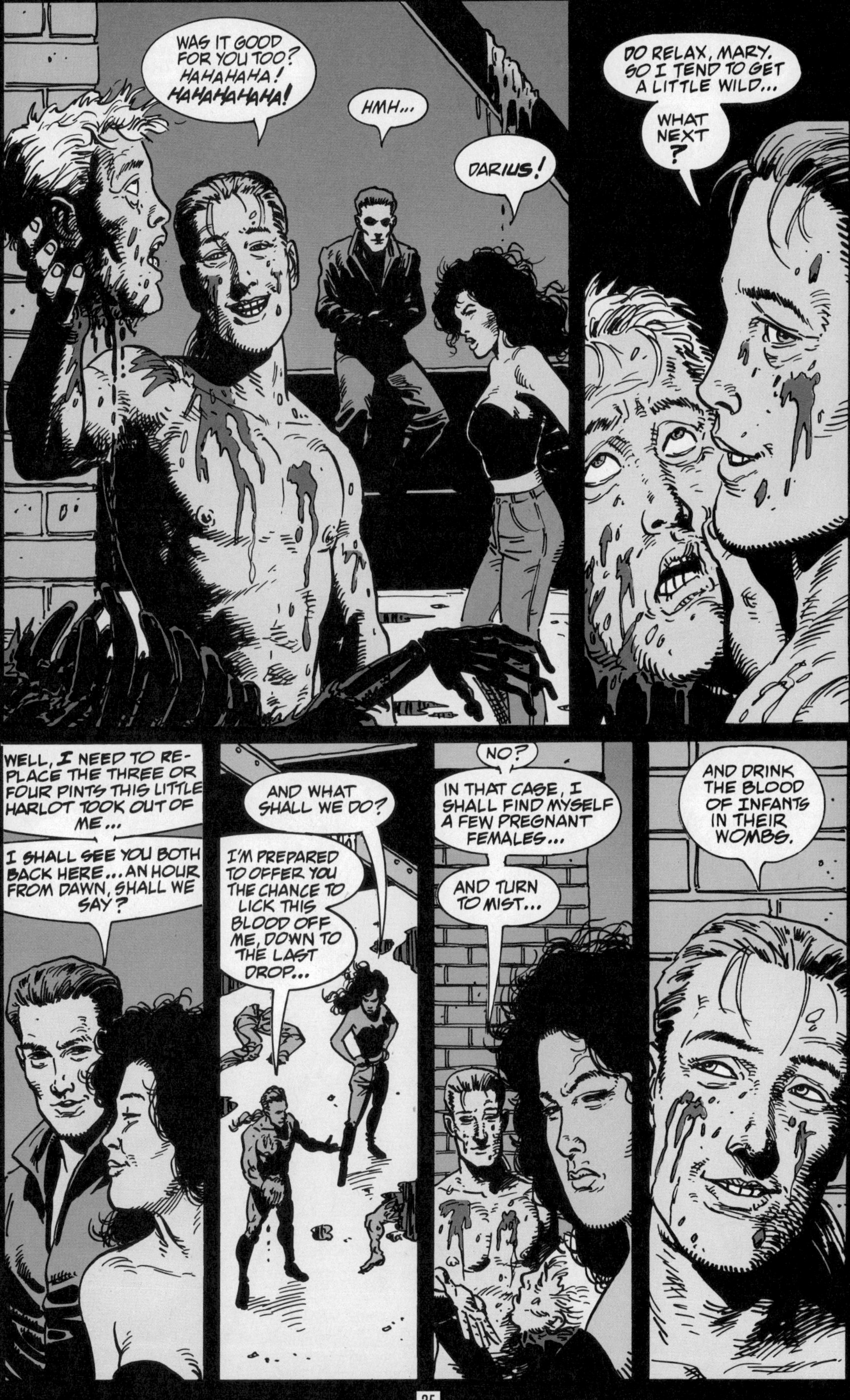
WAS IT GOOD FOR YOU TOO? HAHAHAHA! HAHAHAHAHA!
HMH...
DARIUS!
DO RELAX, MARY. SO I TEND TO GET A LITTLE WILD...
WHAT NEXT?
WELL, I NEED TO RE-PLACE THE THREE OR FOUR PINTS THIS LITTLE HARLOT TOOK OUT OF ME...
I SHALL SEE YOU BOTH BACK HERE... AN HOUR FROM DAWN, SHALL WE SAY?
AND WHAT SHALL WE DO?
I'M PREPARED TO OFFER YOU THE CHANCE TO LICK THIS BLOOD OFF ME, DOWN TO THE LAST DROP...
NO?
IN THAT CASE, I SHALL FIND MYSELF A FEW PREGNANT FEMALES...
AND TURN TO MIST...
AND DRINK THE BLOOD OF INFANTS IN THEIR WOMBS.

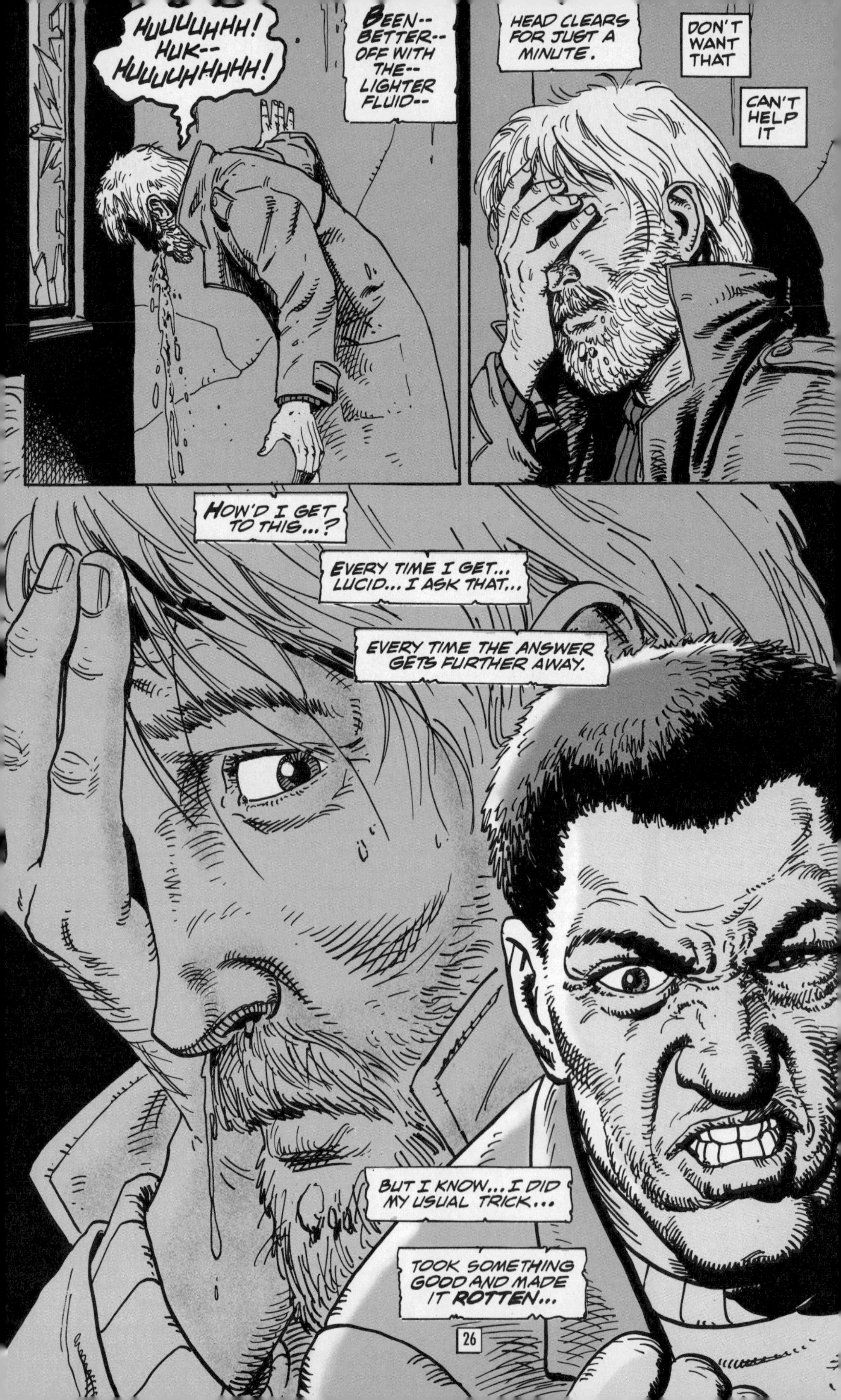
HUUUUHHH! HUK-- HUUUUHHHHH!
BEEN-- BETTER-- OFF WITH THE-- LIGHTER FLUID--
HEAD CLEARS FOR JUST A MINUTE.
DON'T WANT THAT
CAN'T HELP IT
HOW'D I GET TO THIS...?
EVERY TIME I GET... LUCID... I ASK THAT...
EVERY TIME THE ANSWER GETS FURTHER AWAY.
BUT I KNOW... I DID MY USUAL TRICK...
TOOK SOMETHING GOOD AND MADE IT ROTTEN...

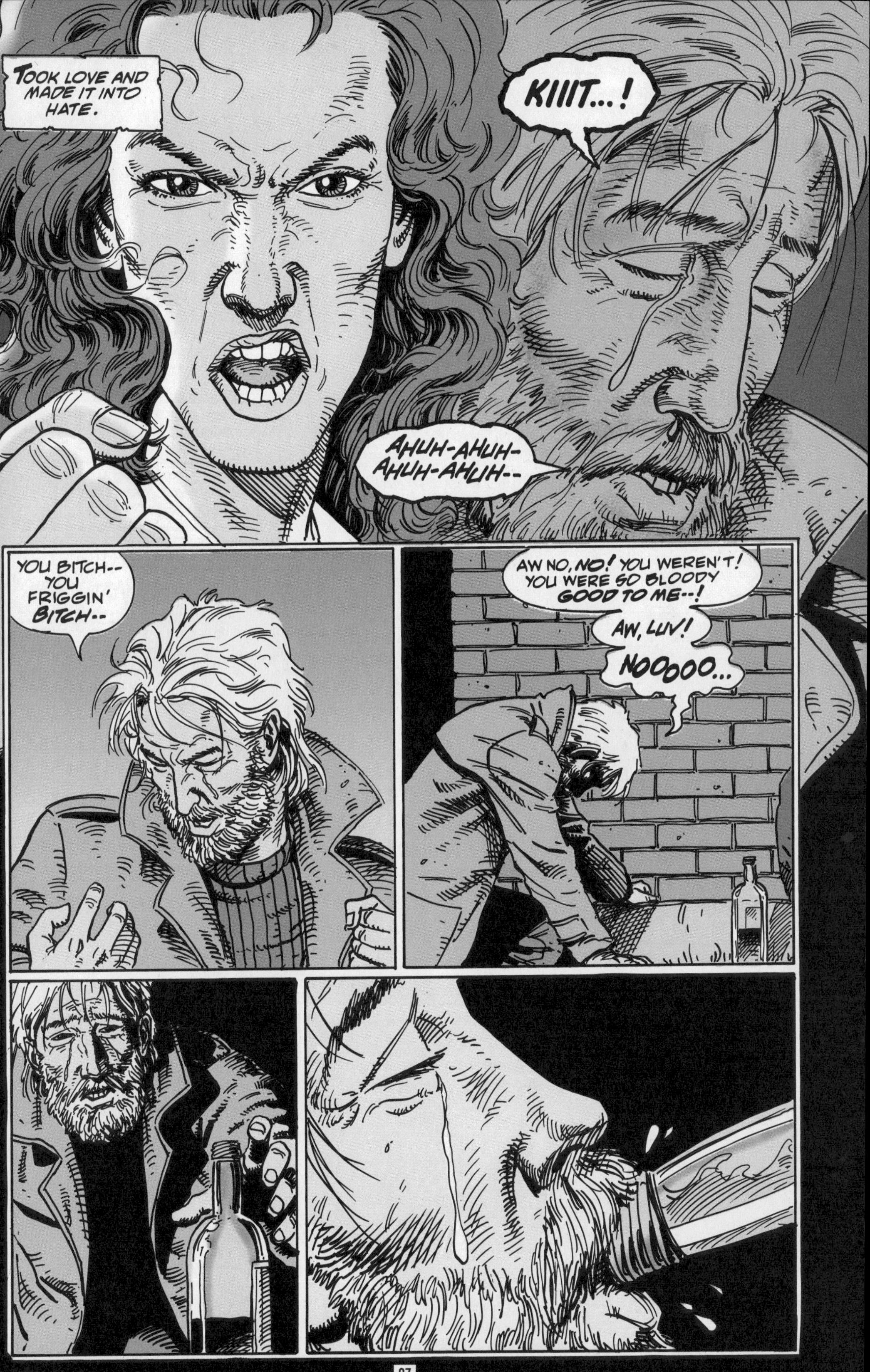
TOOK LOVE AND MADE IT INTO HATE.
KIIIT...!
AHUH-AHUH-AHUH-AHUH--
YOU BITCH--YOU FRIGGIN' BITCH--
AW NO, NO! YOU WEREN'T! YOU WERE SO BLOODY GOOD TO ME--!
AW, LUV!
NOOOOO...

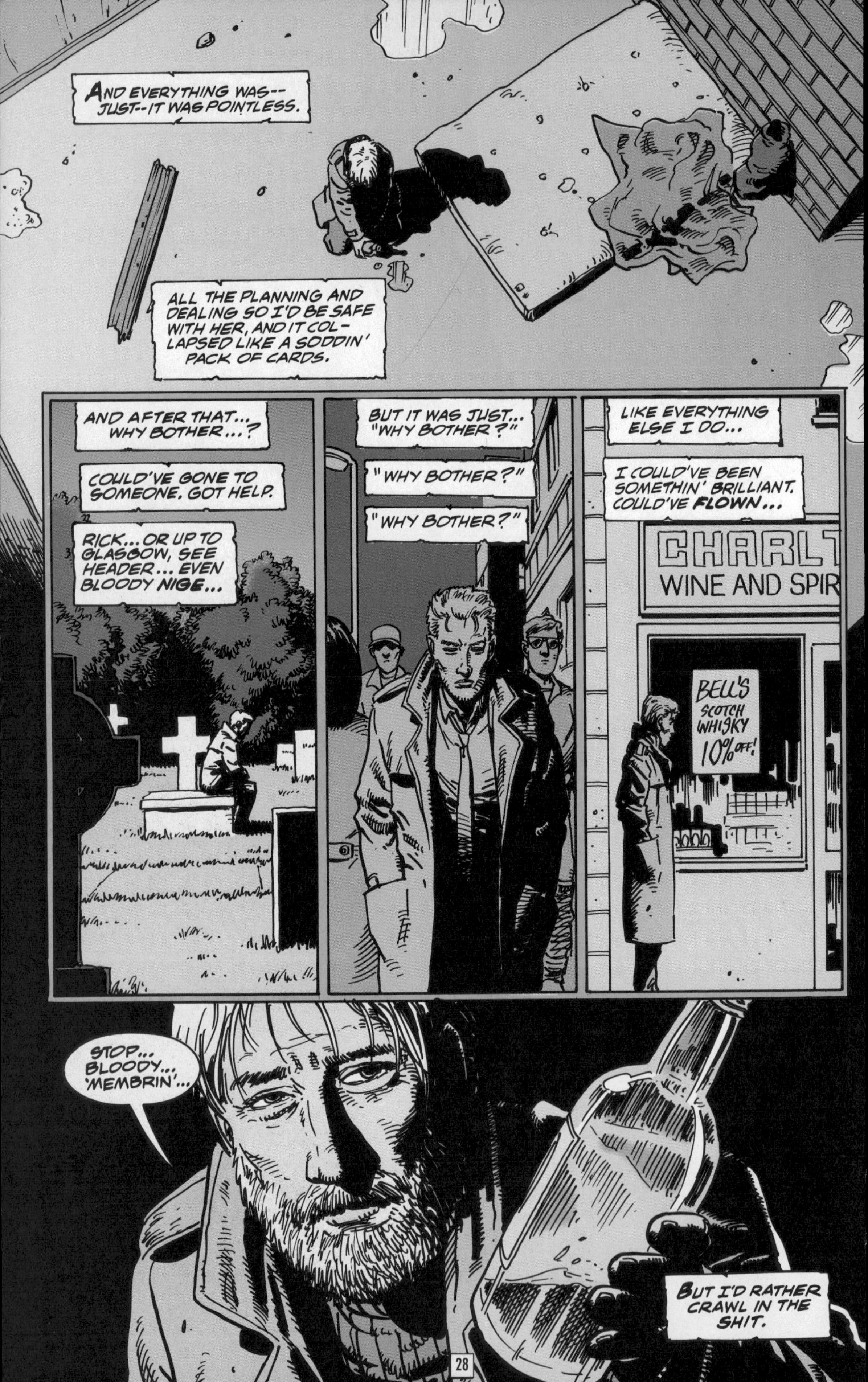
AND EVERYTHING WAS-- JUST--IT WAS POINTLESS.
ALL THE PLANNING AND DEALING SO I'D BE SAFE WITH HER, AND IT COL-LAPSED LIKE A SODDIN' PACK OF CARDS.
AND AFTER THAT... WHY BOTHER...?
COULD'VE GONE TO SOMEONE. GOT HELP.
RICK... OR UP TO GLASGOW, SEE HEADER... EVEN BLOODY NIGE...
BUT IT WAS JUST... "WHY BOTHER?"
"WHY BOTHER?"
"WHY BOTHER?"
LIKE EVERYTHING ELSE I DO...
I COULD'VE BEEN SOMETHIN' BRILLIANT. COULD'VE FLOWN...
CHARLT
WINE AND SPIR
BELL'S SCOTCH WHISKY 10% OFF!
STOP... BLOODY... 'MEMBRIN'...
BUT I'D RATHER CRAWL IN THE SHIT.

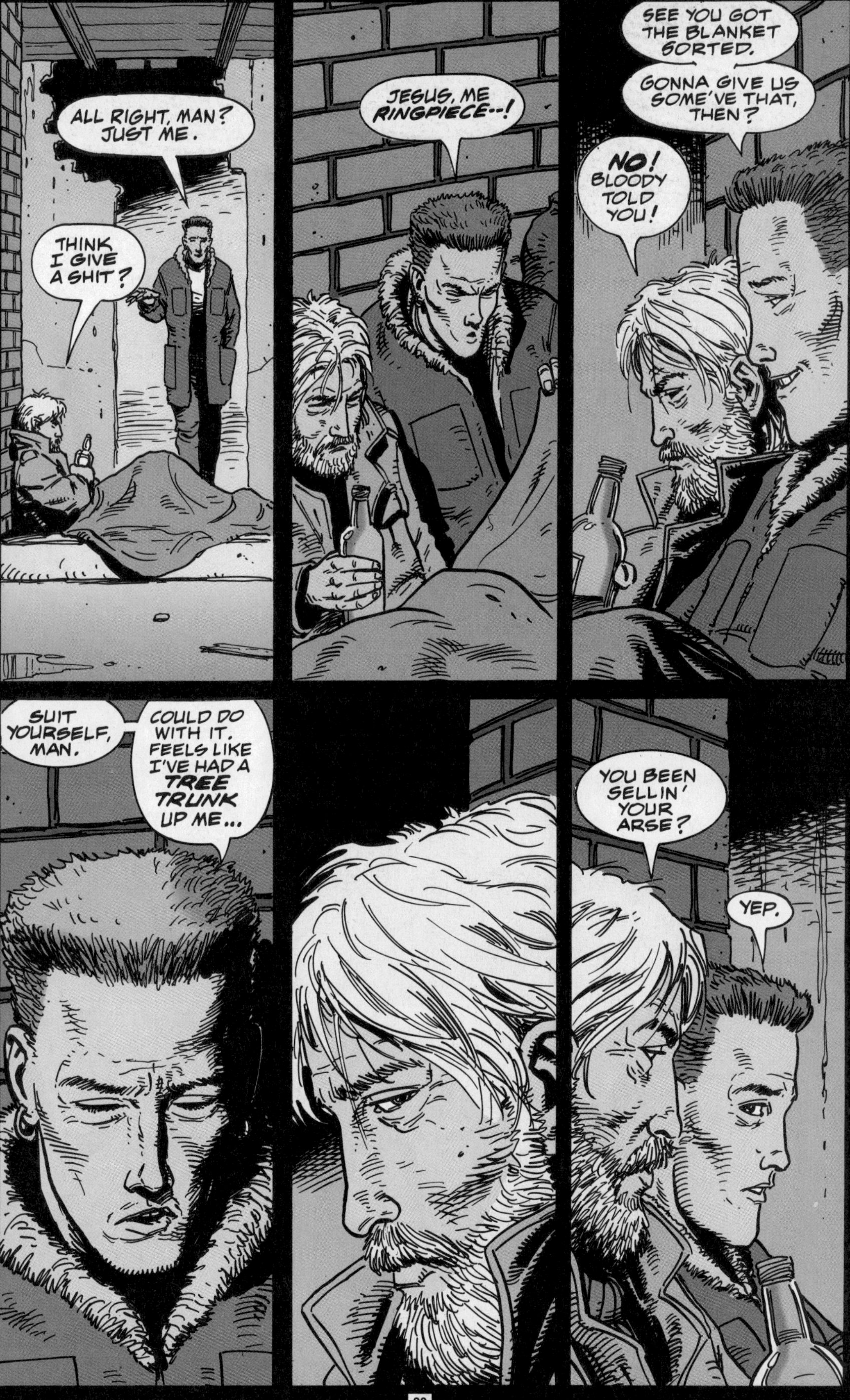
ALL RIGHT, MAN? JUST ME.
THINK I GIVE A SHIT?
JESUS, ME RINGPIECE--!
SEE YOU GOT THE BLANKET SORTED.
GONNA GIVE US SOME'VE THAT, THEN?
NO! BLOODY TOLD YOU!
SUIT YOURSELF, MAN.
COULD DO WITH IT. FEELS LIKE I'VE HAD A TREE TRUNK UP ME...
YOU BEEN SELLIN' YOUR ARSE?
YEP.

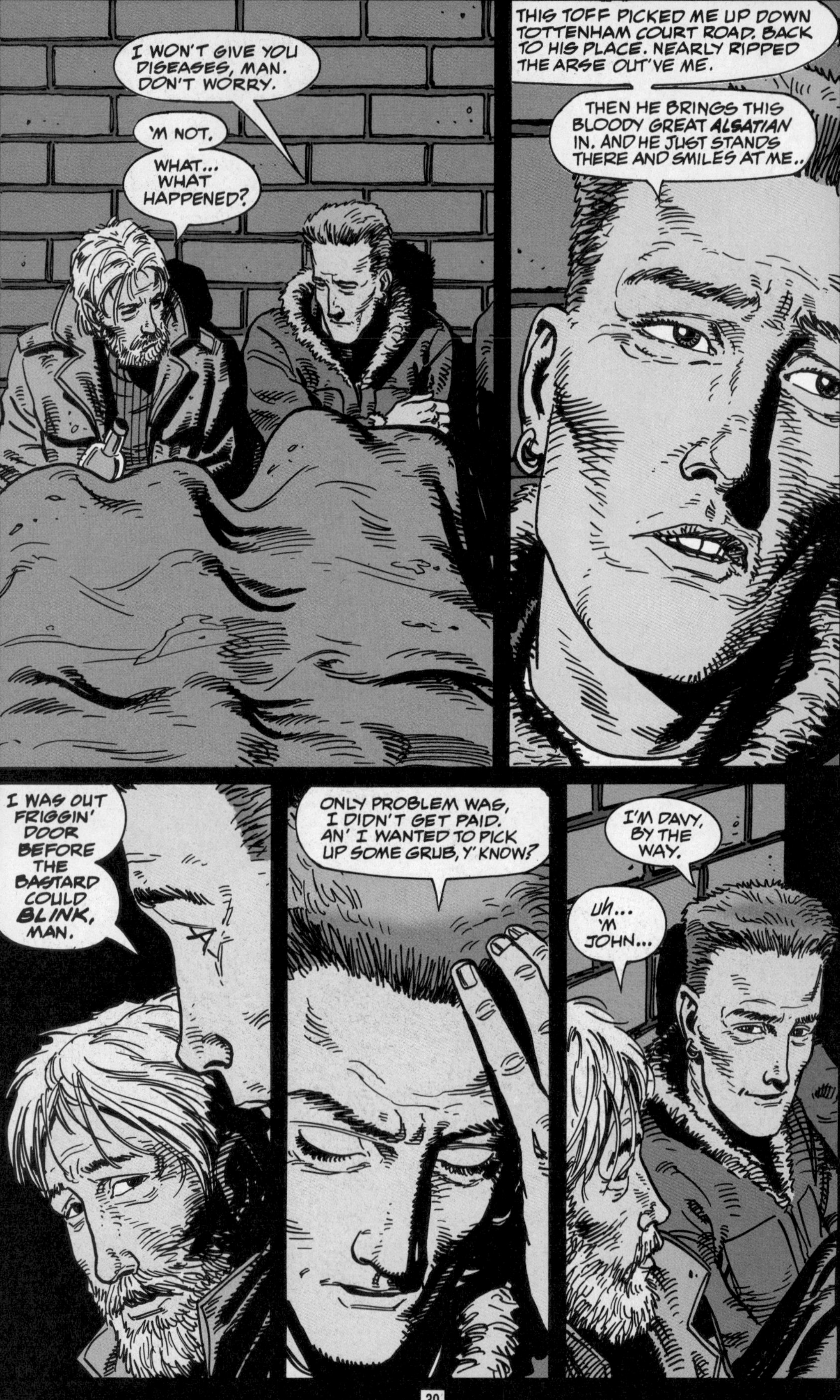
I WON'T GIVE YOU DISEASES, MAN. DON'T WORRY.
'M NOT.
WHAT... WHAT HAPPENED?
THIS TOFF PICKED ME UP DOWN TOTTENHAM COURT ROAD. BACK TO HIS PLACE. NEARLY RIPPED THE ARSE OUT'VE ME.
THEN HE BRINGS THIS BLOODY GREAT ALSATIAN IN. AND HE JUST STANDS THERE AND SMILES AT ME..
I WAS OUT FRIGGIN' DOOR BEFORE THE BASTARD COULD BLINK, MAN.
ONLY PROBLEM WAS, I DIDN'T GET PAID. AN' I WANTED TO PICK UP SOME GRUB, Y'KNOW?
I'M DAVY, BY THE WAY.
UH... 'M JOHN...

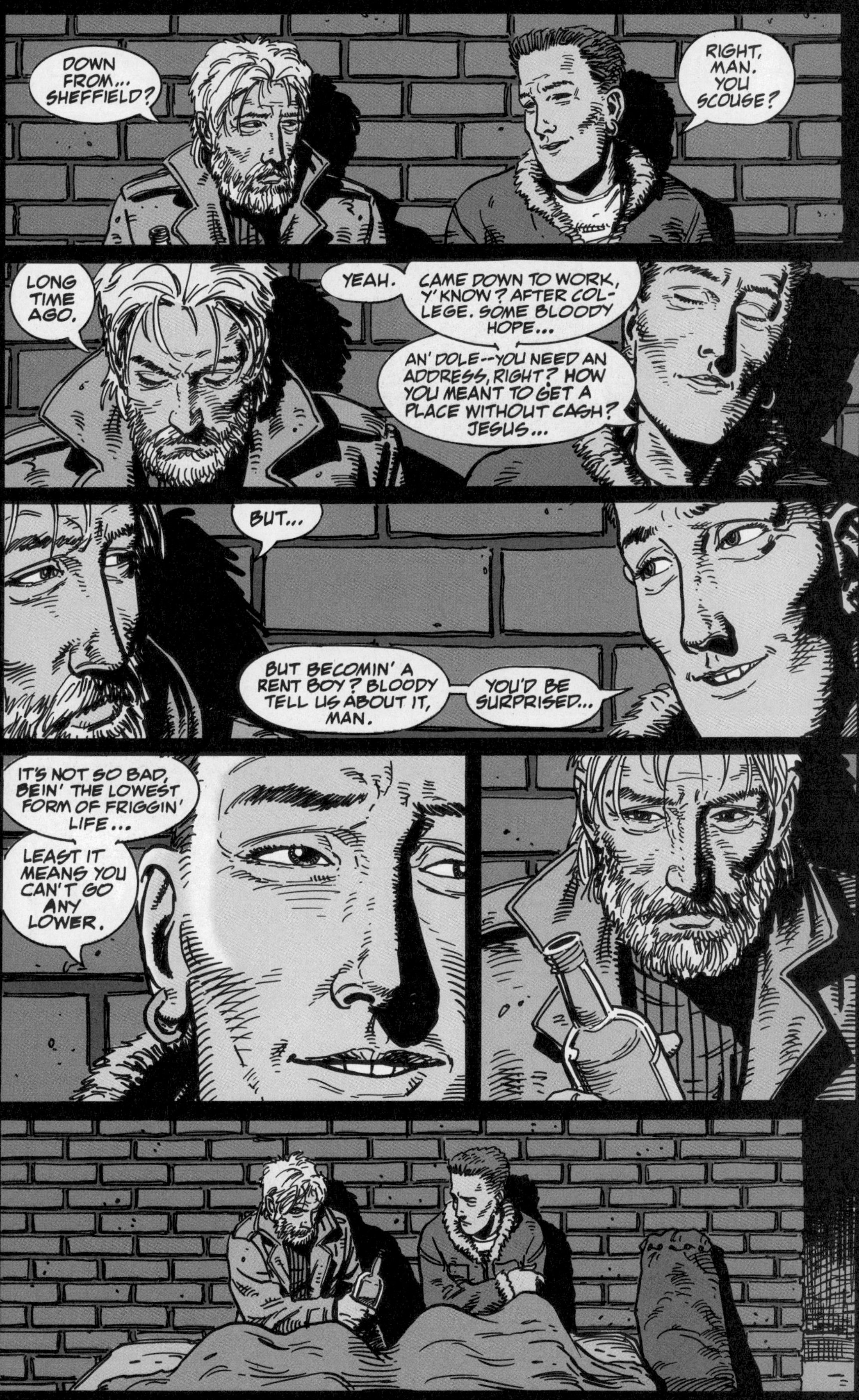
DOWN FROM... SHEFFIELD?
RIGHT, MAN. YOU SCOUSE?
LONG TIME AGO.
YEAH.
CAME DOWN TO WORK, Y'KNOW? AFTER COL-LEGE. SOME BLOODY HOPE...
AN' DOLE--YOU NEED AN ADDRESS, RIGHT? HOW YOU MEANT TO GET A PLACE WITHOUT CASH? JESUS...
BUT...
BUT BECOMIN' A RENT BOY? BLOODY TELL US ABOUT IT, MAN.
YOU'D BE SURPRISED...
IT'S NOT SO BAD, BEIN' THE LOWEST FORM OF FRIGGIN' LIFE...
LEAST IT MEANS YOU CAN'T GO ANY LOWER.

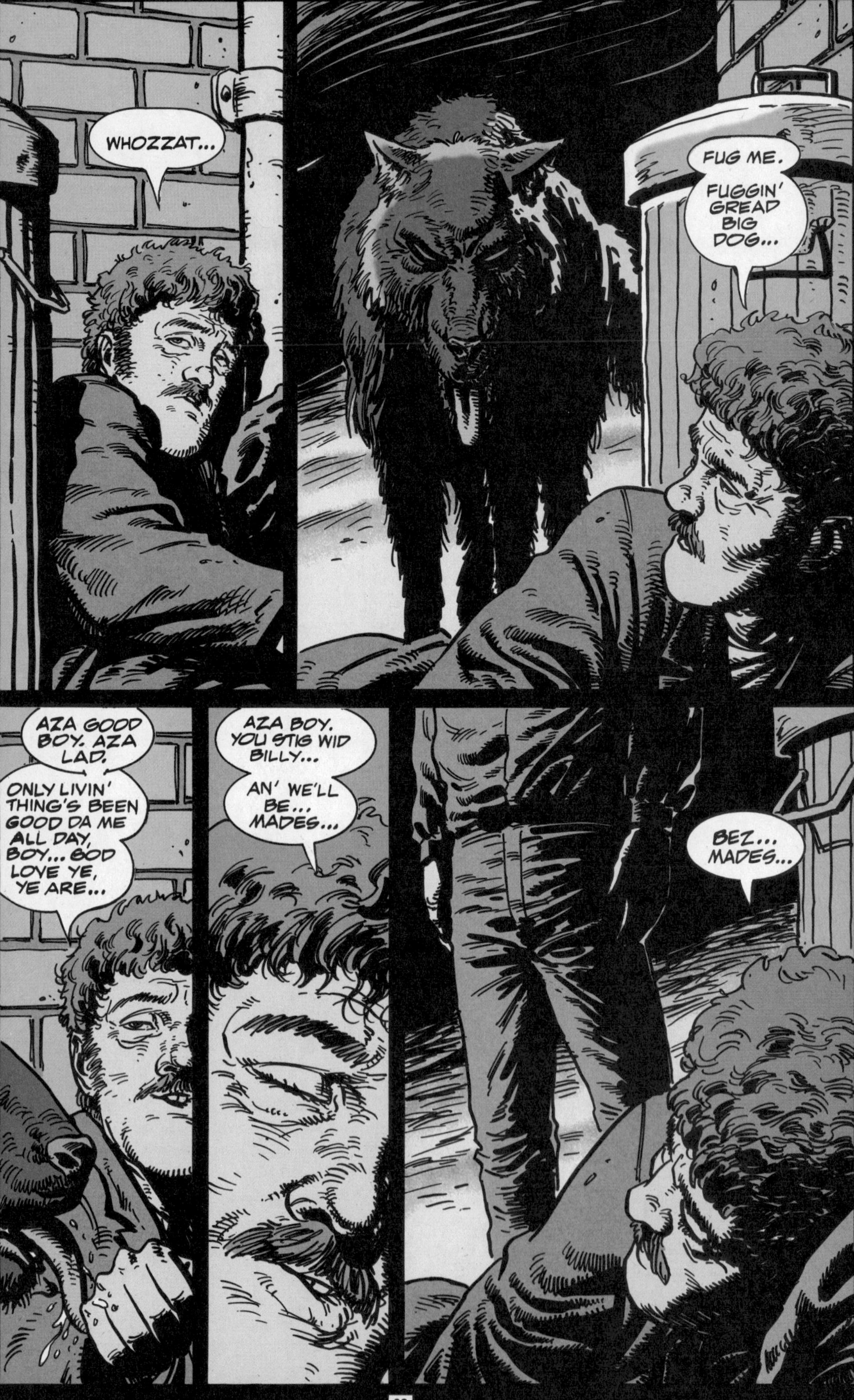
WHOZZAT...
FUG ME.
FUGGIN' GREAD BIG DOG...
AZA GOOD BOY. AZA LAD.
ONLY LIVIN' THING'S BEEN GOOD DA ME ALL DAY, BOY... GOD LOVE YE, YE ARE...
AZA BOY. YOU STIG WID BILLY...
AN' WE'LL BE... MADES...
BEZ... MADES...

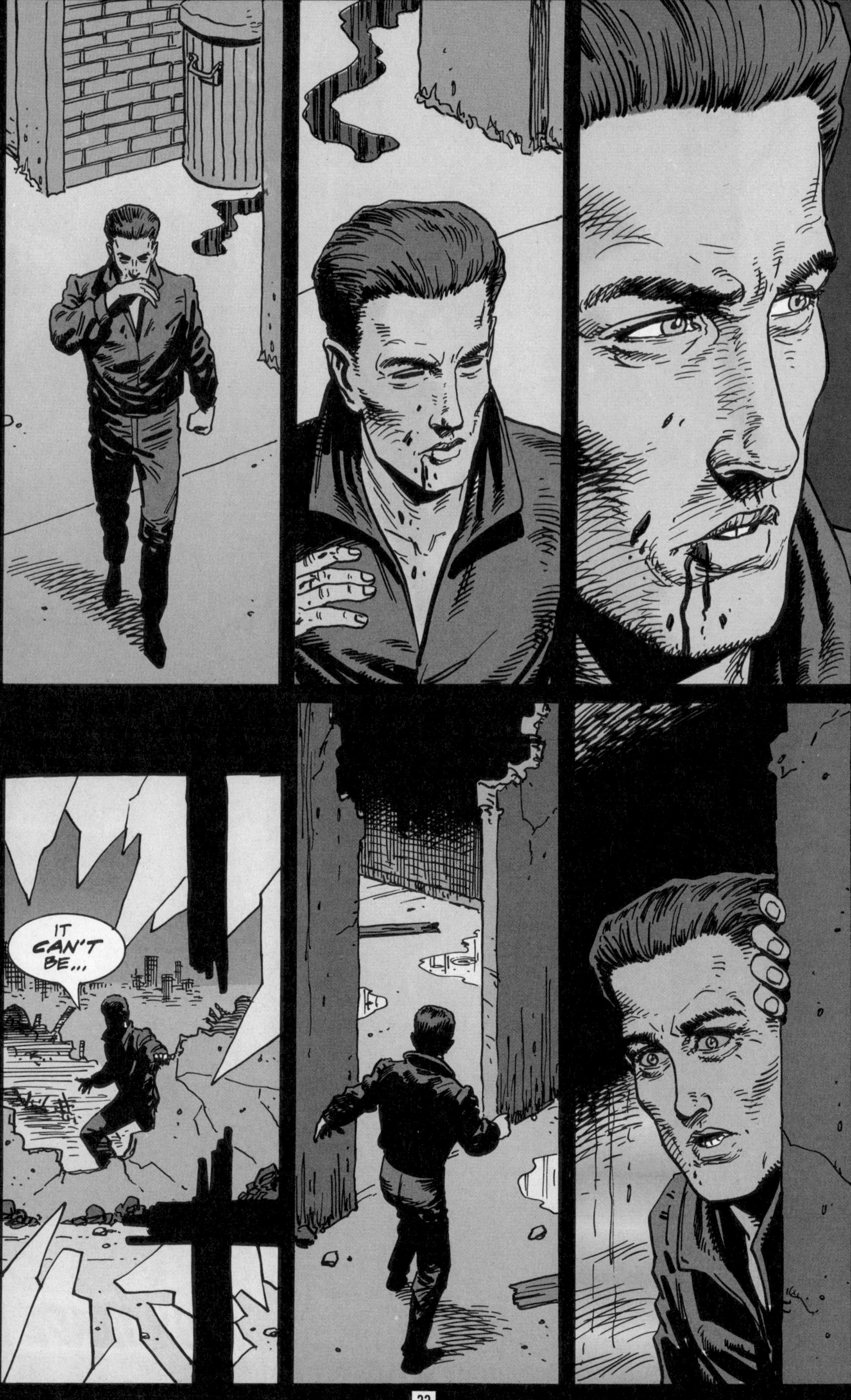
IT CAN'T BE...

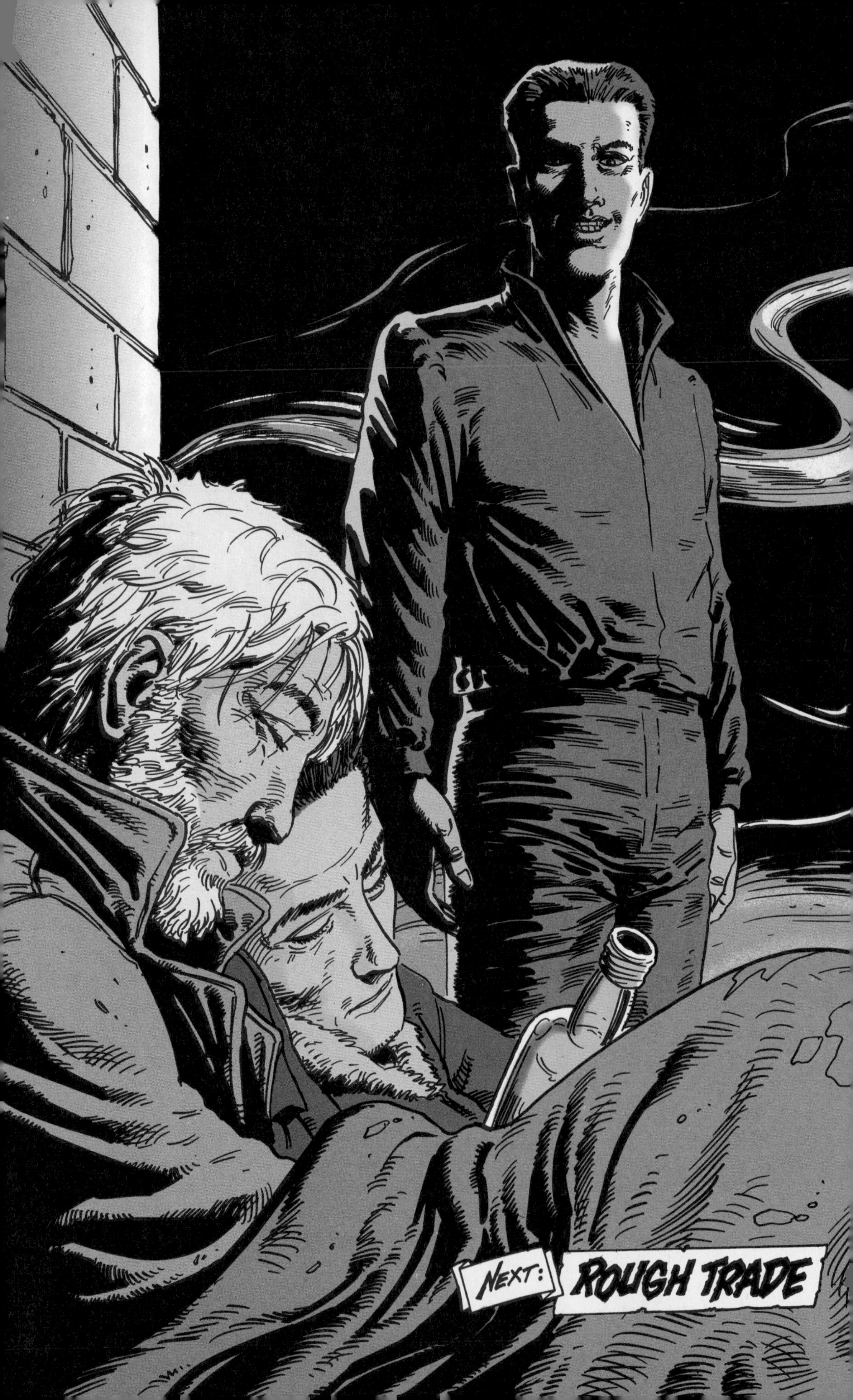
NEXT: ROUGH TRADE

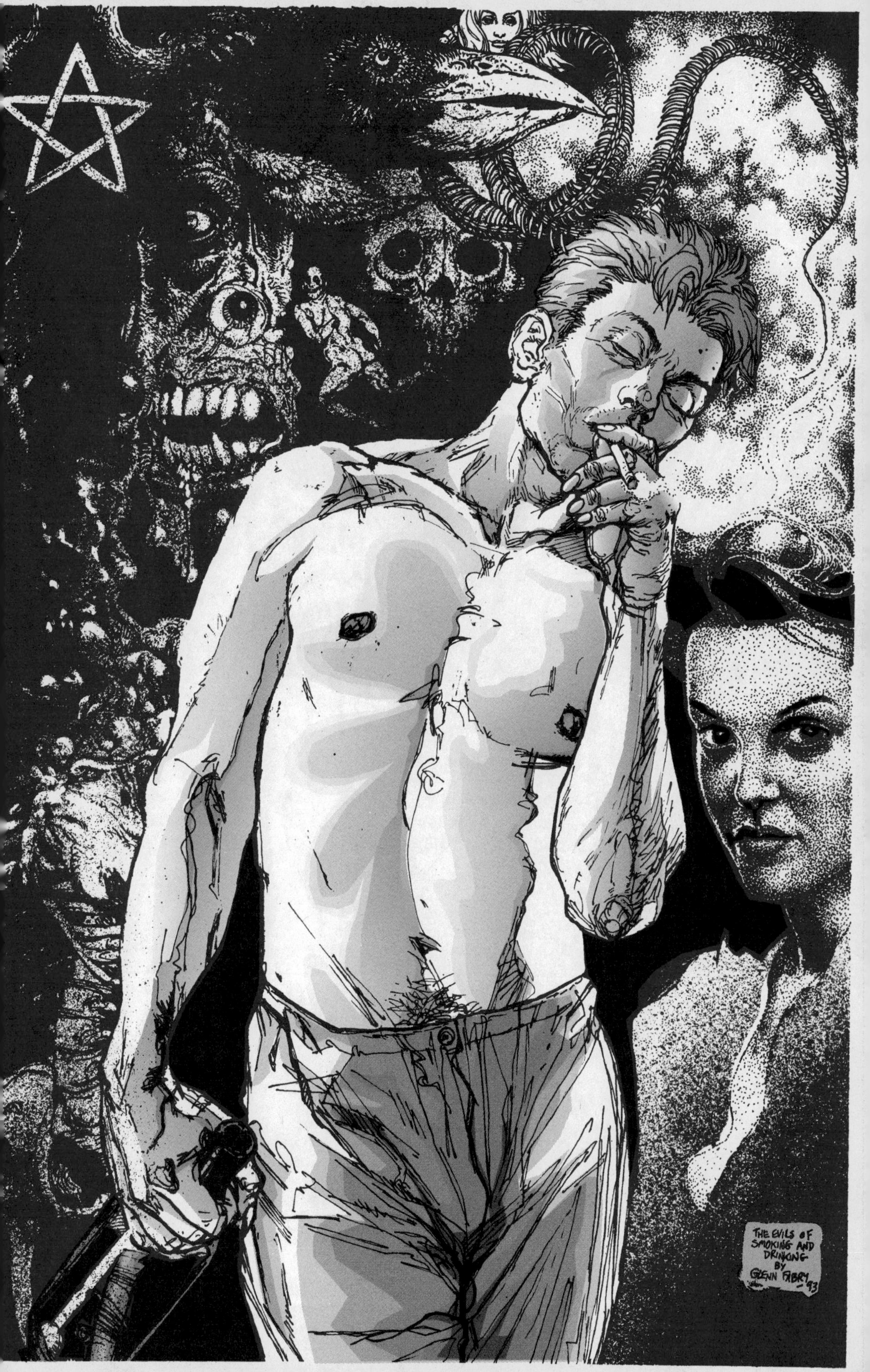
THE EVILS OF
SMOKING AND
DRINKING
BY
GLENN FABRY
-93

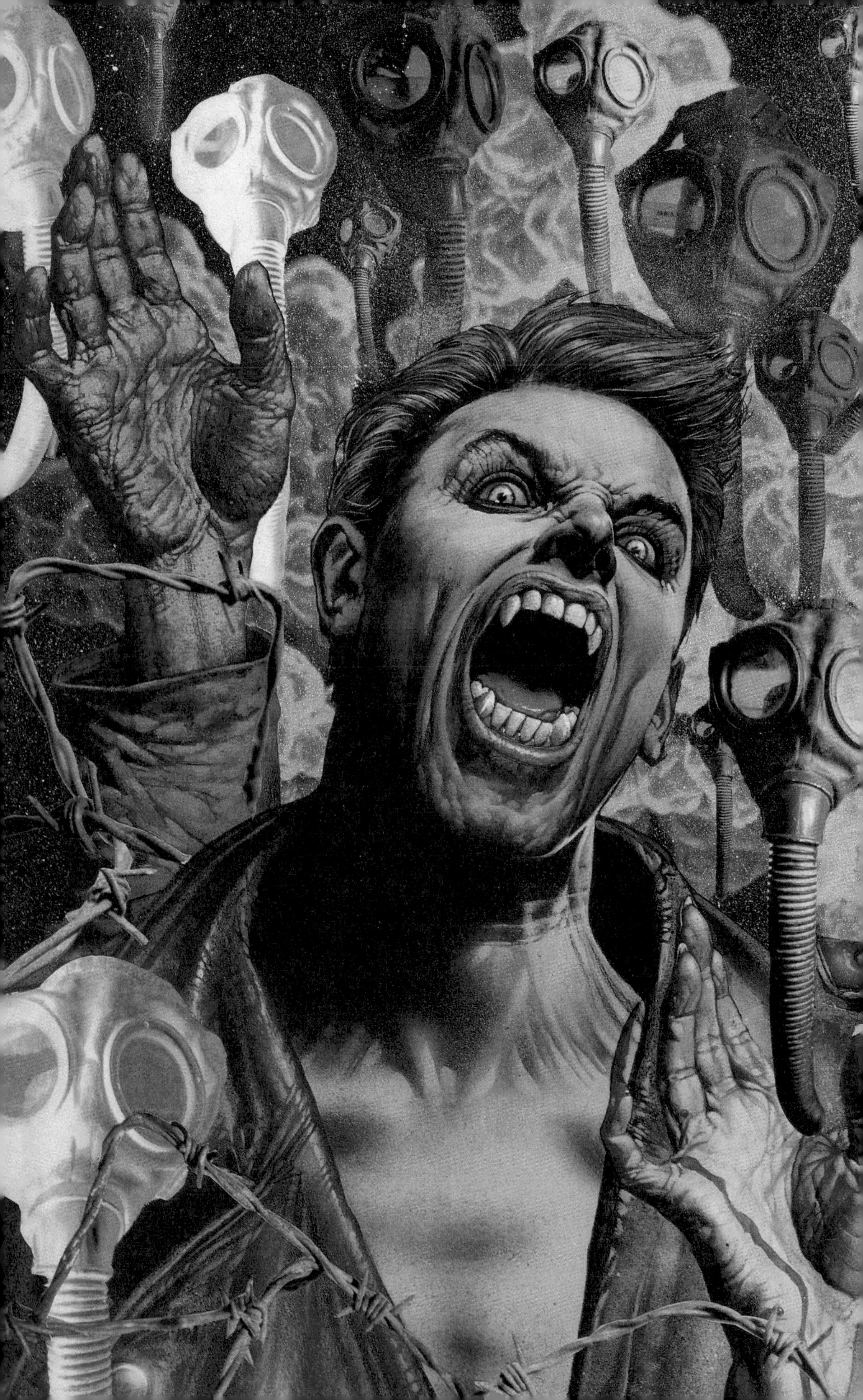

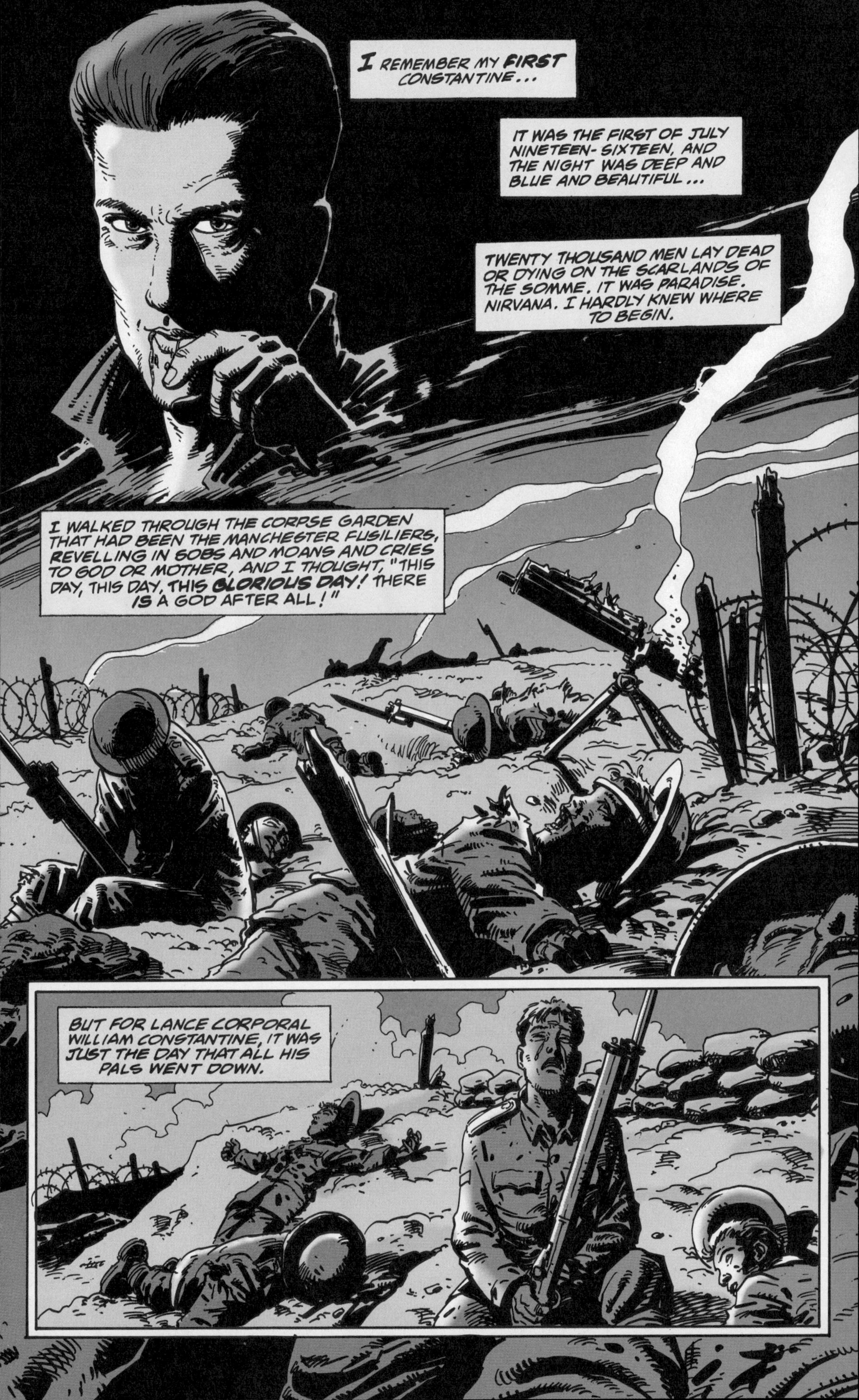
I REMEMBER MY FIRST CONSTANTINE...
IT WAS THE FIRST OF JULY NINETEEN- SIXTEEN, AND THE NIGHT WAS DEEP AND BLUE AND BEAUTIFUL...
TWENTY THOUSAND MEN LAY DEAD OR DYING ON THE SCARLANDS OF THE SOMME. IT WAS PARADISE. NIRVANA. I HARDLY KNEW WHERE TO BEGIN.
I WALKED THROUGH THE CORPSE GARDEN THAT HAD BEEN THE MANCHESTER FUSILIERS, REVELLING IN SOBS AND MOANS AND CRIES TO GOD OR MOTHER, AND I THOUGHT, "THIS DAY, THIS DAY, THIS GLORIOUS DAY! THERE IS A GOD AFTER ALL!"
BUT FOR LANCE CORPORAL WILLIAM CONSTANTINE, IT WAS JUST THE DAY THAT ALL HIS PALS WENT DOWN.

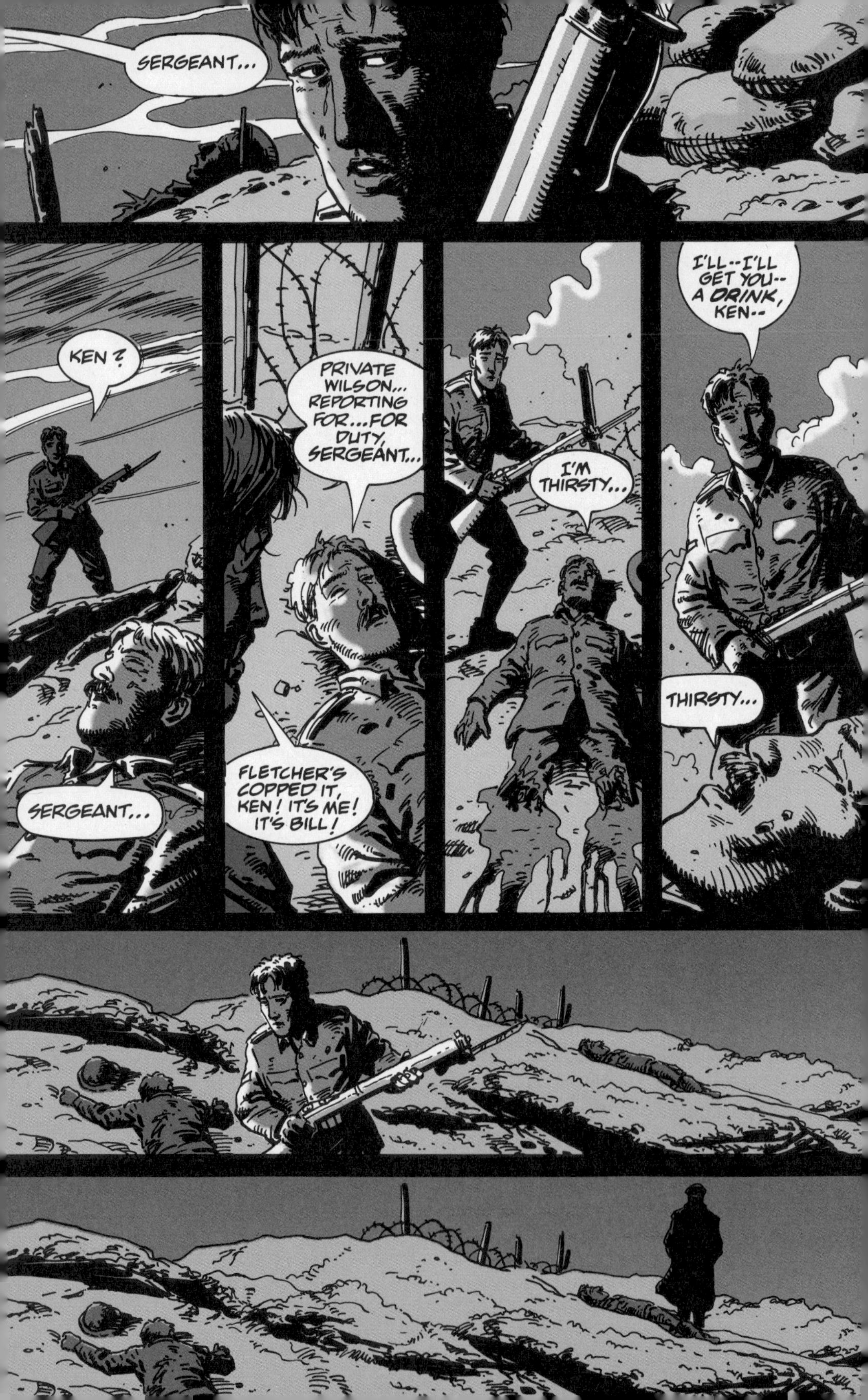
SERGEANT...
KEN?
SERGEANT...
PRIVATE WILSON... REPORTING FOR... FOR DUTY, SERGEANT...
FLETCHER'S COPPED IT, KEN! IT'S ME! IT'S BILL!
I'M THIRSTY...
I'LL--I'LL GET YOU-- A DRINK, KEN--
THIRSTY...

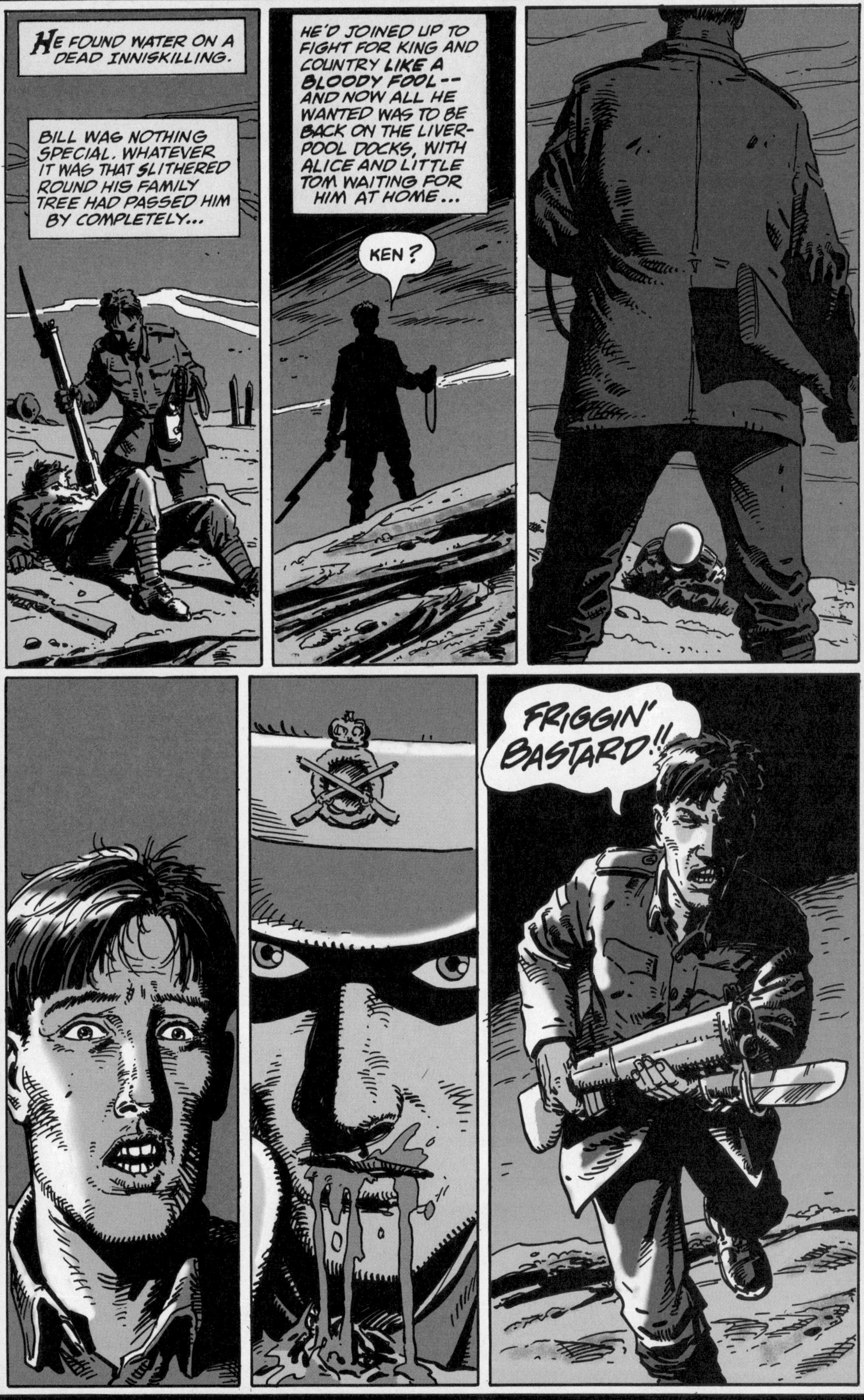
HE FOUND WATER ON A DEAD INNISKILLING.
BILL WAS NOTHING SPECIAL. WHATEVER IT WAS THAT SLITHERED ROUND HIS FAMILY TREE HAD PASSED HIM BY COMPLETELY...
HE'D JOINED UP TO FIGHT FOR KING AND COUNTRY LIKE A BLOODY FOOL -- AND NOW ALL HE WANTED WAS TO BE BACK ON THE LIVER-POOL DOCKS, WITH ALICE AND LITTLE TOM WAITING FOR HIM AT HOME...
KEN?
FRIGGIN' BASTARD!!

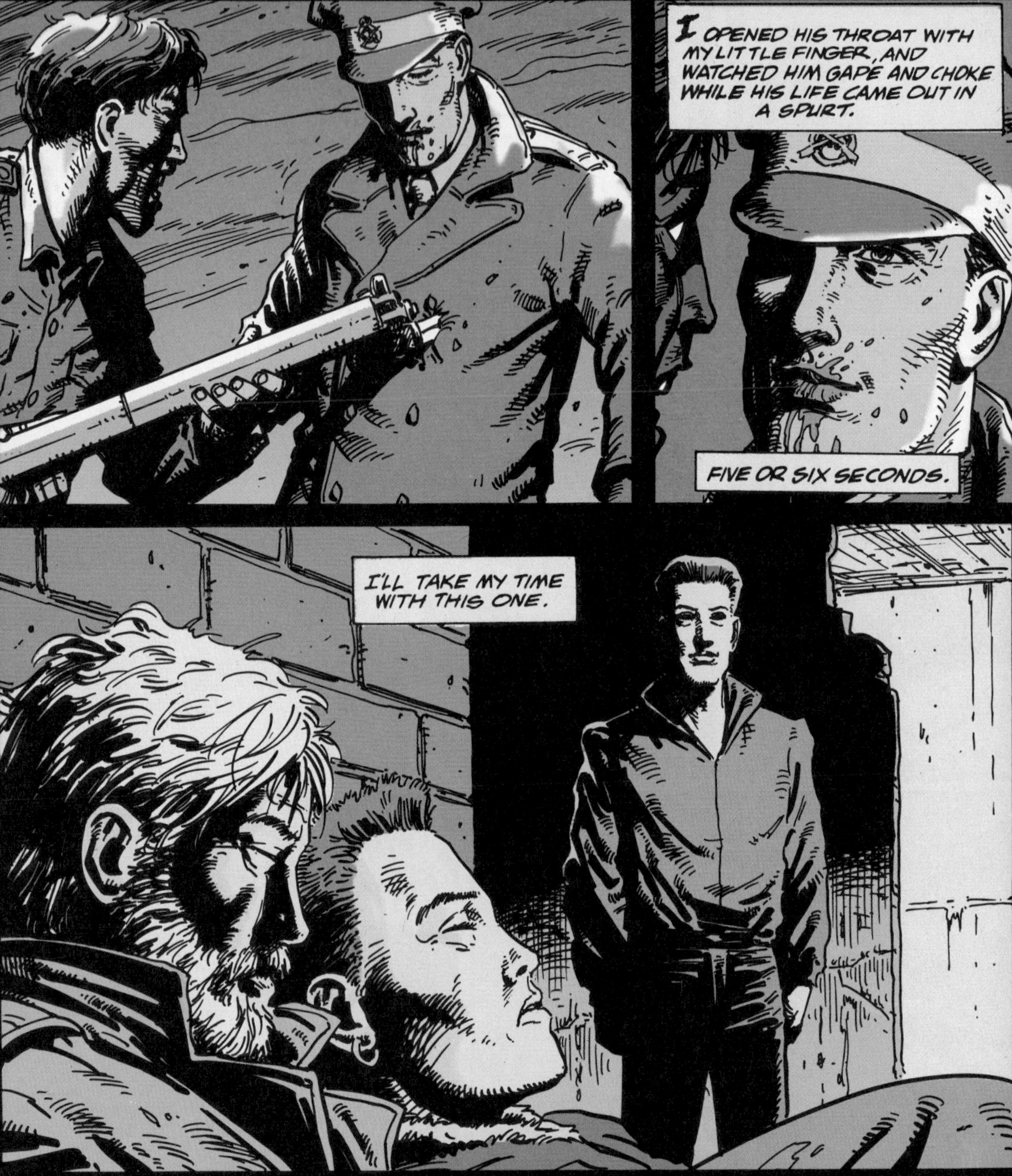
I OPENED HIS THROAT WITH MY LITTLE FINGER, AND WATCHED HIM GAPE AND CHOKE WHILE HIS LIFE CAME OUT IN A SPURT.
FIVE OR SIX SECONDS.
I'LL TAKE MY TIME WITH THIS ONE.

ROUGH TRADE

GARTH ENNIS • *writer* **STEVE DILLON** • *artist* **TOM ZIUKO** • *colors*
GASPAR • *letters* **JULIE ROTTENBERG** • *assistant editor* **STUART MOORE** • *editor*

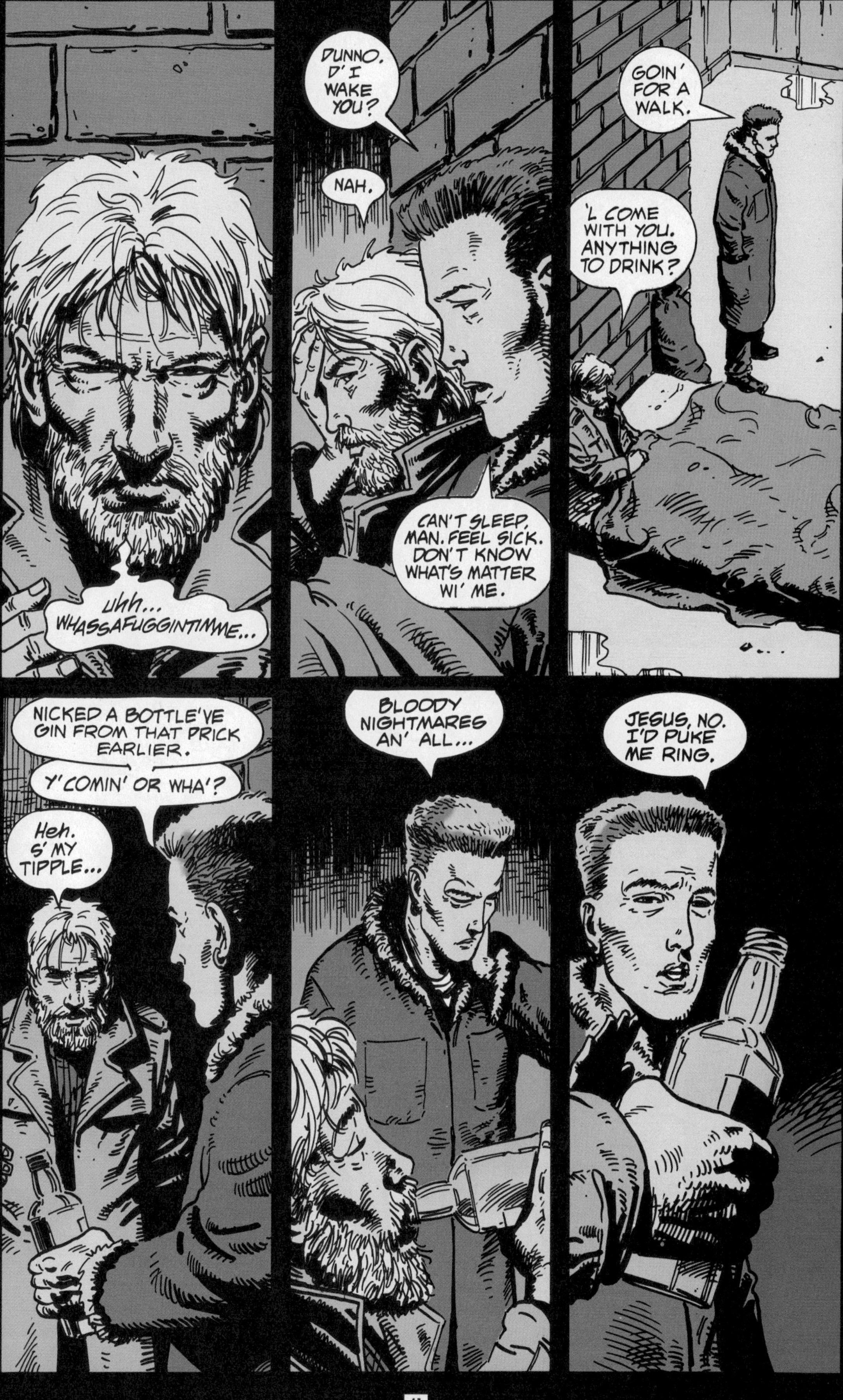
uhh... WHASSAFUGGINTIMME...
DUNNO. D' I WAKE YOU?
NAH.
CAN'T SLEEP, MAN. FEEL SICK. DON'T KNOW WHAT'S MATTER WI' ME.
GOIN' FOR A WALK.
'L COME WITH YOU. ANYTHING TO DRINK?
NICKED A BOTTLE'VE GIN FROM THAT PRICK EARLIER.
Y'COMIN' OR WHA'?
Heh. S' MY TIPPLE...
BLOODY NIGHTMARES AN' ALL...
JESUS, NO. I'D PUKE ME RING.

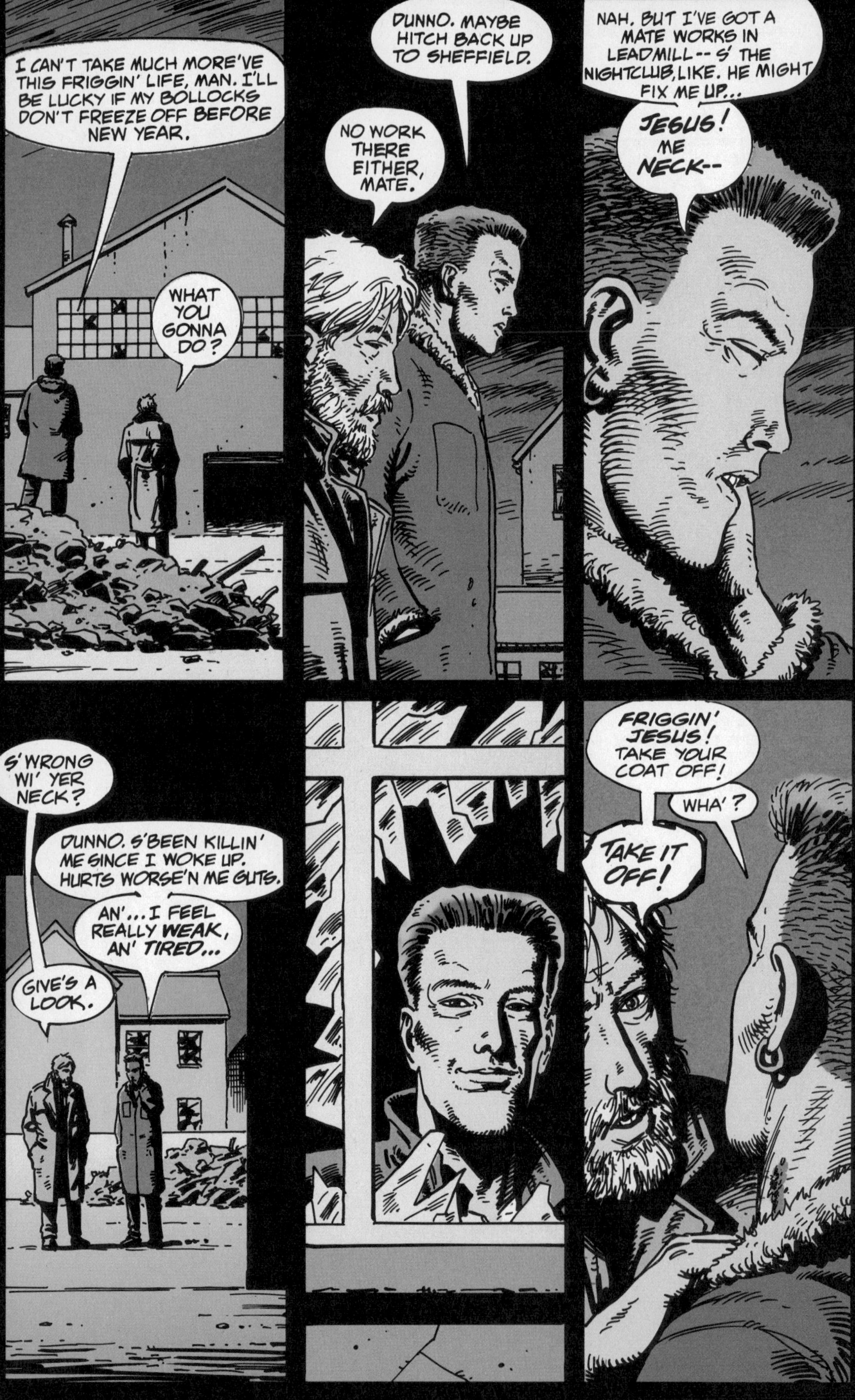
I CAN'T TAKE MUCH MORE'VE THIS FRIGGIN' LIFE, MAN. I'LL BE LUCKY IF MY BOLLOCKS DON'T FREEZE OFF BEFORE NEW YEAR.
WHAT YOU GONNA DO?
DUNNO. MAYBE HITCH BACK UP TO SHEFFIELD.
NO WORK THERE EITHER, MATE.
NAH. BUT I'VE GOT A MATE WORKS IN LEADMILL-- S' THE NIGHTCLUB, LIKE. HE MIGHT FIX ME UP...
JESUS! ME NECK--
S'WRONG WI' YER NECK?
DUNNO. S'BEEN KILLIN' ME SINCE I WOKE UP. HURTS WORSE'N ME GUTS.
AN'... I FEEL REALLY WEAK, AN' TIRED...
GIVE'S A LOOK.
FRIGGIN' JESUS! TAKE YOUR COAT OFF!
WHA'?
TAKE IT OFF!

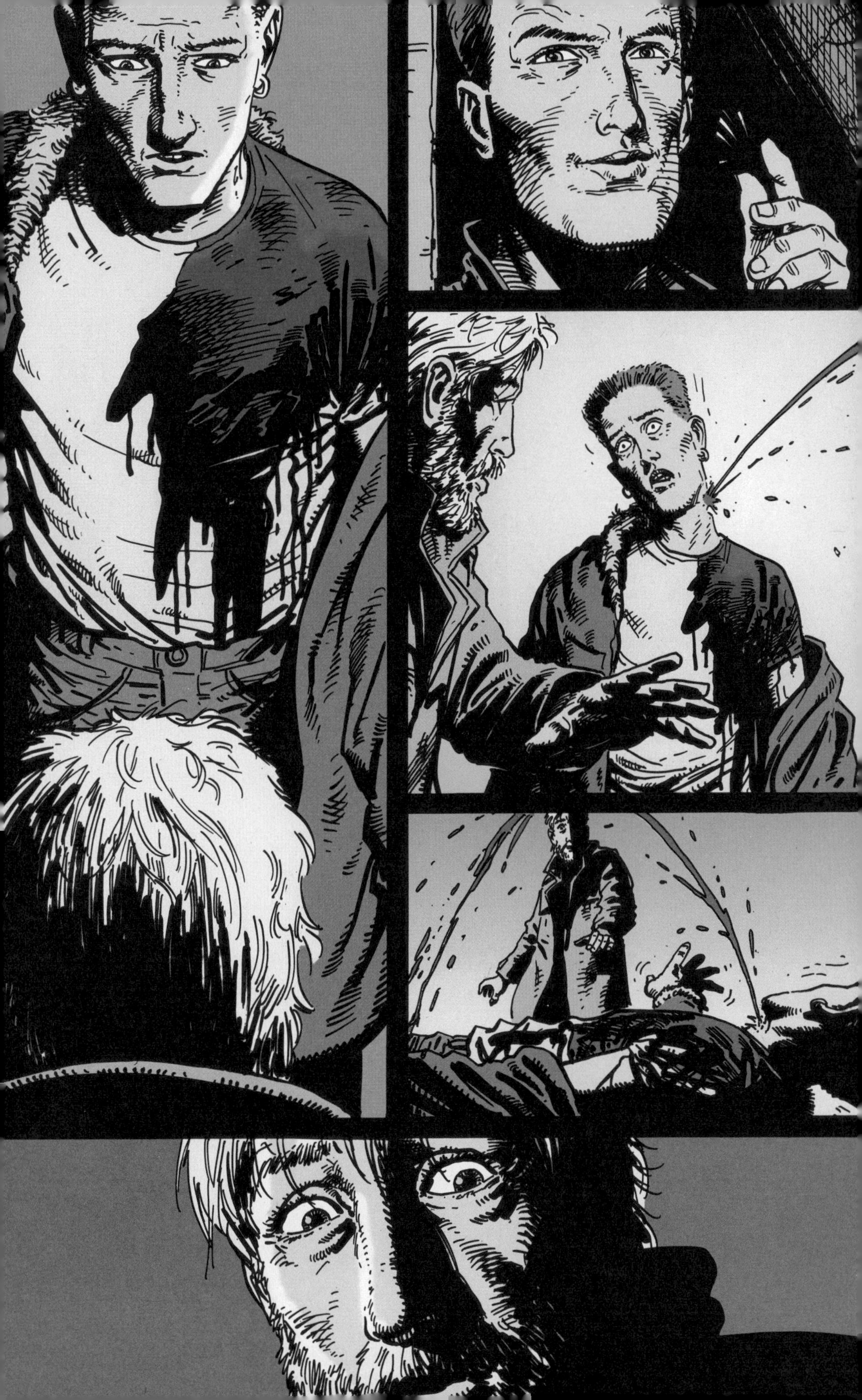

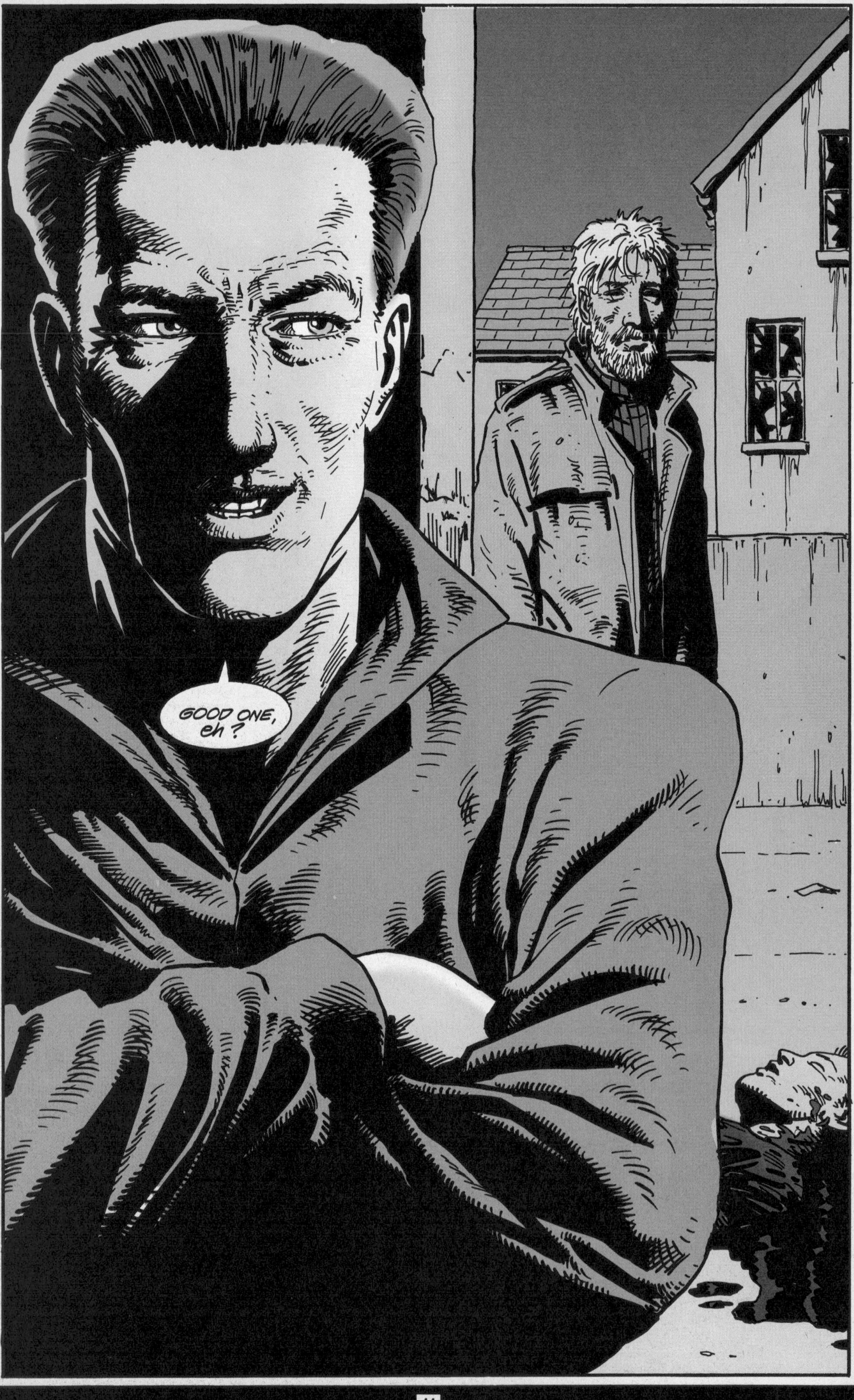
GOOD ONE, eh ?

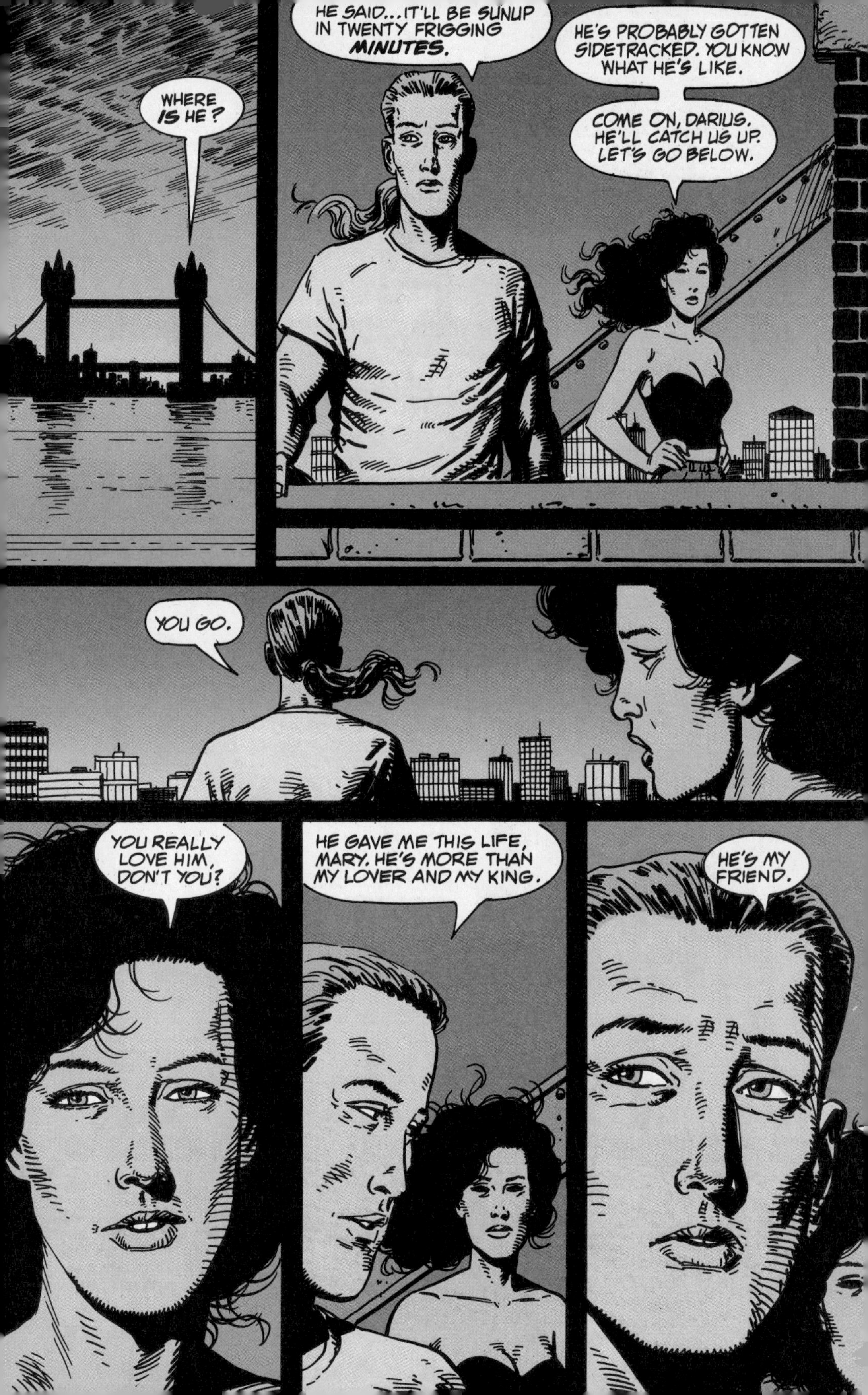
WHERE IS HE?
HE SAID... IT'LL BE SUNUP IN TWENTY FRIGGING MINUTES.
HE'S PROBABLY GOTTEN SIDETRACKED. YOU KNOW WHAT HE'S LIKE.
COME ON, DARIUS. HE'LL CATCH US UP. LET'S GO BELOW.
YOU GO.
YOU REALLY LOVE HIM, DON'T YOU?
HE GAVE ME THIS LIFE, MARY. HE'S MORE THAN MY LOVER AND MY KING.
HE'S MY FRIEND.

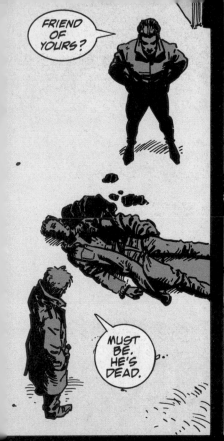

FRIEND OF YOURS?

MUST BE. HE'S DEAD.

HEH.

HE HAD AIDS, YOU KNOW. YOU CAN TASTE IT IN THE BLOOD. WERE YOU SCREWING HIM?

NO.

WELL, IN ABOUT TEN MINUTES IT WON'T MATTER ANYWAY.

SO WHAT HAPPENED TO THE JOYS OF REAL LIFE, THEN? NOT LISTENING TO THE BIRDS SING, OR WATCHING THE SUN COME UP?

CAN'T YOU KISS A GIRL AND KNOW SHE LOVES YOU ANYMORE?

OF COURSE NOT.

THAT'S ALWAYS THE PROBLEM WITH YOU PEOPLE.

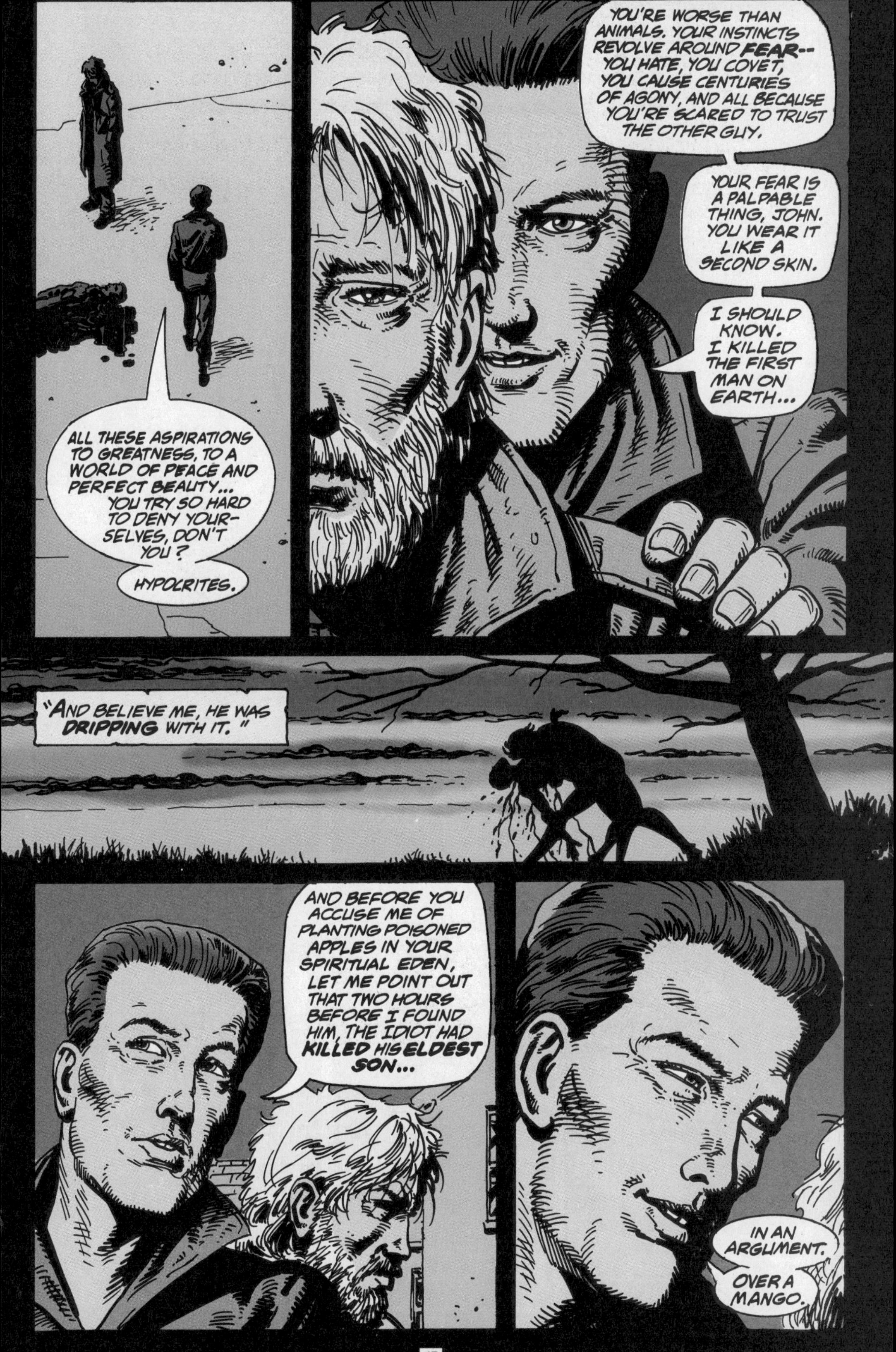
ALL THESE ASPIRATIONS TO GREATNESS, TO A WORLD OF PEACE AND PERFECT BEAUTY...
YOU TRY SO HARD TO DENY YOURSELVES, DON'T YOU?
HYPOCRITES.
YOU'RE WORSE THAN ANIMALS. YOUR INSTINCTS REVOLVE AROUND FEAR-- YOU HATE, YOU COVET, YOU CAUSE CENTURIES OF AGONY, AND ALL BECAUSE YOU'RE SCARED TO TRUST THE OTHER GUY.
YOUR FEAR IS A PALPABLE THING, JOHN. YOU WEAR IT LIKE A SECOND SKIN.
I SHOULD KNOW. I KILLED THE FIRST MAN ON EARTH...
"AND BELIEVE ME, HE WAS DRIPPING WITH IT."
AND BEFORE YOU ACCUSE ME OF PLANTING POISONED APPLES IN YOUR SPIRITUAL EDEN, LET ME POINT OUT THAT TWO HOURS BEFORE I FOUND HIM, THE IDIOT HAD KILLED HIS ELDEST SON...
IN AN ARGUMENT.
OVER A MANGO.

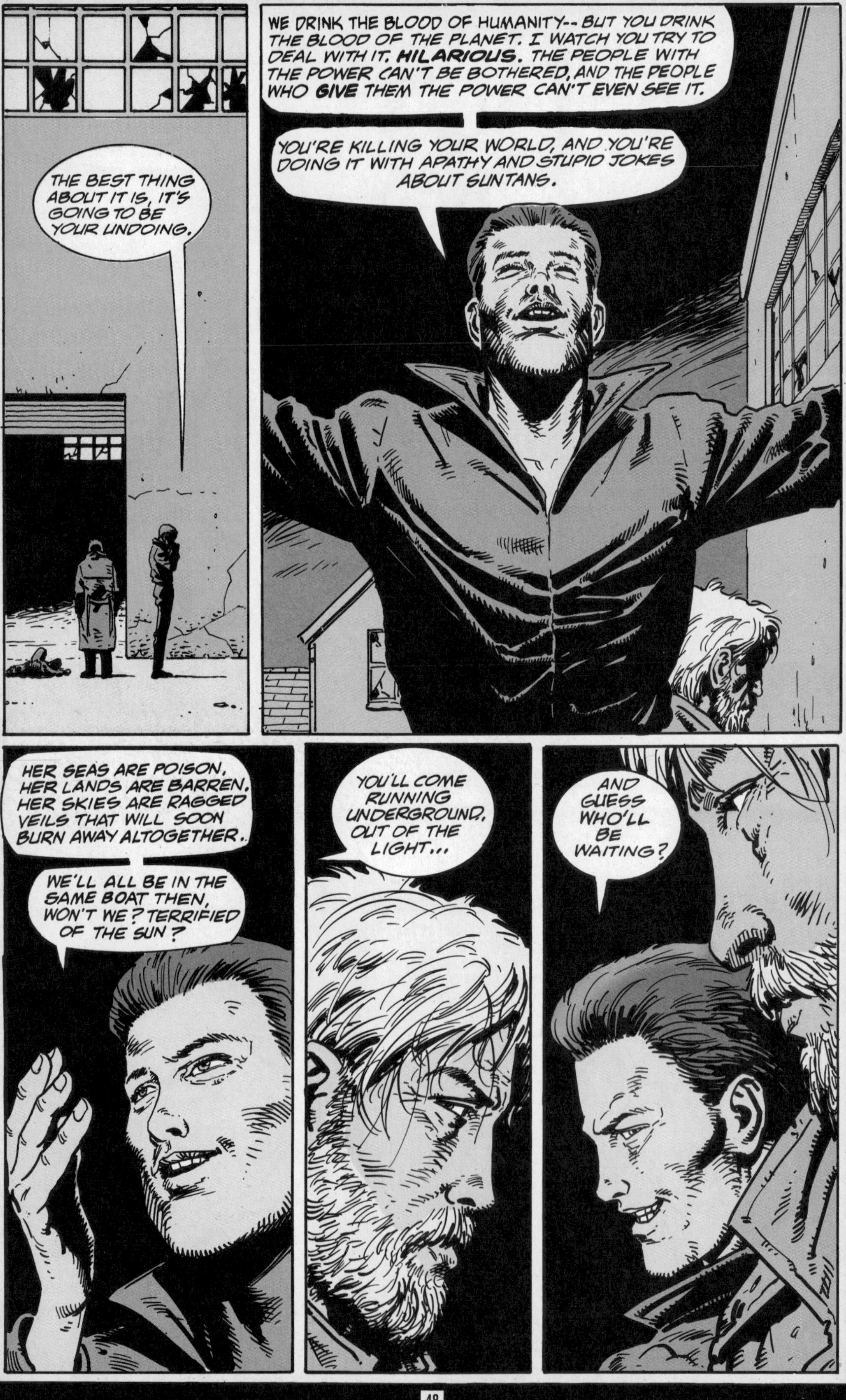
THE BEST THING ABOUT IT IS, IT'S GOING TO BE YOUR UNDOING.
WE DRINK THE BLOOD OF HUMANITY-- BUT YOU DRINK THE BLOOD OF THE PLANET. I WATCH YOU TRY TO DEAL WITH IT. HILARIOUS. THE PEOPLE WITH THE POWER CAN'T BE BOTHERED, AND THE PEOPLE WHO GIVE THEM THE POWER CAN'T EVEN SEE IT.
YOU'RE KILLING YOUR WORLD, AND YOU'RE DOING IT WITH APATHY AND STUPID JOKES ABOUT SUNTANS.
HER SEAS ARE POISON, HER LANDS ARE BARREN. HER SKIES ARE RAGGED VEILS THAT WILL SOON BURN AWAY ALTOGETHER..
WE'LL ALL BE IN THE SAME BOAT THEN, WON'T WE? TERRIFIED OF THE SUN?
YOU'LL COME RUNNING UNDERGROUND, OUT OF THE LIGHT...
AND GUESS WHO'LL BE WAITING?

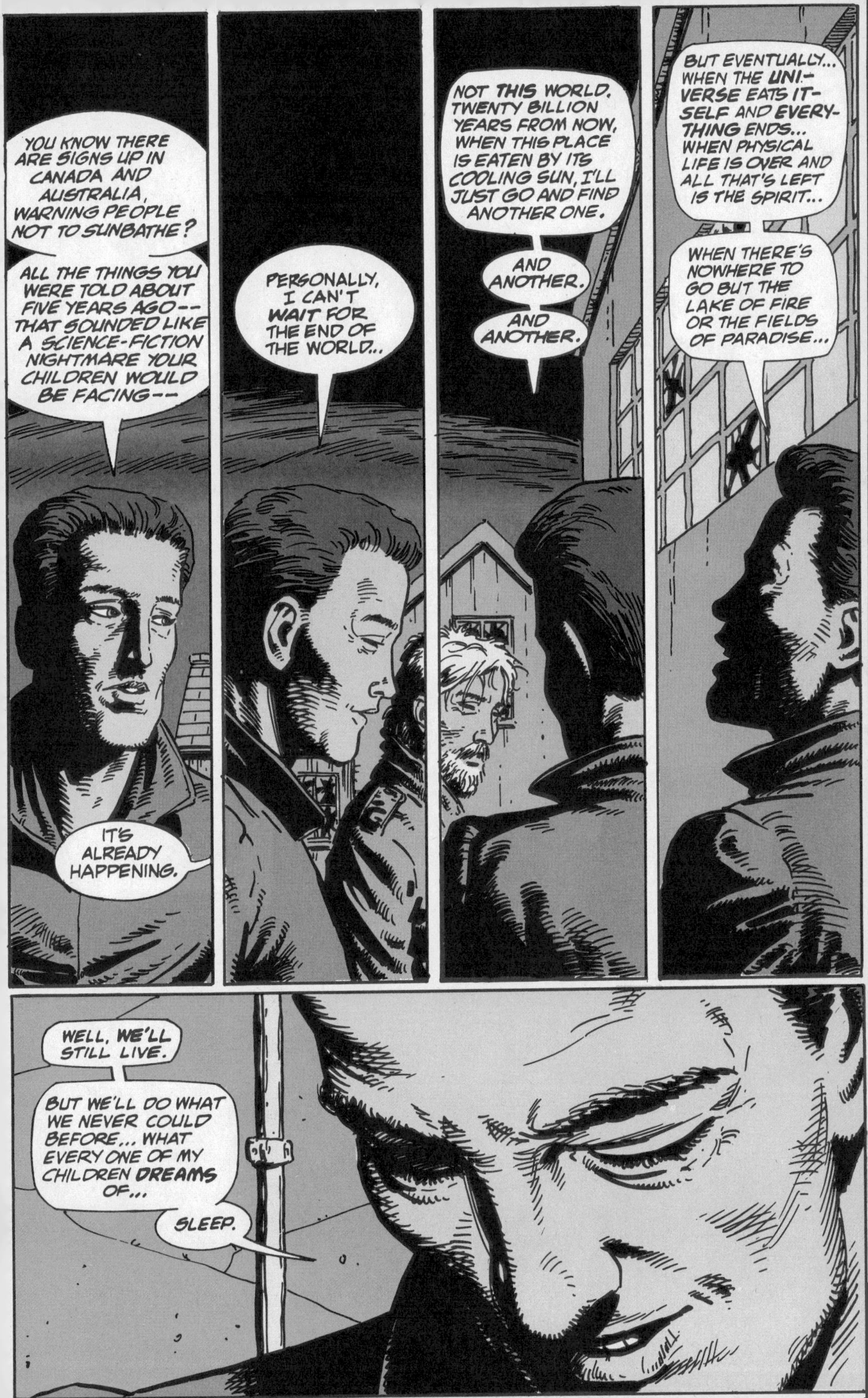
YOU KNOW THERE ARE SIGNS UP IN CANADA AND AUSTRALIA, WARNING PEOPLE NOT TO SUNBATHE?
ALL THE THINGS YOU WERE TOLD ABOUT FIVE YEARS AGO-- THAT SOUNDED LIKE A SCIENCE-FICTION NIGHTMARE YOUR CHILDREN WOULD BE FACING--
IT'S ALREADY HAPPENING.
PERSONALLY, I CAN'T WAIT FOR THE END OF THE WORLD...
NOT THIS WORLD. TWENTY BILLION YEARS FROM NOW, WHEN THIS PLACE IS EATEN BY ITS COOLING SUN, I'LL JUST GO AND FIND ANOTHER ONE.
AND ANOTHER.
AND ANOTHER.
BUT EVENTUALLY... WHEN THE UNI-VERSE EATS IT-SELF AND EVERY-THING ENDS... WHEN PHYSICAL LIFE IS OVER AND ALL THAT'S LEFT IS THE SPIRIT...
WHEN THERE'S NOWHERE TO GO BUT THE LAKE OF FIRE OR THE FIELDS OF PARADISE...
WELL, WE'LL STILL LIVE.
BUT WE'LL DO WHAT WE NEVER COULD BEFORE... WHAT EVERY ONE OF MY CHILDREN DREAMS OF...
SLEEP.

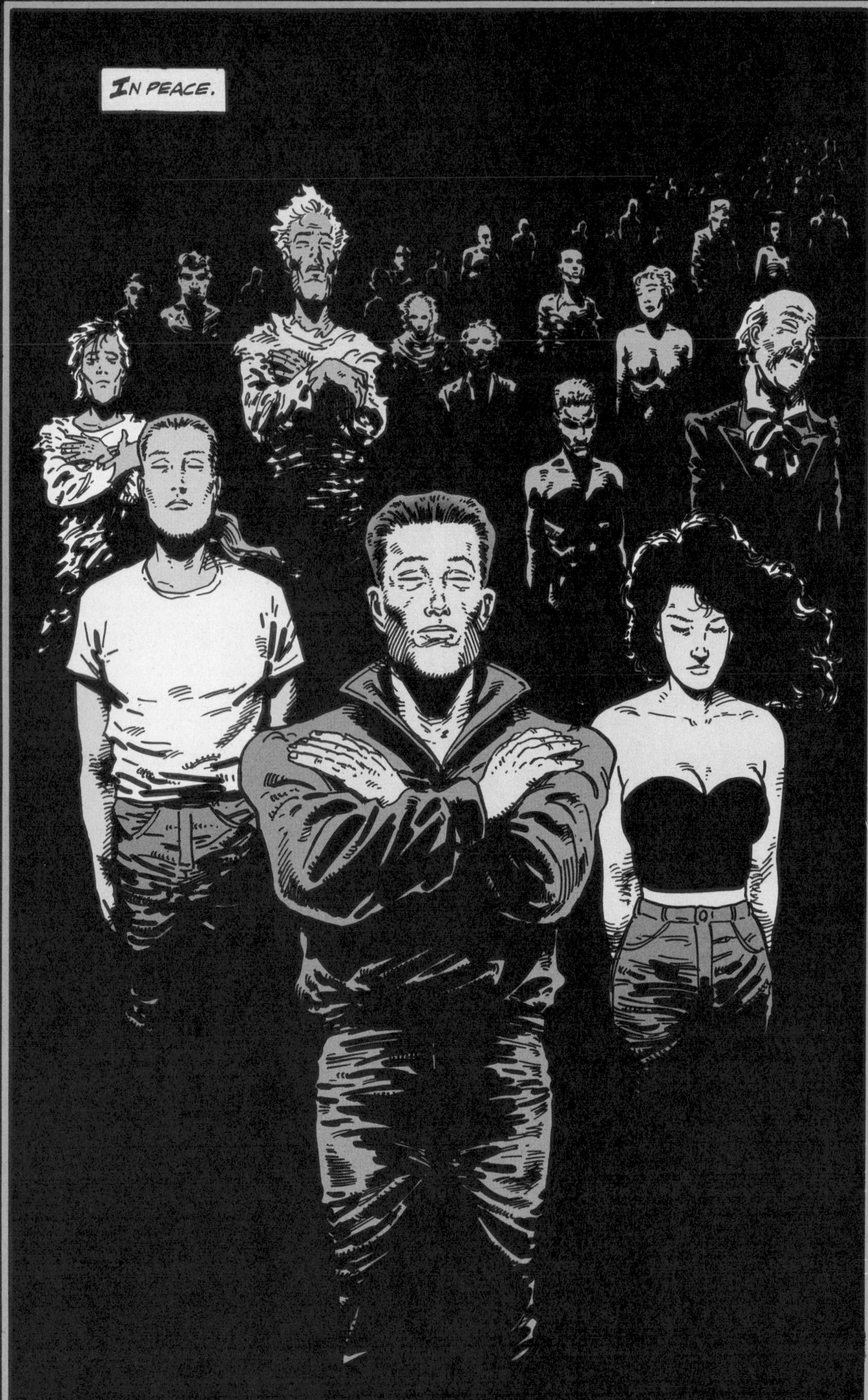
IN PEACE.

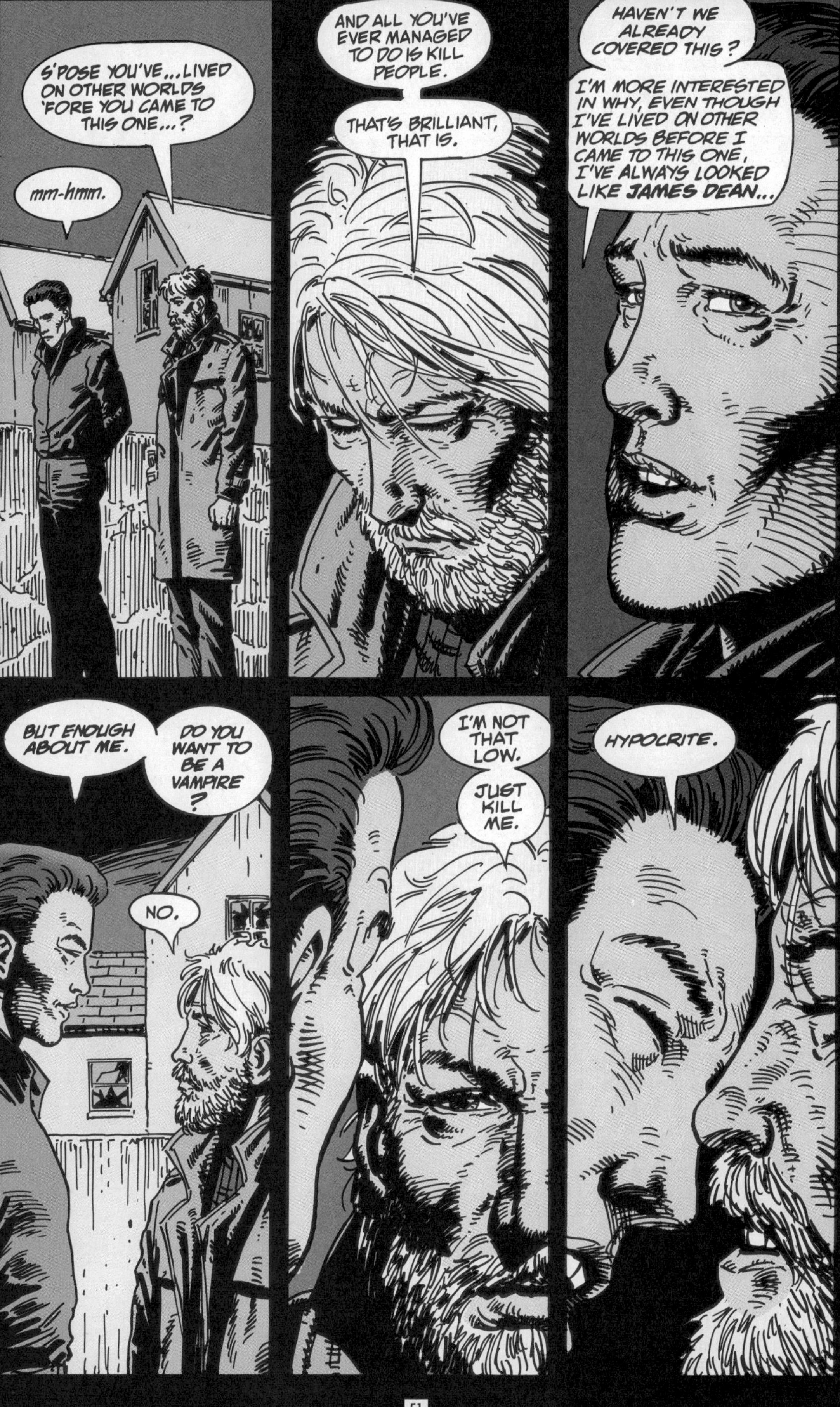

S'POSE YOU'VE...LIVED ON OTHER WORLDS 'FORE YOU CAME TO THIS ONE...?
mm-hmm.
AND ALL YOU'VE EVER MANAGED TO DO IS KILL PEOPLE.
THAT'S BRILLIANT, THAT IS.
HAVEN'T WE ALREADY COVERED THIS?
I'M MORE INTERESTED IN WHY, EVEN THOUGH I'VE LIVED ON OTHER WORLDS BEFORE I CAME TO THIS ONE, I'VE ALWAYS LOOKED LIKE JAMES DEAN...
BUT ENOUGH ABOUT ME.
DO YOU WANT TO BE A VAMPIRE?
NO.
I'M NOT THAT LOW.
JUST KILL ME.
HYPOCRITE.

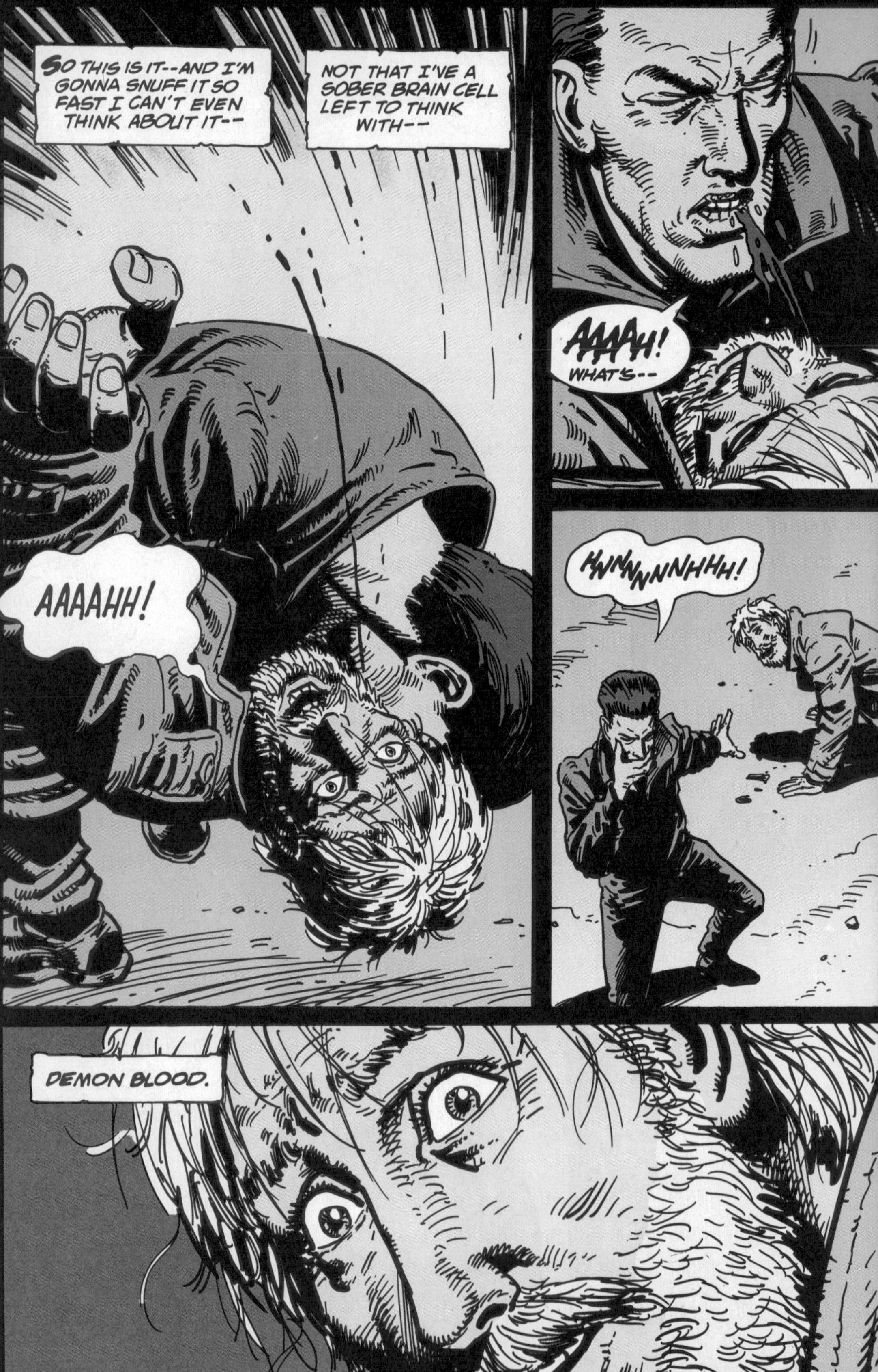
SO THIS IS IT--AND I'M GONNA SNUFF IT SO FAST I CAN'T EVEN THINK ABOUT IT--
NOT THAT I'VE A SOBER BRAIN CELL LEFT TO THINK WITH--
AAAAHH!
AAAAH! WHAT'S--
HNNNNNNHHH!
DEMON BLOOD.

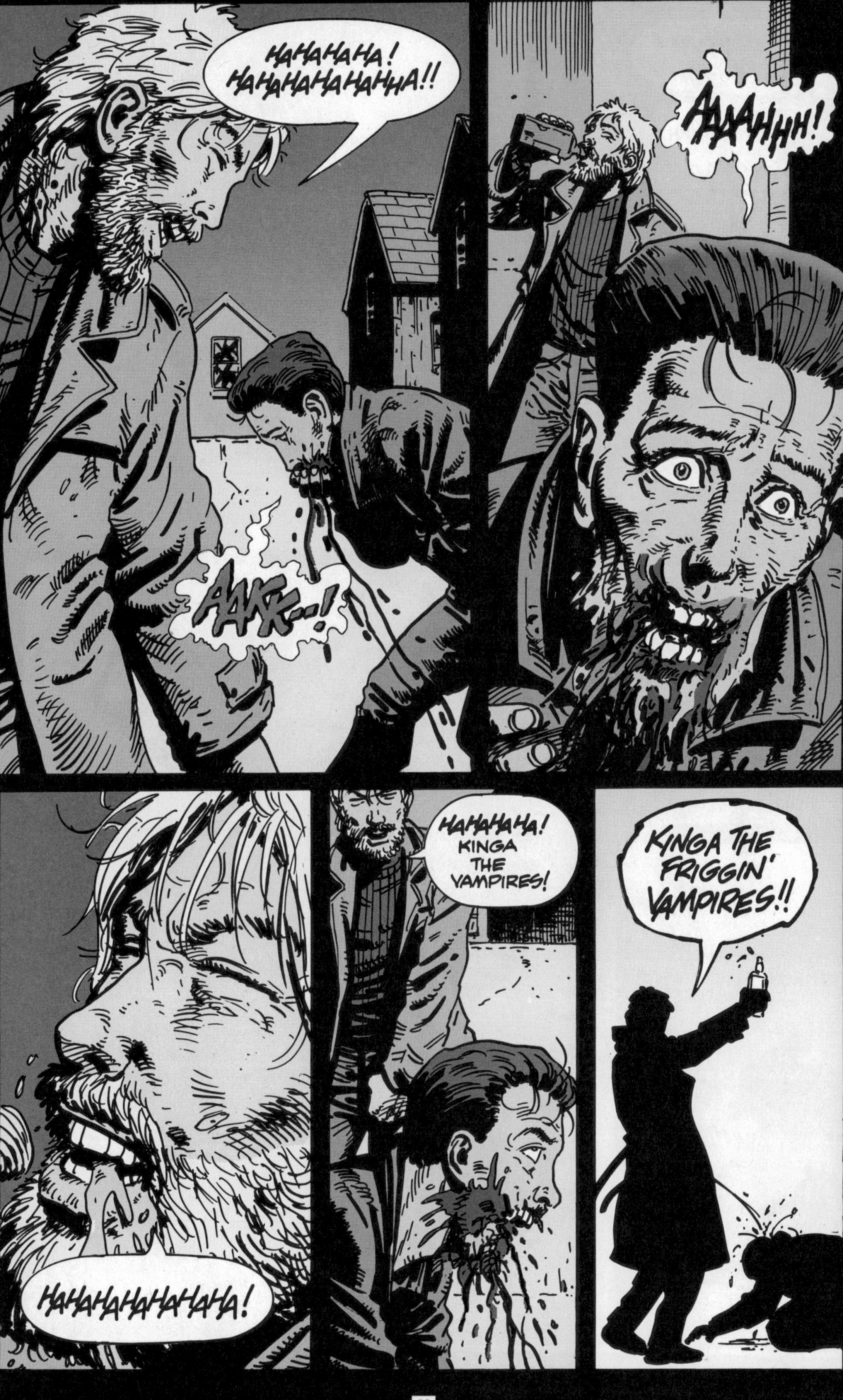
HAHAHAHA!
HAHAHAHAHAHAHHA!!
AAAAHHH!
AAKK--!
HAHAHAHAHAHAHAHA!
HAHAHAHA! KINGA THE VAMPIRES!
KINGA THE FRIGGIN' VAMPIRES!!

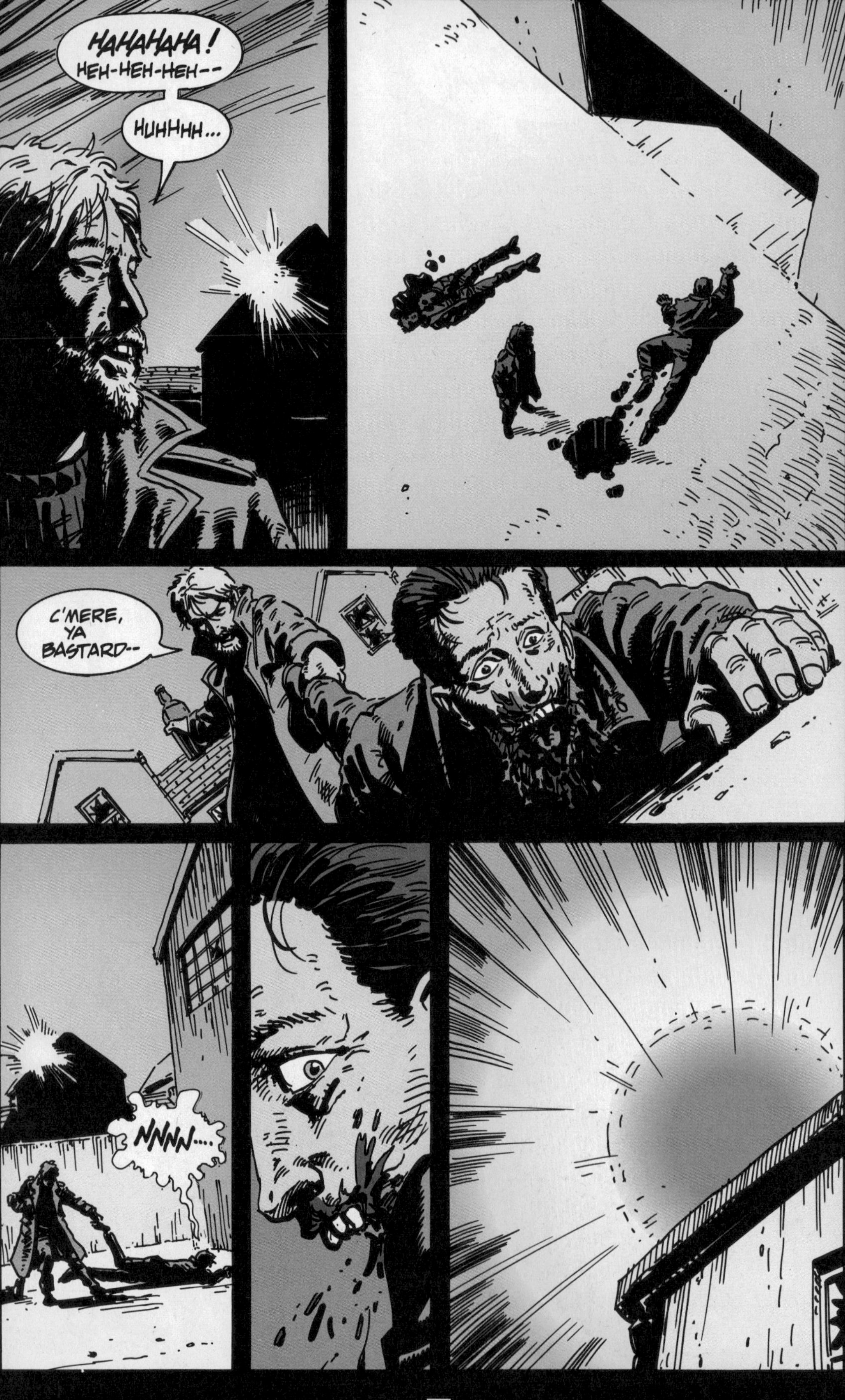
HAHAHAHA!
HEH-HEH-HEH--
HUHHHH...
C'MERE, YA BASTARD--
NNNN....

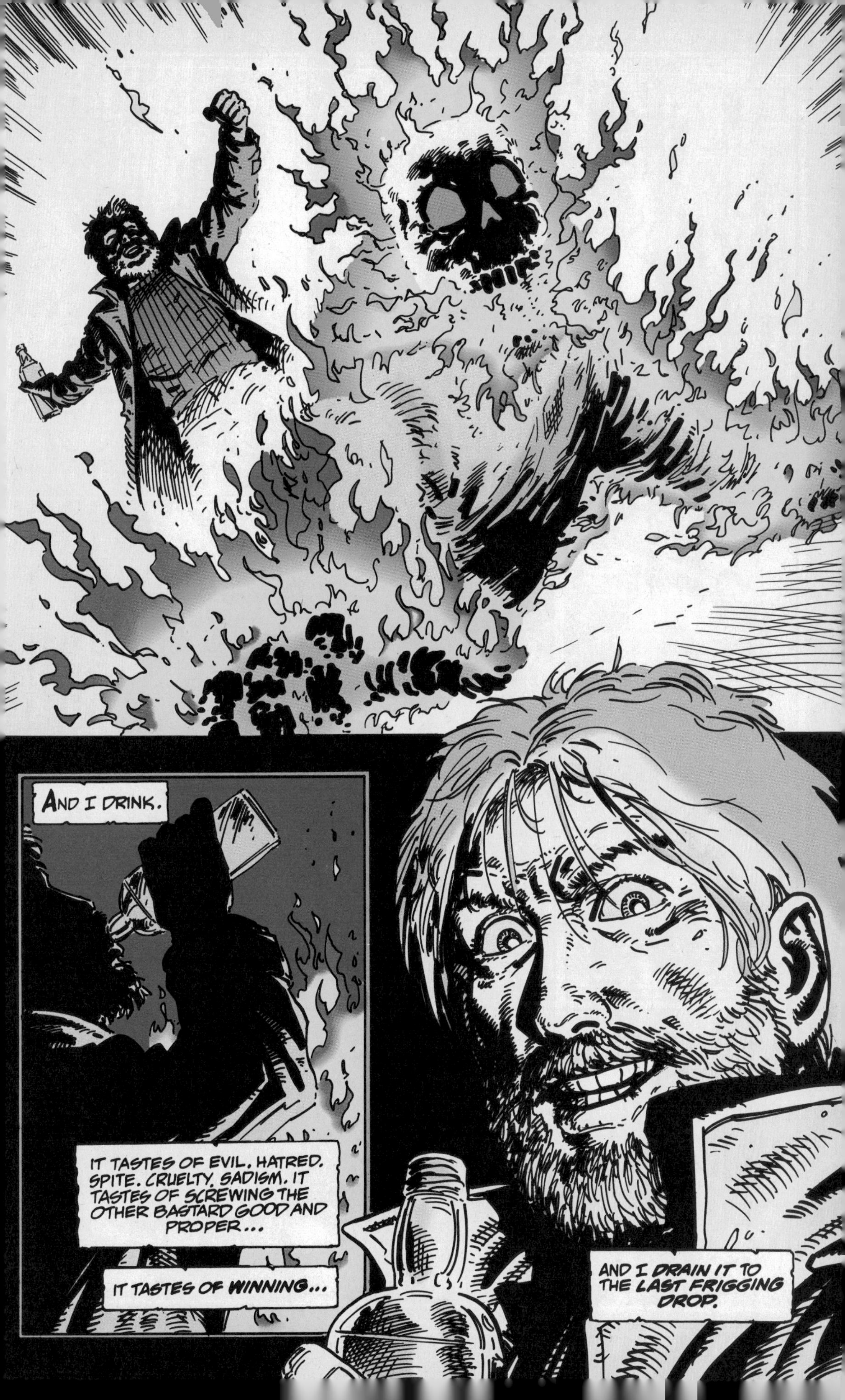
AND I DRINK.
IT TASTES OF EVIL. HATRED. SPITE. CRUELTY. SADISM. IT TASTES OF SCREWING THE OTHER BASTARD GOOD AND PROPER...
IT TASTES OF WINNING...
AND I DRAIN IT TO THE LAST FRIGGING DROP.

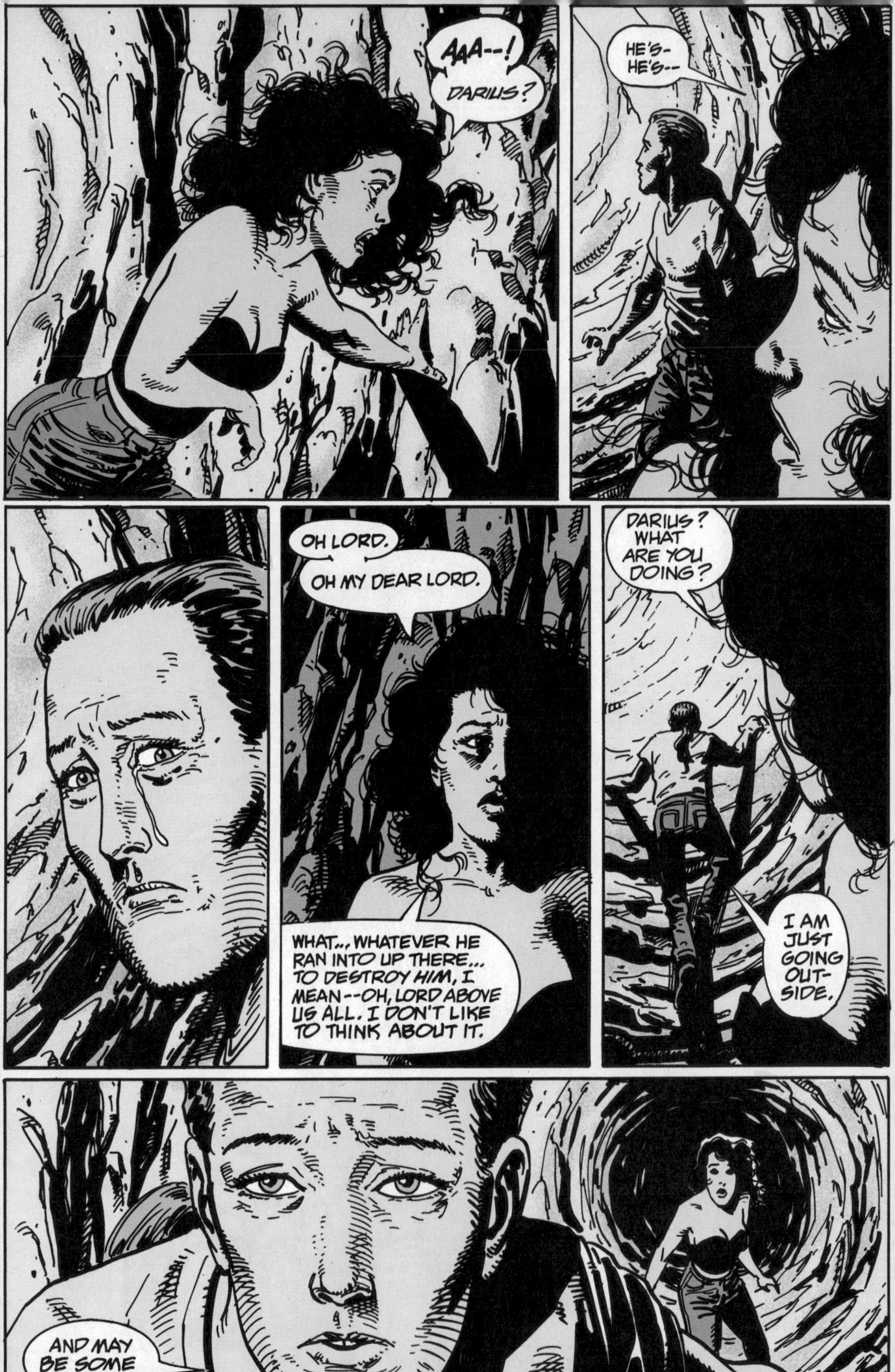
AAA--!
DARIUS?
HE'S-
HE'S--
OH LORD.
OH MY DEAR LORD.
WHAT... WHATEVER HE RAN INTO UP THERE... TO DESTROY HIM, I MEAN--OH, LORD ABOVE US ALL. I DON'T LIKE TO THINK ABOUT IT.
DARIUS? WHAT ARE YOU DOING?
I AM JUST GOING OUT-SIDE.
AND MAY BE SOME TIME.

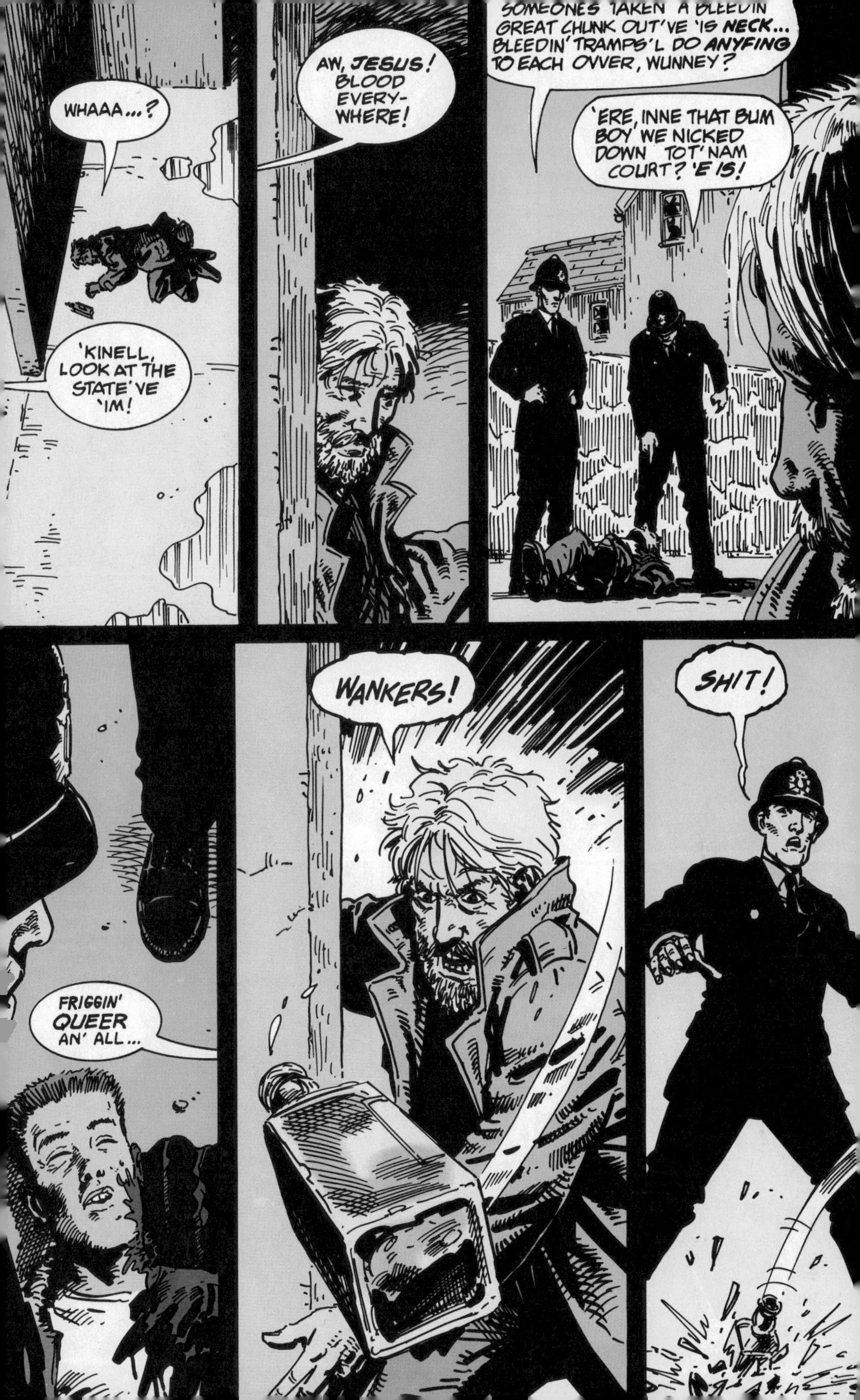
WHAAA...?
'KINELL, LOOK AT THE STATE'VE 'IM!
AW, JESUS! BLOOD EVERY-WHERE!
SOMEONE'S TAKEN A BLEEDIN GREAT CHUNK OUT'VE 'IS NECK... BLEEDIN' TRAMPS'L DO ANYFING TO EACH OVVER, WUNNEY?
'ERE, INNE THAT BUM BOY WE NICKED DOWN TOT'NAM COURT? 'E IS!
FRIGGIN' QUEER AN' ALL...
WANKERS!
SHIT!

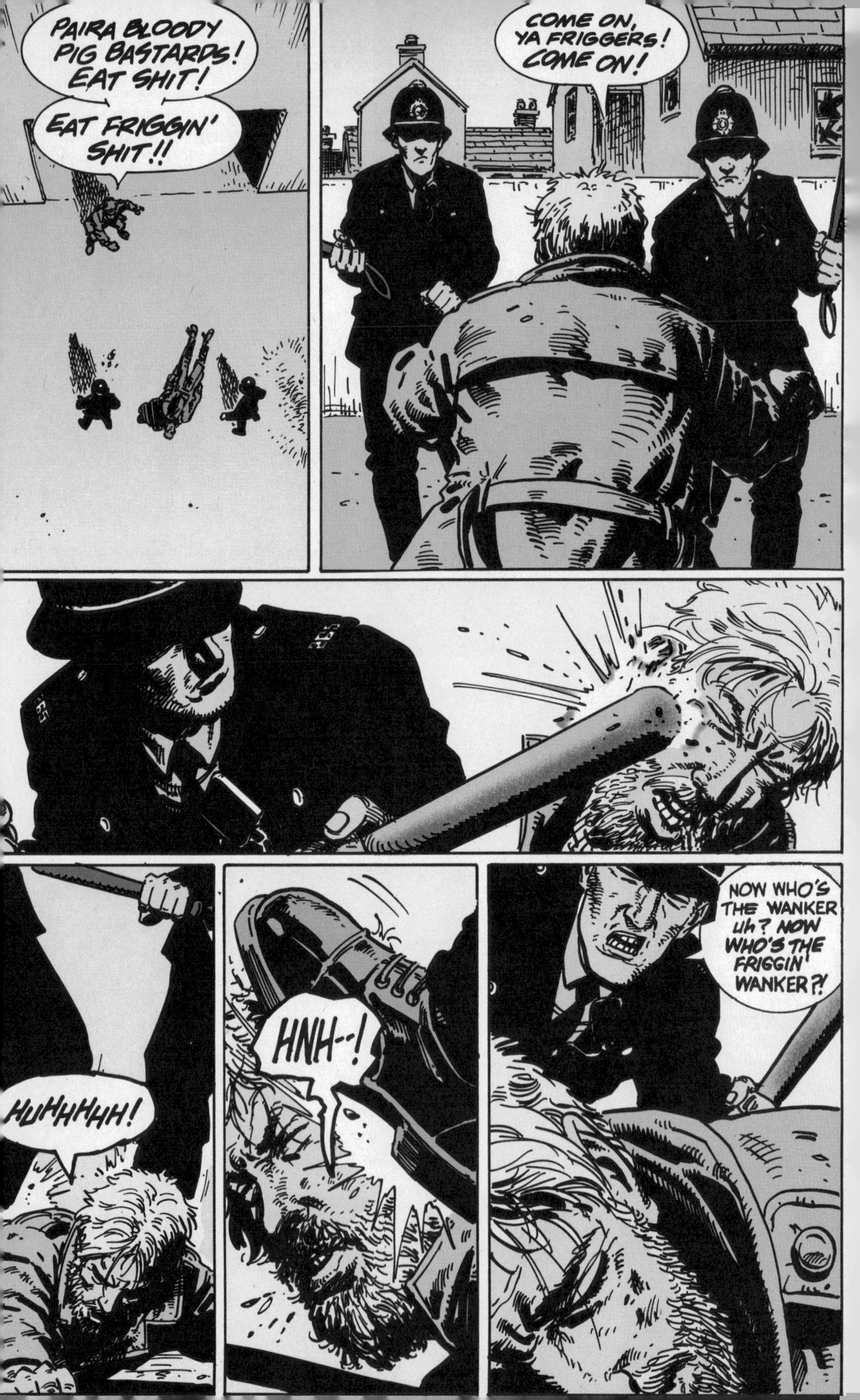
PAIRA BLOODY PIG BASTARDS! EAT SHIT!
EAT FRIGGIN' SHIT!!
COME ON, YA FRIGGERS! COME ON!
HUHHHHH!
HNH--!
NOW WHO'S THE WANKER uh? NOW WHO'S THE FRIGGIN' WANKER?!

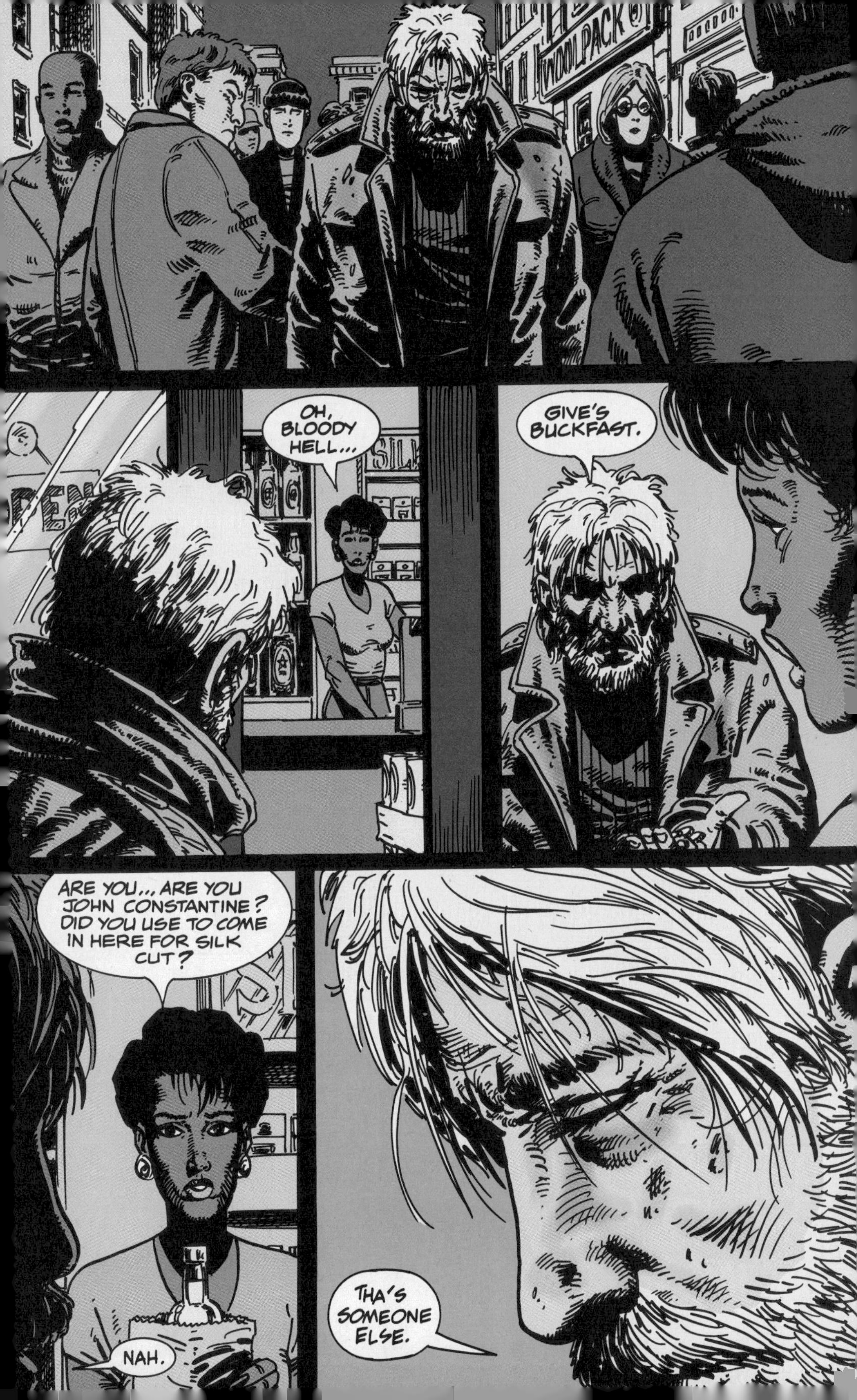
WOOLPACK
OH, BLOODY HELL...
GIVE'S BUCKFAST.
ARE YOU... ARE YOU JOHN CONSTANTINE? DID YOU USE TO COME IN HERE FOR SILK CUT?
NAH.
THA'S SOMEONE ELSE.

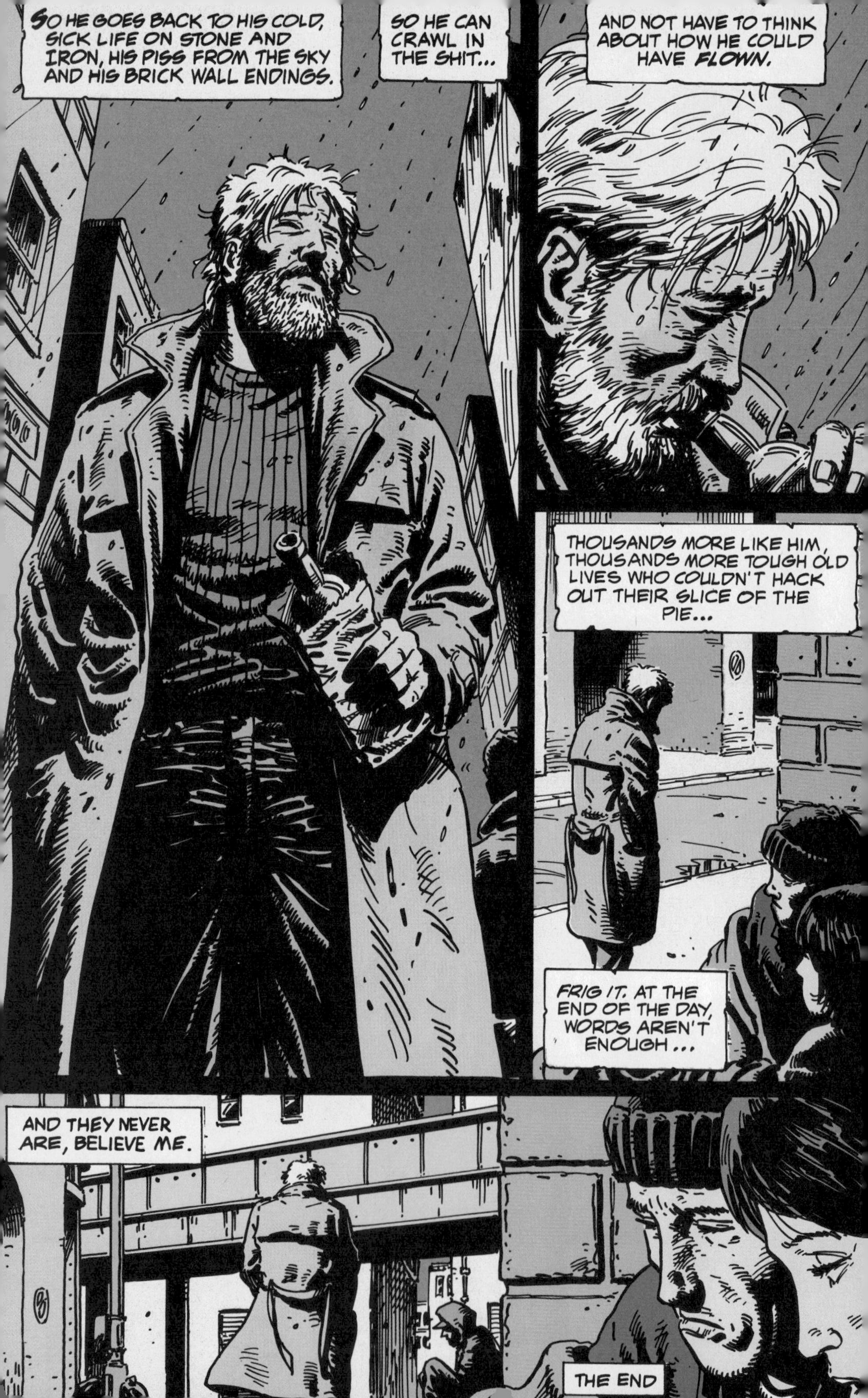
SO HE GOES BACK TO HIS COLD, SICK LIFE ON STONE AND IRON, HIS PISS FROM THE SKY AND HIS BRICK WALL ENDINGS.
SO HE CAN CRAWL IN THE SHIT...
AND NOT HAVE TO THINK ABOUT HOW HE COULD HAVE FLOWN.
THOUSANDS MORE LIKE HIM, THOUSANDS MORE TOUGH OLD LIVES WHO COULDN'T HACK OUT THEIR SLICE OF THE PIE...
FRIG IT. AT THE END OF THE DAY, WORDS AREN'T ENOUGH...
AND THEY NEVER ARE, BELIEVE ME.
THE END

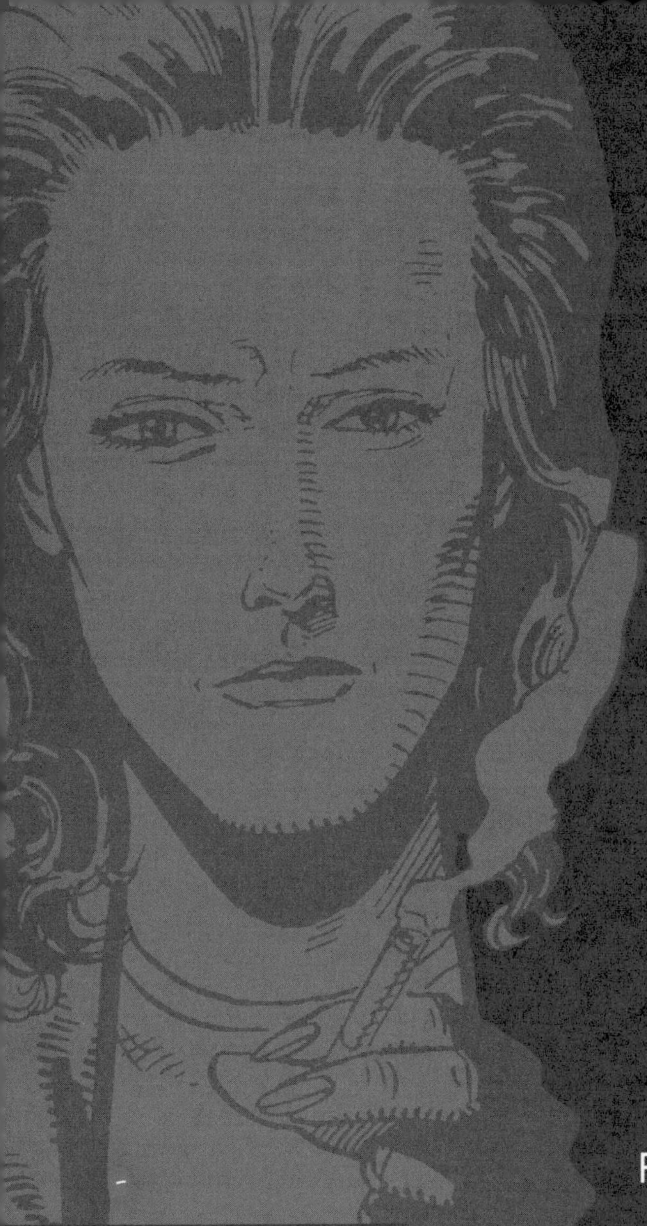

FALL AND RISE

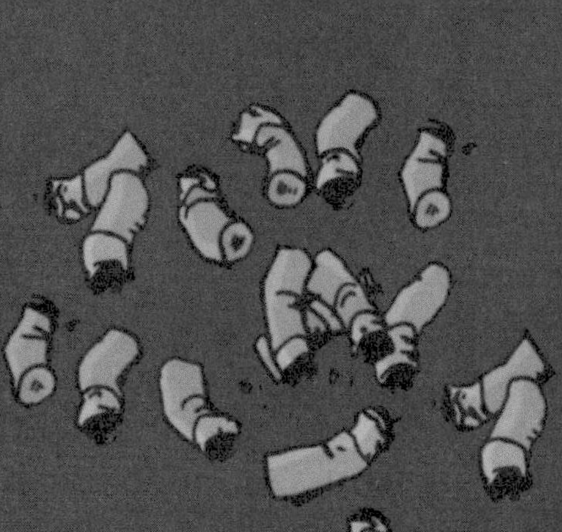

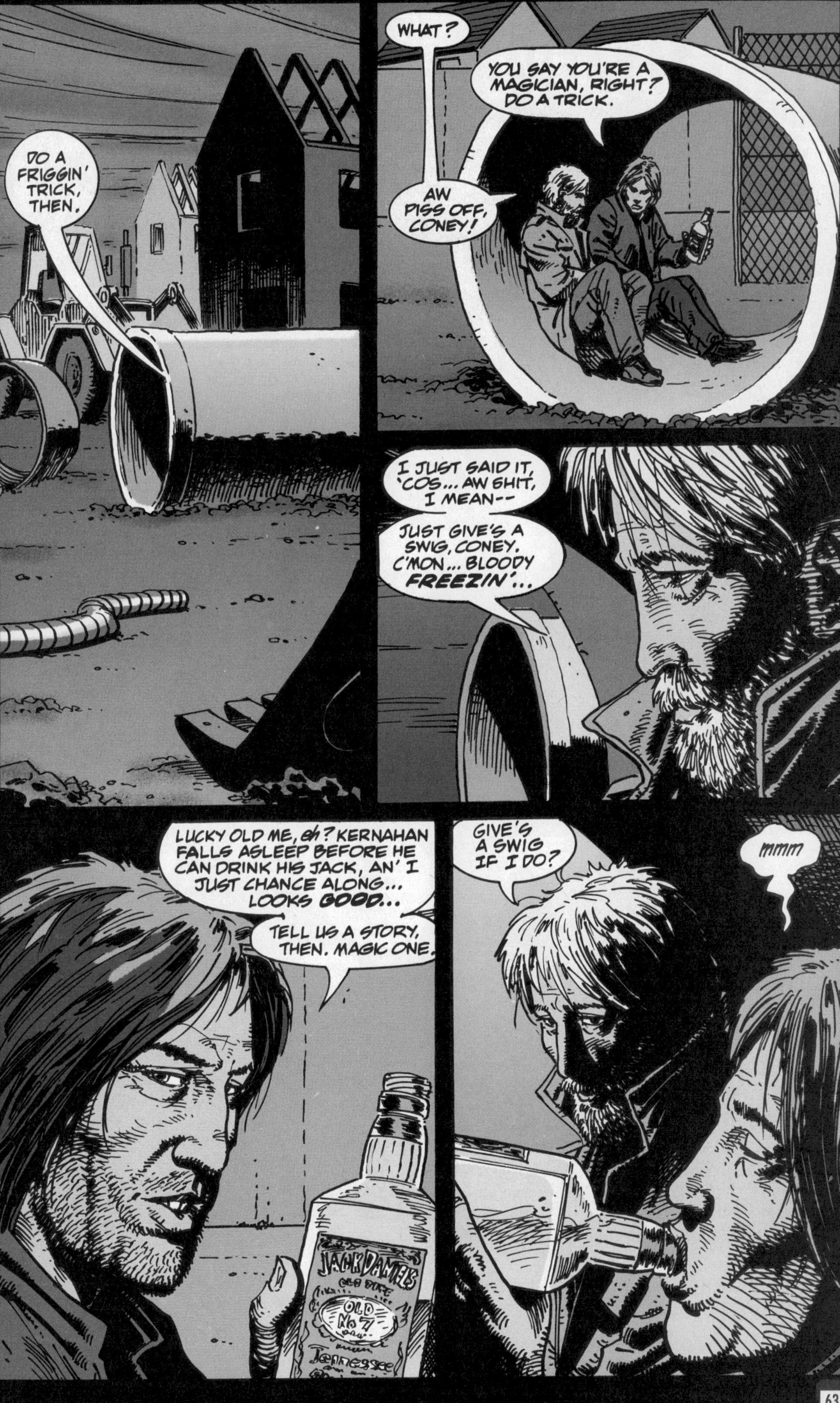
DO A FRIGGIN' TRICK, THEN.
WHAT?
YOU SAY YOU'RE A MAGICIAN, RIGHT? DO A TRICK.
AW PISS OFF, CONEY!
I JUST SAID IT, 'COS... AW SHIT, I MEAN--
JUST GIVE'S A SWIG, CONEY. C'MON... BLOODY FREEZIN'...
LUCKY OLD ME, eh? KERNAHAN FALLS ASLEEP BEFORE HE CAN DRINK HIS JACK, AN' I JUST CHANCE ALONG... LOOKS GOOD...
TELL US A STORY, THEN. MAGIC ONE.
GIVE'S A SWIG IF I DO?
mmm

TAINTED LOVE

GARTH ENNIS • writer
STEVE DILLON • artist
TOM ZIUKO • colors
gaspar • letters
JULIE ROTTENBERG • asst. editor
STUART MOORE • editor

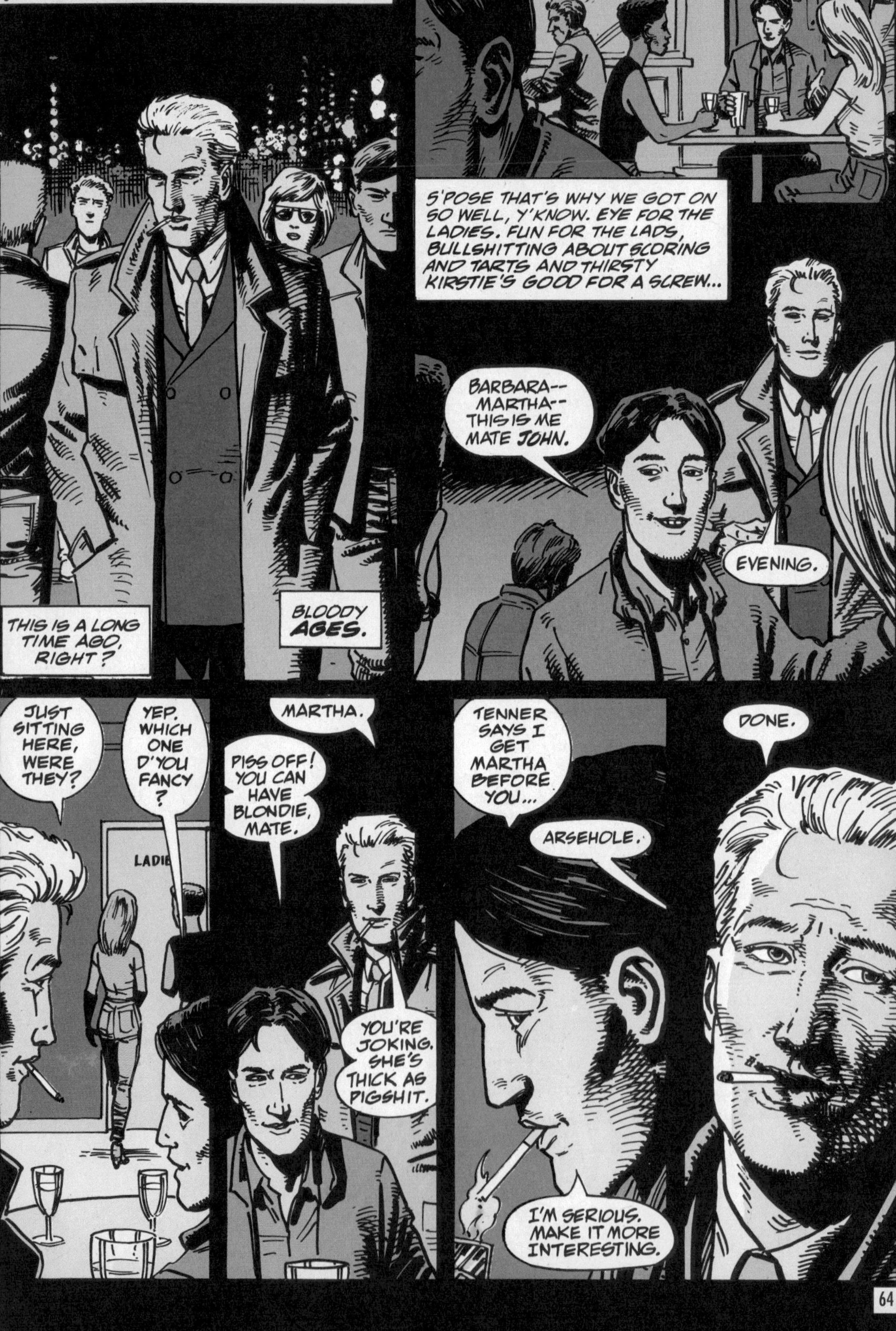
THIS IS A LONG TIME AGO, RIGHT?
BLOODY AGES.
MATE OF MINE CALLED SETH. REAL SMOOTH OPERATOR. HAD TO BEAT THE BIRDS OFF WITH A BIG SHITTY STICK.
NOT THAT I HAD MUCH TROUBLE IN THAT DEPARTMENT...
S'POSE THAT'S WHY WE GOT ON SO WELL, Y'KNOW. EYE FOR THE LADIES. FUN FOR THE LADS, BULLSHITTING ABOUT SCORING AND TARTS AND THIRSTY KIRSTIE'S GOOD FOR A SCREW...
BARBARA-- MARTHA-- THIS IS ME MATE JOHN.
EVENING.
JUST SITTING HERE, WERE THEY?
YEP. WHICH ONE D'YOU FANCY?
LADIE
MARTHA.
PISS OFF! YOU CAN HAVE BLONDIE, MATE.
YOU'RE JOKING. SHE'S THICK AS PIGSHIT.
TENNER SAYS I GET MARTHA BEFORE YOU...
DONE.
ARSEHOLE.
I'M SERIOUS. MAKE IT MORE INTERESTING.

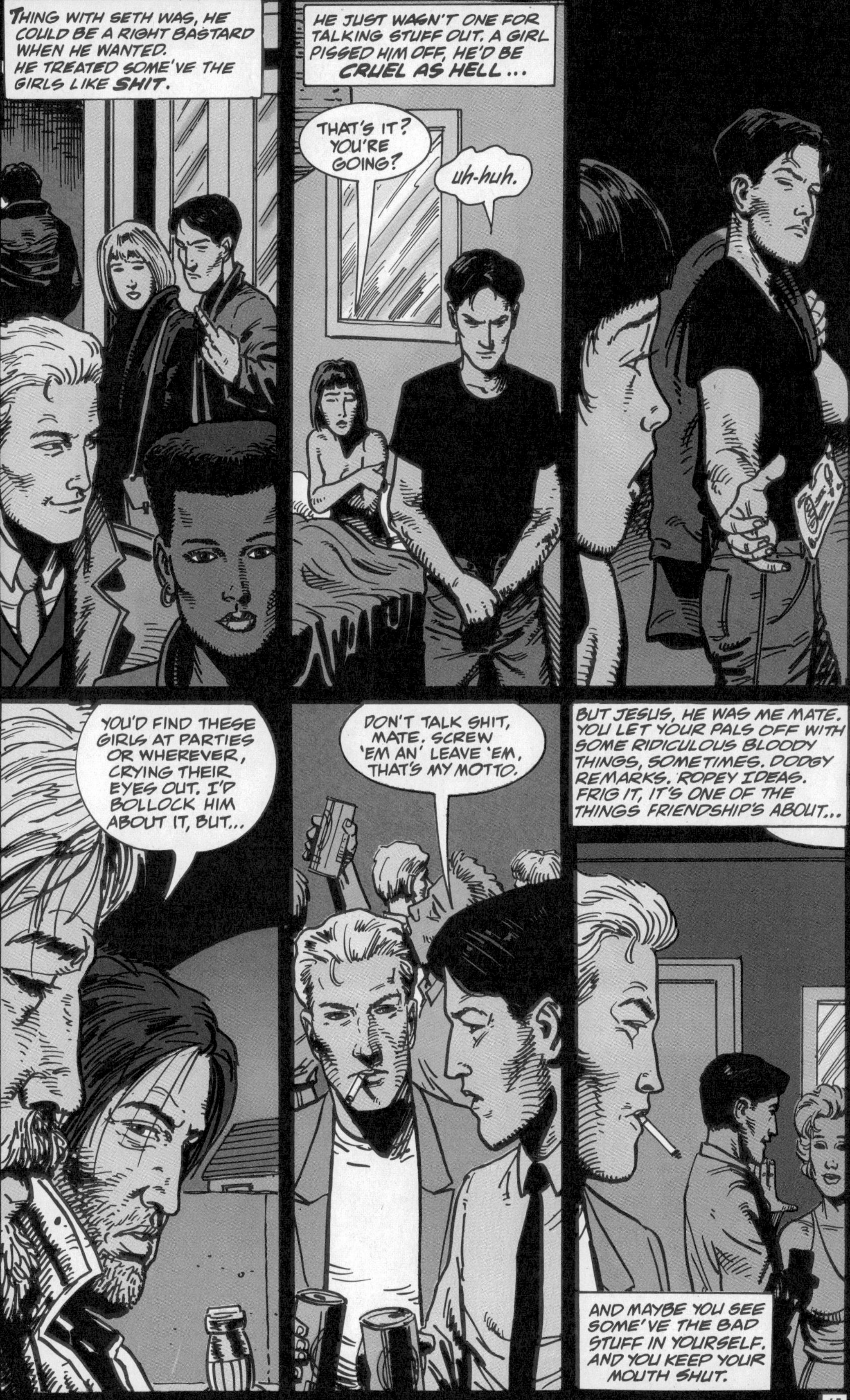
THING WITH SETH WAS, HE COULD BE A RIGHT BASTARD WHEN HE WANTED. HE TREATED SOME'VE THE GIRLS LIKE SHIT.
HE JUST WASN'T ONE FOR TALKING STUFF OUT. A GIRL PISSED HIM OFF, HE'D BE CRUEL AS HELL...
THAT'S IT? YOU'RE GOING?
uh-huh.
YOU'D FIND THESE GIRLS AT PARTIES OR WHEREVER, CRYING THEIR EYES OUT. I'D BOLLOCK HIM ABOUT IT, BUT...
DON'T TALK SHIT, MATE. SCREW 'EM AN' LEAVE 'EM, THAT'S MY MOTTO.
BUT JESUS, HE WAS ME MATE. YOU LET YOUR PALS OFF WITH SOME RIDICULOUS BLOODY THINGS, SOMETIMES. DODGY REMARKS. ROPEY IDEAS. FRIG IT, IT'S ONE OF THE THINGS FRIENDSHIP'S ABOUT...
AND MAYBE YOU SEE SOME'VE THE BAD STUFF IN YOURSELF. AND YOU KEEP YOUR MOUTH SHUT.

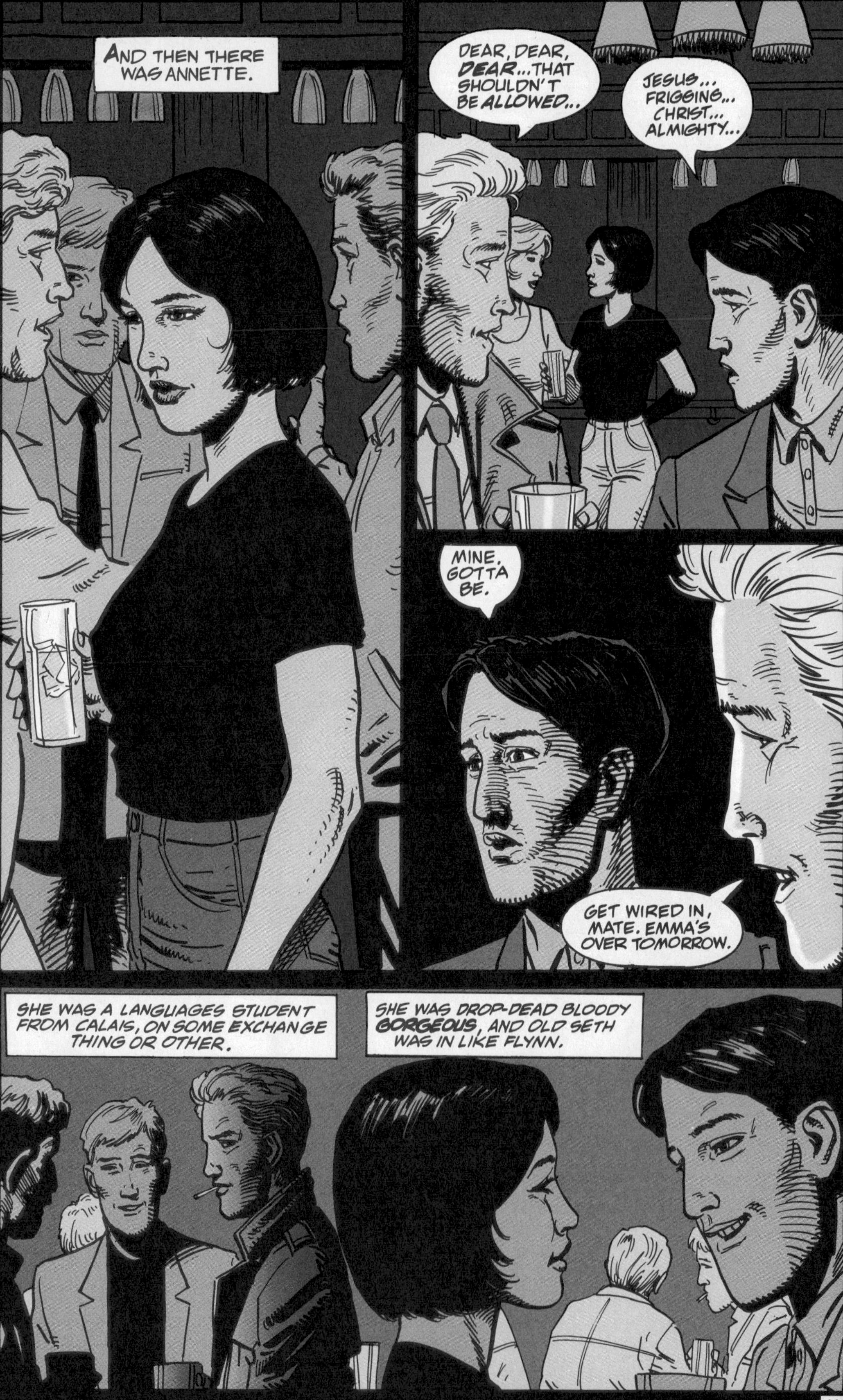
AND THEN THERE WAS ANNETTE.
DEAR, DEAR, DEAR...THAT SHOULDN'T BE ALLOWED...
JESUS... FRIGGING... CHRIST... ALMIGHTY...
MINE. GOTTA BE.
GET WIRED IN, MATE. EMMA'S OVER TOMORROW.
SHE WAS A LANGUAGES STUDENT FROM CALAIS, ON SOME EXCHANGE THING OR OTHER.
SHE WAS DROP-DEAD BLOODY GORGEOUS, AND OLD SETH WAS IN LIKE FLYNN.

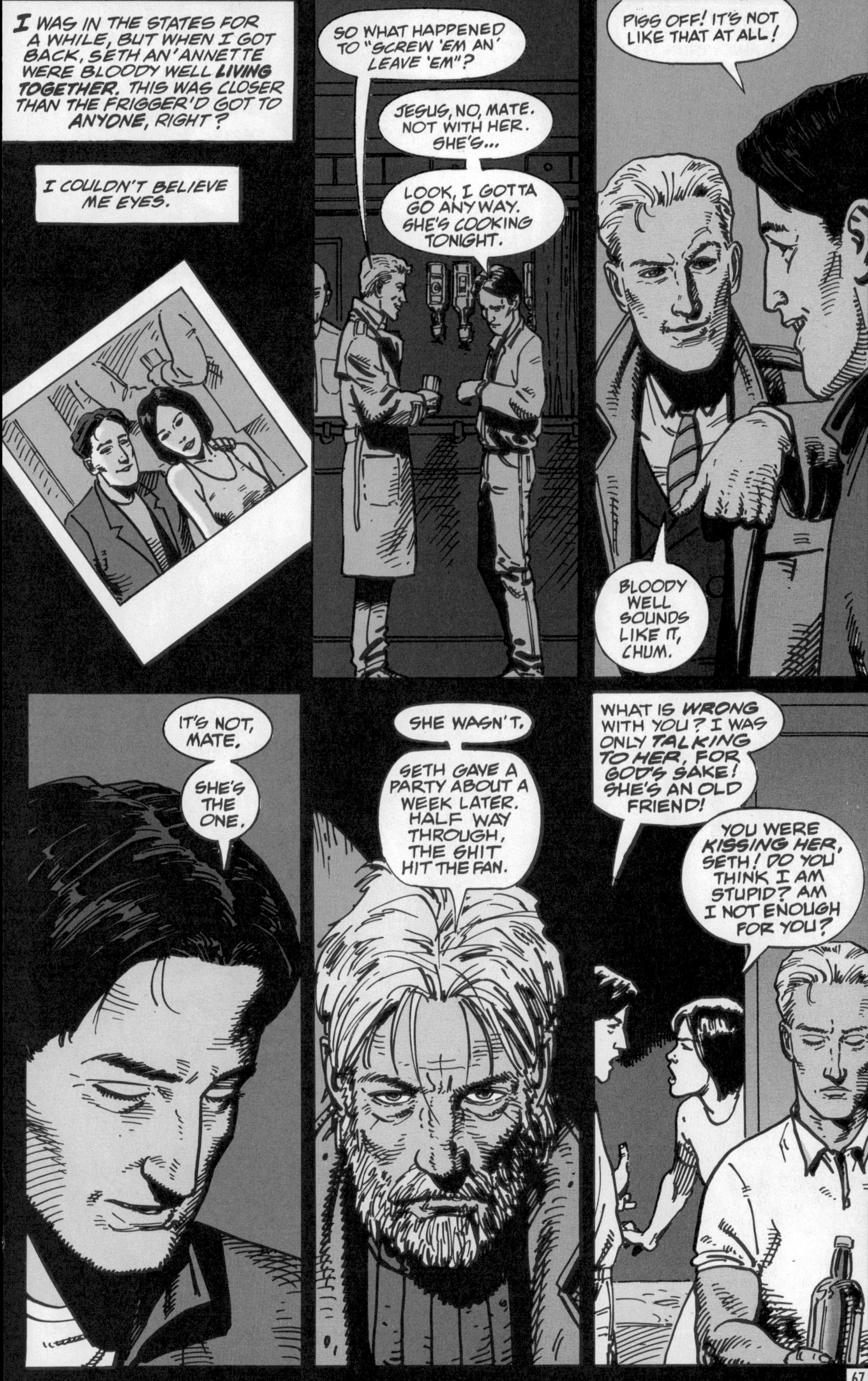

I WAS IN THE STATES FOR A WHILE, BUT WHEN I GOT BACK, SETH AN' ANNETTE WERE BLOODY WELL LIVING TOGETHER. THIS WAS CLOSER THAN THE FRIGGER'D GOT TO ANYONE, RIGHT?
I COULDN'T BELIEVE ME EYES.
SO WHAT HAPPENED TO "SCREW 'EM AN' LEAVE 'EM"?
JESUS, NO, MATE. NOT WITH HER. SHE'S...
LOOK, I GOTTA GO ANYWAY. SHE'S COOKING TONIGHT.
PISS OFF! IT'S NOT LIKE THAT AT ALL!
BLOODY WELL SOUNDS LIKE IT, CHUM.
IT'S NOT, MATE.
SHE'S THE ONE.
SHE WASN'T.
SETH GAVE A PARTY ABOUT A WEEK LATER. HALF WAY THROUGH, THE SHIT HIT THE FAN.
WHAT IS WRONG WITH YOU? I WAS ONLY TALKING TO HER, FOR GOD'S SAKE! SHE'S AN OLD FRIEND!
YOU WERE KISSING HER, SETH! DO YOU THINK I AM STUPID? AM I NOT ENOUGH FOR YOU?

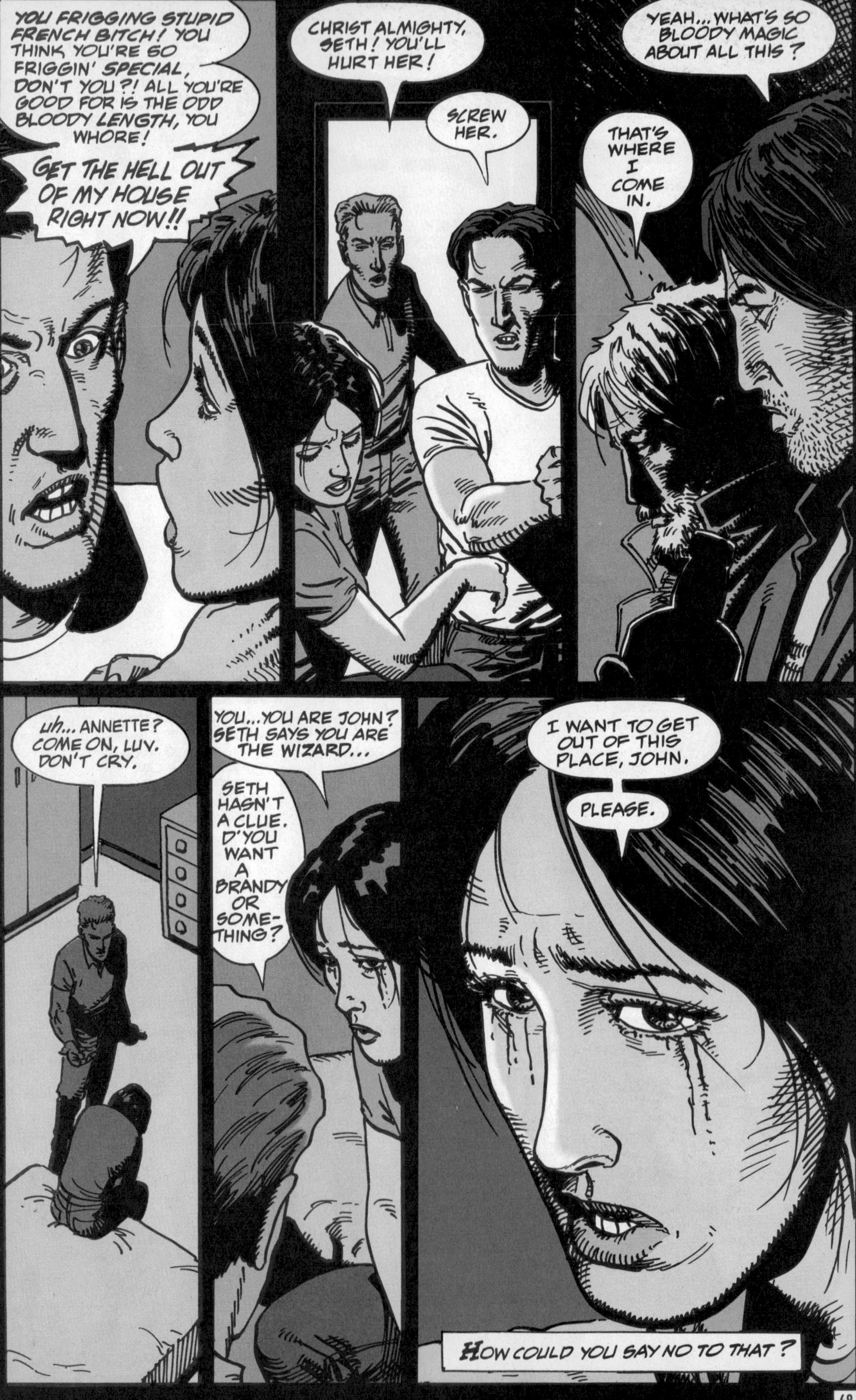
YOU FRIGGING STUPID FRENCH BITCH! YOU THINK YOU'RE SO FRIGGIN' SPECIAL, DON'T YOU?! ALL YOU'RE GOOD FOR IS THE ODD BLOODY LENGTH, YOU WHORE!
GET THE HELL OUT OF MY HOUSE RIGHT NOW!!
CHRIST ALMIGHTY, SETH! YOU'LL HURT HER!
SCREW HER.
YEAH... WHAT'S SO BLOODY MAGIC ABOUT ALL THIS?
THAT'S WHERE I COME IN.
uh... ANNETTE? COME ON, LUV. DON'T CRY.
YOU... YOU ARE JOHN? SETH SAYS YOU ARE THE WIZARD...
SETH HASN'T A CLUE. D'YOU WANT A BRANDY OR SOMETHING?
I WANT TO GET OUT OF THIS PLACE, JOHN.
PLEASE.
HOW COULD YOU SAY NO TO THAT?

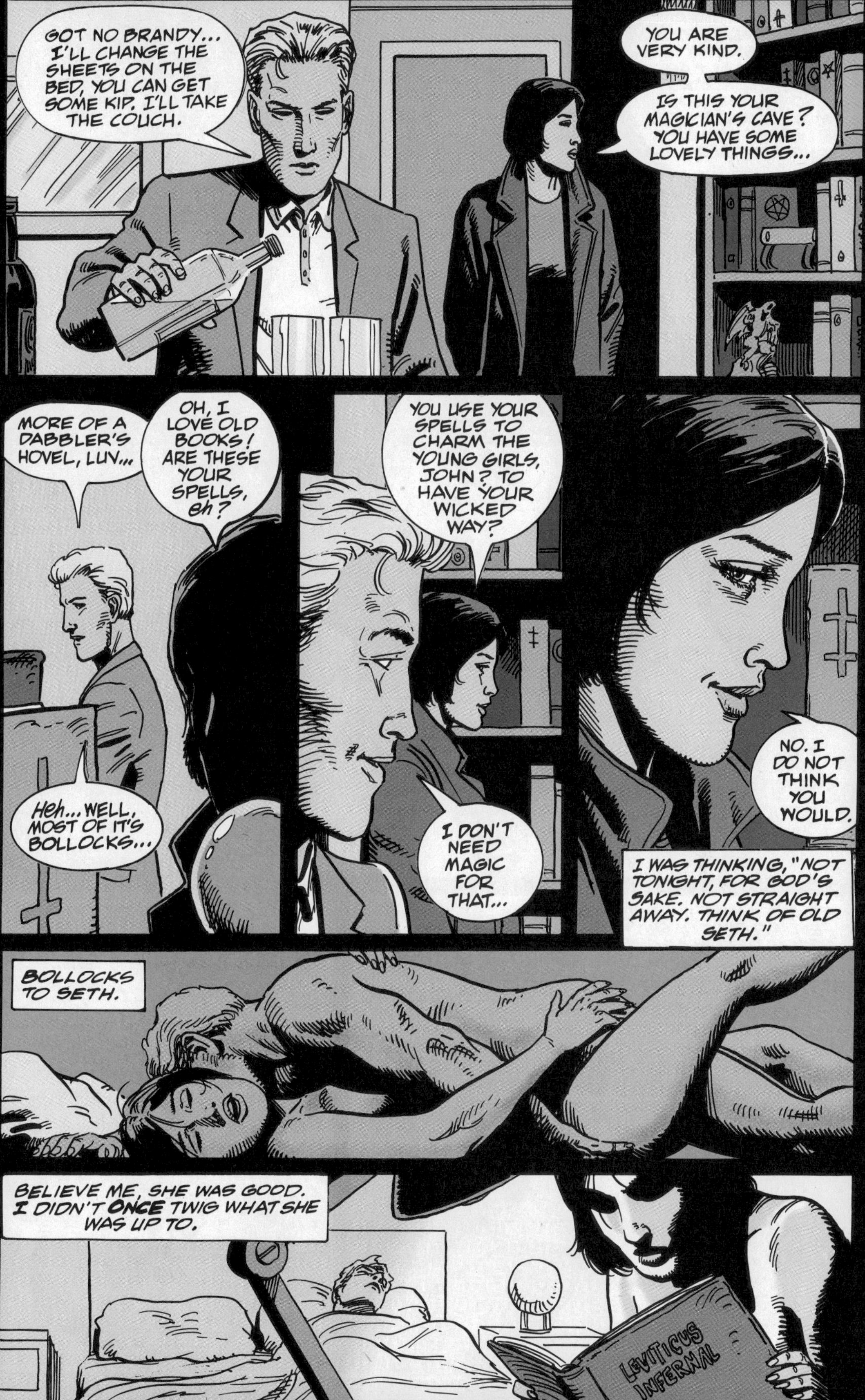
GOT NO BRANDY... I'LL CHANGE THE SHEETS ON THE BED, YOU CAN GET SOME KIP. I'LL TAKE THE COUCH.
YOU ARE VERY KIND.
IS THIS YOUR MAGICIAN'S CAVE? YOU HAVE SOME LOVELY THINGS...
MORE OF A DABBLER'S HOVEL, LUV...
OH, I LOVE OLD BOOKS! ARE THESE YOUR SPELLS, EH?
HEH... WELL, MOST OF IT'S BOLLOCKS...
YOU USE YOUR SPELLS TO CHARM THE YOUNG GIRLS, JOHN? TO HAVE YOUR WICKED WAY?
I DON'T NEED MAGIC FOR THAT...
NO. I DO NOT THINK YOU WOULD.
I WAS THINKING, "NOT TONIGHT, FOR GOD'S SAKE. NOT STRAIGHT AWAY. THINK OF OLD SETH."
BOLLOCKS TO SETH.
BELIEVE ME, SHE WAS GOOD. I DIDN'T ONCE TWIG WHAT SHE WAS UP TO.
LEVITICUS INFERNAL

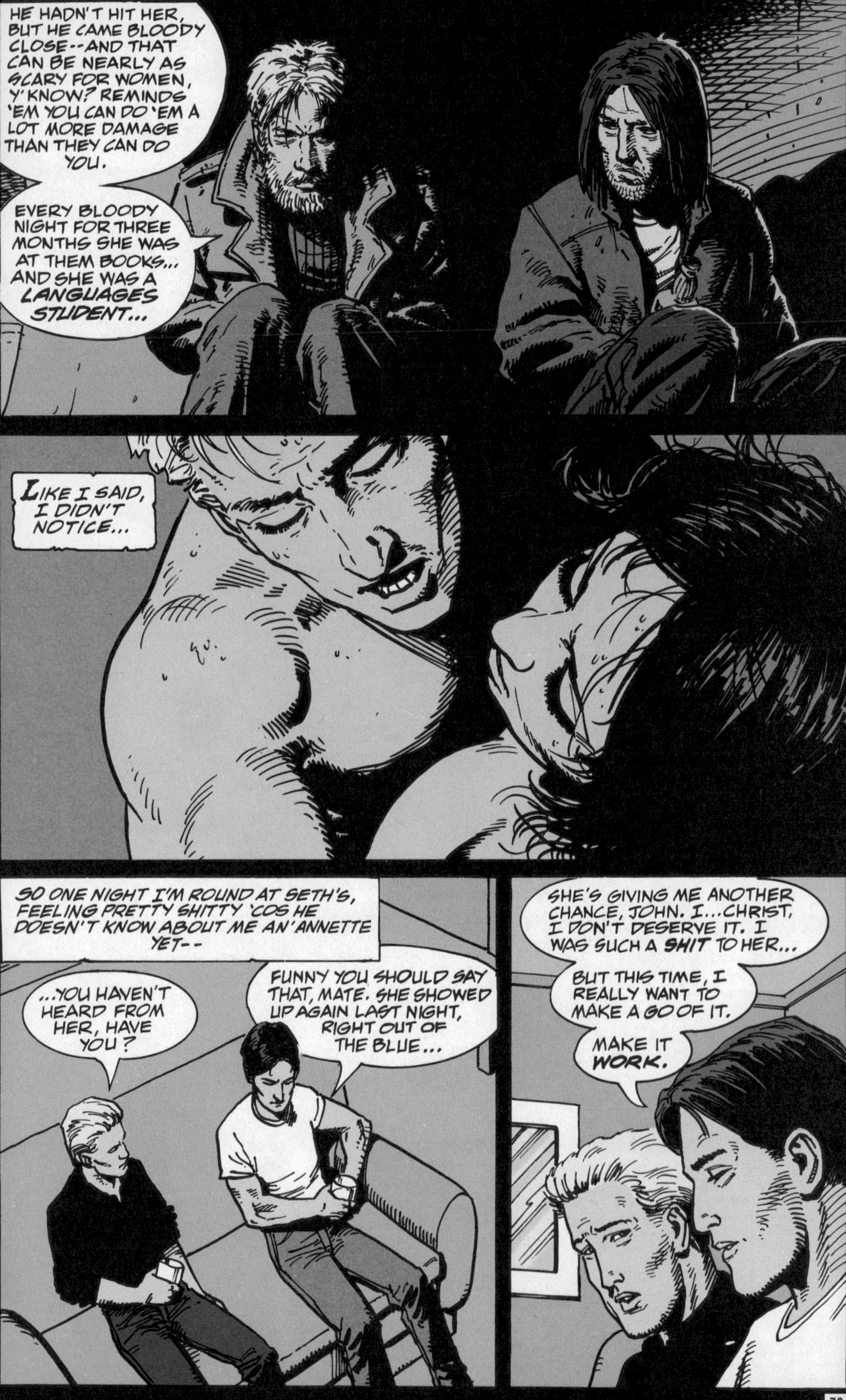
HE HADN'T HIT HER, BUT HE CAME BLOODY CLOSE--AND THAT CAN BE NEARLY AS SCARY FOR WOMEN, Y'KNOW? REMINDS 'EM YOU CAN DO 'EM A LOT MORE DAMAGE THAN THEY CAN DO YOU.
EVERY BLOODY NIGHT FOR THREE MONTHS SHE WAS AT THEM BOOKS... AND SHE WAS A LANGUAGES STUDENT...
LIKE I SAID, I DIDN'T NOTICE...
SO ONE NIGHT I'M ROUND AT SETH'S, FEELING PRETTY SHITTY 'COS HE DOESN'T KNOW ABOUT ME AN' ANNETTE YET--
...YOU HAVEN'T HEARD FROM HER, HAVE YOU?
FUNNY YOU SHOULD SAY THAT, MATE. SHE SHOWED UP AGAIN LAST NIGHT, RIGHT OUT OF THE BLUE...
SHE'S GIVING ME ANOTHER CHANCE, JOHN. I...CHRIST, I DON'T DESERVE IT. I WAS SUCH A SHIT TO HER...
BUT THIS TIME, I REALLY WANT TO MAKE A GO OF IT.
MAKE IT WORK.

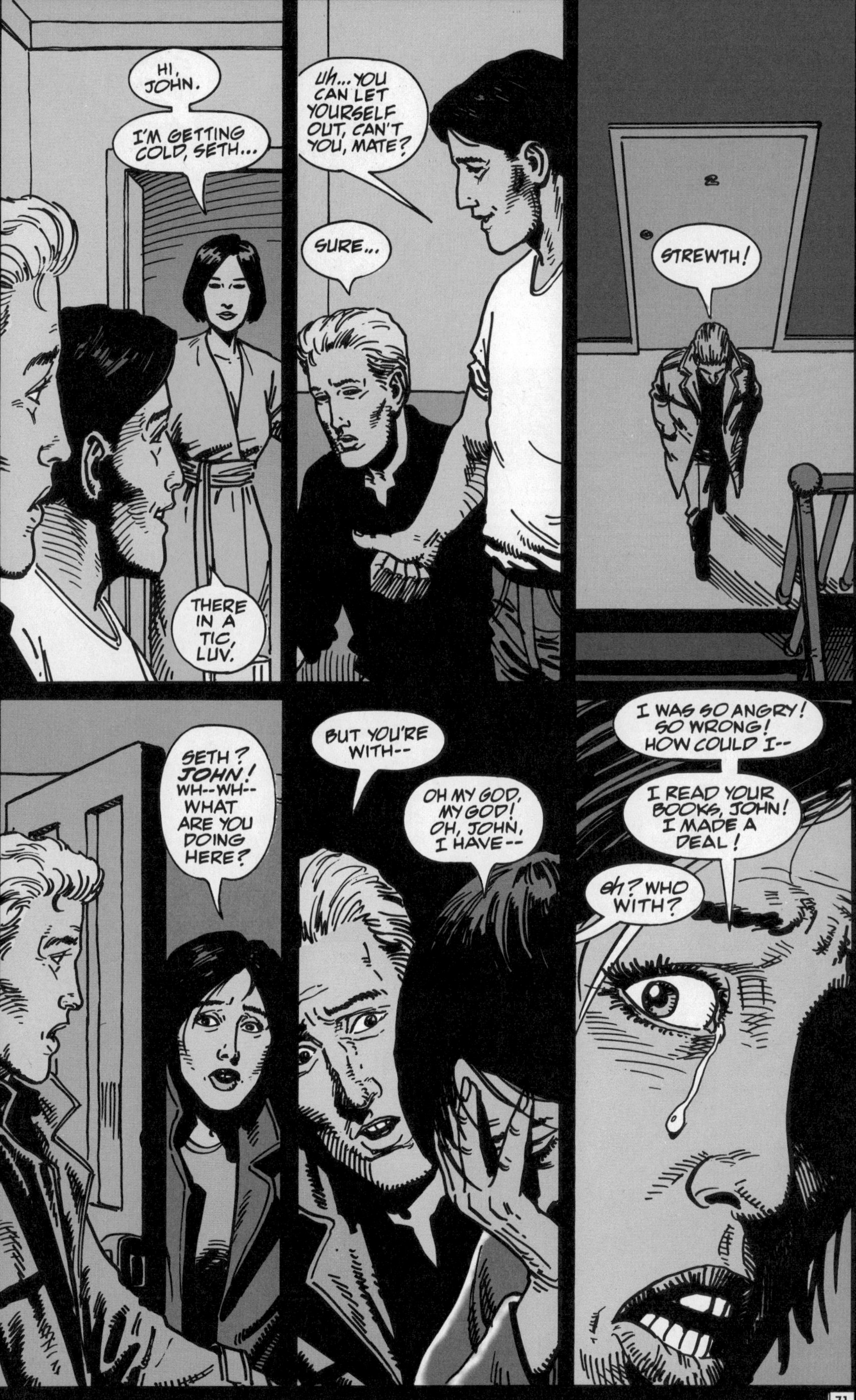
HI, JOHN.
I'M GETTING COLD, SETH...
THERE IN A TIC, LUV.
UH... YOU CAN LET YOURSELF OUT, CAN'T YOU, MATE?
SURE...
STREWTH!
SETH? JOHN! WH--WH-- WHAT ARE YOU DOING HERE?
BUT YOU'RE WITH--
OH MY GOD, MY GOD! OH, JOHN, I HAVE--
I WAS SO ANGRY! SO WRONG! HOW COULD I--
I READ YOUR BOOKS, JOHN! I MADE A DEAL!
OH? WHO WITH?

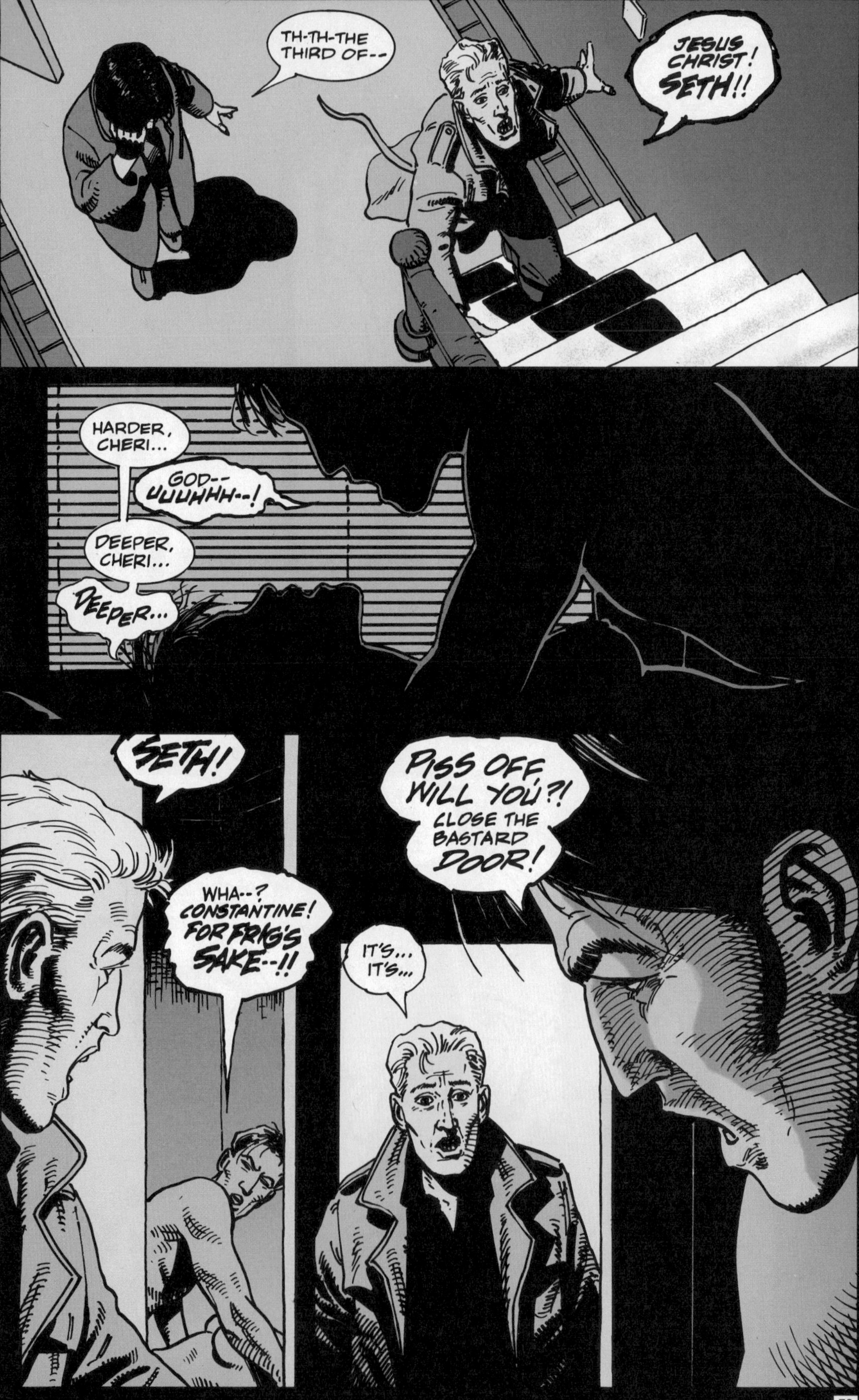
TH-TH-THE THIRD OF--
JESUS CHRIST! SETH!!
HARDER, CHERI...
GOD-- UUUHHH--!
DEEPER, CHERI...
DEEPER...
SETH!
PISS OFF, WILL YOU?! CLOSE THE BASTARD DOOR!
WHA--? CONSTANTINE! FOR FRIG'S SAKE--!!
IT'S... IT'S...

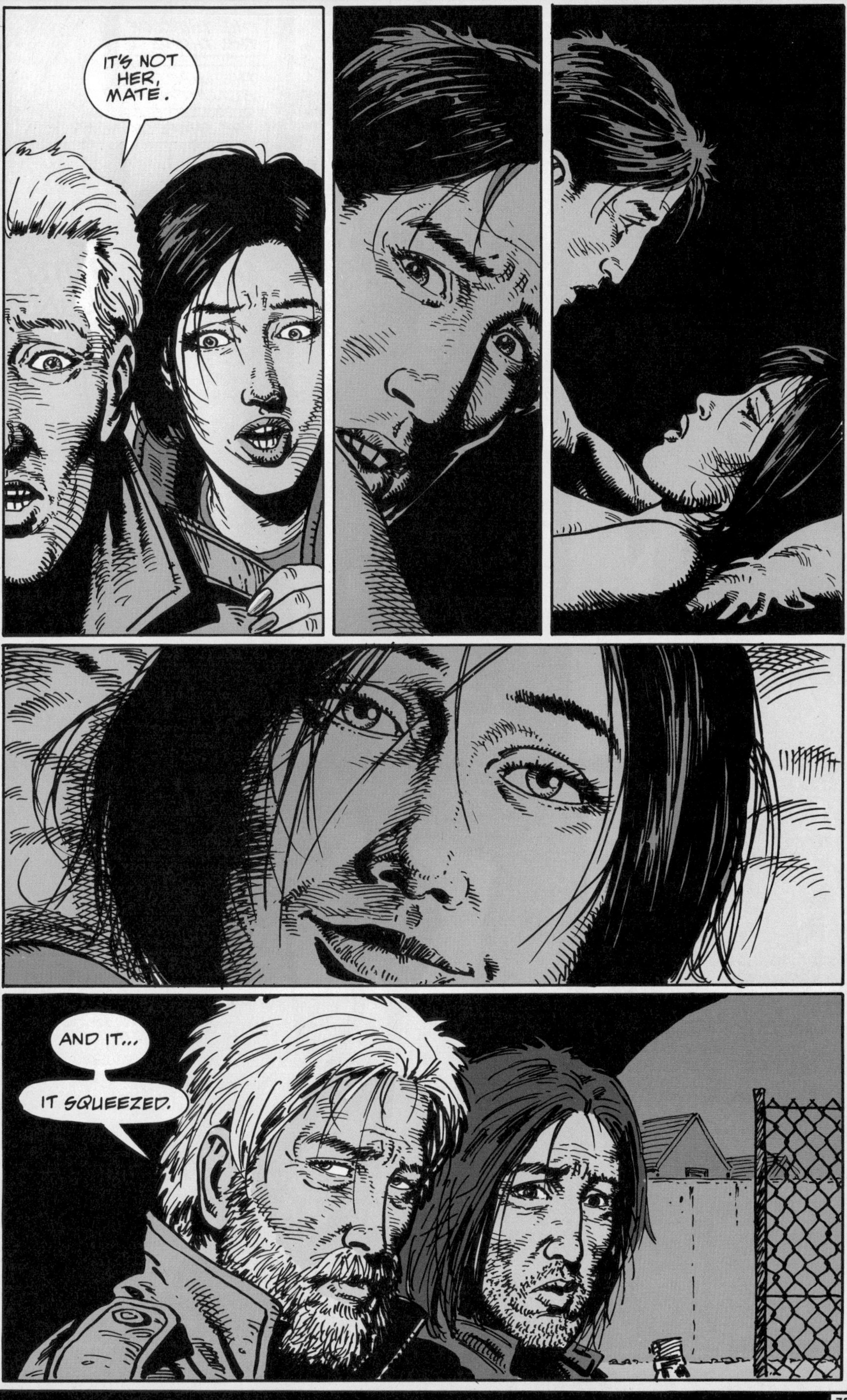
IT'S NOT HER, MATE.
AND IT...
IT SQUEEZED.

NOGODAAAAHHHH

RUN! FOR CHRIST'S SAKE, YOU STUPID COW! RUN!!

SCREW THIS!

AAAAAHHHH

AAAAAHHHH

THE THIRD OF THE THREE.

THE LORD OF A BILLION FACES.

THE SHAPECHANGER.

AAAAAAAAA-HUK!!

SPTOOCH!

BE SEEING YOU.

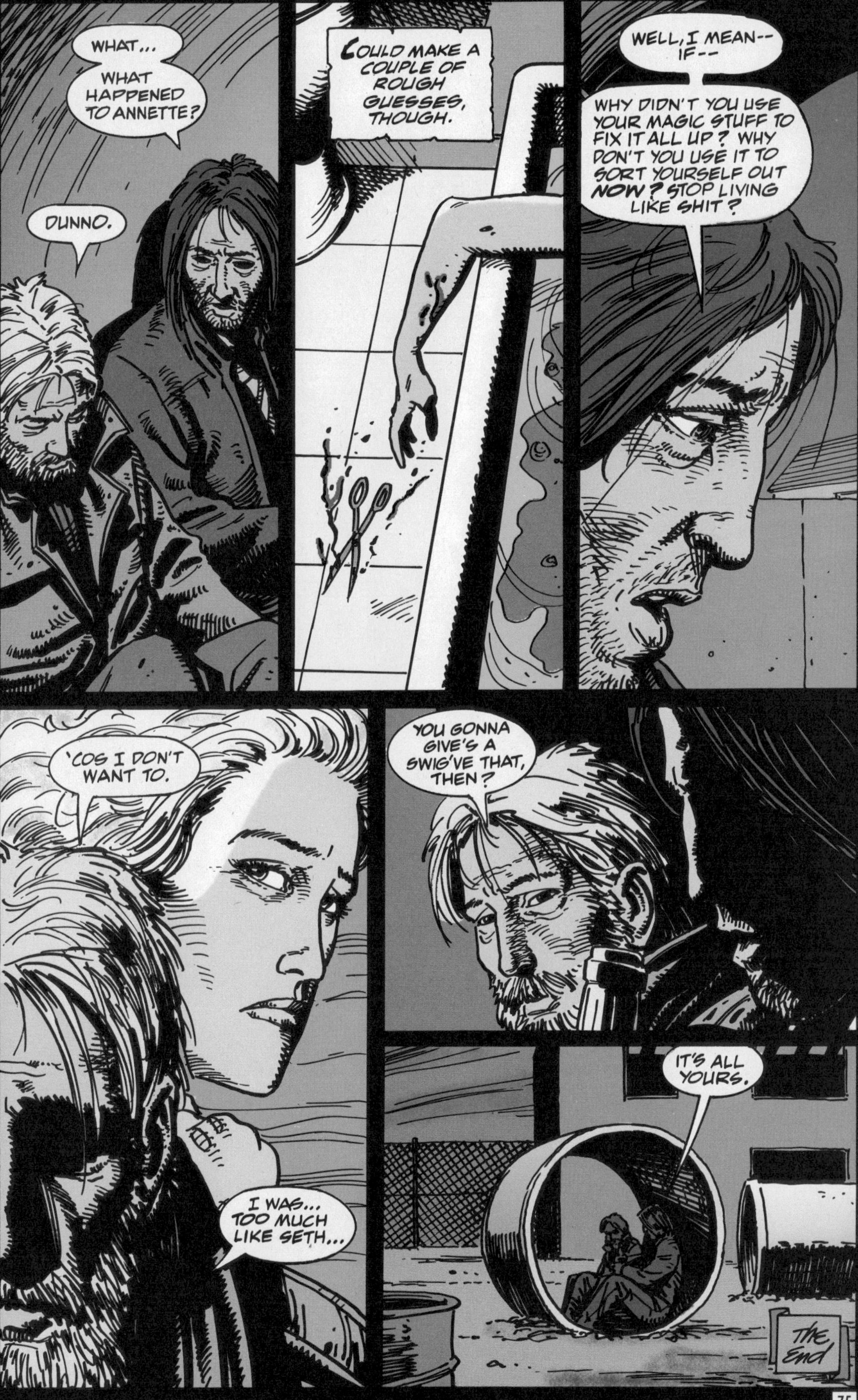
WHAT...
WHAT HAPPENED TO ANNETTE?
DUNNO.
COULD MAKE A COUPLE OF ROUGH GUESSES, THOUGH.
WELL, I MEAN-- IF--
WHY DIDN'T YOU USE YOUR MAGIC STUFF TO FIX IT ALL UP? WHY DON'T YOU USE IT TO SORT YOURSELF OUT NOW? STOP LIVING LIKE SHIT?
'COS I DON'T WANT TO.
I WAS... TOO MUCH LIKE SETH...
YOU GONNA GIVE'S A SWIG'VE THAT, THEN?
IT'S ALL YOURS.
THE END

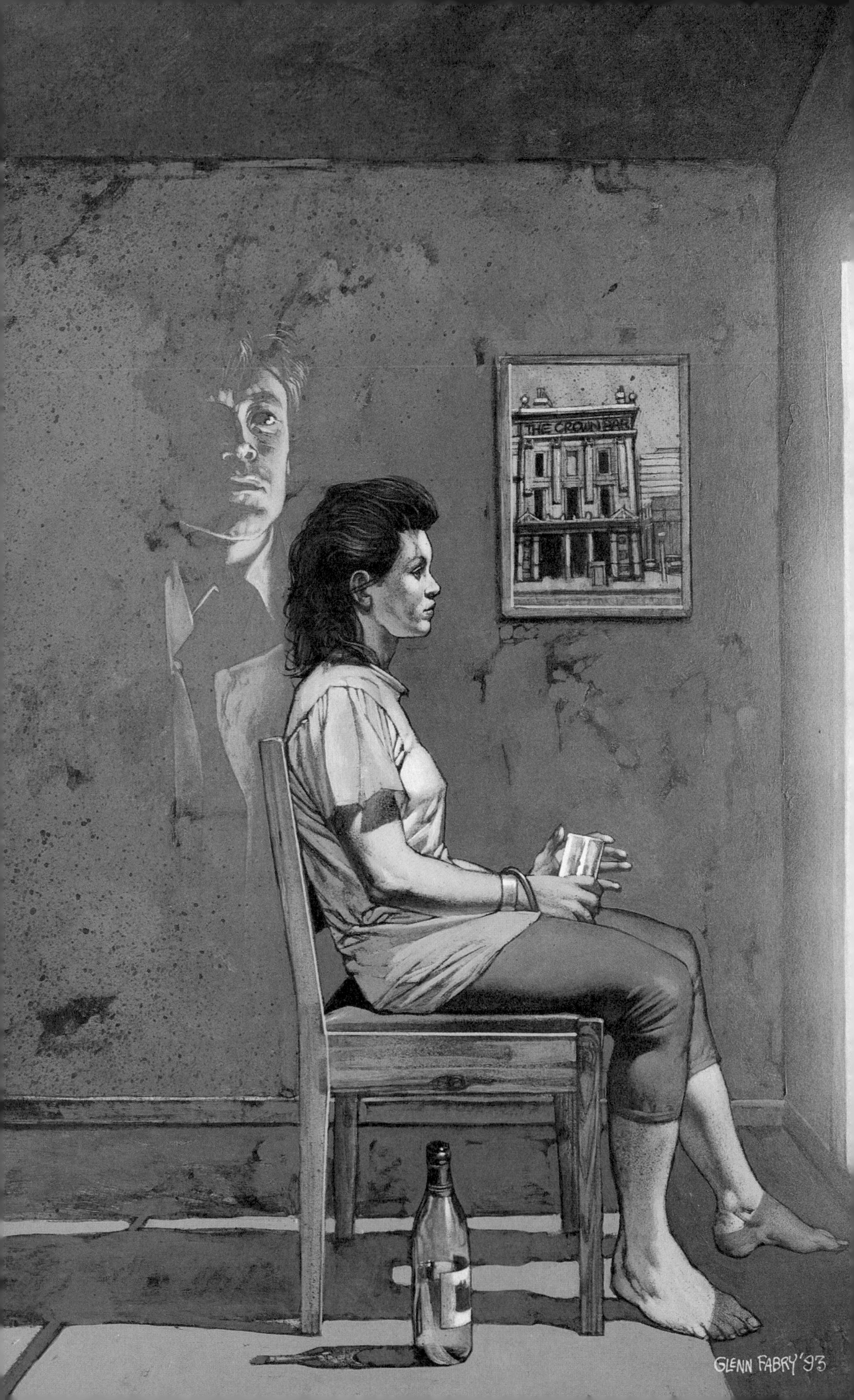
THE CROWN BAR
GLENN FABRY '93

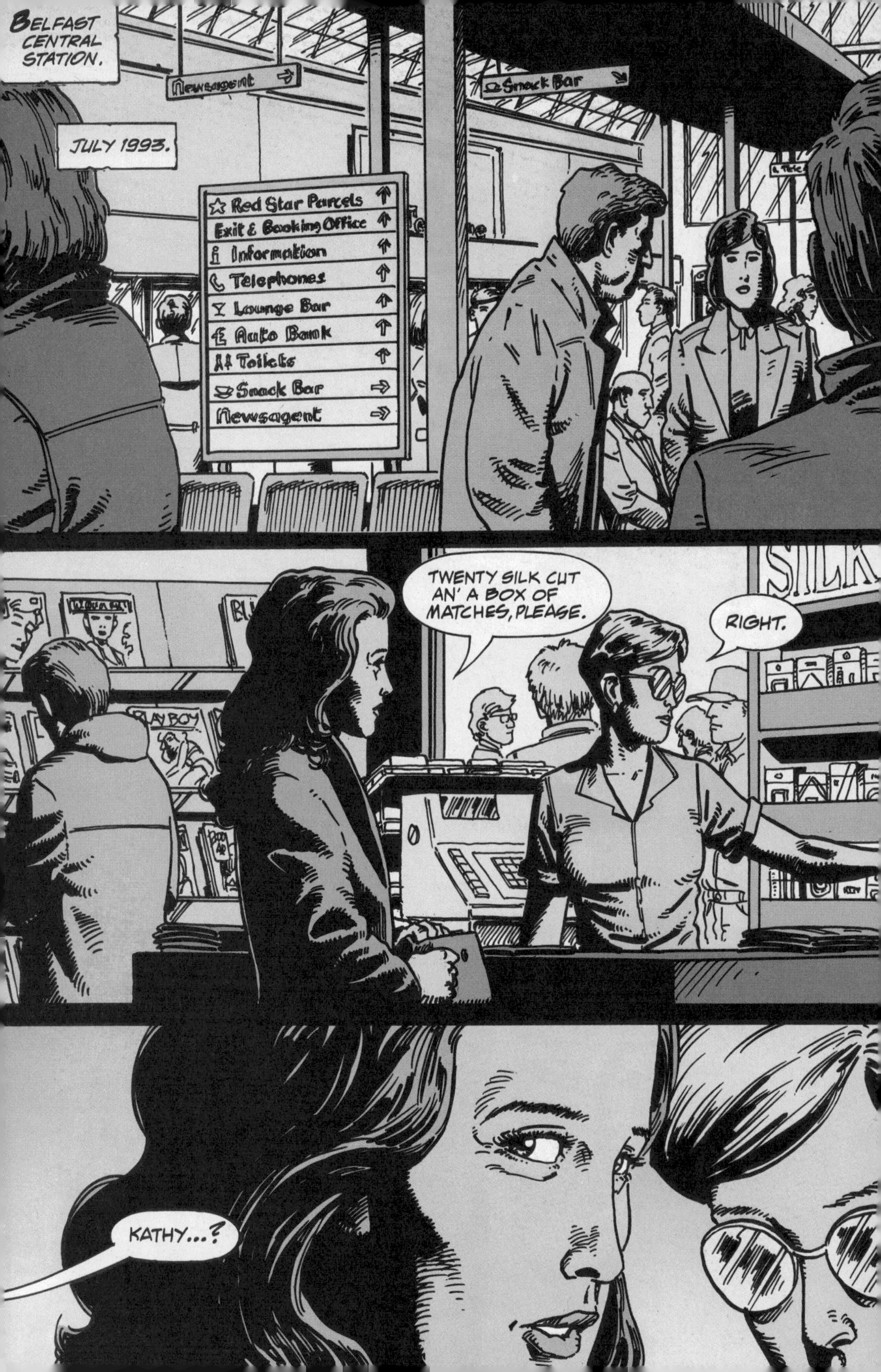
BELFAST CENTRAL STATION.
Newsagent
Snack Bar
JULY 1993.
Red Star Parcels
Exit & Booking Office
Information
Telephones
Lounge Bar
Auto Bank
Toilets
Snack Bar
Newsagent
PLAYBOY
SILK
TWENTY SILK CUT AN' A BOX OF MATCHES, PLEASE.
RIGHT.
KATHY...?

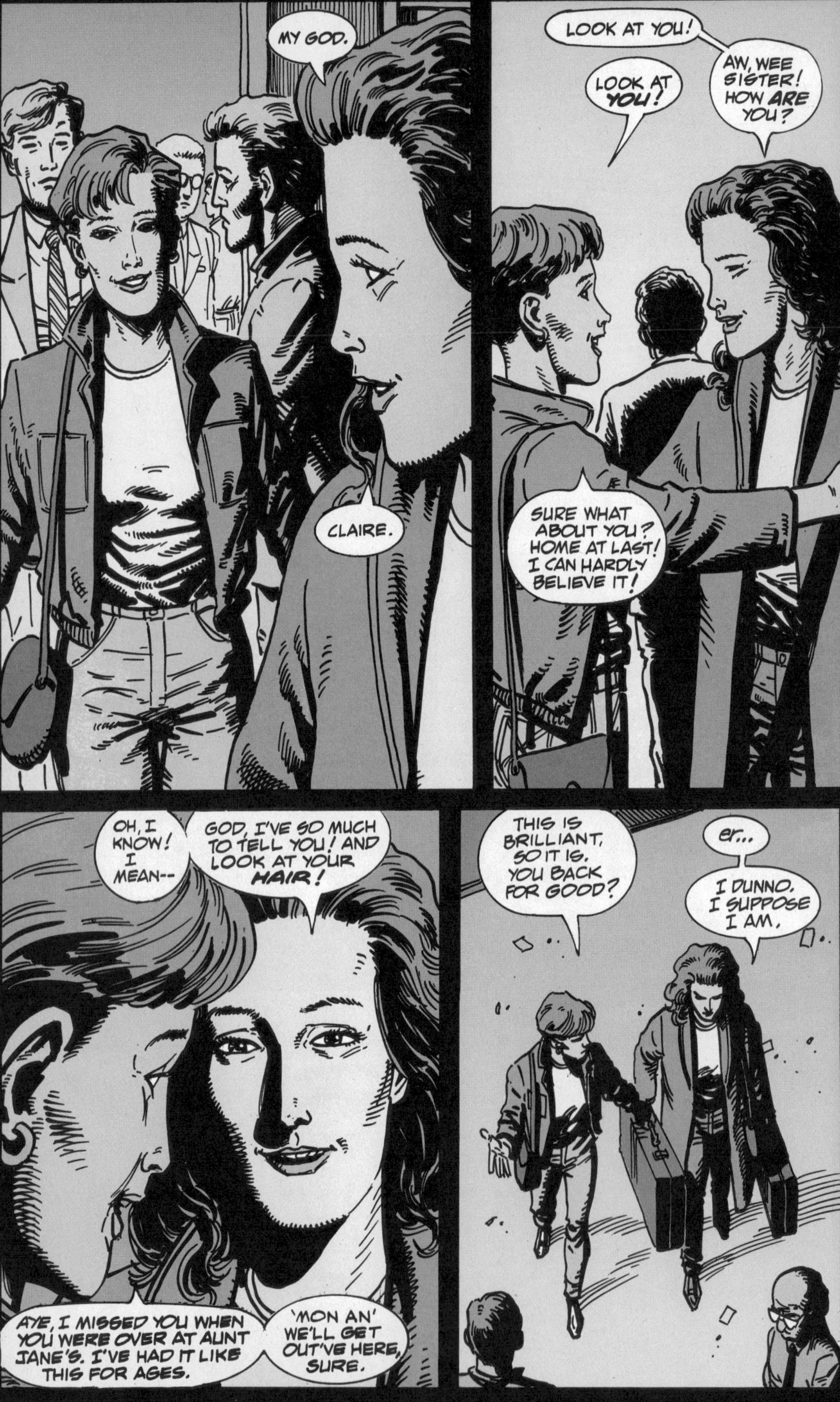
MY GOD.
CLAIRE.
LOOK AT YOU!
LOOK AT YOU!
AW, WEE SISTER! HOW ARE YOU?
SURE WHAT ABOUT YOU? HOME AT LAST! I CAN HARDLY BELIEVE IT!
OH, I KNOW! I MEAN--
GOD, I'VE SO MUCH TO TELL YOU! AND LOOK AT YOUR HAIR!
AYE, I MISSED YOU WHEN YOU WERE OVER AT AUNT JANE'S. I'VE HAD IT LIKE THIS FOR AGES.
'MON AN' WE'LL GET OUT'VE HERE, SURE.
THIS IS BRILLIANT, SO IT IS. YOU BACK FOR GOOD?
er...
I DUNNO. I SUPPOSE I AM.

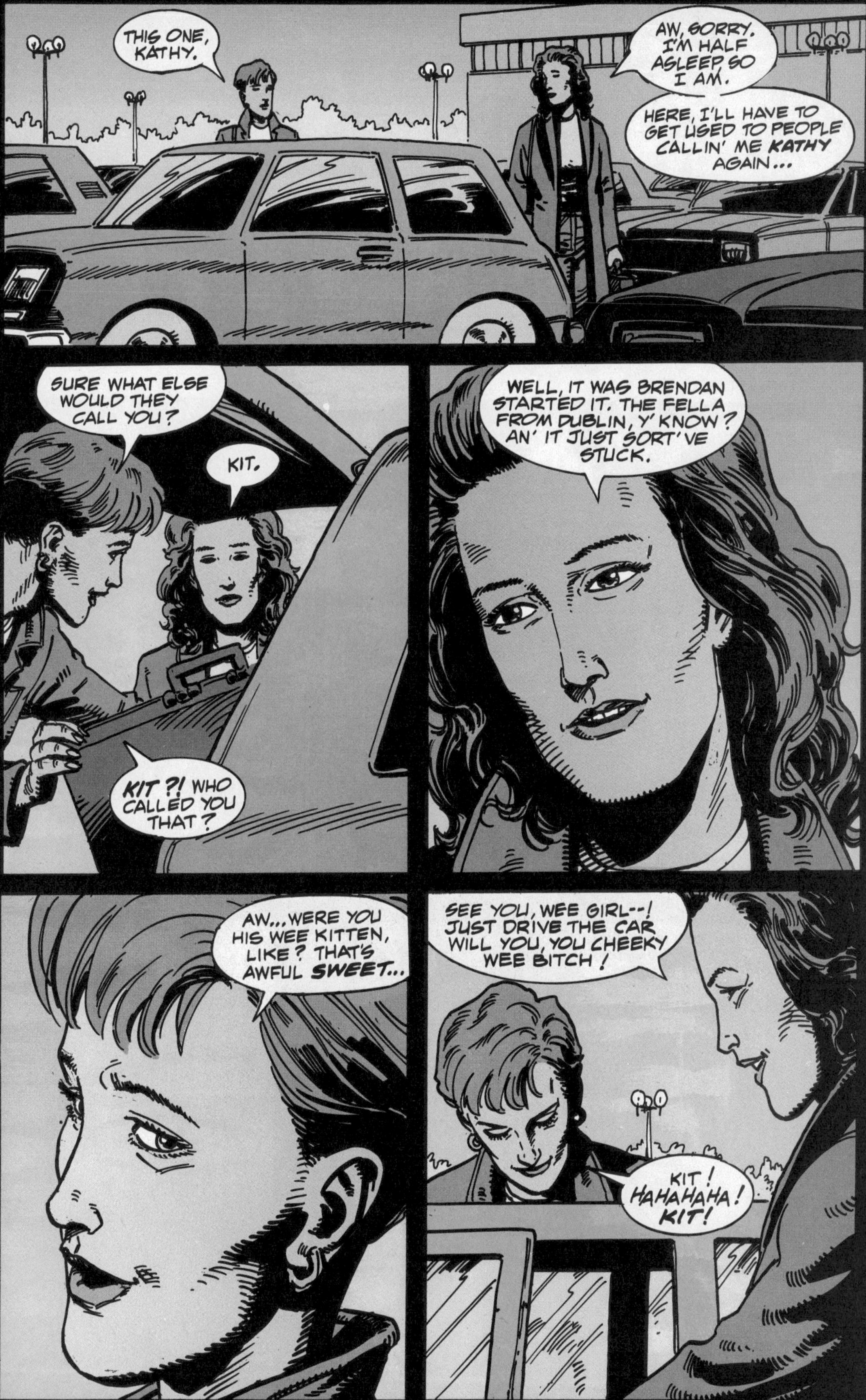
THIS ONE, KATHY.
AW, SORRY. I'M HALF ASLEEP SO I AM.
HERE, I'LL HAVE TO GET USED TO PEOPLE CALLIN' ME KATHY AGAIN...
SURE WHAT ELSE WOULD THEY CALL YOU?
KIT.
KIT?! WHO CALLED YOU THAT?
WELL, IT WAS BRENDAN STARTED IT. THE FELLA FROM DUBLIN, Y' KNOW? AN' IT JUST SORT'VE STUCK.
AW... WERE YOU HIS WEE KITTEN, LIKE? THAT'S AWFUL SWEET...
SEE YOU, WEE GIRL--! JUST DRIVE THE CAR WILL YOU, YOU CHEEKY WEE BITCH!
KIT! HAHAHAHA! KIT!

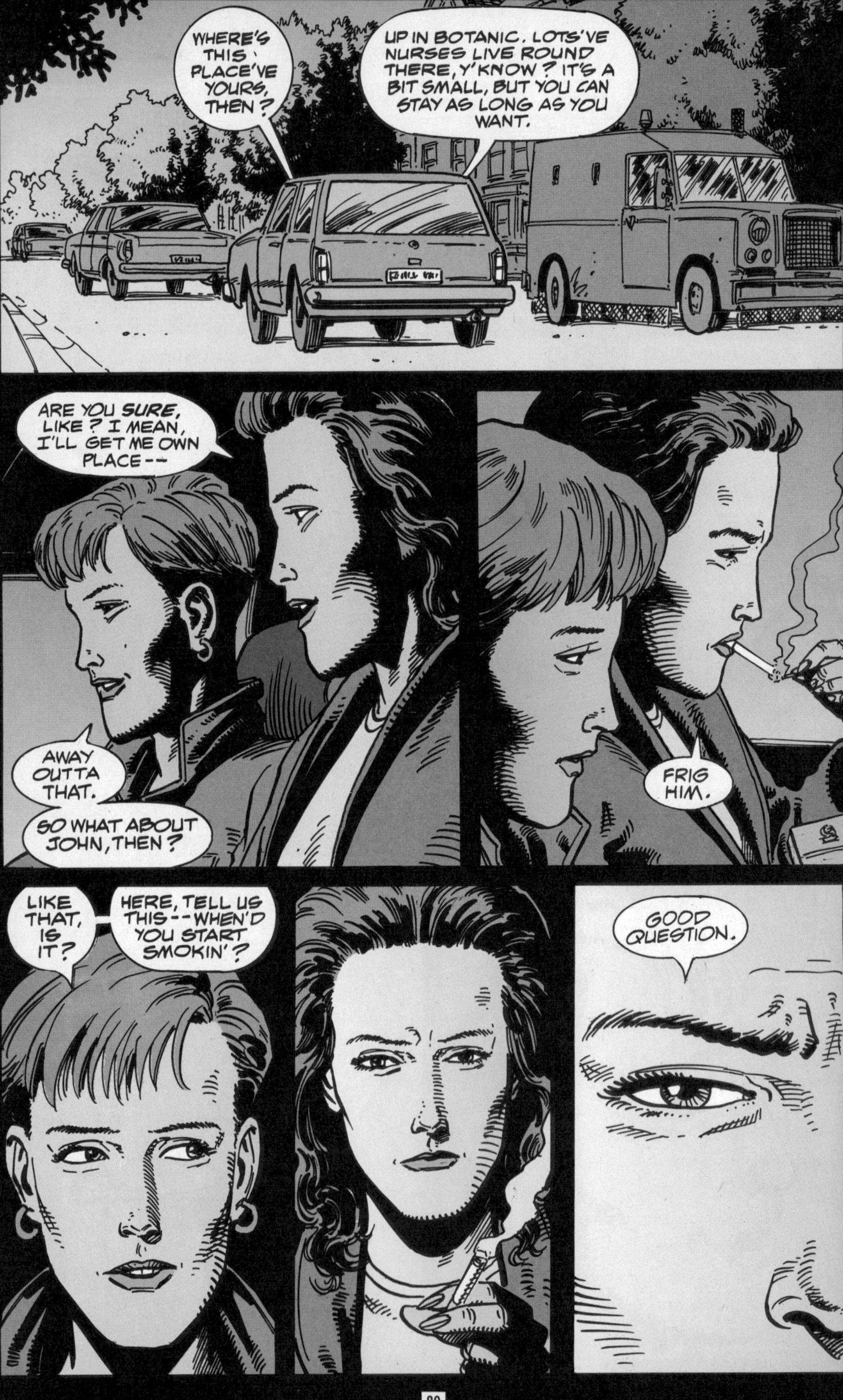
WHERE'S THIS PLACE'VE YOURS, THEN?
UP IN BOTANIC. LOTS'VE NURSES LIVE ROUND THERE, Y'KNOW? IT'S A BIT SMALL, BUT YOU CAN STAY AS LONG AS YOU WANT.
ARE YOU SURE, LIKE? I MEAN, I'LL GET ME OWN PLACE--
AWAY OUTTA THAT.
SO WHAT ABOUT JOHN, THEN?
FRIG HIM.
LIKE THAT, IS IT?
HERE, TELL US THIS--WHEN'D YOU START SMOKIN'?
GOOD QUESTION.

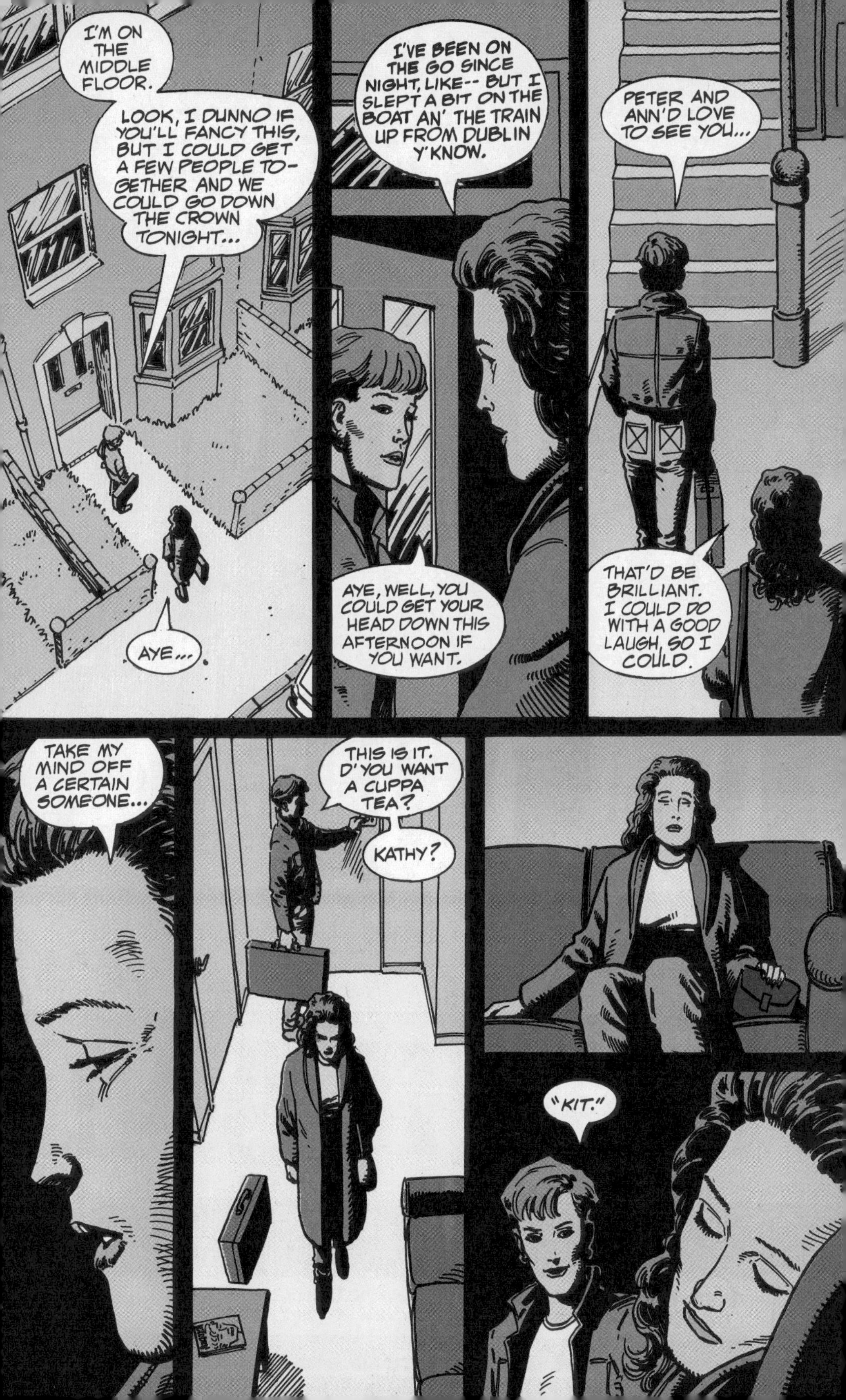
I'M ON THE MIDDLE FLOOR.
LOOK, I DUNNO IF YOU'LL FANCY THIS, BUT I COULD GET A FEW PEOPLE TOGETHER AND WE COULD GO DOWN THE CROWN TONIGHT...
AYE...
I'VE BEEN ON THE GO SINCE NIGHT, LIKE-- BUT I SLEPT A BIT ON THE BOAT AN' THE TRAIN UP FROM DUBLIN Y'KNOW.
AYE, WELL, YOU COULD GET YOUR HEAD DOWN THIS AFTERNOON IF YOU WANT.
PETER AND ANN'D LOVE TO SEE YOU...
THAT'D BE BRILLIANT. I COULD DO WITH A GOOD LAUGH, SO I COULD.
TAKE MY MIND OFF A CERTAIN SOMEONE...
THIS IS IT. D'YOU WANT A CUPPA TEA?
KATHY?
"KIT."

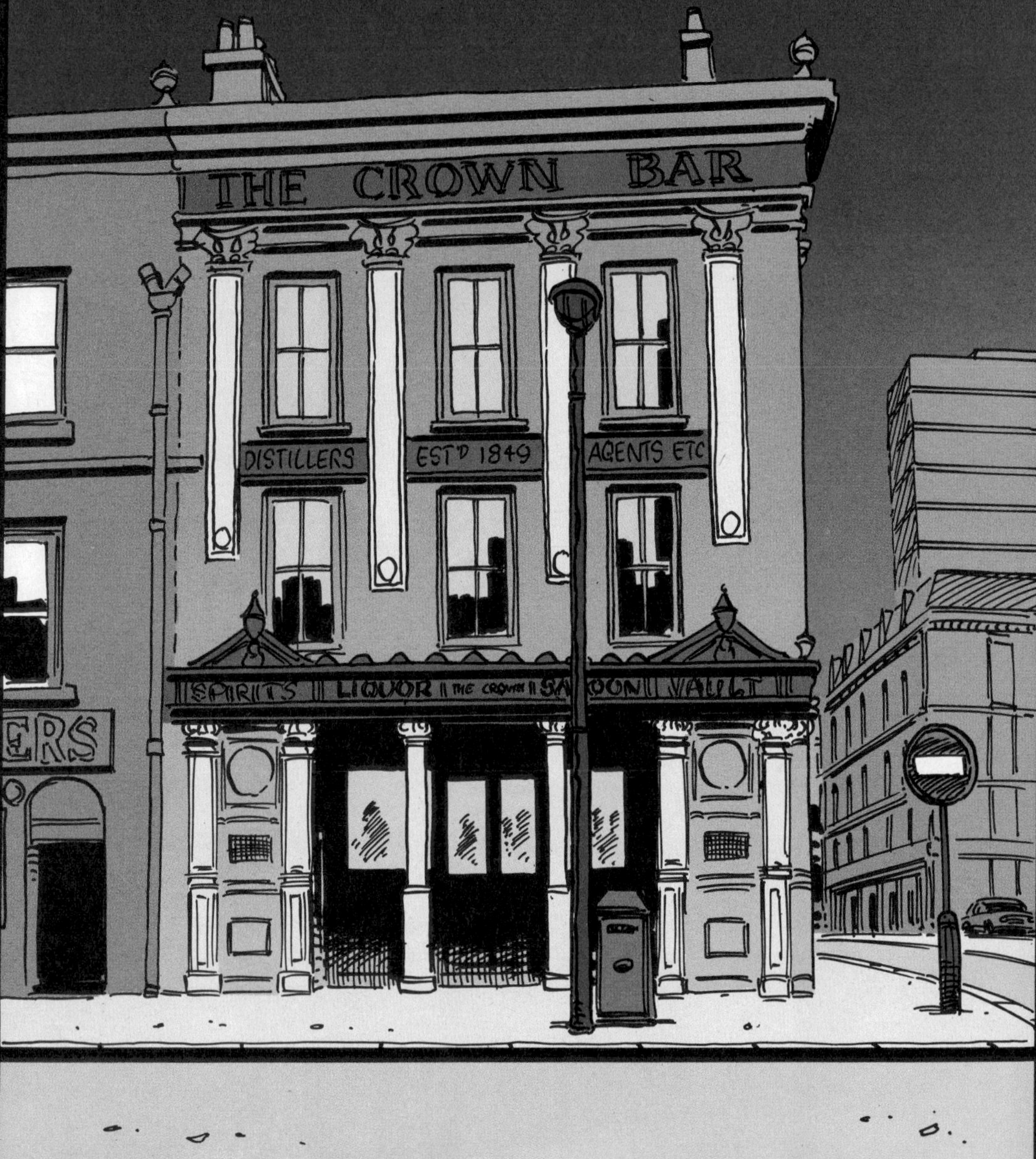
THE CROWN BAR
DISTILLERS
EST'D 1849
AGENTS ETC
SPIRITS
LIQUOR
THE CROWN
SALOON
VAULT
ERS

HEARTLAND

GARTH ENNIS • *writer* **STEVE DILLON** • *artist* **STUART CHAIFETZ** • *colors*
GASPAR • *letters* **JULIE ROTTENBERG** • *asst. editor* **STUART MOORE** • *editor*

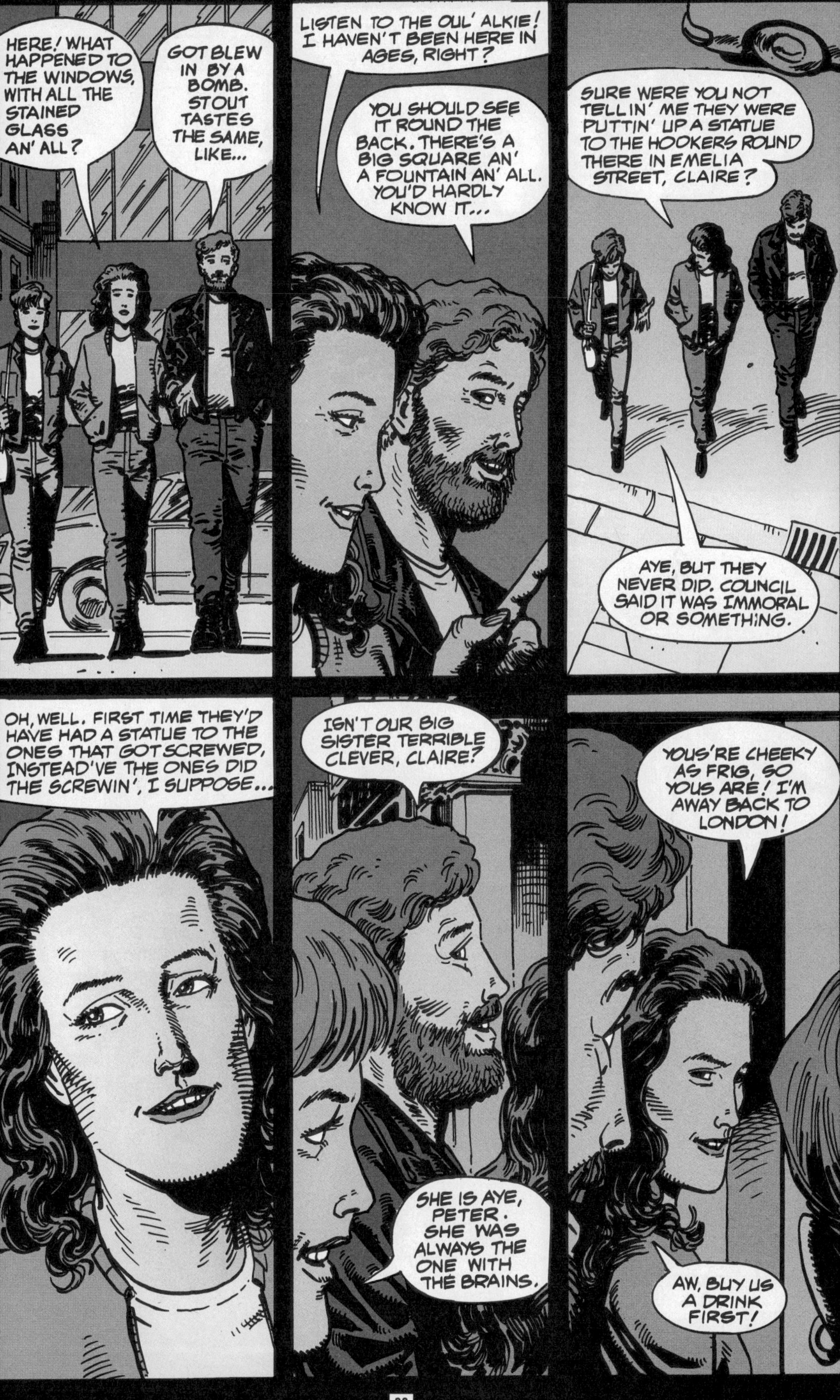
HERE! WHAT HAPPENED TO THE WINDOWS, WITH ALL THE STAINED GLASS AN' ALL?
GOT BLEW IN BY A BOMB. STOUT TASTES THE SAME, LIKE...
LISTEN TO THE OUL' ALKIE! I HAVEN'T BEEN HERE IN AGES, RIGHT?
YOU SHOULD SEE IT ROUND THE BACK. THERE'S A BIG SQUARE AN' A FOUNTAIN AN' ALL. YOU'D HARDLY KNOW IT...
SURE WERE YOU NOT TELLIN' ME THEY WERE PUTTIN' UP A STATUE TO THE HOOKERS ROUND THERE IN EMELIA STREET, CLAIRE?
AYE, BUT THEY NEVER DID. COUNCIL SAID IT WAS IMMORAL OR SOMETHING.
OH, WELL. FIRST TIME THEY'D HAVE HAD A STATUE TO THE ONES THAT GOT SCREWED, INSTEAD'VE THE ONES DID THE SCREWIN', I SUPPOSE...
ISN'T OUR BIG SISTER TERRIBLE CLEVER, CLAIRE?
SHE IS AYE, PETER. SHE WAS ALWAYS THE ONE WITH THE BRAINS.
YOUS'RE CHEEKY AS FRIG, SO YOUS ARE! I'M AWAY BACK TO LONDON!
AW, BUY US A DRINK FIRST!

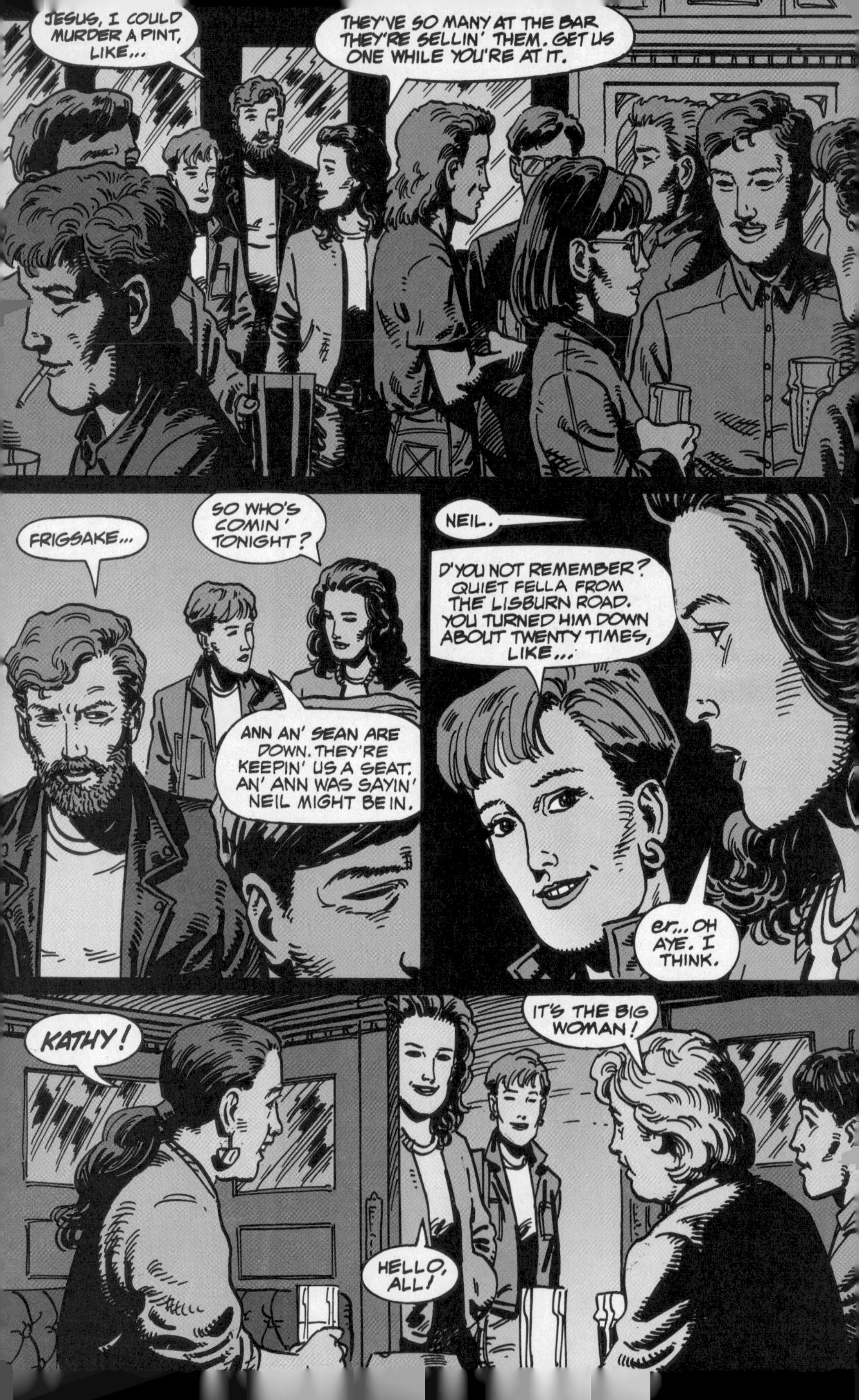
JESUS, I COULD MURDER A PINT, LIKE...
THEY'VE SO MANY AT THE BAR THEY'RE SELLIN' THEM. GET US ONE WHILE YOU'RE AT IT.
FRIGSAKE...
SO WHO'S COMIN' TONIGHT?
ANN AN' SEAN ARE DOWN. THEY'RE KEEPIN' US A SEAT. AN' ANN WAS SAYIN' NEIL MIGHT BE IN.
NEIL.
D'YOU NOT REMEMBER? QUIET FELLA FROM THE LISBURN ROAD. YOU TURNED HIM DOWN ABOUT TWENTY TIMES, LIKE...
er... OH AYE. I THINK.
KATHY!
IT'S THE BIG WOMAN!
HELLO, ALL!

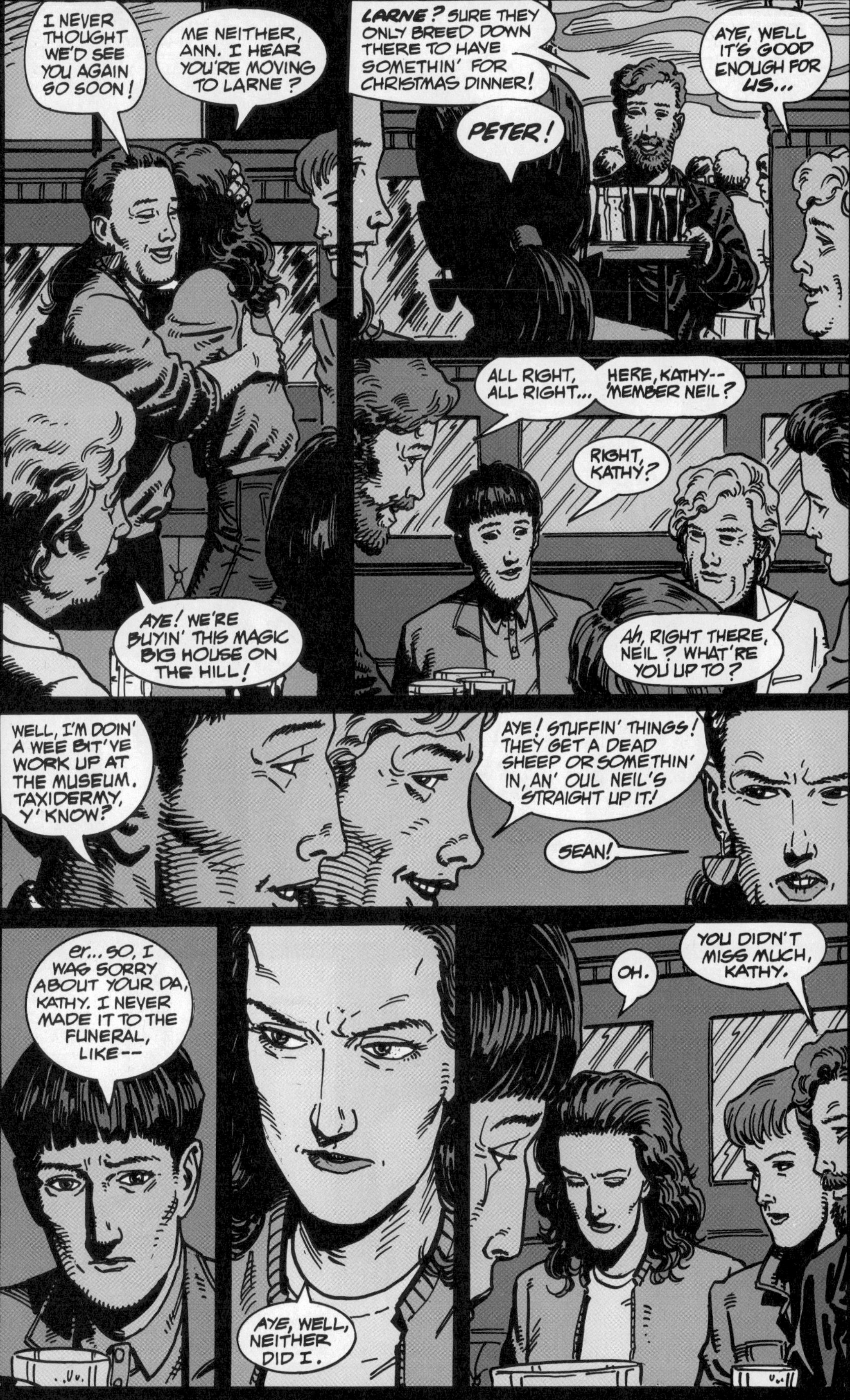
I NEVER THOUGHT WE'D SEE YOU AGAIN SO SOON!
ME NEITHER, ANN. I HEAR YOU'RE MOVING TO LARNE?
AYE! WE'RE BUYIN' THIS MAGIC BIG HOUSE ON THE HILL!
LARNE? SURE THEY ONLY BREED DOWN THERE TO HAVE SOMETHIN' FOR CHRISTMAS DINNER!
PETER!
AYE, WELL IT'S GOOD ENOUGH FOR US...
ALL RIGHT, ALL RIGHT...
HERE, KATHY--'MEMBER NEIL?
RIGHT, KATHY?
Ah, RIGHT THERE, NEIL? WHAT'RE YOU UP TO?
WELL, I'M DOIN' A WEE BIT'VE WORK UP AT THE MUSEUM. TAXIDERMY, Y' KNOW?
AYE! STUFFIN' THINGS! THEY GET A DEAD SHEEP OR SOMETHIN' IN, AN' OUL NEIL'S STRAIGHT UP IT!
SEAN!
er... SO, I WAS SORRY ABOUT YOUR DA, KATHY. I NEVER MADE IT TO THE FUNERAL, LIKE--
AYE, WELL, NEITHER DID I.
OH.
YOU DIDN'T MISS MUCH, KATHY.

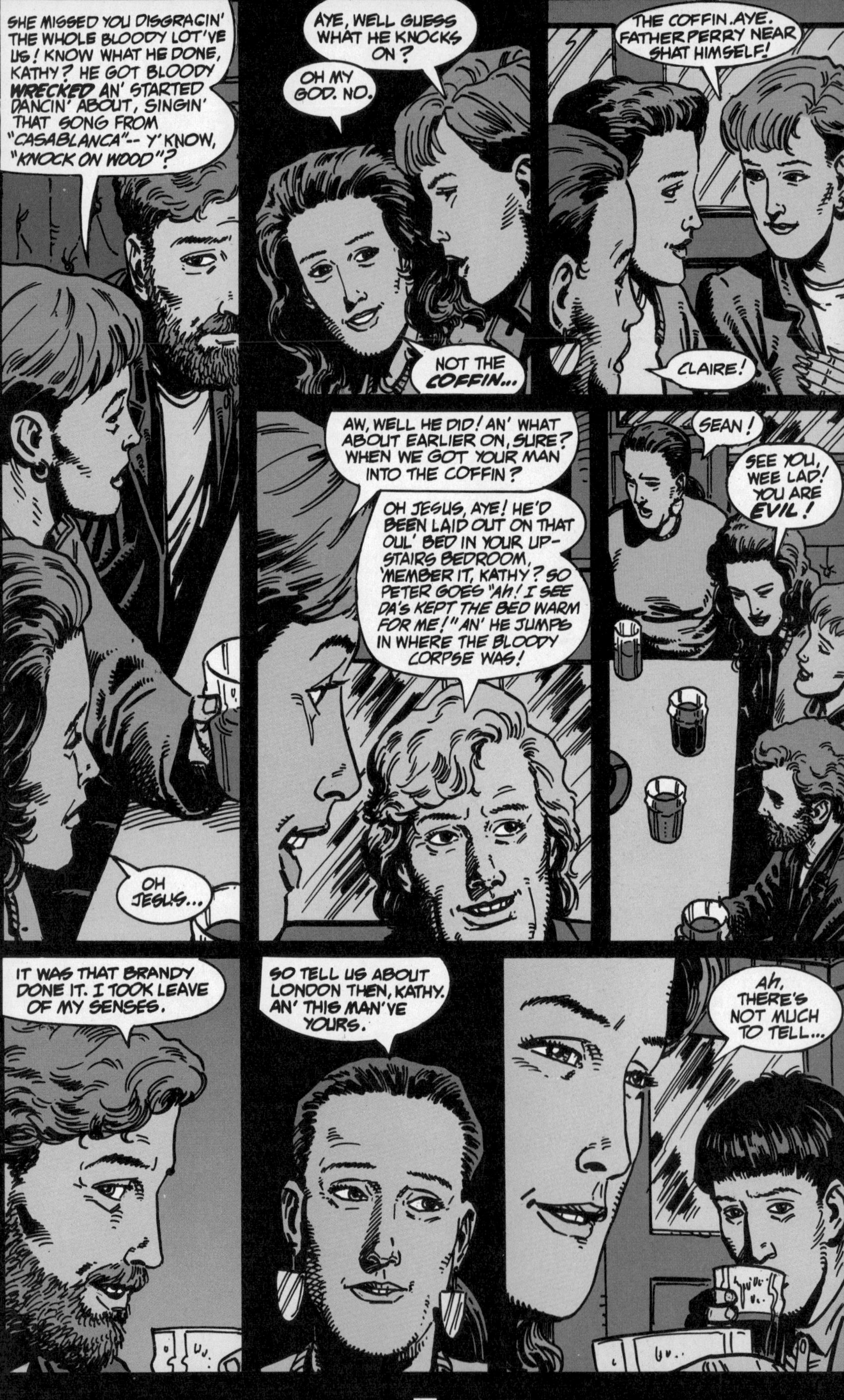
SHE MISSED YOU DISGRACIN' THE WHOLE BLOODY LOT'VE US! KNOW WHAT HE DONE, KATHY? HE GOT BLOODY WRECKED AN' STARTED DANCIN' ABOUT, SINGIN' THAT SONG FROM "CASABLANCA"-- Y' KNOW, "KNOCK ON WOOD"?
AYE, WELL GUESS WHAT HE KNOCKS ON?
OH MY GOD. NO.
NOT THE COFFIN...
THE COFFIN. AYE. FATHER PERRY NEAR SHAT HIMSELF!
CLAIRE!
OH JESUS...
AW, WELL HE DID! AN' WHAT ABOUT EARLIER ON, SURE? WHEN WE GOT YOUR MAN INTO THE COFFIN?
OH JESUS, AYE! HE'D BEEN LAID OUT ON THAT OUL' BED IN YOUR UP-STAIRS BEDROOM, 'MEMBER IT, KATHY? SO PETER GOES "Ah! I SEE DA'S KEPT THE BED WARM FOR ME!" AN' HE JUMPS IN WHERE THE BLOODY CORPSE WAS!
SEAN!
SEE YOU, WEE LAD! YOU ARE EVIL!
IT WAS THAT BRANDY DONE IT. I TOOK LEAVE OF MY SENSES.
SO TELL US ABOUT LONDON THEN, KATHY. AN' THIS MAN'VE YOURS.
Ah, THERE'S NOT MUCH TO TELL...

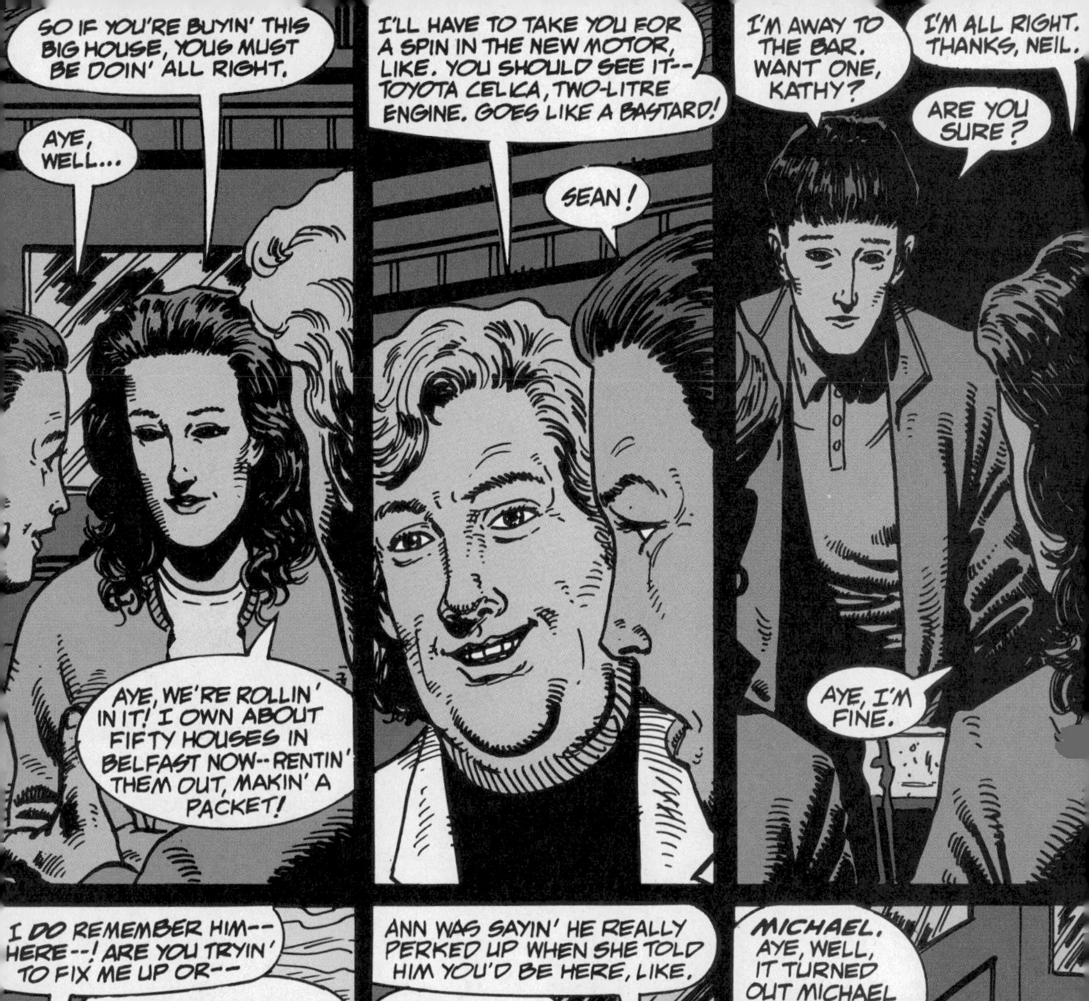
SO IF YOU'RE BUYIN' THIS BIG HOUSE, YOUS MUST BE DOIN' ALL RIGHT.
AYE, WELL...
AYE, WE'RE ROLLIN' IN IT! I OWN ABOUT FIFTY HOUSES IN BELFAST NOW--RENTIN' THEM OUT, MAKIN' A PACKET!
I'LL HAVE TO TAKE YOU FOR A SPIN IN THE NEW MOTOR, LIKE. YOU SHOULD SEE IT--TOYOTA CELICA, TWO-LITRE ENGINE. GOES LIKE A BASTARD!
SEAN!
I'M AWAY TO THE BAR. WANT ONE, KATHY?
I'M ALL RIGHT. THANKS, NEIL.
ARE YOU SURE?
AYE, I'M FINE.
I DO REMEMBER HIM--HERE--! ARE YOU TRYIN' TO FIX ME UP OR--
FLIPSAKE, WOULD YOU CREDIT ME WITH SOME BLOODY SENSE! BUT I BETTER TELL YOU, LIKE--I THINK HE IS AFTER YOU...
OH, JESUS...
ANN WAS SAYIN' HE REALLY PERKED UP WHEN SHE TOLD HIM YOU'D BE HERE, LIKE.
AW, BRILLIANT. GREAT.
WHAT HAPPENED TO THAT FELLA YOU WERE GOIN' OUT WITH, BY THE WAY? MARTIN?
MICHAEL. AYE, WELL, IT TURNED OUT MICHAEL HAD A WEE SURPRISE FOR ME...
AN EXTRA DICK?

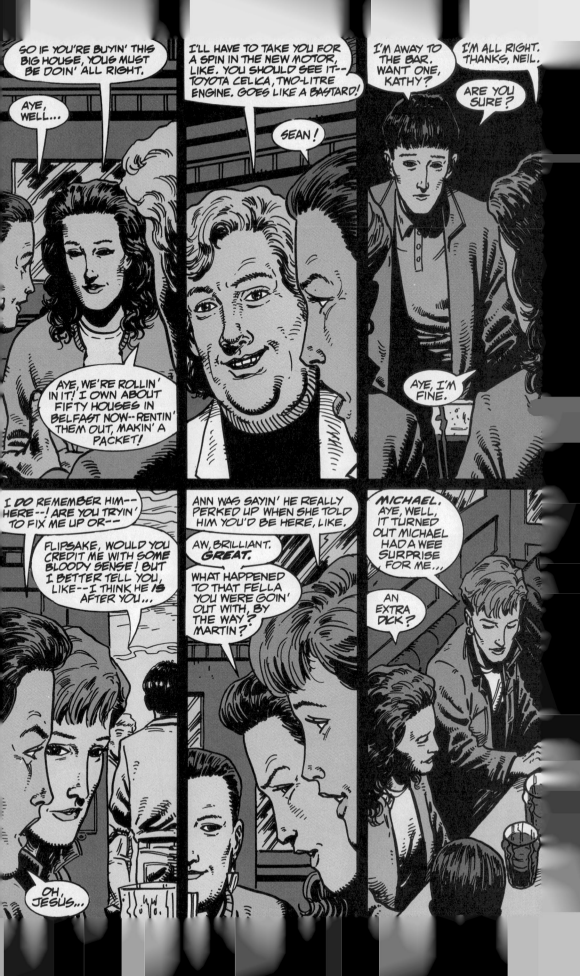

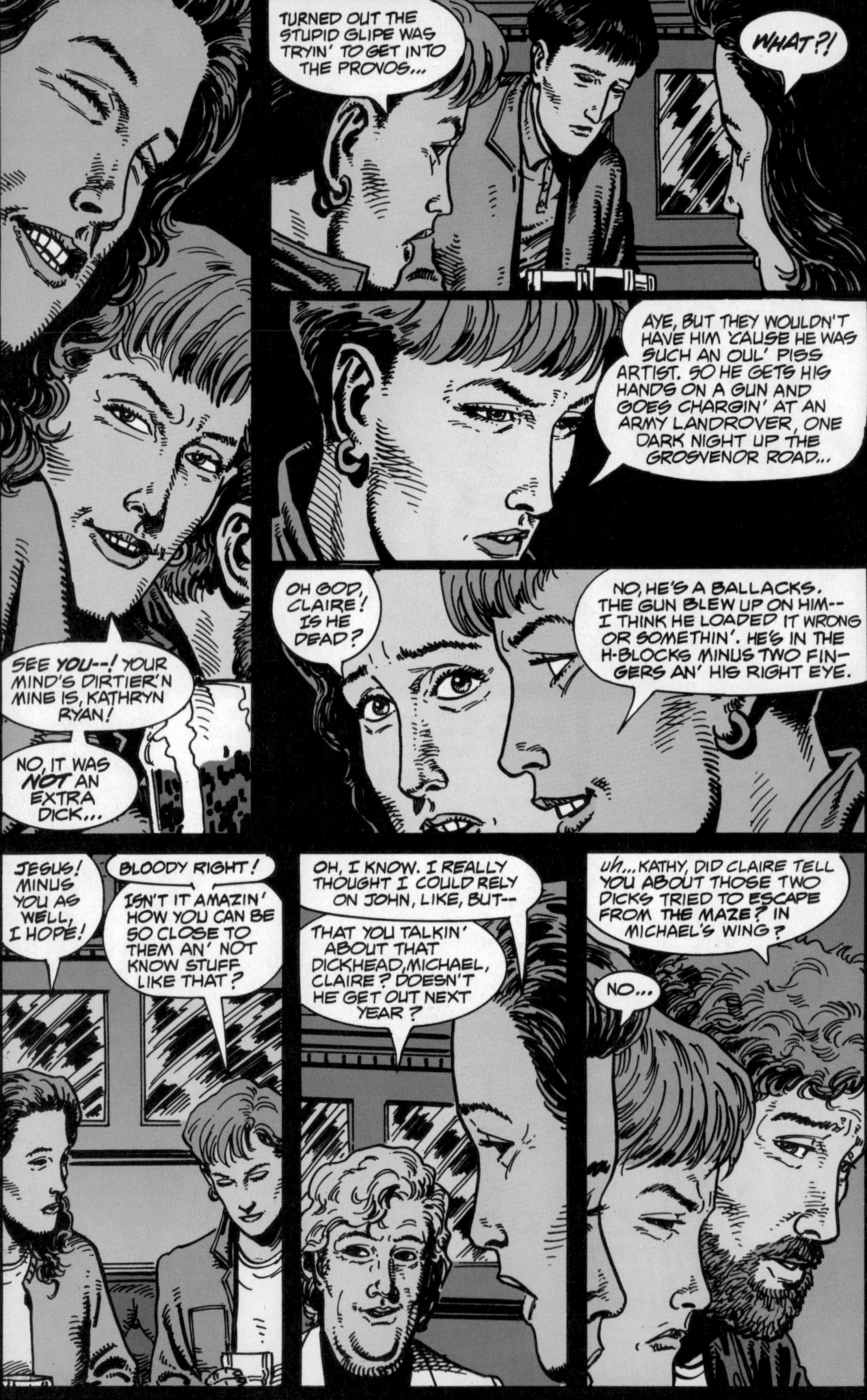

TURNED OUT THE STUPID GLIPE WAS TRYIN' TO GET INTO THE PROVOS...
WHAT?!
SEE YOU--! YOUR MIND'S DIRTIER'N MINE IS, KATHRYN RYAN!
NO, IT WAS NOT AN EXTRA DICK...
AYE, BUT THEY WOULDN'T HAVE HIM 'CAUSE HE WAS SUCH AN OUL' PISS ARTIST. SO HE GETS HIS HANDS ON A GUN AND GOES CHARGIN' AT AN ARMY LANDROVER, ONE DARK NIGHT UP THE GROSVENOR ROAD...
OH GOD, CLAIRE! IS HE DEAD?
NO, HE'S A BALLACKS. THE GUN BLEW UP ON HIM-- I THINK HE LOADED IT WRONG OR SOMETHIN'. HE'S IN THE H-BLOCKS MINUS TWO FINGERS AN' HIS RIGHT EYE.
JESUS! MINUS YOU AS WELL, I HOPE!
BLOODY RIGHT!
ISN'T IT AMAZIN' HOW YOU CAN BE SO CLOSE TO THEM AN' NOT KNOW STUFF LIKE THAT?
OH, I KNOW. I REALLY THOUGHT I COULD RELY ON JOHN, LIKE, BUT--
THAT YOU TALKIN' ABOUT THAT DICKHEAD, MICHAEL, CLAIRE? DOESN'T HE GET OUT NEXT YEAR?
uh... KATHY, DID CLAIRE TELL YOU ABOUT THOSE TWO DICKS TRIED TO ESCAPE FROM THE MAZE? IN MICHAEL'S WING?
NO...

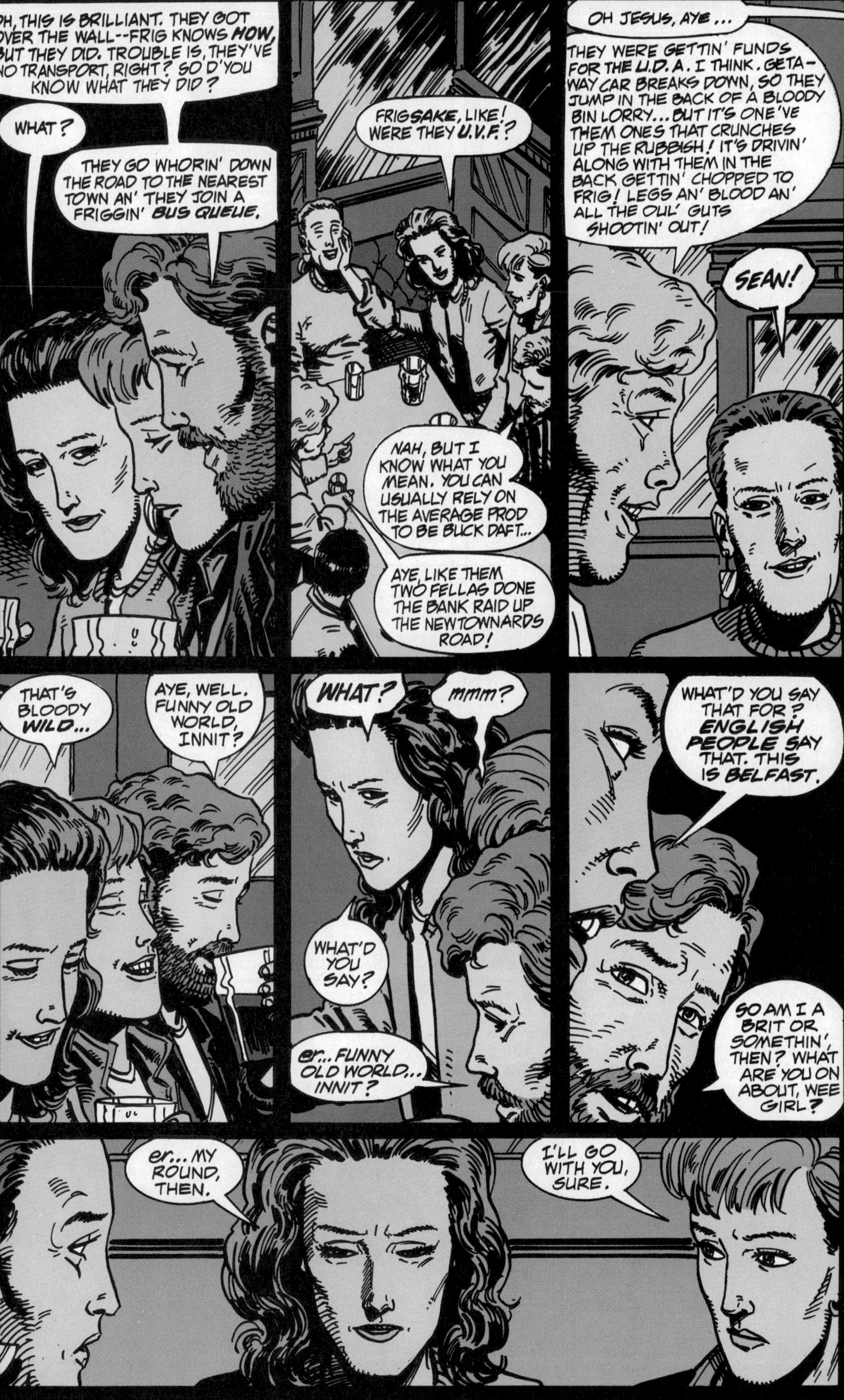
OH, THIS IS BRILLIANT. THEY GOT OVER THE WALL--FRIG KNOWS HOW, BUT THEY DID. TROUBLE IS, THEY'VE NO TRANSPORT, RIGHT? SO D'YOU KNOW WHAT THEY DID?
WHAT?
THEY GO WHORIN' DOWN THE ROAD TO THE NEAREST TOWN AN' THEY JOIN A FRIGGIN' BUS QUEUE.
FRIGSAKE, LIKE! WERE THEY U.V.F.?
NAH, BUT I KNOW WHAT YOU MEAN. YOU CAN USUALLY RELY ON THE AVERAGE PROD TO BE BUCK DAFT...
AYE, LIKE THEM TWO FELLAS DONE THE BANK RAID UP THE NEWTOWNARDS ROAD!
OH JESUS, AYE ...
THEY WERE GETTIN' FUNDS FOR THE U.D.A. I THINK. GETAWAY CAR BREAKS DOWN, SO THEY JUMP IN THE BACK OF A BLOODY BIN LORRY... BUT IT'S ONE 'VE THEM ONES THAT CRUNCHES UP THE RUBBISH! IT'S DRIVIN' ALONG WITH THEM IN THE BACK GETTIN' CHOPPED TO FRIG! LEGS AN' BLOOD AN' ALL THE OUL' GUTS SHOOTIN' OUT!
SEAN!
THAT'S BLOODY WILD...
AYE, WELL. FUNNY OLD WORLD, INNIT?
WHAT?
mmm?
WHAT'D YOU SAY?
er... FUNNY OLD WORLD... INNIT?
WHAT'D YOU SAY THAT FOR? ENGLISH PEOPLE SAY THAT. THIS IS BELFAST.
SO AM I A BRIT OR SOMETHIN', THEN? WHAT ARE YOU ON ABOUT, WEE GIRL?
er... MY ROUND, THEN.
I'LL GO WITH YOU, SURE.

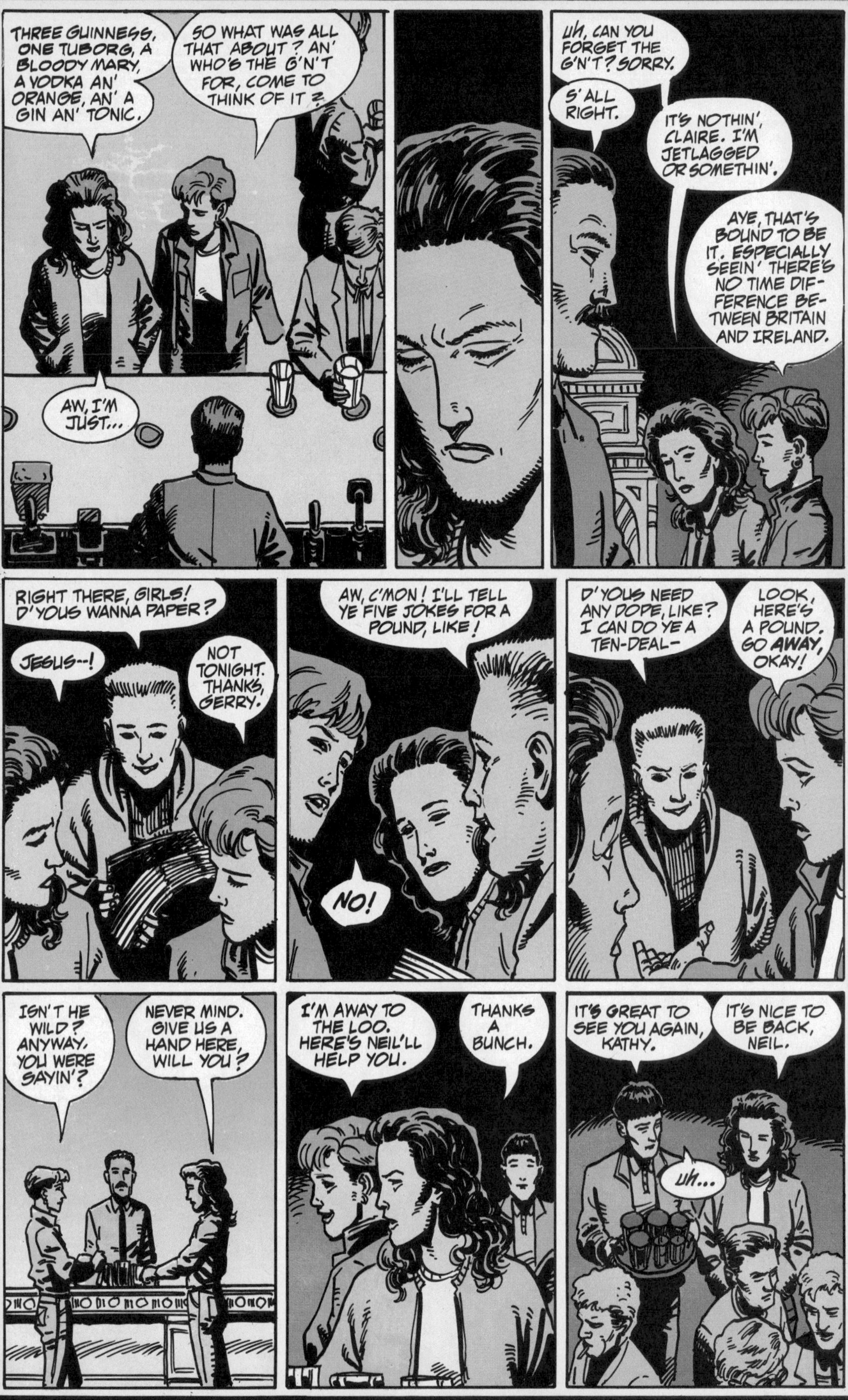
THREE GUINNESS, ONE TUBORG, A BLOODY MARY, A VODKA AN' ORANGE, AN' A GIN AN' TONIC.
SO WHAT WAS ALL THAT ABOUT? AN' WHO'S THE G'N'T FOR, COME TO THINK OF IT?
AW, I'M JUST...
UH, CAN YOU FORGET THE G'N'T? SORRY.
S' ALL RIGHT.
IT'S NOTHIN', CLAIRE. I'M JETLAGGED OR SOMETHIN'.
AYE, THAT'S BOUND TO BE IT. ESPECIALLY SEEIN' THERE'S NO TIME DIFFERENCE BETWEEN BRITAIN AND IRELAND.
RIGHT THERE, GIRLS! D'YOUS WANNA PAPER?
JESUS--!
NOT TONIGHT. THANKS, GERRY.
AW, C'MON! I'LL TELL YE FIVE JOKES FOR A POUND, LIKE!
NO!
D'YOUS NEED ANY DOPE, LIKE? I CAN DO YE A TEN-DEAL-
LOOK, HERE'S A POUND. GO AWAY, OKAY!
ISN'T HE WILD? ANYWAY, YOU WERE SAYIN'?
NEVER MIND. GIVE US A HAND HERE, WILL YOU?
I'M AWAY TO THE LOO. HERE'S NEIL'LL HELP YOU.
THANKS A BUNCH.
IT'S GREAT TO SEE YOU AGAIN, KATHY.
IT'S NICE TO BE BACK, NEIL.
UH...

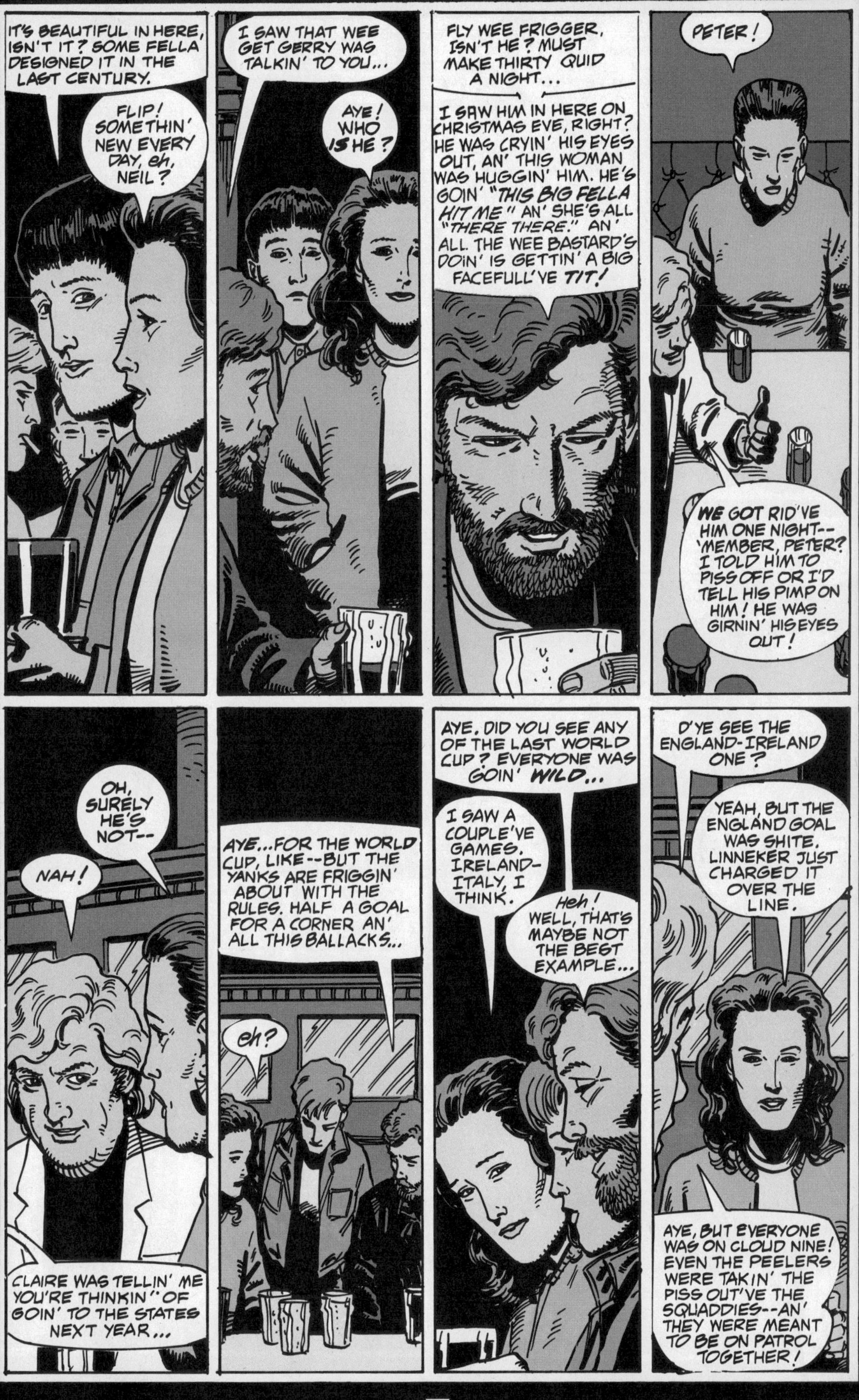
IT'S BEAUTIFUL IN HERE, ISN'T IT? SOME FELLA DESIGNED IT IN THE LAST CENTURY.
FLIP! SOMETHIN' NEW EVERY DAY, eh, NEIL?
I SAW THAT WEE GET GERRY WAS TALKIN' TO YOU...
AYE! WHO IS HE?
FLY WEE FRIGGER, ISN'T HE? MUST MAKE THIRTY QUID A NIGHT...
I SAW HIM IN HERE ON CHRISTMAS EVE, RIGHT? HE WAS CRYIN' HIS EYES OUT, AN' THIS WOMAN WAS HUGGIN' HIM. HE'S GOIN' "THIS BIG FELLA HIT ME" AN' SHE'S ALL "THERE THERE." AN' ALL. THE WEE BASTARD'S DOIN' IS GETTIN' A BIG FACEFULL'VE TIT!
PETER!
WE GOT RID'VE HIM ONE NIGHT-- 'MEMBER, PETER? I TOLD HIM TO PISS OFF OR I'D TELL HIS PIMP ON HIM! HE WAS GIRNIN' HIS EYES OUT!
OH, SURELY HE'S NOT--
NAH!
CLAIRE WAS TELLIN' ME YOU'RE THINKIN' OF GOIN' TO THE STATES NEXT YEAR...
AYE...FOR THE WORLD CUP, LIKE--BUT THE YANKS ARE FRIGGIN' ABOUT WITH THE RULES. HALF A GOAL FOR A CORNER AN' ALL THIS BALLACKS...
eh?
AYE. DID YOU SEE ANY OF THE LAST WORLD CUP? EVERYONE WAS GOIN' WILD...
I SAW A COUPLE'VE GAMES. IRELAND-ITALY, I THINK.
Heh! WELL, THAT'S MAYBE NOT THE BEST EXAMPLE...
D'YE SEE THE ENGLAND-IRELAND ONE?
YEAH, BUT THE ENGLAND GOAL WAS SHITE. LINNEKER JUST CHARGED IT OVER THE LINE.
AYE, BUT EVERYONE WAS ON CLOUD NINE! EVEN THE PEELERS WERE TAKIN' THE PISS OUT'VE THE SQUADDIES--AN' THEY WERE MEANT TO BE ON PATROL TOGETHER!

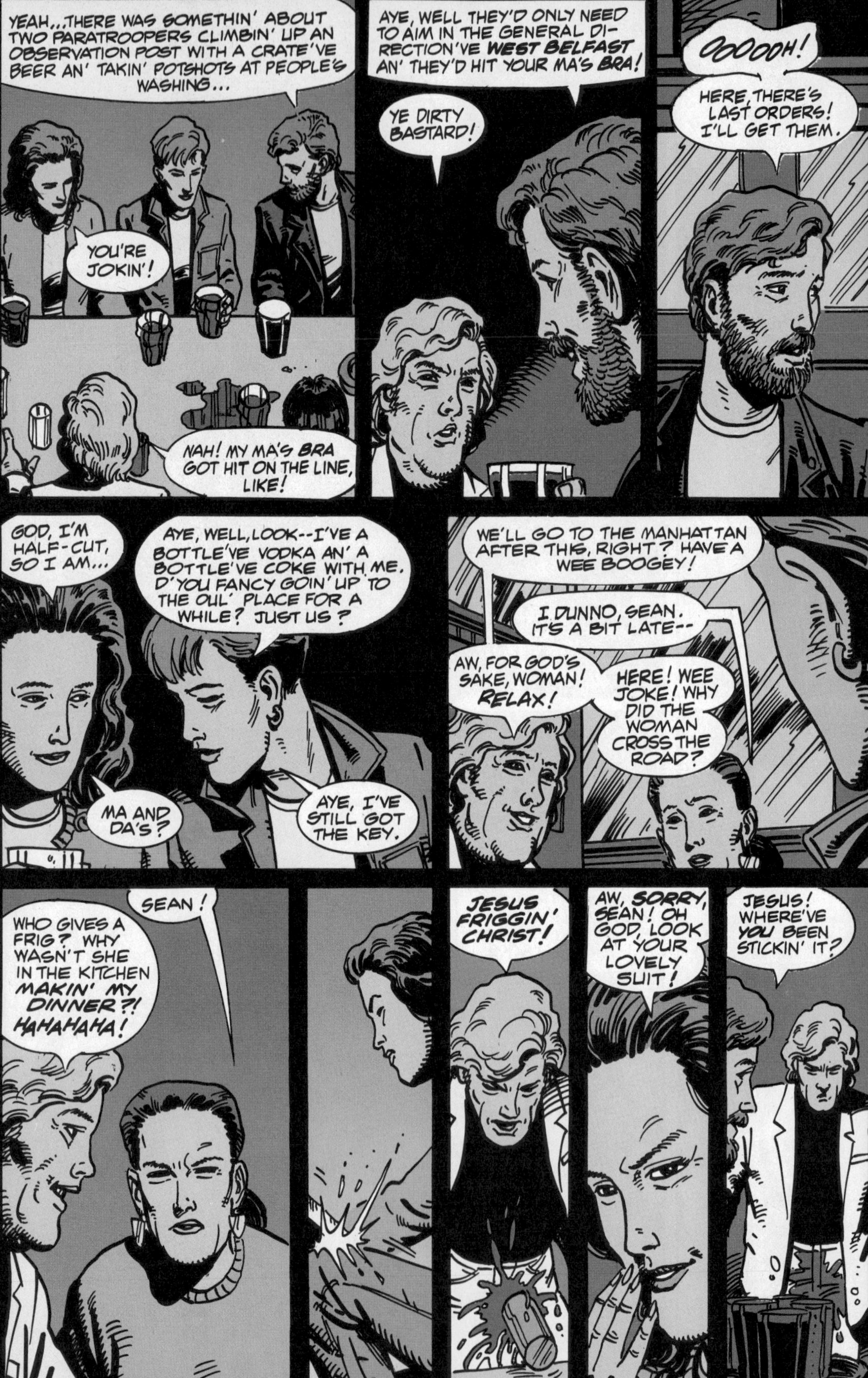

YEAH...THERE WAS SOMETHIN' ABOUT TWO PARATROOPERS CLIMBIN' UP AN OBSERVATION POST WITH A CRATE'VE BEER AN' TAKIN' POTSHOTS AT PEOPLE'S WASHING...
YOU'RE JOKIN'!
NAH! MY MA'S BRA GOT HIT ON THE LINE, LIKE!
AYE, WELL THEY'D ONLY NEED TO AIM IN THE GENERAL DI-RECTION'VE WEST BELFAST AN' THEY'D HIT YOUR MA'S BRA!
YE DIRTY BASTARD!
OOOOOOH!
HERE, THERE'S LAST ORDERS! I'LL GET THEM.
GOD, I'M HALF-CUT, SO I AM...
AYE, WELL, LOOK--I'VE A BOTTLE'VE VODKA AN' A BOTTLE'VE COKE WITH ME. D'YOU FANCY GOIN' UP TO THE OUL' PLACE FOR A WHILE? JUST US?
MA AND DA'S?
AYE, I'VE STILL GOT THE KEY.
WE'LL GO TO THE MANHATTAN AFTER THIS, RIGHT? HAVE A WEE BOOGEY!
I DUNNO, SEAN. IT'S A BIT LATE--
AW, FOR GOD'S SAKE, WOMAN! RELAX!
HERE! WEE JOKE! WHY DID THE WOMAN CROSS THE ROAD?
SEAN!
WHO GIVES A FRIG? WHY WASN'T SHE IN THE KITCHEN MAKIN' MY DINNER?! HAHAHAHA!
JESUS FRIGGIN' CHRIST!
AW, SORRY, SEAN! OH GOD, LOOK AT YOUR LOVELY SUIT!
JESUS! WHERE'VE YOU BEEN STICKIN' IT?

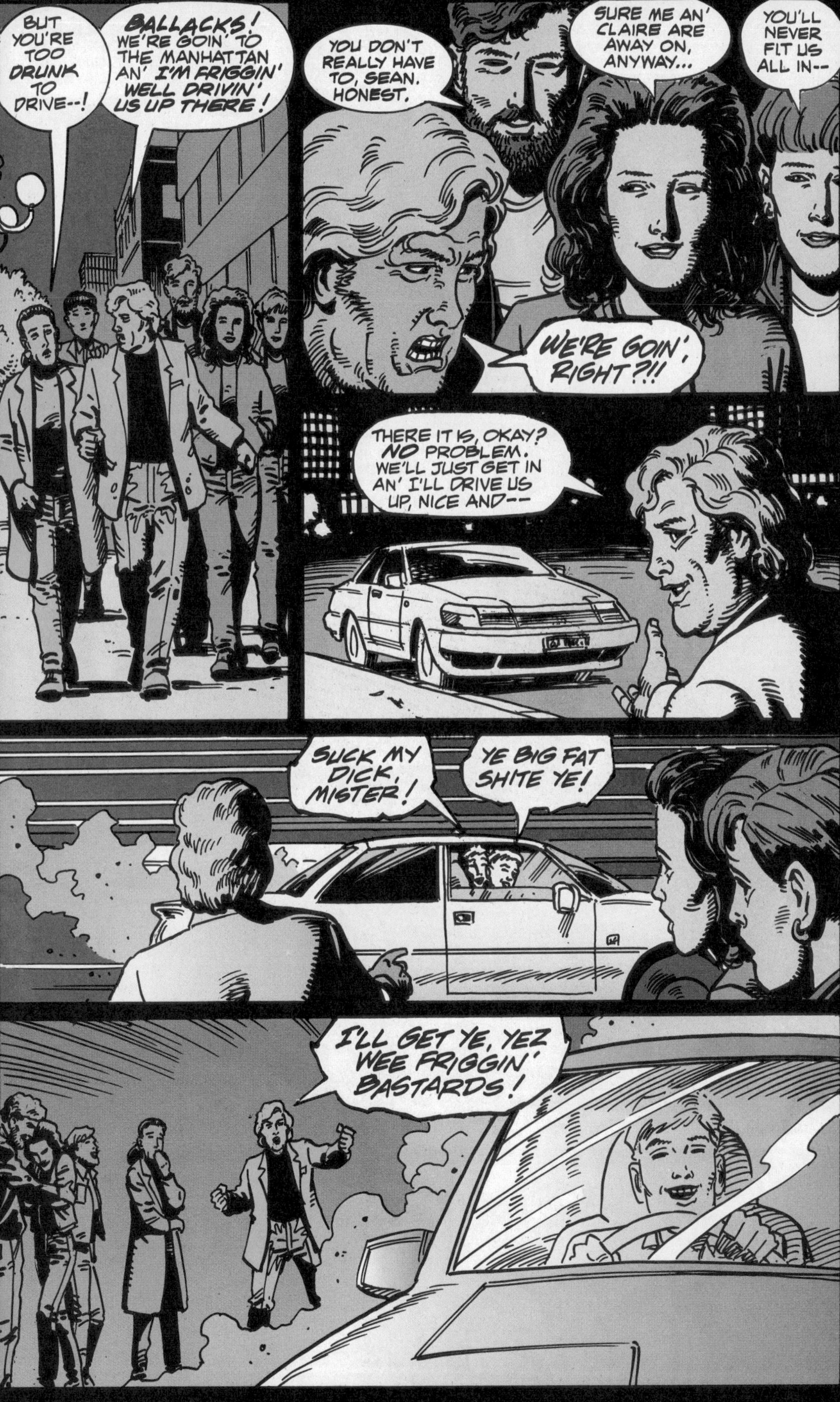
BUT YOU'RE TOO DRUNK TO DRIVE--!
BALLACKS! WE'RE GOIN' TO THE MANHATTAN AN' I'M FRIGGIN' WELL DRIVIN' US UP THERE!
YOU DON'T REALLY HAVE TO, SEAN. HONEST.
SURE ME AN' CLAIRE ARE AWAY ON, ANYWAY...
YOU'LL NEVER FIT US ALL IN--
WE'RE GOIN', RIGHT?!!
THERE IT IS, OKAY? NO PROBLEM. WE'LL JUST GET IN AN' I'LL DRIVE US UP, NICE AND--
SUCK MY DICK, MISTER!
YE BIG FAT SHITE YE!
I'LL GET YE, YEZ WEE FRIGGIN' BASTARDS!

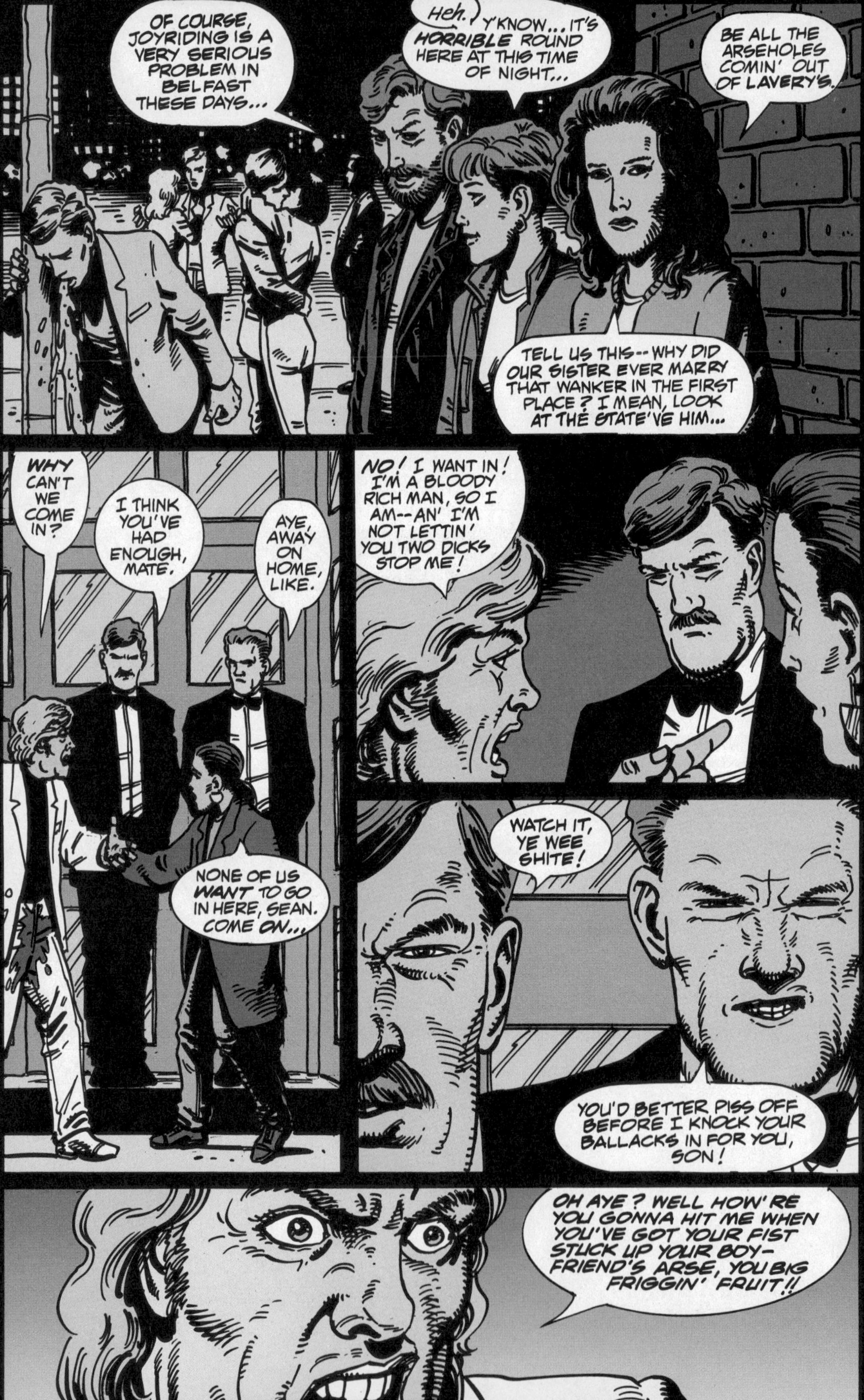
OF COURSE, JOYRIDING IS A VERY SERIOUS PROBLEM IN BELFAST THESE DAYS...
Heh. Y'KNOW... IT'S HORRIBLE ROUND HERE AT THIS TIME OF NIGHT...
BE ALL THE ARSEHOLES COMIN' OUT OF LAVERY'S.
TELL US THIS-- WHY DID OUR SISTER EVER MARRY THAT WANKER IN THE FIRST PLACE? I MEAN, LOOK AT THE STATE'VE HIM...
WHY CAN'T WE COME IN?
I THINK YOU'VE HAD ENOUGH, MATE.
AYE, AWAY ON HOME, LIKE.
NONE OF US WANT TO GO IN HERE, SEAN. COME ON...
NO! I WANT IN! I'M A BLOODY RICH MAN, SO I AM-- AN' I'M NOT LETTIN' YOU TWO DICKS STOP ME!
WATCH IT, YE WEE SHITE!
YOU'D BETTER PISS OFF BEFORE I KNOCK YOUR BALLACKS IN FOR YOU, SON!
OH AYE? WELL HOW'RE YOU GONNA HIT ME WHEN YOU'VE GOT YOUR FIST STUCK UP YOUR BOY-FRIEND'S ARSE, YOU BIG FRIGGIN' FRUIT!!

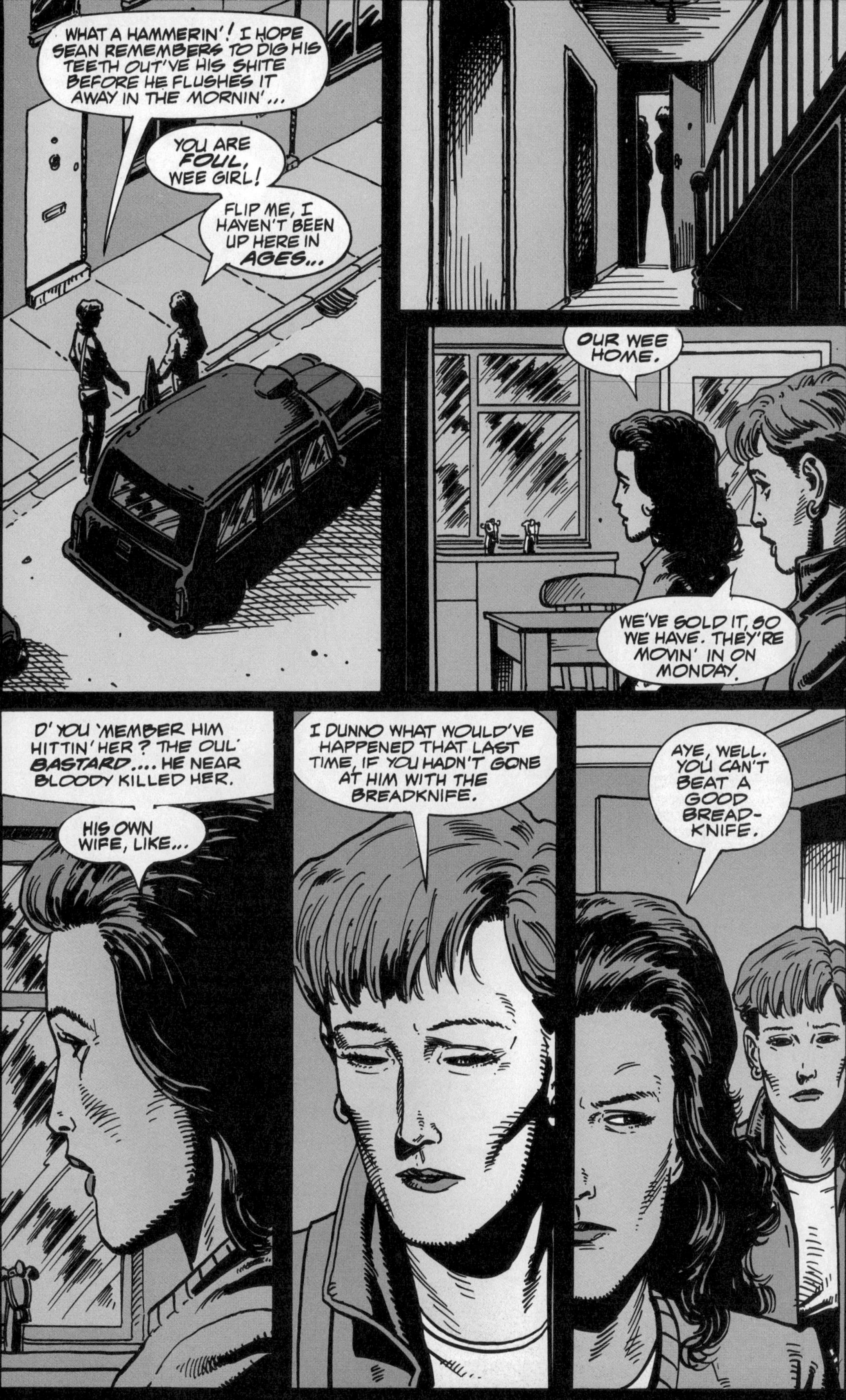
WHAT A HAMMERIN'! I HOPE SEAN REMEMBERS TO DIG HIS TEETH OUT'VE HIS SHITE BEFORE HE FLUSHES IT AWAY IN THE MORNIN'...
YOU ARE FOUL, WEE GIRL!
FLIP ME, I HAVEN'T BEEN UP HERE IN AGES...
OUR WEE HOME.
WE'VE SOLD IT, SO WE HAVE. THEY'RE MOVIN' IN ON MONDAY.
D' YOU 'MEMBER HIM HITTIN' HER? THE OUL' BASTARD.... HE NEAR BLOODY KILLED HER.
HIS OWN WIFE, LIKE...
I DUNNO WHAT WOULD'VE HAPPENED THAT LAST TIME, IF YOU HADN'T GONE AT HIM WITH THE BREADKNIFE.
AYE, WELL. YOU CAN'T BEAT A GOOD BREAD-KNIFE.

...AN' I JUST DON'T KNOW ANYMORE.

I MEAN, HE LIKED ME BECAUSE HE COULD RELAX WITH ME, Y'KNOW? HE HAD THIS SORT'VE FRONT FOR EVERYONE ELSE, BUT UNDERNEATH IT, HE WAS A NICE FELLA.

OR HE WAS DOIN' HIS BEST TO BE, ANYWAY.

DID HE LOVE YOU?

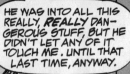

HE...

HE WAS INTO ALL THIS REALLY, *REALLY* DANGEROUS STUFF, BUT HE DIDN'T LET ANY OF IT TOUCH ME. UNTIL THAT LAST TIME, ANYWAY.

BUT AT THE END, RIGHT, WHEN I TOLD HIM I WAS LEAVIN'--HE WAS SAYIN' THINGS I *NEVER* THOUGHT I'D HEAR OUT'VE HIM. HE STOPPED JUST SHORT OF TELLIN' ME HE LOVED ME...

YOU'VE NO IDEA WHAT THAT MEANT, COMIN' FROM HIM.

AND...?

WELL, I....AW, I JUST WOULDN'T LISTEN TO HIM. YOU KNOW WHAT I'M LIKE.

AN' THEN HE CALLED ME *COLD*.

AN' YOU ATE THE HEAD OFF HIM.

AYE.

NOK NOK

EH?

IT'S THREE IN THE BLOODY MORNIN'...

NEIL?

KATHY...

KATHY, LOOK... I WANTED TO... I MEAN... I WAS JUST WONDERIN', LIKE... I HEARD YOU AN' CLAIRE SAYIN' YE WERE COMIN' UP HERE...

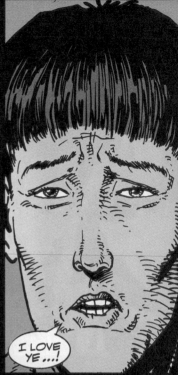

KATHY...

I LOVE YE...!

GO ON HOME, NEIL, YOU'RE DRUNK.

BUT...

GO ON.

RIGHT.

GOODNIGHT, NEIL.

JESUS.

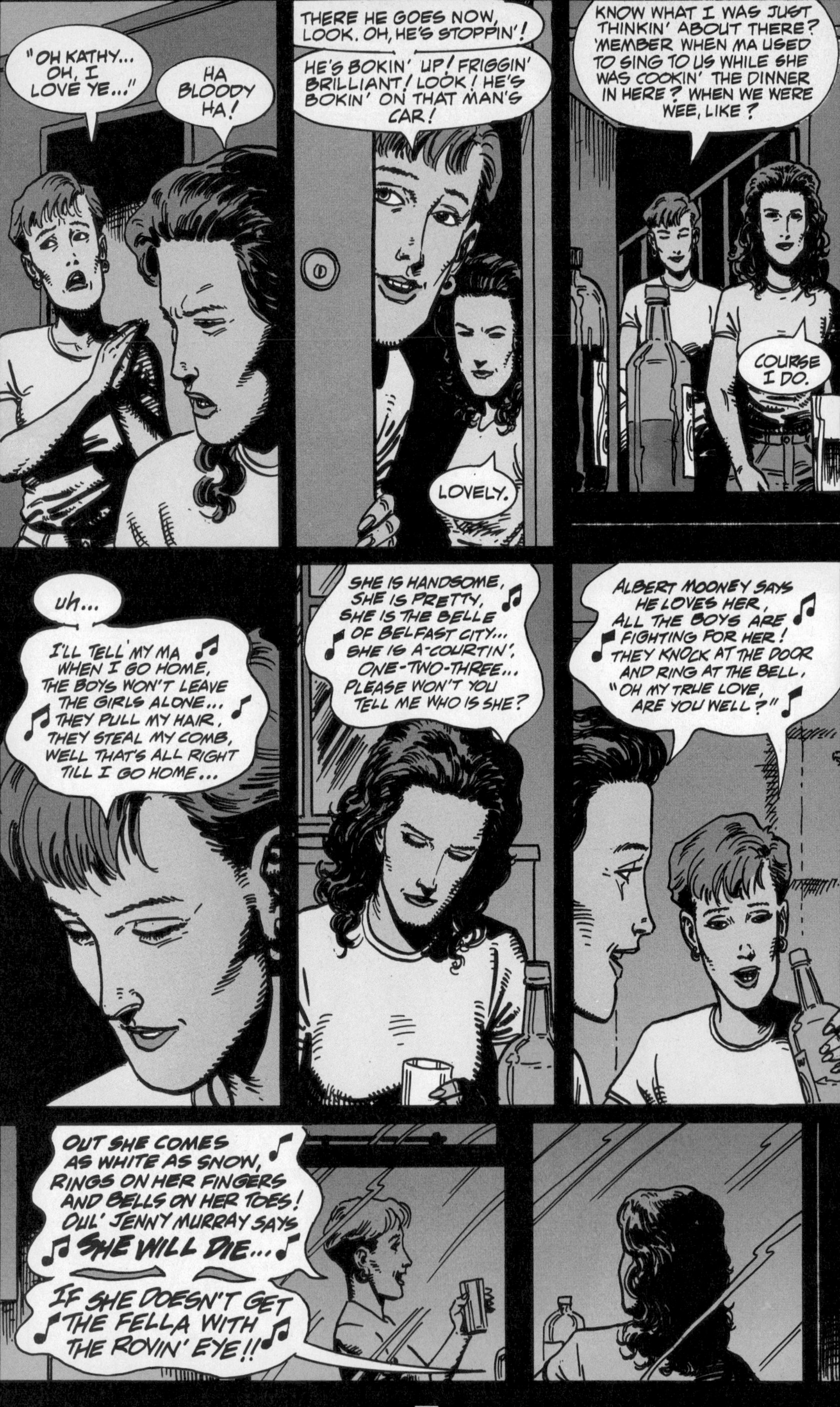
"OH KATHY... OH, I LOVE YE..."
HA BLOODY HA!
THERE HE GOES NOW, LOOK. OH, HE'S STOPPIN'!
HE'S BOKIN' UP! FRIGGIN' BRILLIANT! LOOK! HE'S BOKIN' ON THAT MAN'S CAR!
LOVELY.
KNOW WHAT I WAS JUST THINKIN' ABOUT THERE? 'MEMBER WHEN MA USED TO SING TO US WHILE SHE WAS COOKIN' THE DINNER IN HERE? WHEN WE WERE WEE, LIKE?
COURSE I DO.
uh...
I'LL TELL MY MA WHEN I GO HOME, THE BOYS WON'T LEAVE THE GIRLS ALONE... THEY PULL MY HAIR, THEY STEAL MY COMB, WELL THAT'S ALL RIGHT TILL I GO HOME...
SHE IS HANDSOME, SHE IS PRETTY, SHE IS THE BELLE OF BELFAST CITY... SHE IS A-COURTIN', ONE-TWO-THREE... PLEASE WON'T YOU TELL ME WHO IS SHE?
ALBERT MOONEY SAYS HE LOVES HER, ALL THE BOYS ARE FIGHTING FOR HER! THEY KNOCK AT THE DOOR AND RING AT THE BELL, "OH MY TRUE LOVE, ARE YOU WELL?"
OUT SHE COMES AS WHITE AS SNOW, RINGS ON HER FINGERS AND BELLS ON HER TOES! OUL' JENNY MURRAY SAYS SHE WILL DIE...
IF SHE DOESN'T GET THE FELLA WITH THE ROVIN' EYE!!

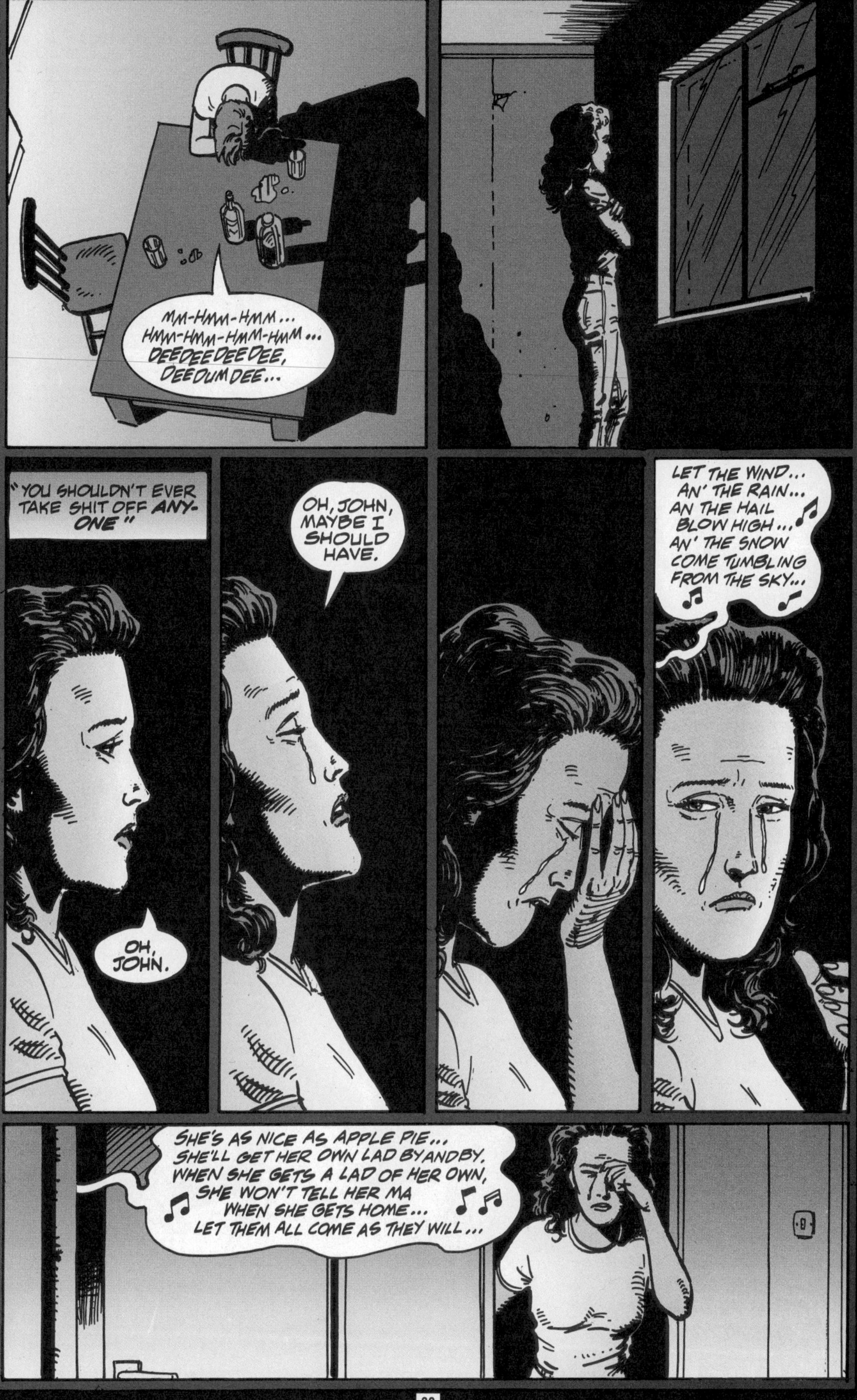
MM-HMM-HMM...
HMM-HMM-HMM-HMM...
DEEDEEDEEDEE,
DEEDUMDEE...
"YOU SHOULDN'T EVER TAKE SHIT OFF ANY-ONE"
OH, JOHN.
OH, JOHN, MAYBE I SHOULD HAVE.
LET THE WIND... AN' THE RAIN... AN THE HAIL BLOW HIGH... AN' THE SNOW COME TUMBLING FROM THE SKY...
SHE'S AS NICE AS APPLE PIE... SHE'LL GET HER OWN LAD BY AND BY. WHEN SHE GETS A LAD OF HER OWN, SHE WON'T TELL HER MA WHEN SHE GETS HOME... LET THEM ALL COME AS THEY WILL...

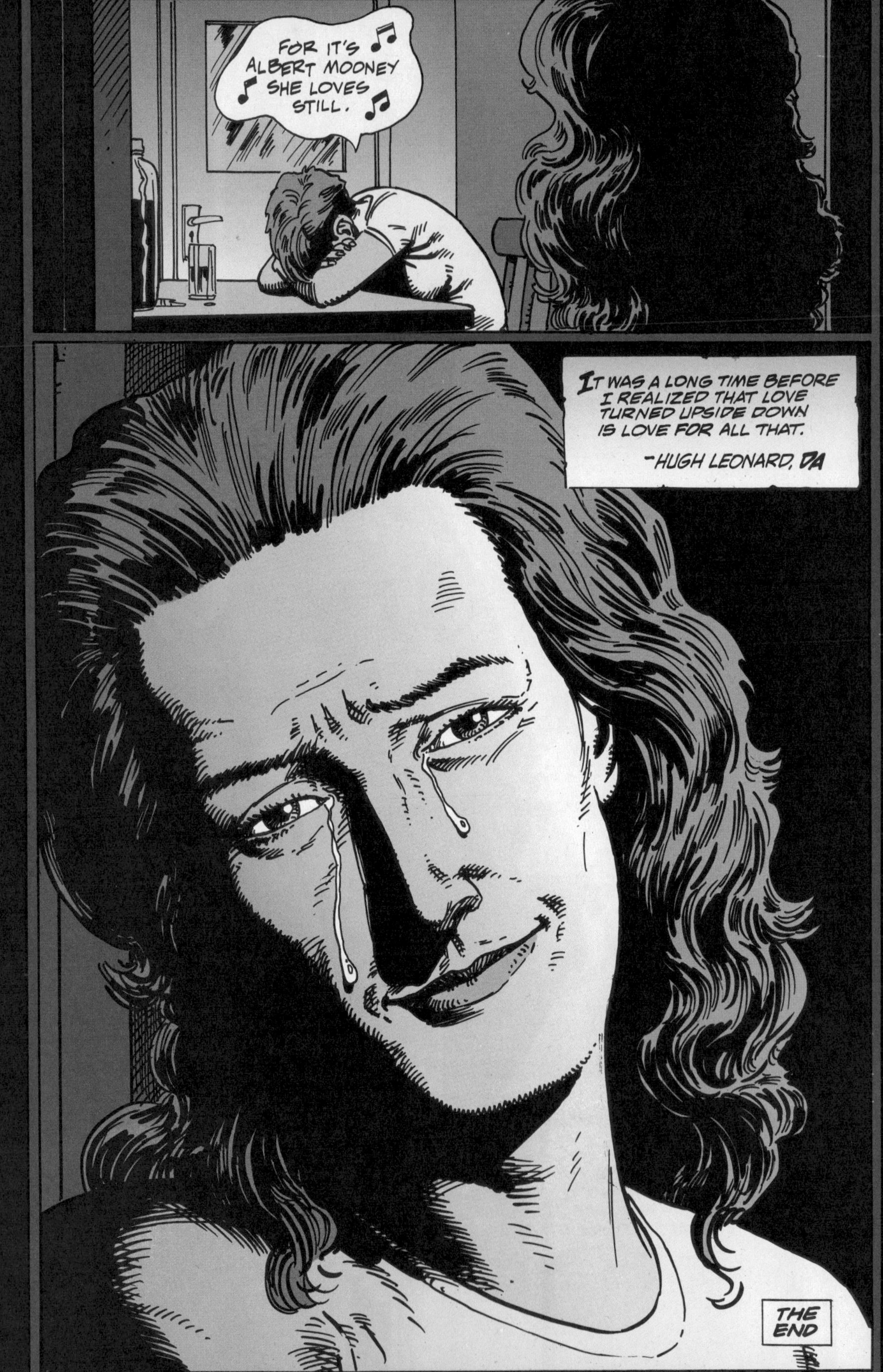
FOR IT'S ALBERT MOONEY SHE LOVES STILL.
IT WAS A LONG TIME BEFORE I REALIZED THAT LOVE TURNED UPSIDE DOWN IS LOVE FOR ALL THAT.
-HUGH LEONARD, DA
THE END

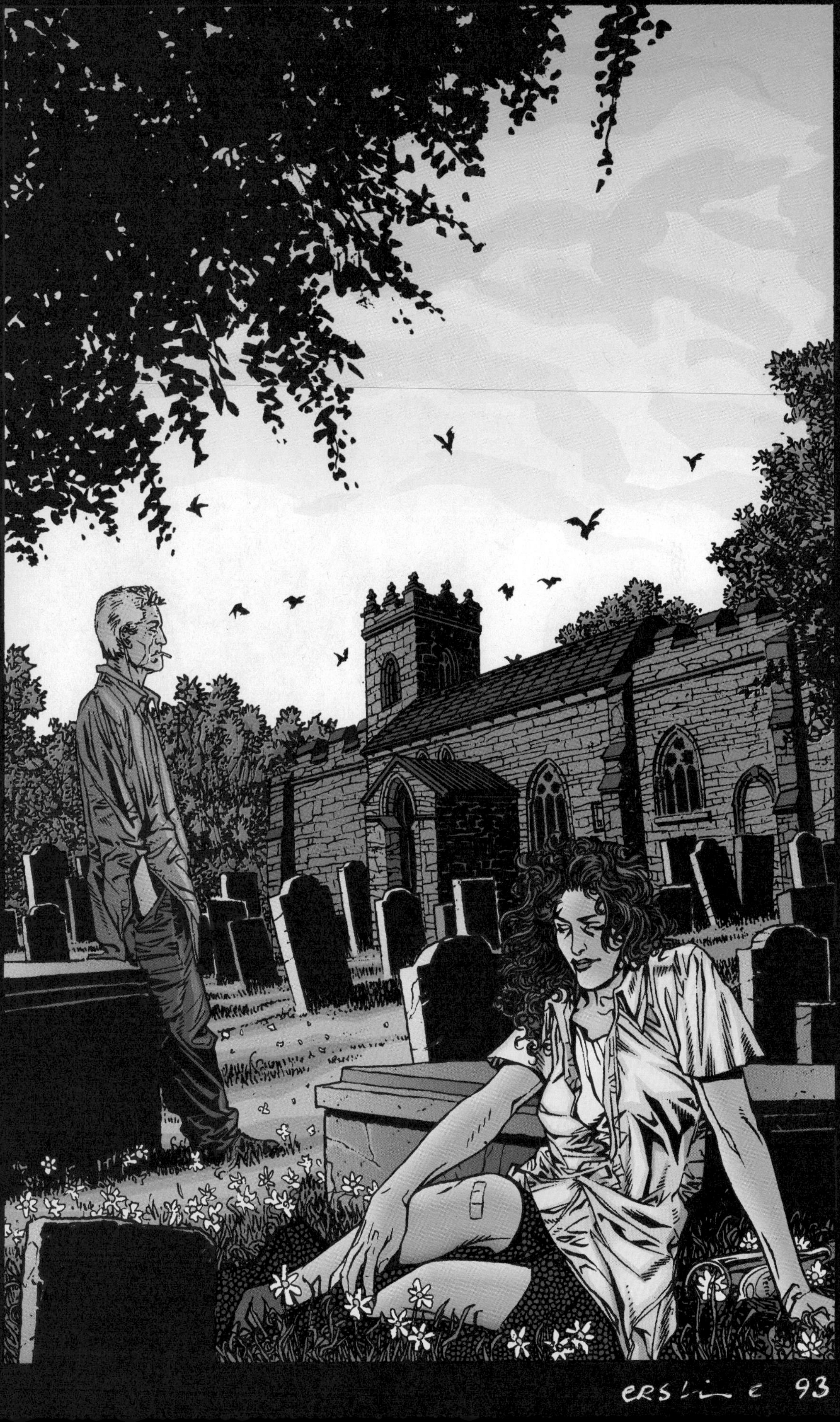
ERSKINE 93

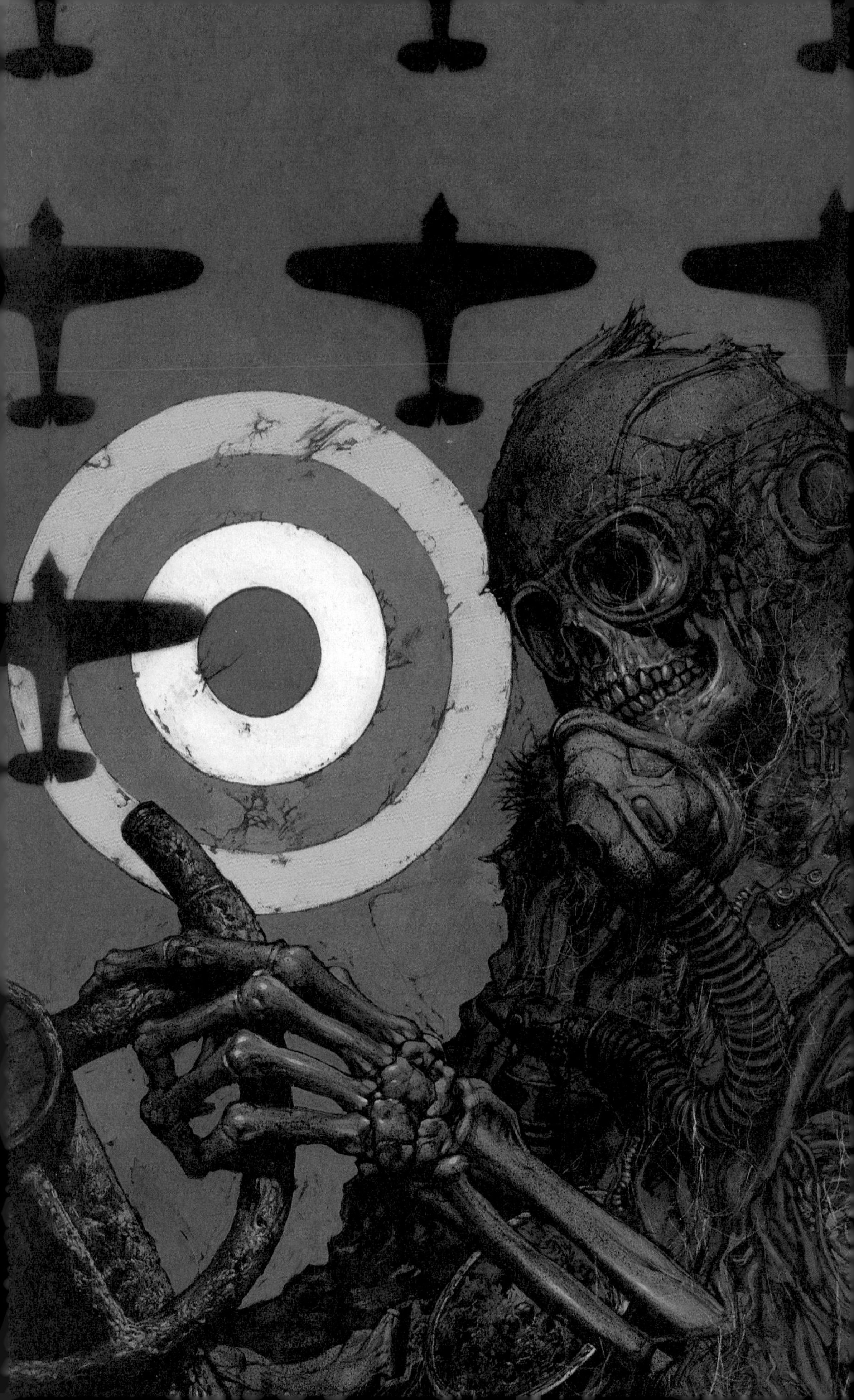

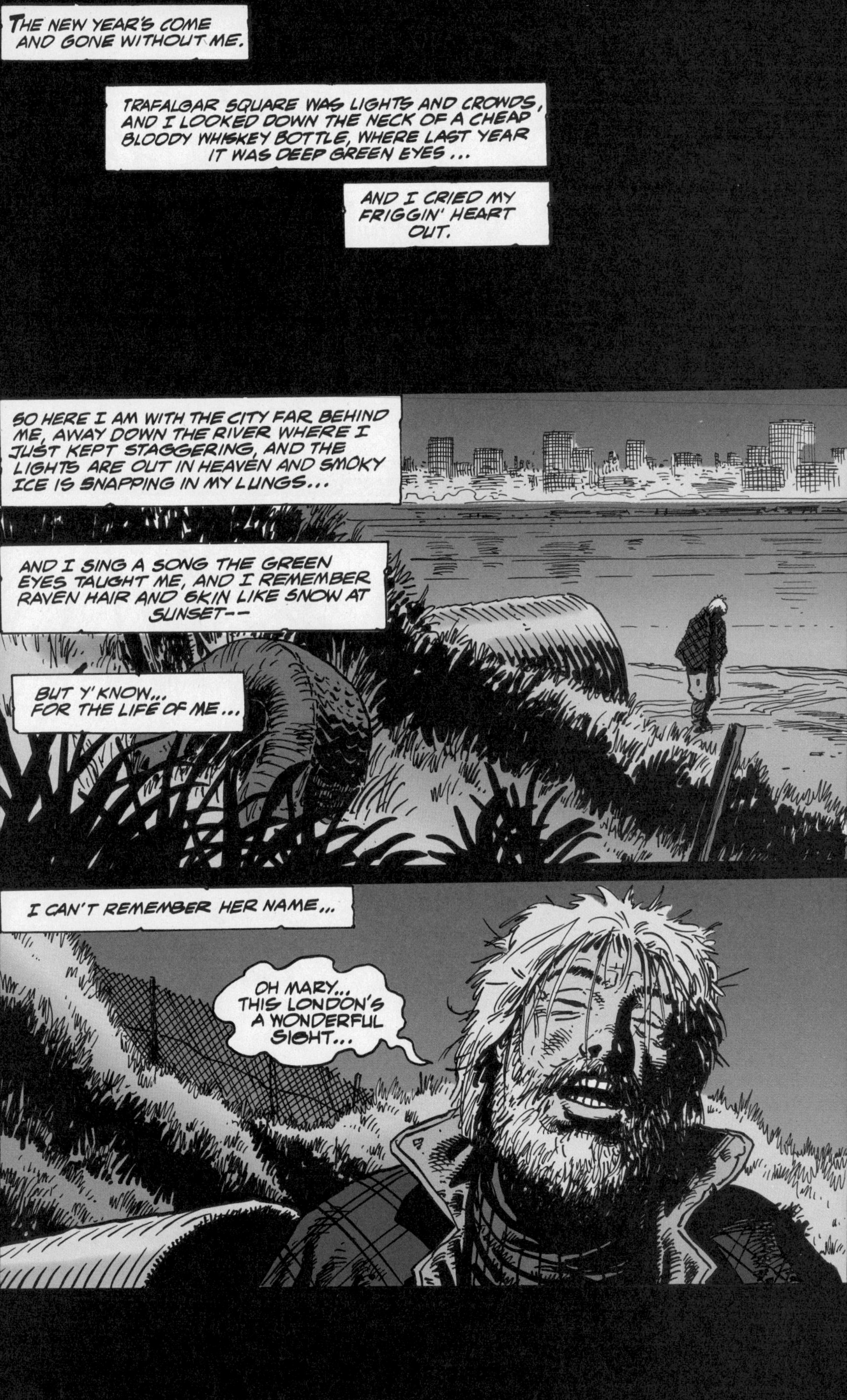
THE NEW YEAR'S COME AND GONE WITHOUT ME.
TRAFALGAR SQUARE WAS LIGHTS AND CROWDS, AND I LOOKED DOWN THE NECK OF A CHEAP BLOODY WHISKEY BOTTLE, WHERE LAST YEAR IT WAS DEEP GREEN EYES...
AND I CRIED MY FRIGGIN' HEART OUT.
SO HERE I AM WITH THE CITY FAR BEHIND ME, AWAY DOWN THE RIVER WHERE I JUST KEPT STAGGERING, AND THE LIGHTS ARE OUT IN HEAVEN AND SMOKY ICE IS SNAPPING IN MY LUNGS...
AND I SING A SONG THE GREEN EYES TAUGHT ME, AND I REMEMBER RAVEN HAIR AND SKIN LIKE SNOW AT SUNSET--
BUT Y'KNOW... FOR THE LIFE OF ME...
I CAN'T REMEMBER HER NAME...
OH MARY... THIS LONDON'S A WONDERFUL SIGHT...

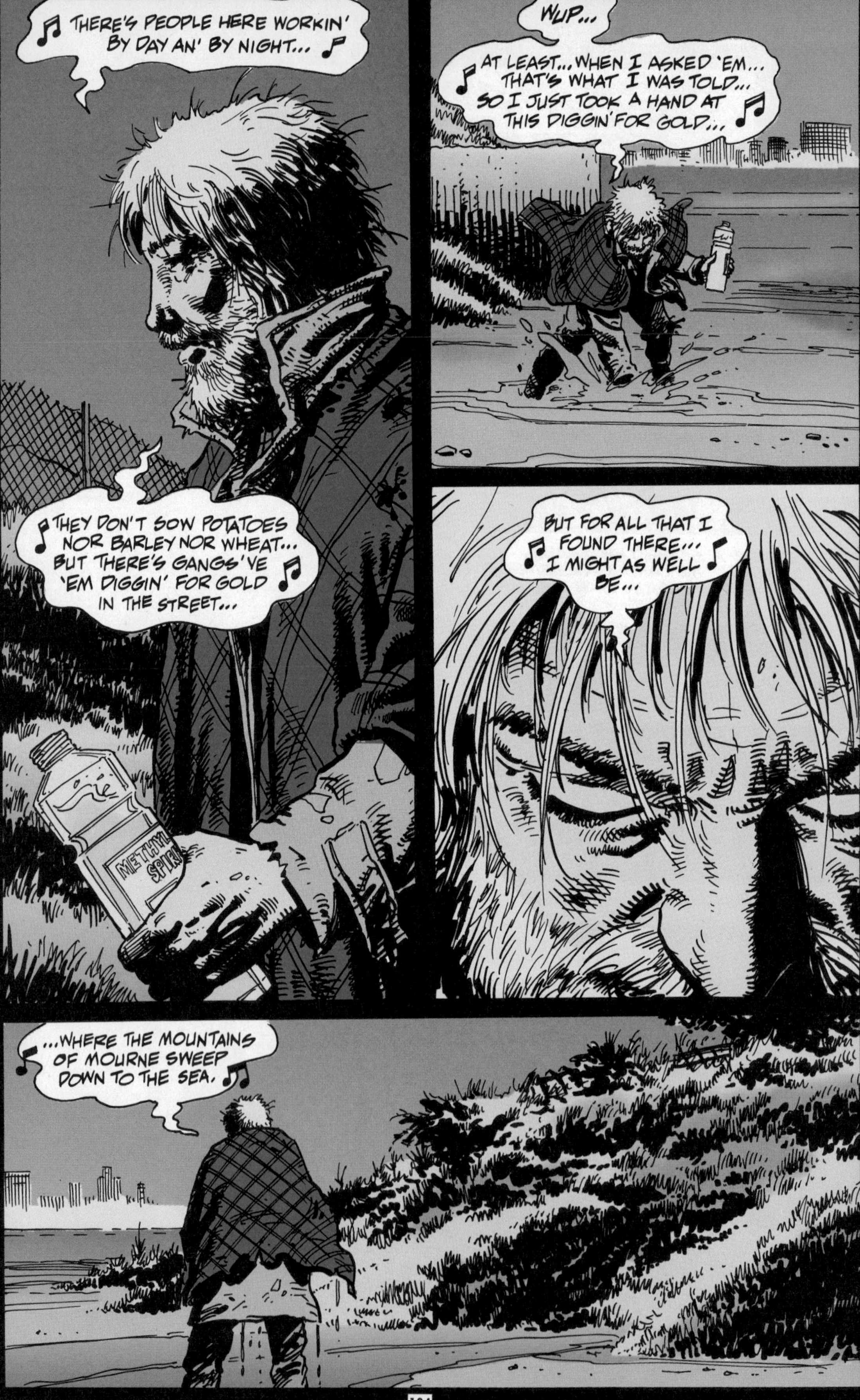
THERE'S PEOPLE HERE WORKIN' BY DAY AN' BY NIGHT...
THEY DON'T SOW POTATOES NOR BARLEY NOR WHEAT... BUT THERE'S GANGS'VE 'EM DIGGIN' FOR GOLD IN THE STREET...
METHYL SPIRI
WUP...
AT LEAST... WHEN I ASKED 'EM... THAT'S WHAT I WAS TOLD... SO I JUST TOOK A HAND AT THIS DIGGIN' FOR GOLD...
BUT FOR ALL THAT I FOUND THERE... I MIGHT AS WELL BE...
...WHERE THE MOUNTAINS OF MOURNE SWEEP DOWN TO THE SEA.

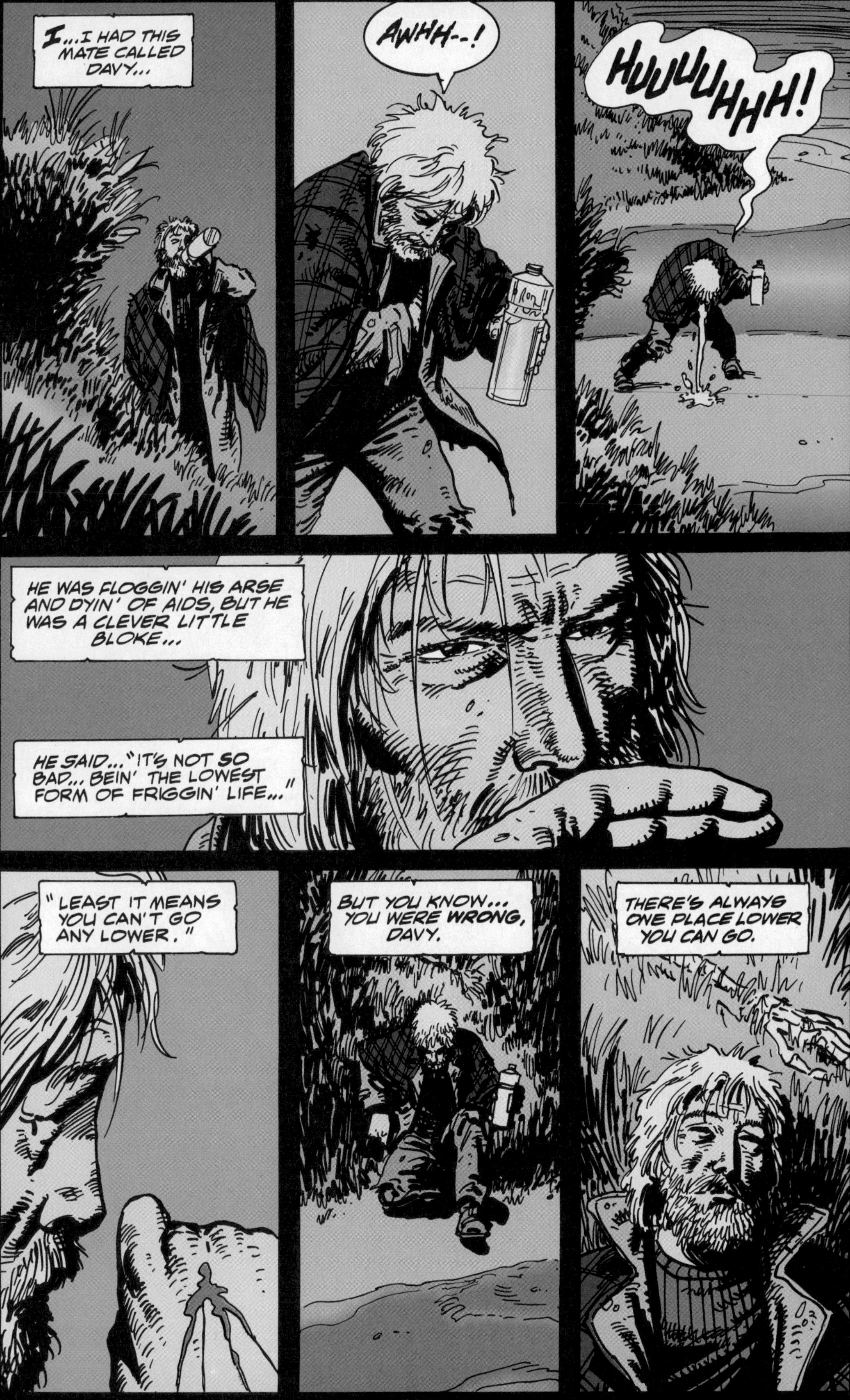
I...I HAD THIS MATE CALLED DAVY...
AWHH--!
HUUUUHHH!
HE WAS FLOGGIN' HIS ARSE AND DYIN' OF AIDS, BUT HE WAS A CLEVER LITTLE BLOKE...
HE SAID..."IT'S NOT SO BAD... BEIN' THE LOWEST FORM OF FRIGGIN' LIFE..."
"LEAST IT MEANS YOU CAN'T GO ANY LOWER."
BUT YOU KNOW... YOU WERE WRONG, DAVY.
THERE'S ALWAYS ONE PLACE LOWER YOU CAN GO.

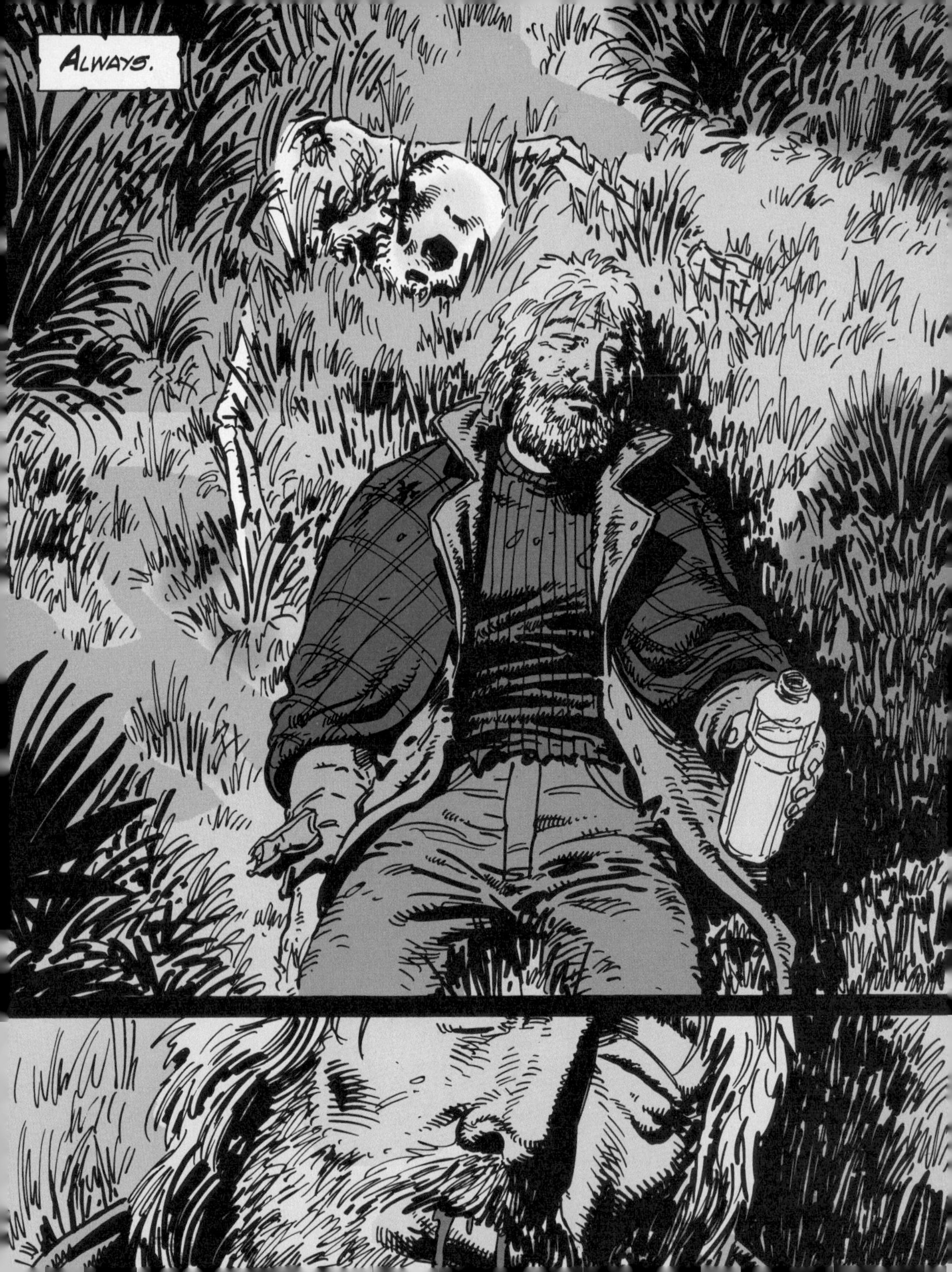
ALWAYS.

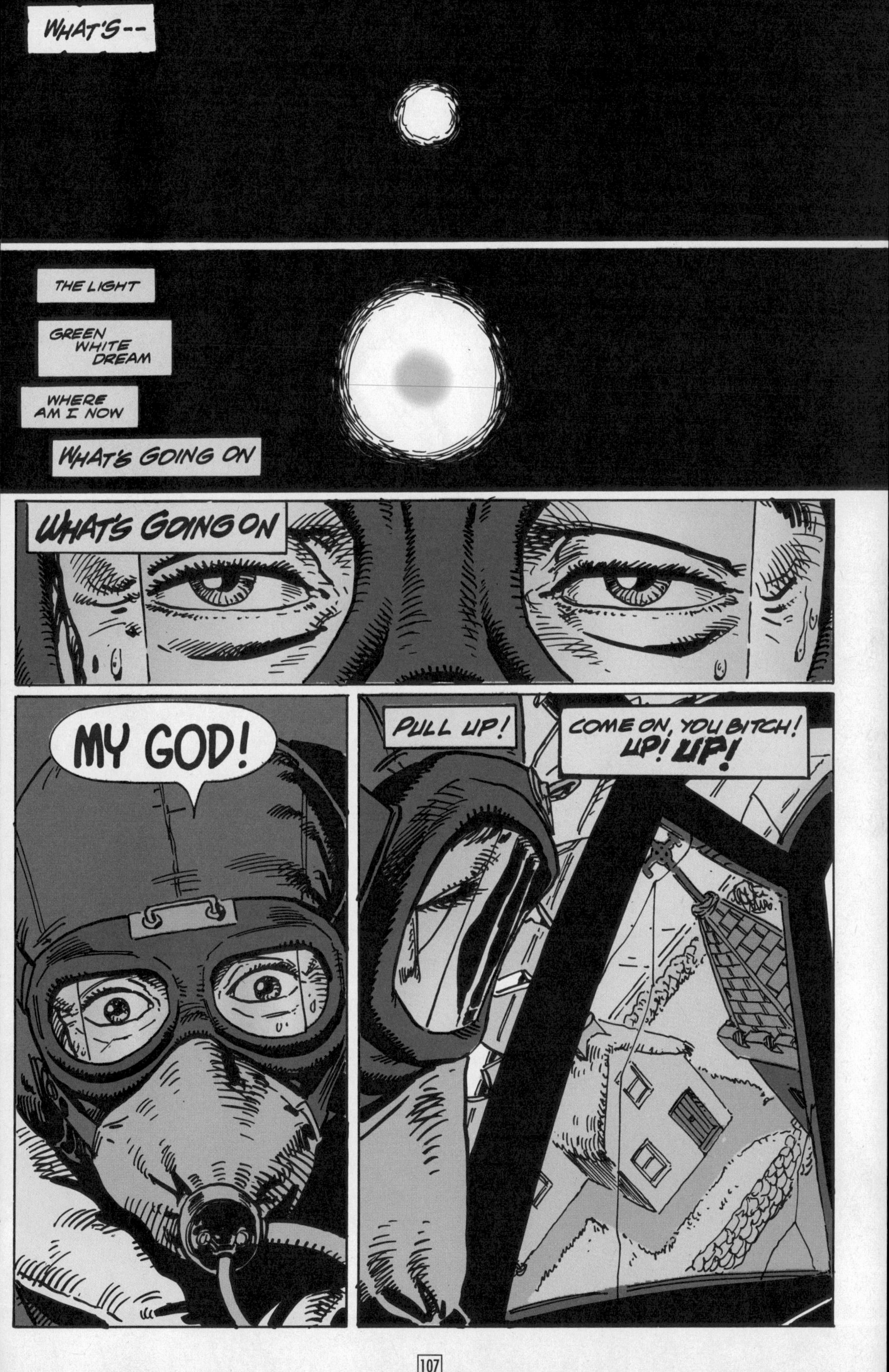
WHAT'S--
THE LIGHT
GREEN WHITE DREAM
WHERE AM I NOW
WHAT'S GOING ON
WHAT'S GOING ON
MY GOD!
PULL UP!
COME ON, YOU BITCH! UP! UP!

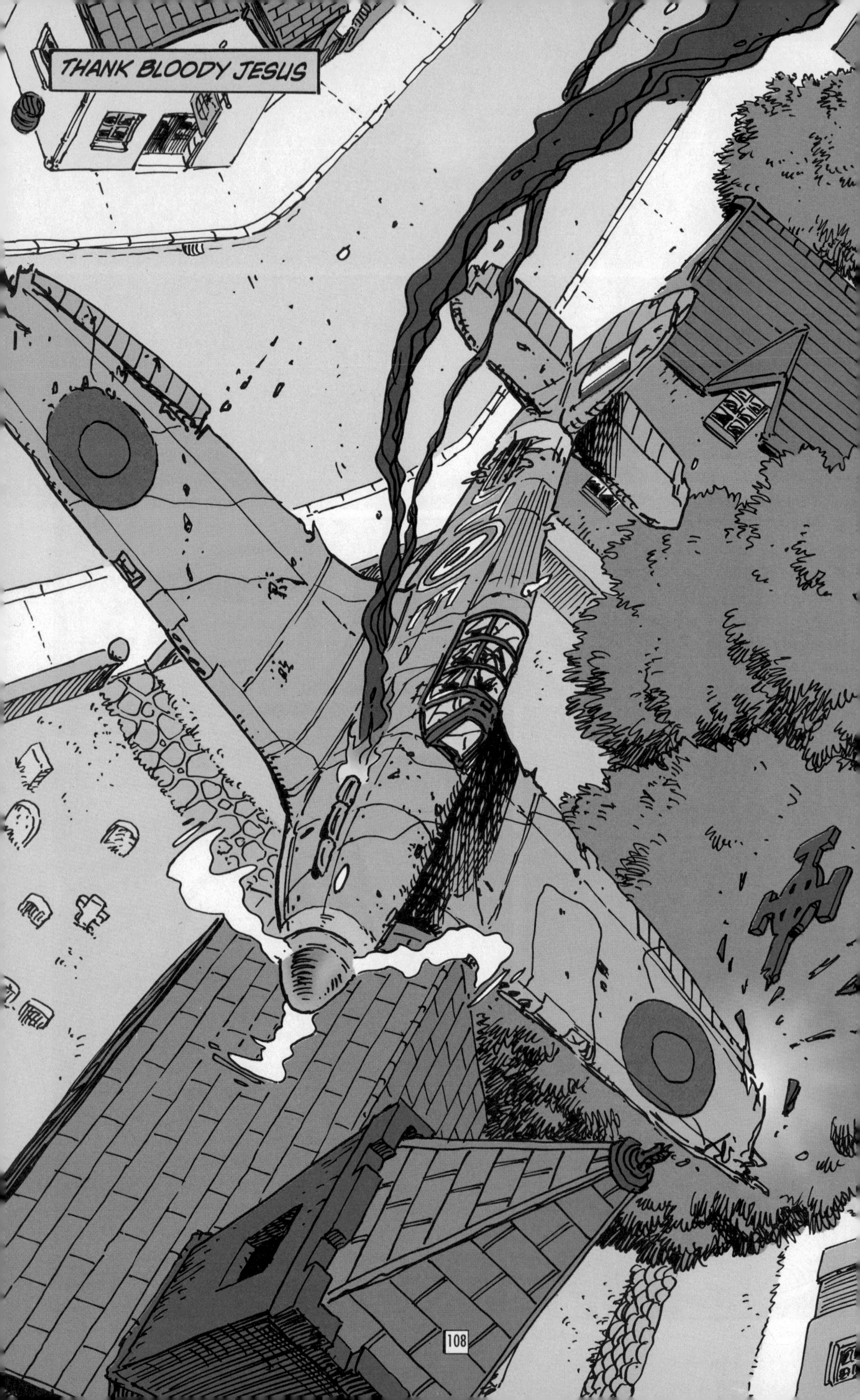
THANK BLOODY JESUS

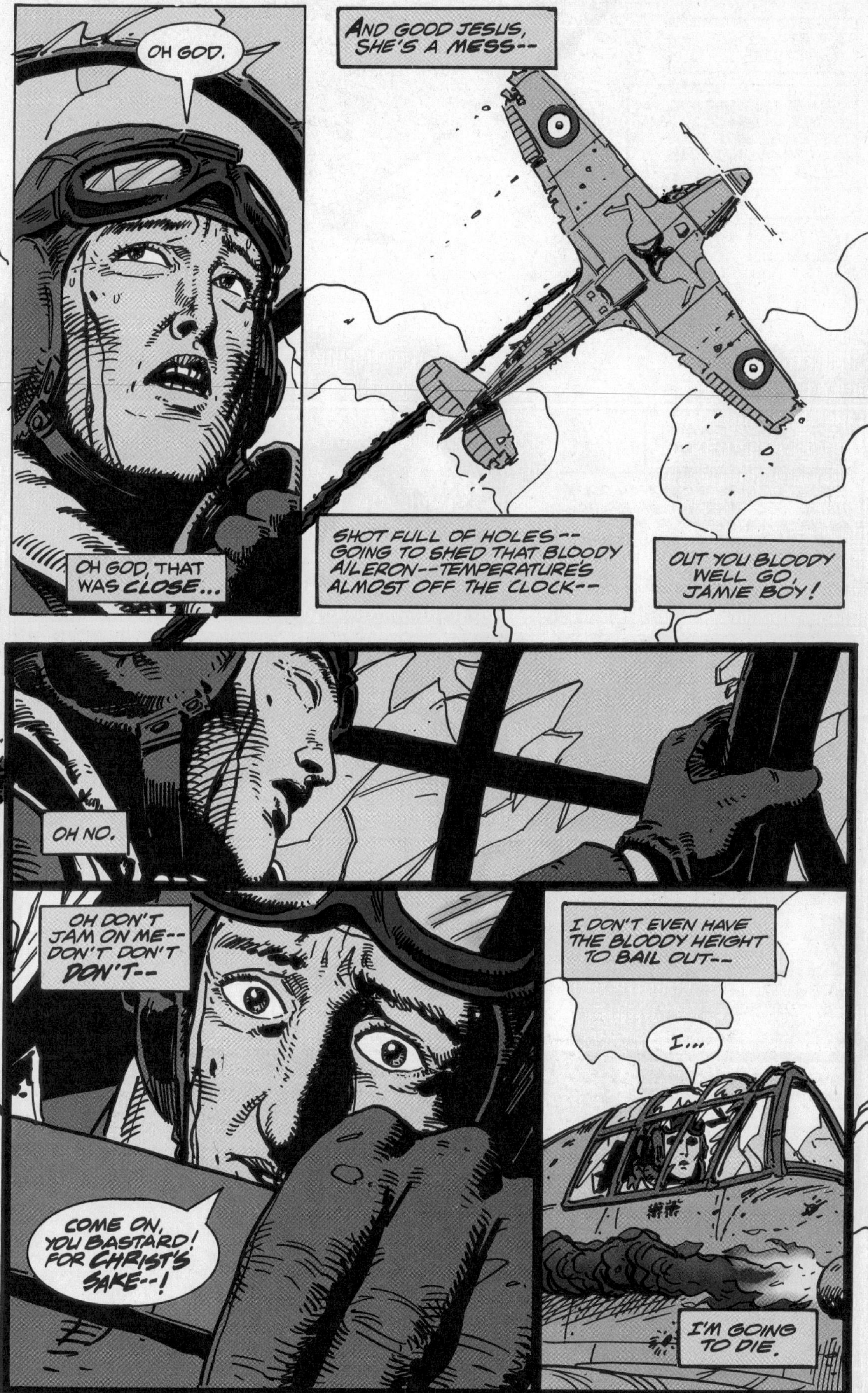
OH GOD.
AND GOOD JESUS, SHE'S A MESS--
OH GOD, THAT WAS CLOSE...
SHOT FULL OF HOLES-- GOING TO SHED THAT BLOODY AILERON--TEMPERATURE'S ALMOST OFF THE CLOCK--
OUT YOU BLOODY WELL GO, JAMIE BOY!
OH NO.
OH DON'T JAM ON ME-- DON'T DON'T DON'T--
COME ON, YOU BASTARD! FOR CHRIST'S SAKE--!
I DON'T EVEN HAVE THE BLOODY HEIGHT TO BAIL OUT--
I...
I'M GOING TO DIE.

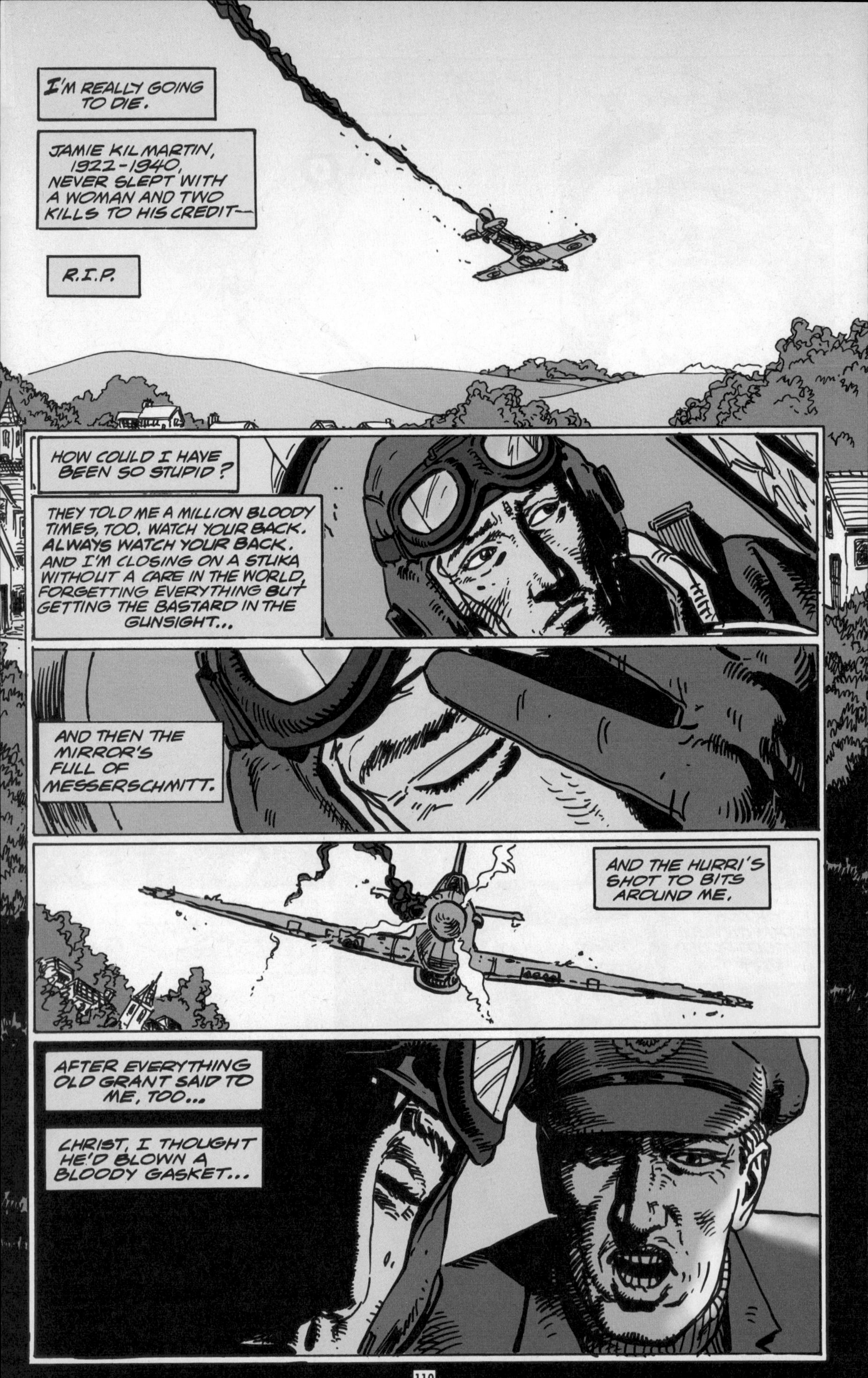
I'M REALLY GOING TO DIE.
JAMIE KILMARTIN, 1922-1940, NEVER SLEPT WITH A WOMAN AND TWO KILLS TO HIS CREDIT—
R.I.P.
HOW COULD I HAVE BEEN SO STUPID?
THEY TOLD ME A MILLION BLOODY TIMES, TOO. WATCH YOUR BACK. ALWAYS WATCH YOUR BACK. AND I'M CLOSING ON A STUKA WITHOUT A CARE IN THE WORLD, FORGETTING EVERYTHING BUT GETTING THE BASTARD IN THE GUNSIGHT...
AND THEN THE MIRROR'S FULL OF MESSERSCHMITT.
AND THE HURRI'S SHOT TO BITS AROUND ME.
AFTER EVERYTHING OLD GRANT SAID TO ME, TOO...
CHRIST, I THOUGHT HE'D BLOWN A BLOODY GASKET...

AH...SQUADRON LEADER GRANT?

eh?

SERGEANT KILMARTIN, SIR. I WAS JUST, er, OUT FOR A WALK BEFORE TURNING IN, AND, WELL--

YOU'RE WONDERING WHY YOUR COMMANDING OFFICER'S SITTING PISSED AS A FART UNDER HIS AIRCRAFT.

HERE.

WELL, I DON'T NORMALLY--

OH, IN CHRIST'S NAME--! TAKE IT!

YOU'RE... BLUE FLIGHT? NICHOLS' WINGMAN?

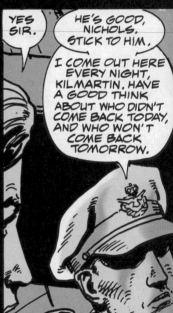

YES SIR.

HE'S GOOD, NICHOLS. STICK TO HIM.

I COME OUT HERE EVERY NIGHT, KILMARTIN. HAVE A GOOD THINK ABOUT WHO DIDN'T COME BACK TODAY, AND WHO WON'T COME BACK TOMORROW.

AND NOT A BLOODY THING I CAN DO ABOUT IT, EITHER.

WELL, IT'S-- ≥ak≤

IT'S SOMETHING WE ALL WORRY ABOUT, ISN'T IT, SIR? WHEN OLD MAN DEATH'S GOING TO COME CALLING...

WHAT?

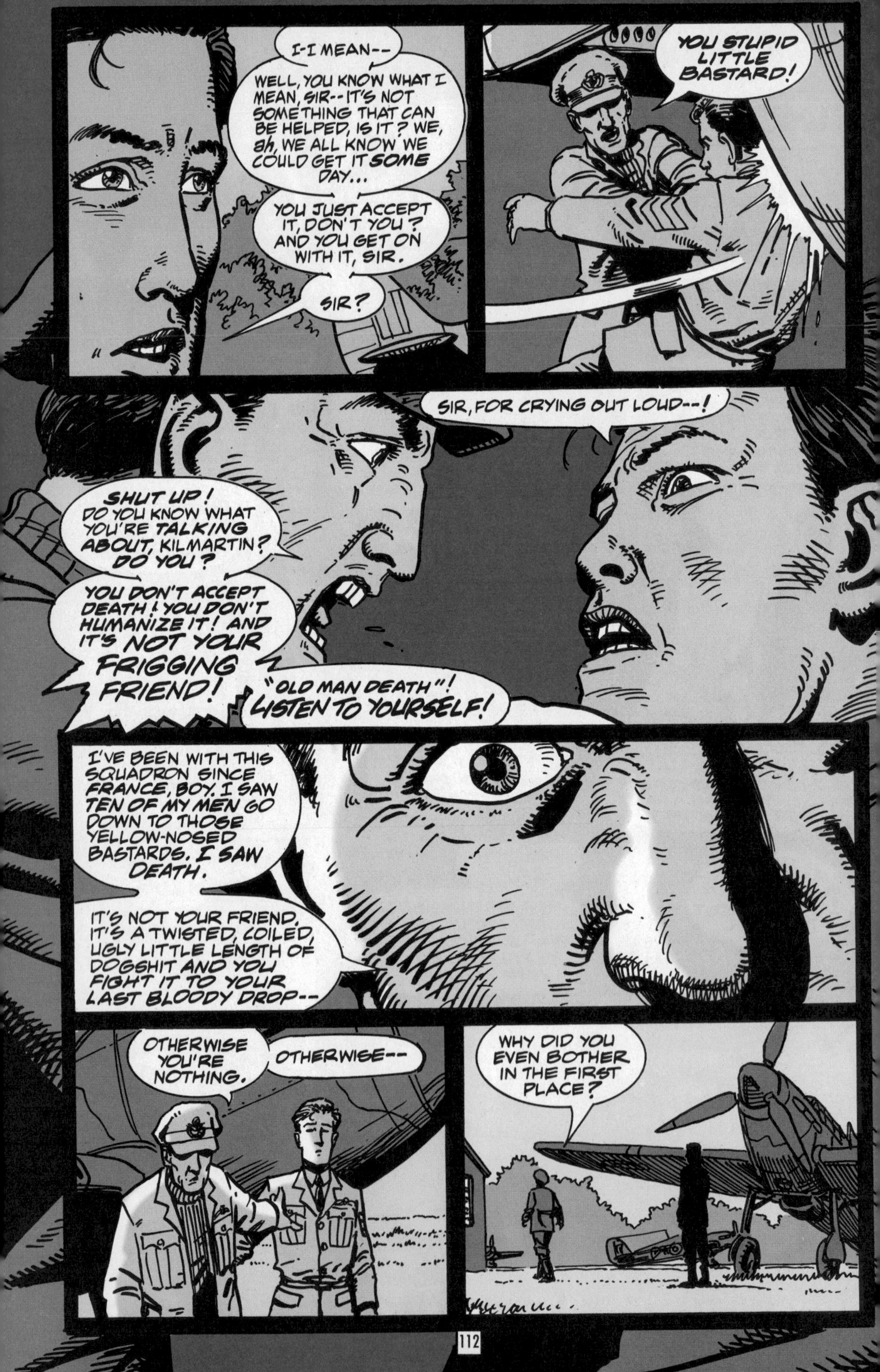
I-I MEAN--
WELL, YOU KNOW WHAT I MEAN, SIR--IT'S NOT SOMETHING THAT CAN BE HELPED, IS IT? WE, ah, WE ALL KNOW WE COULD GET IT SOME DAY...
YOU JUST ACCEPT IT, DON'T YOU? AND YOU GET ON WITH IT, SIR.
SIR?
YOU STUPID LITTLE BASTARD!
SIR, FOR CRYING OUT LOUD--!
SHUT UP! DO YOU KNOW WHAT YOU'RE TALKING ABOUT, KILMARTIN? DO YOU?
YOU DON'T ACCEPT DEATH! YOU DON'T HUMANIZE IT! AND IT'S NOT YOUR FRIGGING FRIEND!
"OLD MAN DEATH"! LISTEN TO YOURSELF!
I'VE BEEN WITH THIS SQUADRON SINCE FRANCE, BOY. I SAW TEN OF MY MEN GO DOWN TO THOSE YELLOW-NOSED BASTARDS. I SAW DEATH.
IT'S NOT YOUR FRIEND. IT'S A TWISTED, COILED, UGLY LITTLE LENGTH OF DOGSHIT AND YOU FIGHT IT TO YOUR LAST BLOODY DROP--
OTHERWISE YOU'RE NOTHING.
OTHERWISE--
WHY DID YOU EVEN BOTHER IN THE FIRST PLACE?

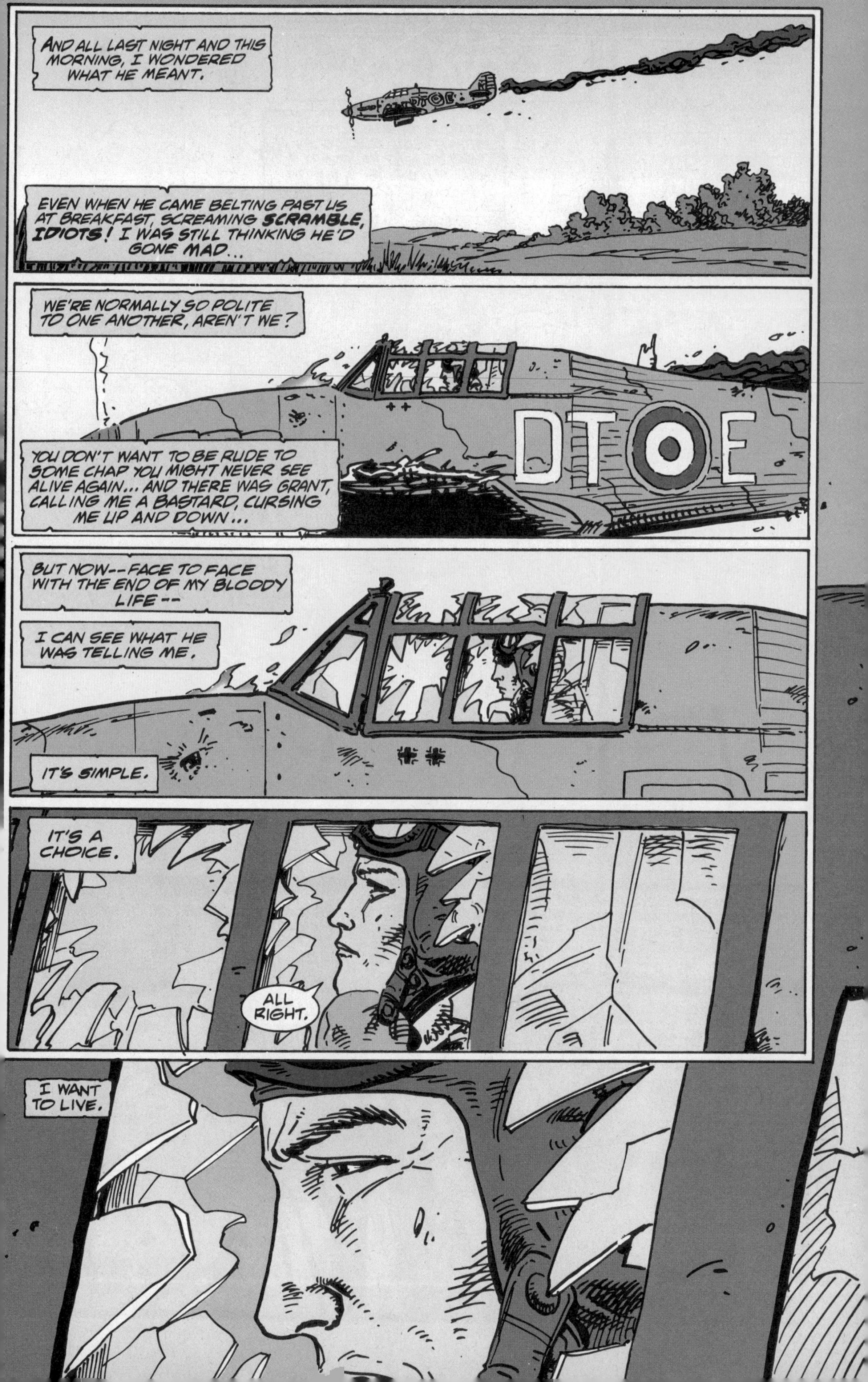
AND ALL LAST NIGHT AND THIS MORNING, I WONDERED WHAT HE MEANT.
EVEN WHEN HE CAME BELTING PAST US AT BREAKFAST, SCREAMING SCRAMBLE, IDIOTS! I WAS STILL THINKING HE'D GONE MAD...
DTOE
WE'RE NORMALLY SO POLITE TO ONE ANOTHER, AREN'T WE?
DTOE
YOU DON'T WANT TO BE RUDE TO SOME CHAP YOU MIGHT NEVER SEE ALIVE AGAIN... AND THERE WAS GRANT, CALLING ME A BASTARD, CURSING ME UP AND DOWN...
BUT NOW--FACE TO FACE WITH THE END OF MY BLOODY LIFE--
I CAN SEE WHAT HE WAS TELLING ME.
IT'S SIMPLE.
IT'S A CHOICE.
ALL RIGHT.
I WANT TO LIVE.

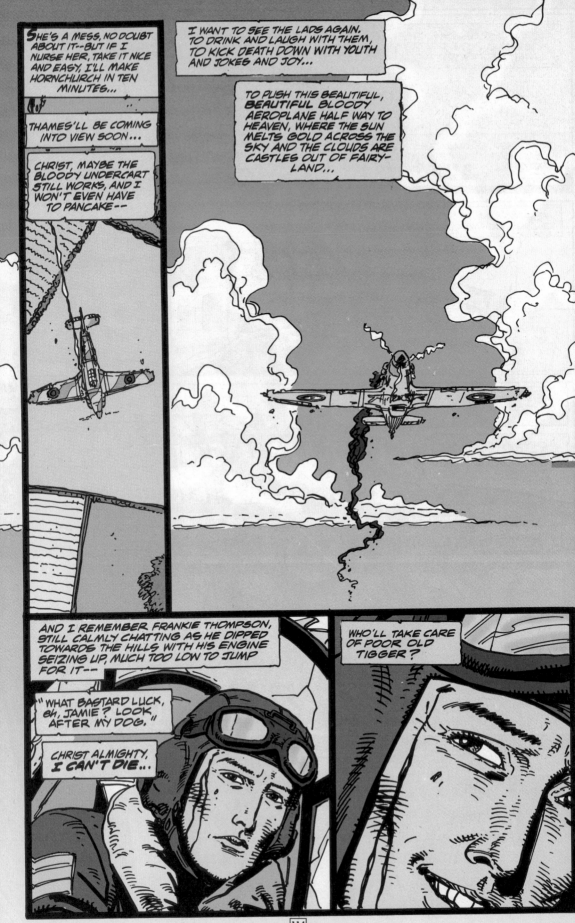

SHE'S A MESS, NO DOUBT ABOUT IT--BUT IF I NURSE HER, TAKE IT NICE AND EASY, I'LL MAKE HORNCHURCH IN TEN MINUTES...

THAMES'LL BE COMING INTO VIEW SOON...

CHRIST, MAYBE THE BLOODY UNDERCART STILL WORKS, AND I WON'T EVEN HAVE TO PANCAKE--

I WANT TO SEE THE LADS AGAIN. TO DRINK AND LAUGH WITH THEM, TO KICK DEATH DOWN WITH YOUTH AND JOKES AND JOY...

TO PUSH THIS BEAUTIFUL, BEAUTIFUL BLOODY AEROPLANE HALF WAY TO HEAVEN, WHERE THE SUN MELTS GOLD ACROSS THE SKY AND THE CLOUDS ARE CASTLES OUT OF FAIRY-LAND...

AND I REMEMBER FRANKIE THOMPSON, STILL CALMLY CHATTING AS HE DIPPED TOWARDS THE HILLS WITH HIS ENGINE SEIZING UP, MUCH TOO LOW TO JUMP FOR IT--

"WHAT BASTARD LUCK, EH, JAMIE? LOOK AFTER MY DOG."

CHRIST ALMIGHTY, I CAN'T DIE...

WHO'LL TAKE CARE OF POOR OLD TIGGER?

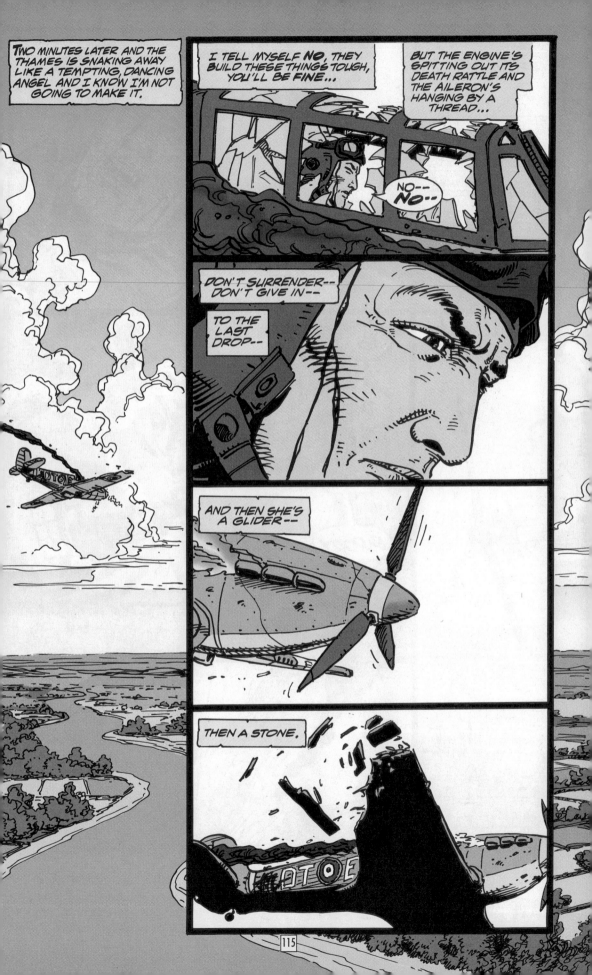

TWO MINUTES LATER AND THE THAMES IS SNAKING AWAY LIKE A TEMPTING, DANCING ANGEL AND I KNOW I'M NOT GOING TO MAKE IT.

I TELL MYSELF **NO**, THEY BUILD THESE THINGS TOUGH, YOU'LL BE FINE...

BUT THE ENGINE'S SPITTING OUT ITS DEATH RATTLE AND THE AILERON'S HANGING BY A THREAD...

NO-- NO--

DON'T SURRENDER-- DON'T GIVE IN--

TO THE LAST DROP--

AND THEN SHE'S A GLIDER--

THEN A STONE.

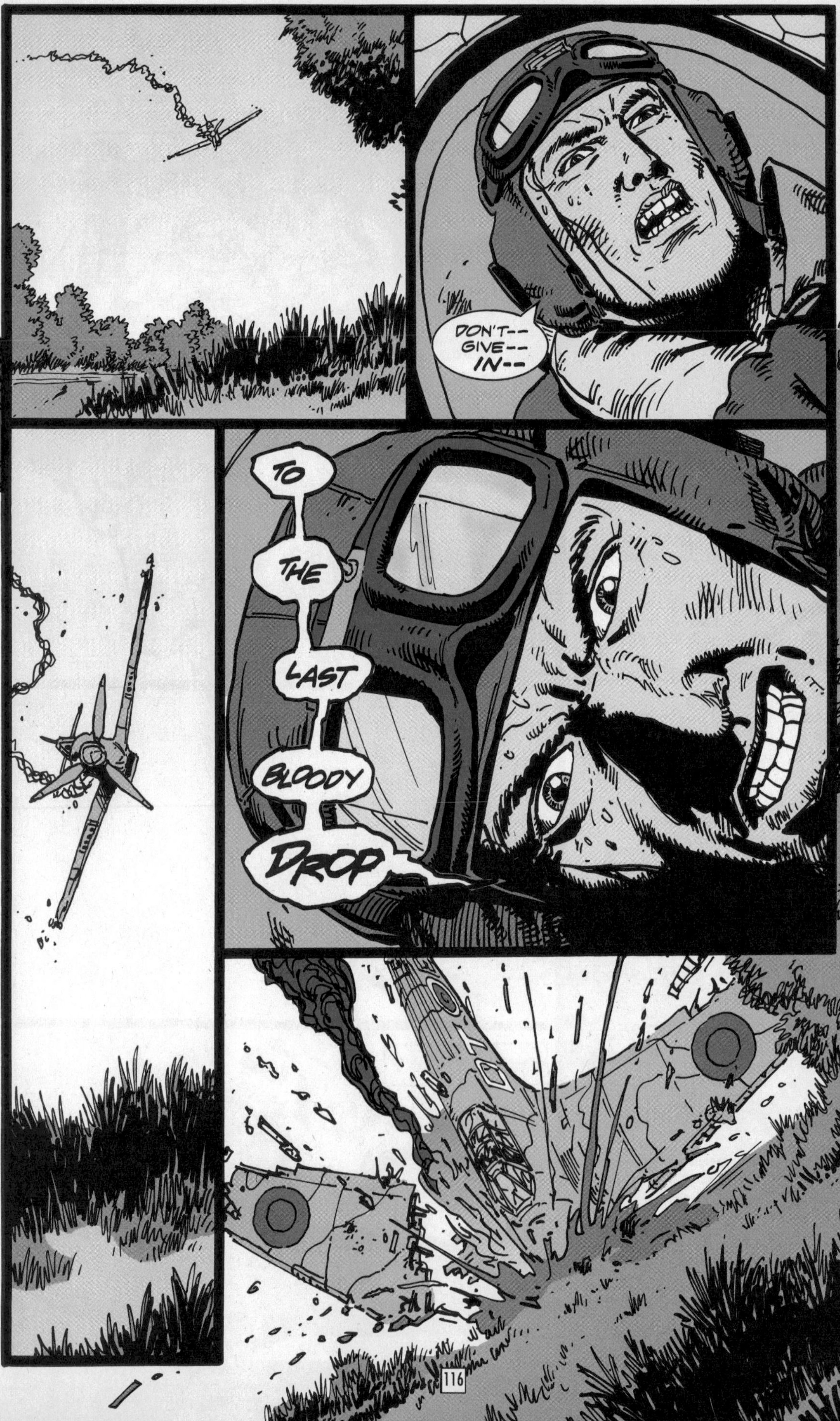
DON'T-- GIVE-- IN--
TO
THE
LAST
BLOODY
DROP

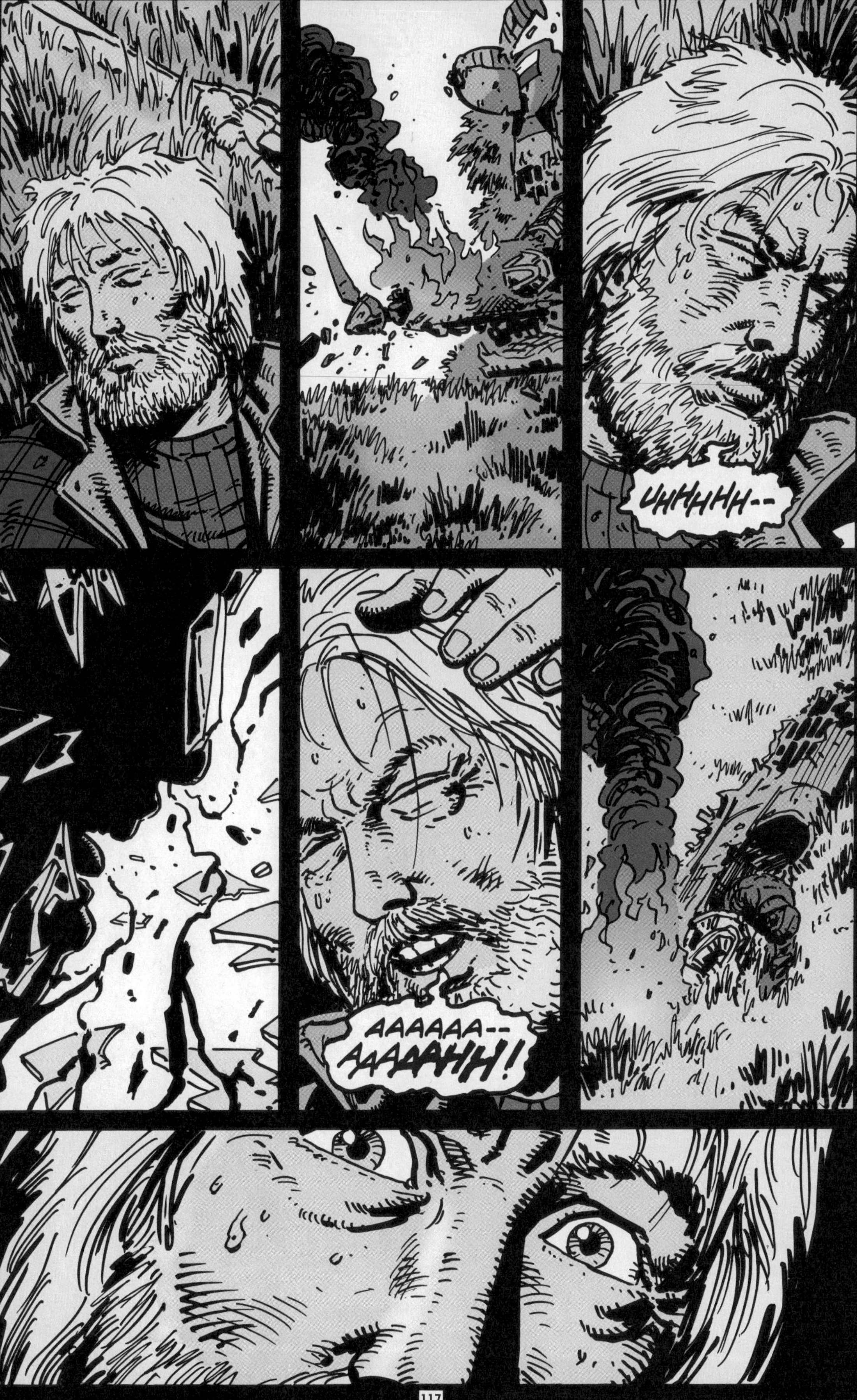
UHHHHH--
AAAAAA--
AAAAAHH!

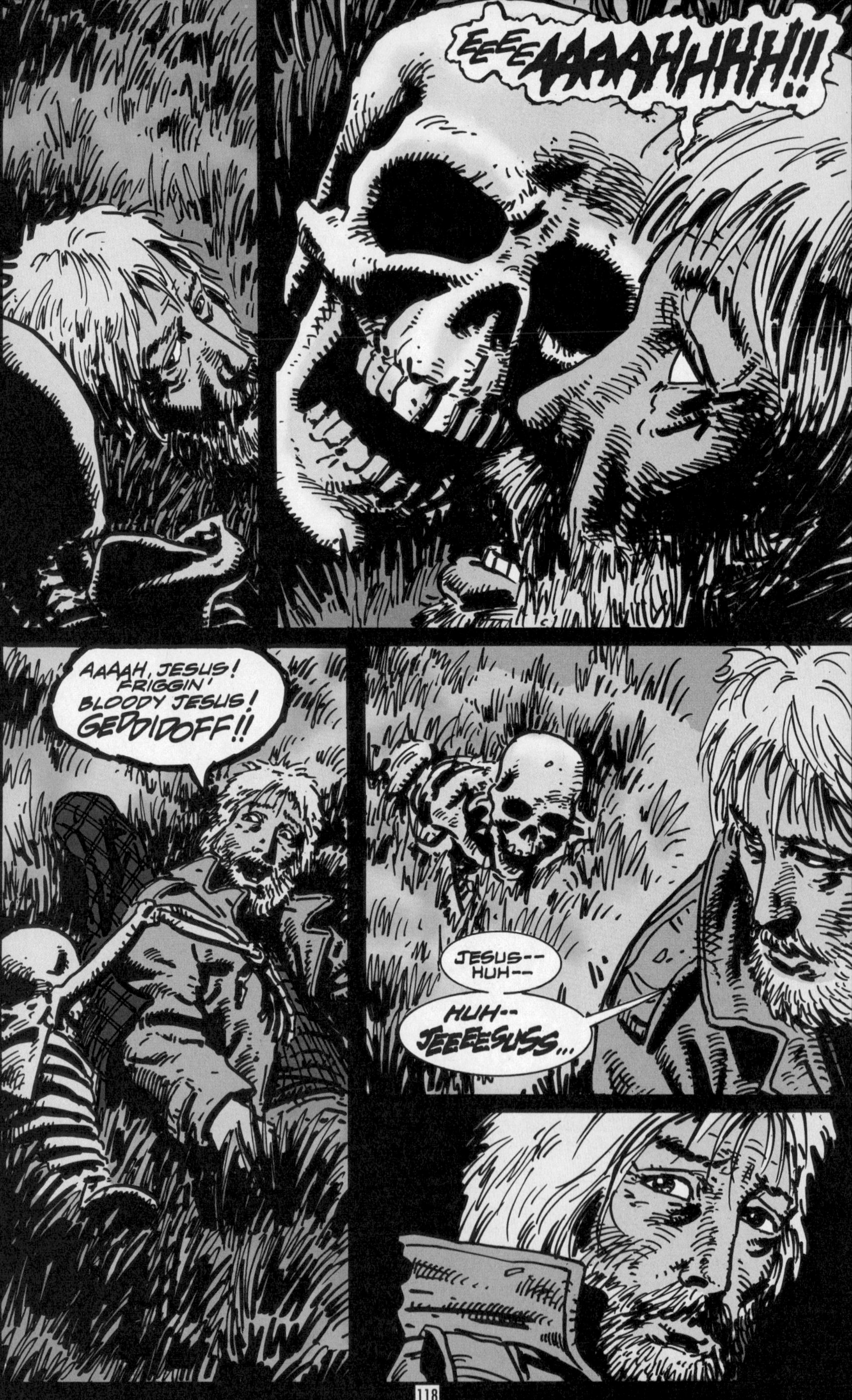
EEEEAAAAHHHH!!
AAAAH, JESUS! FRIGGIN' BLOODY JESUS! GEDDIDOFF!!
JESUS-- HUH--
HUH-- JEEEESUSS...

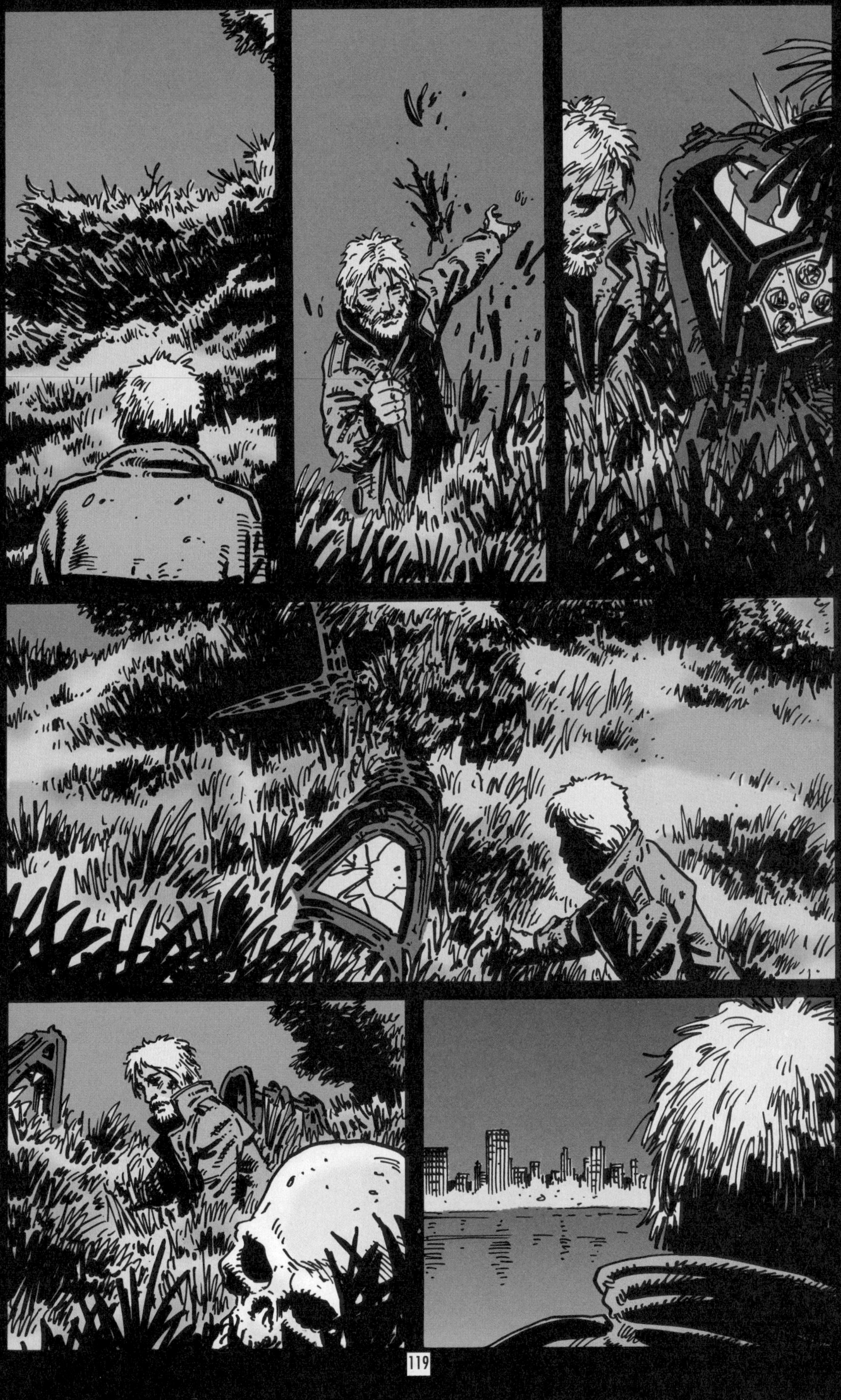

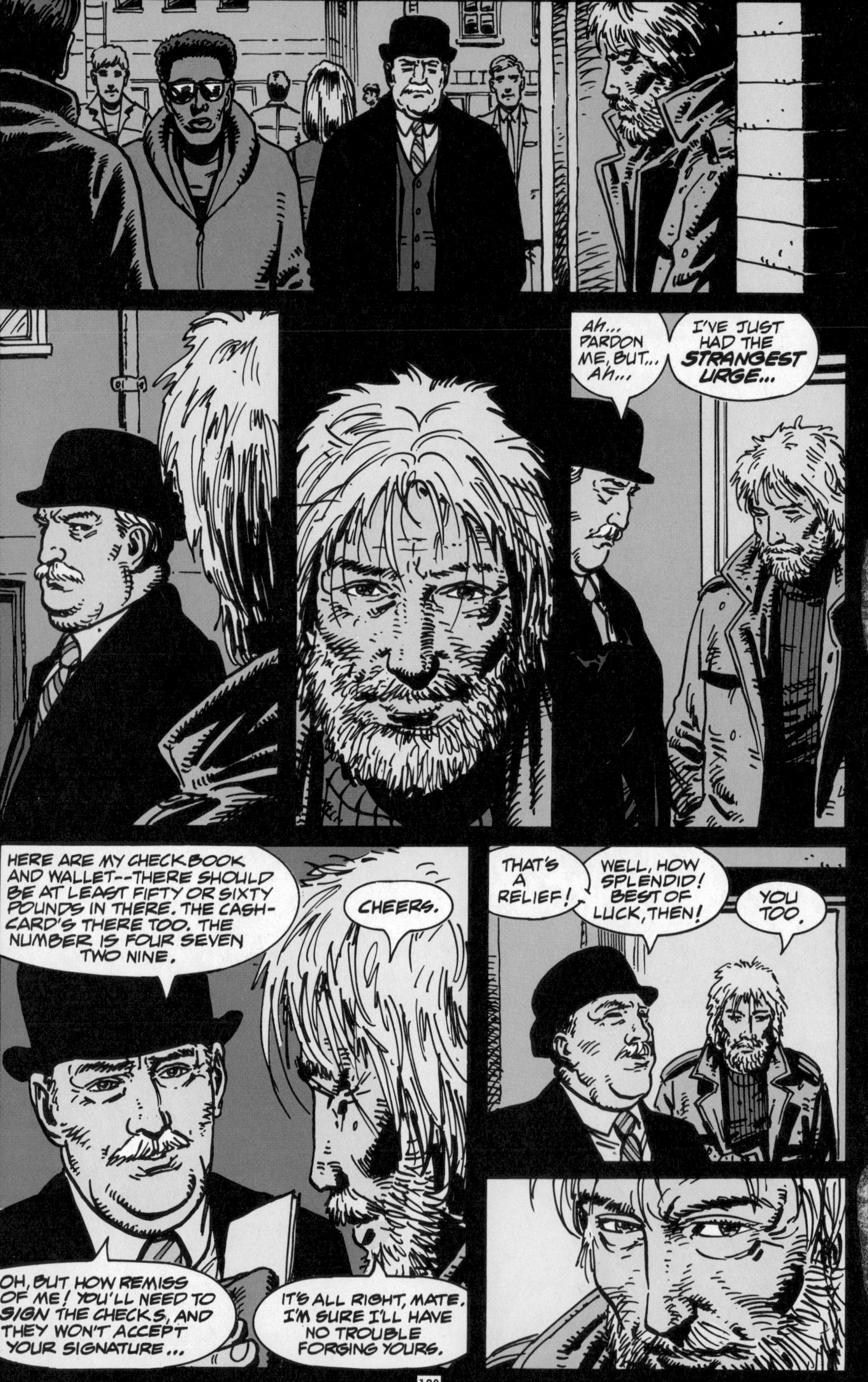

AH... PARDON ME, BUT... AH...
I'VE JUST HAD THE STRANGEST URGE...
HERE ARE MY CHECKBOOK AND WALLET--THERE SHOULD BE AT LEAST FIFTY OR SIXTY POUNDS IN THERE. THE CASH-CARD'S THERE TOO. THE NUMBER IS FOUR SEVEN TWO NINE.
CHEERS.
OH, BUT HOW REMISS OF ME! YOU'LL NEED TO SIGN THE CHECKS, AND THEY WON'T ACCEPT YOUR SIGNATURE...
IT'S ALL RIGHT, MATE. I'M SURE I'LL HAVE NO TROUBLE FORGING YOURS.
THAT'S A RELIEF!
WELL, HOW SPLENDID! BEST OF LUCK, THEN!
YOU TOO.

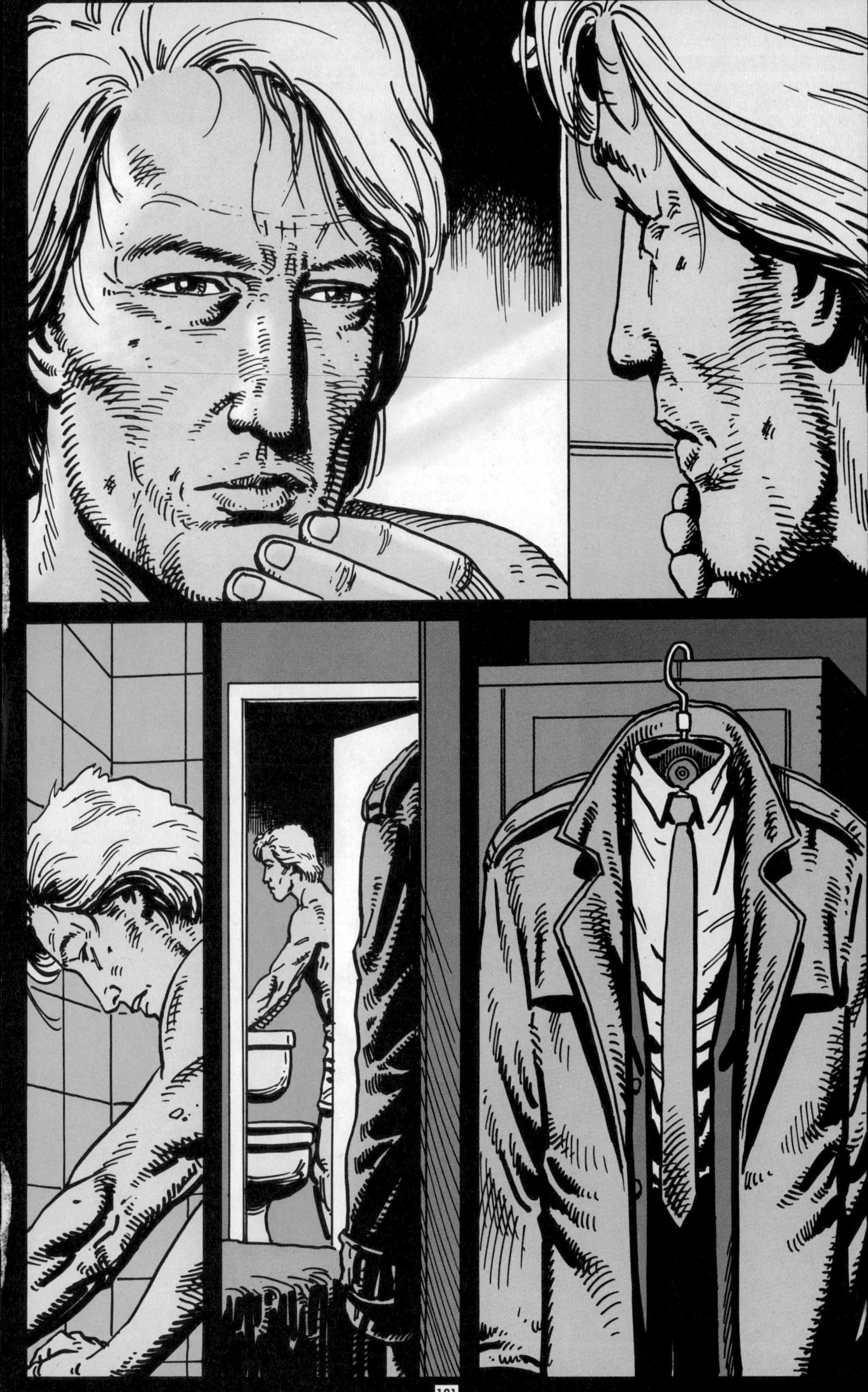

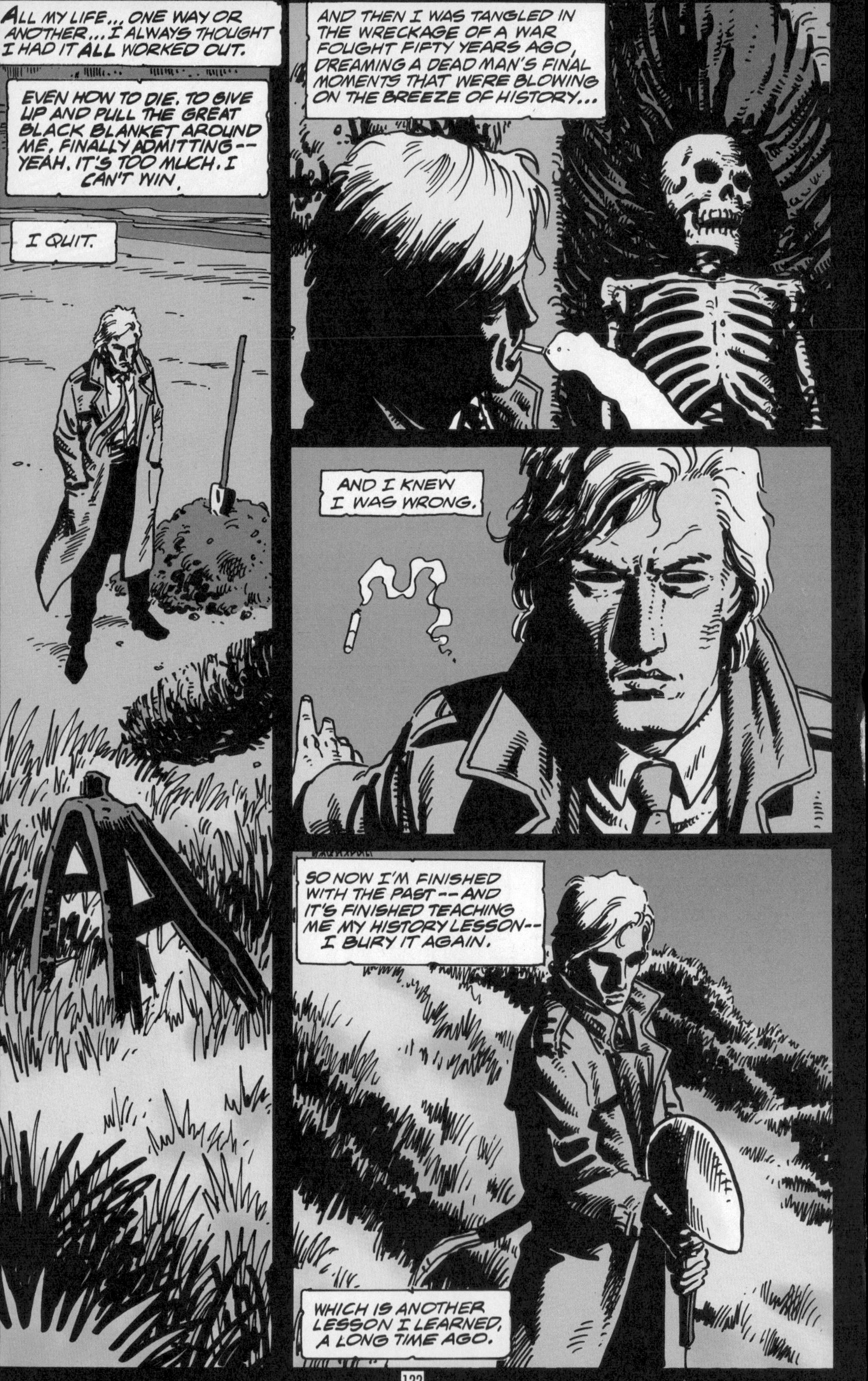
ALL MY LIFE... ONE WAY OR ANOTHER... I ALWAYS THOUGHT I HAD IT ALL WORKED OUT.
EVEN HOW TO DIE. TO GIVE UP AND PULL THE GREAT BLACK BLANKET AROUND ME. FINALLY ADMITTING -- YEAH. IT'S TOO MUCH. I CAN'T WIN.
I QUIT.
AND THEN I WAS TANGLED IN THE WRECKAGE OF A WAR FOUGHT FIFTY YEARS AGO, DREAMING A DEAD MAN'S FINAL MOMENTS THAT WERE BLOWING ON THE BREEZE OF HISTORY...
AND I KNEW I WAS WRONG.
SO NOW I'M FINISHED WITH THE PAST -- AND IT'S FINISHED TEACHING ME MY HISTORY LESSON -- I BURY IT AGAIN.
WHICH IS ANOTHER LESSON I LEARNED, A LONG TIME AGO.

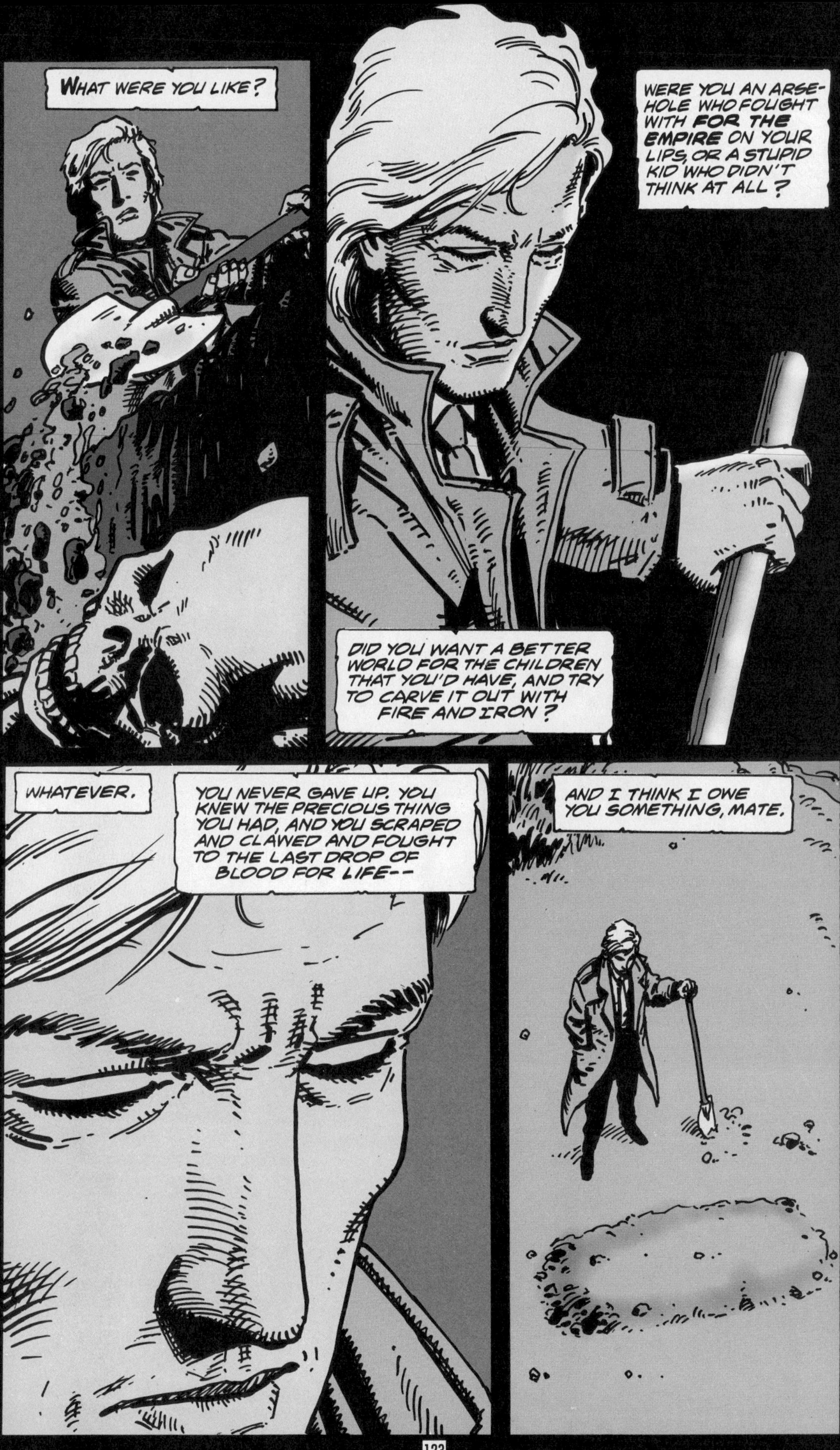
WHAT WERE YOU LIKE?
WERE YOU AN ARSEHOLE WHO FOUGHT WITH FOR THE EMPIRE ON YOUR LIPS, OR A STUPID KID WHO DIDN'T THINK AT ALL?
DID YOU WANT A BETTER WORLD FOR THE CHILDREN THAT YOU'D HAVE, AND TRY TO CARVE IT OUT WITH FIRE AND IRON?
WHATEVER.
YOU NEVER GAVE UP. YOU KNEW THE PRECIOUS THING YOU HAD, AND YOU SCRAPED AND CLAWED AND FOUGHT TO THE LAST DROP OF BLOOD FOR LIFE--
AND I THINK I OWE YOU SOMETHING, MATE.

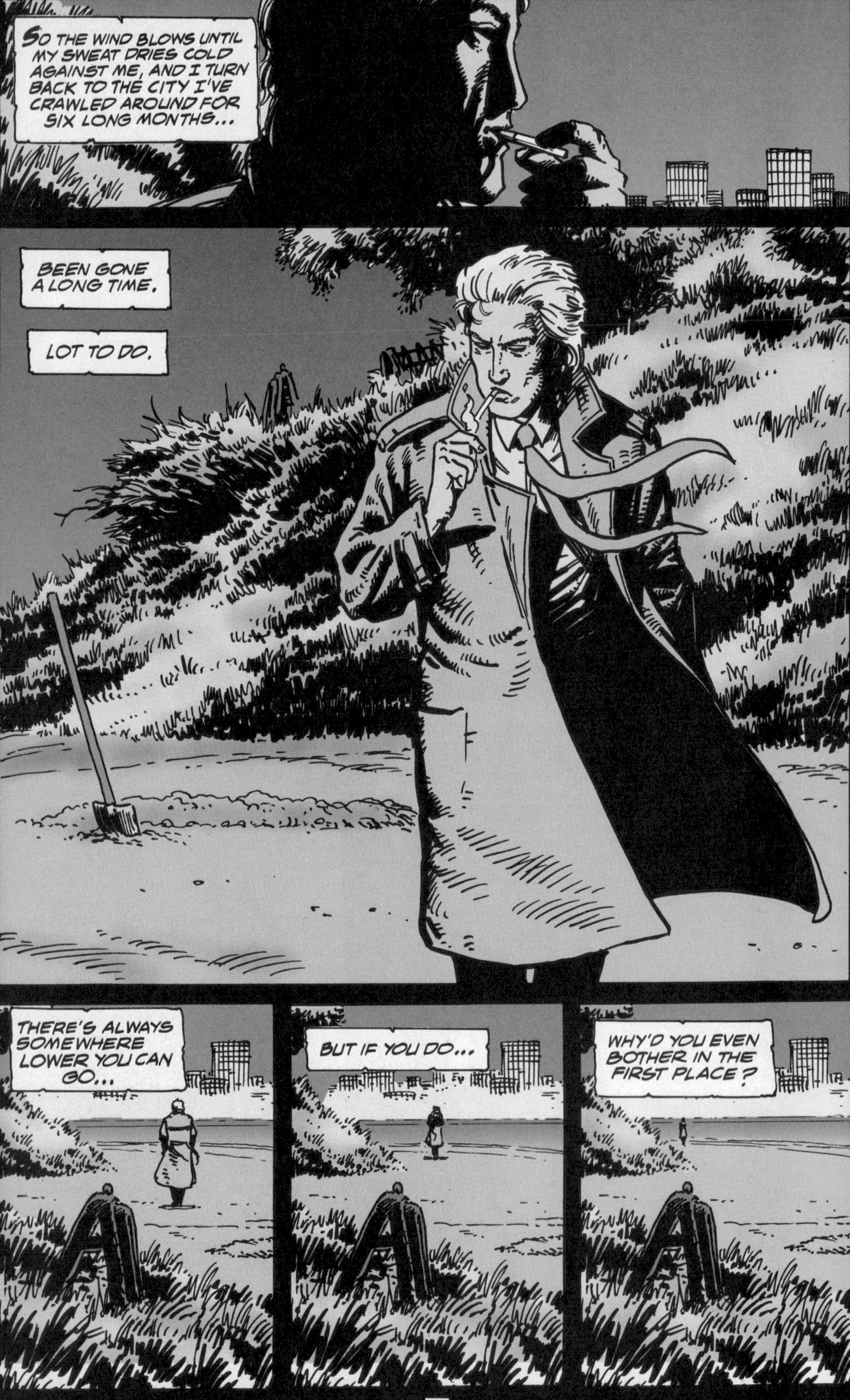

SO THE WIND BLOWS UNTIL MY SWEAT DRIES COLD AGAINST ME, AND I TURN BACK TO THE CITY I'VE CRAWLED AROUND FOR SIX LONG MONTHS...
BEEN GONE A LONG TIME.
LOT TO DO.
THERE'S ALWAYS SOMEWHERE LOWER YOU CAN GO...
BUT IF YOU DO...
WHY'D YOU EVEN BOTHER IN THE FIRST PLACE?

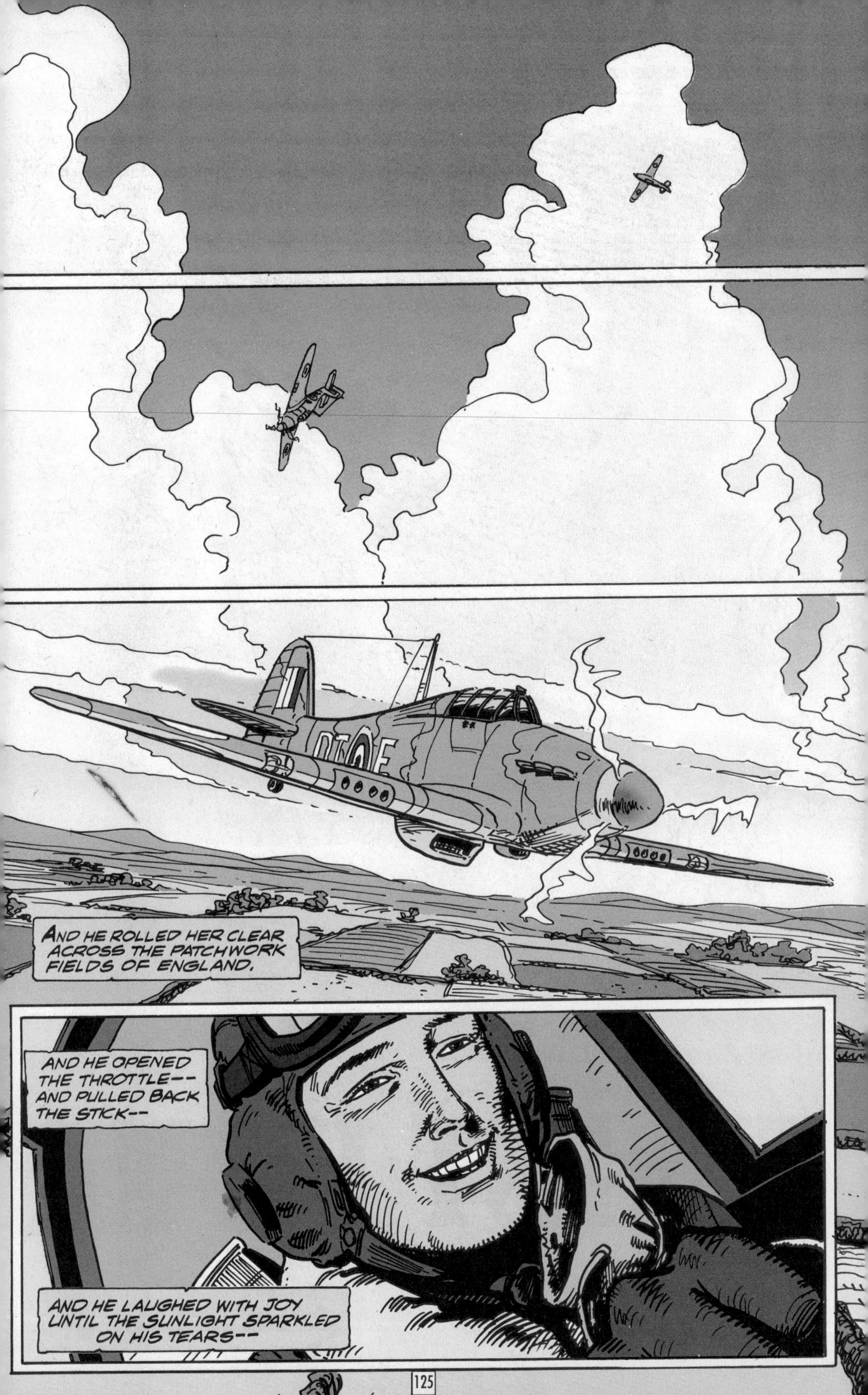
AND HE ROLLED HER CLEAR ACROSS THE PATCHWORK FIELDS OF ENGLAND.
AND HE OPENED THE THROTTLE-- AND PULLED BACK THE STICK--
AND HE LAUGHED WITH JOY UNTIL THE SUNLIGHT SPARKLED ON HIS TEARS--

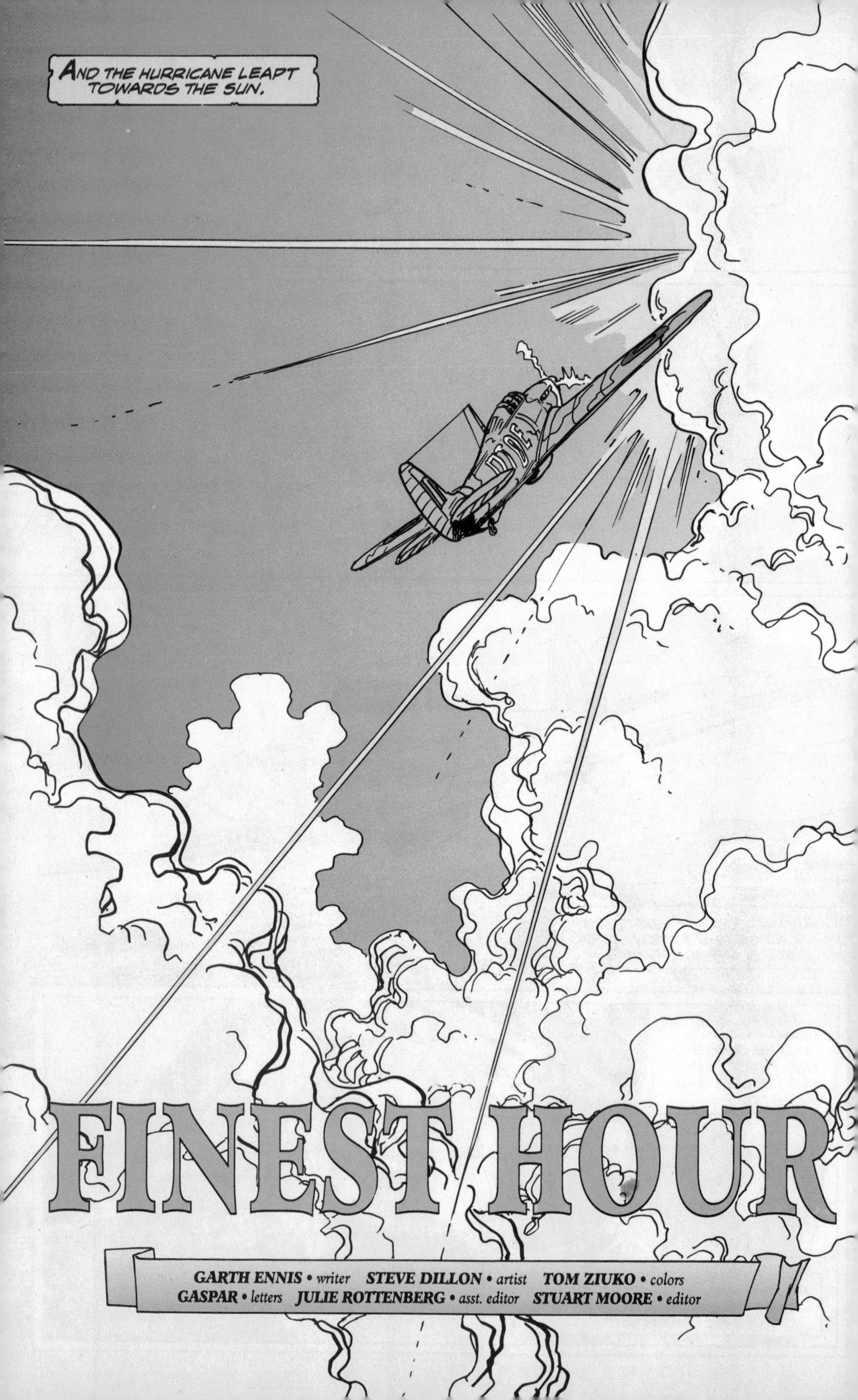
AND THE HURRICANE LEAPT TOWARDS THE SUN.
FINEST HOUR
GARTH ENNIS • writer STEVE DILLON • artist TOM ZIUKO • colors
GASPAR • letters JULIE ROTTENBERG • asst. editor STUART MOORE • editor

CONFESSIONAL

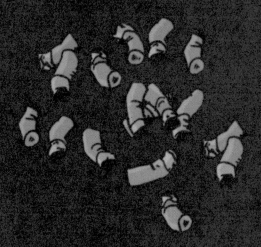

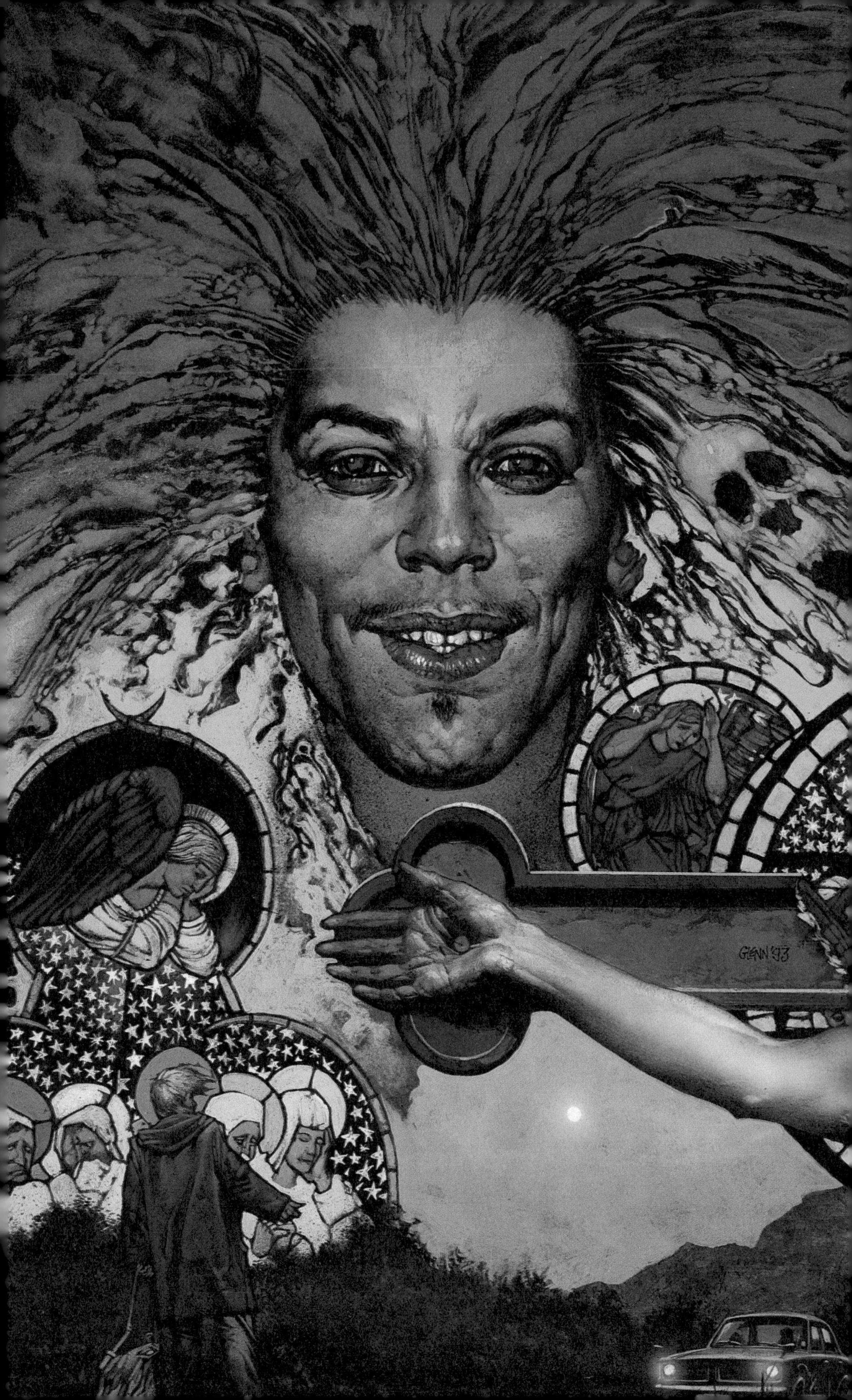
GLENN '93

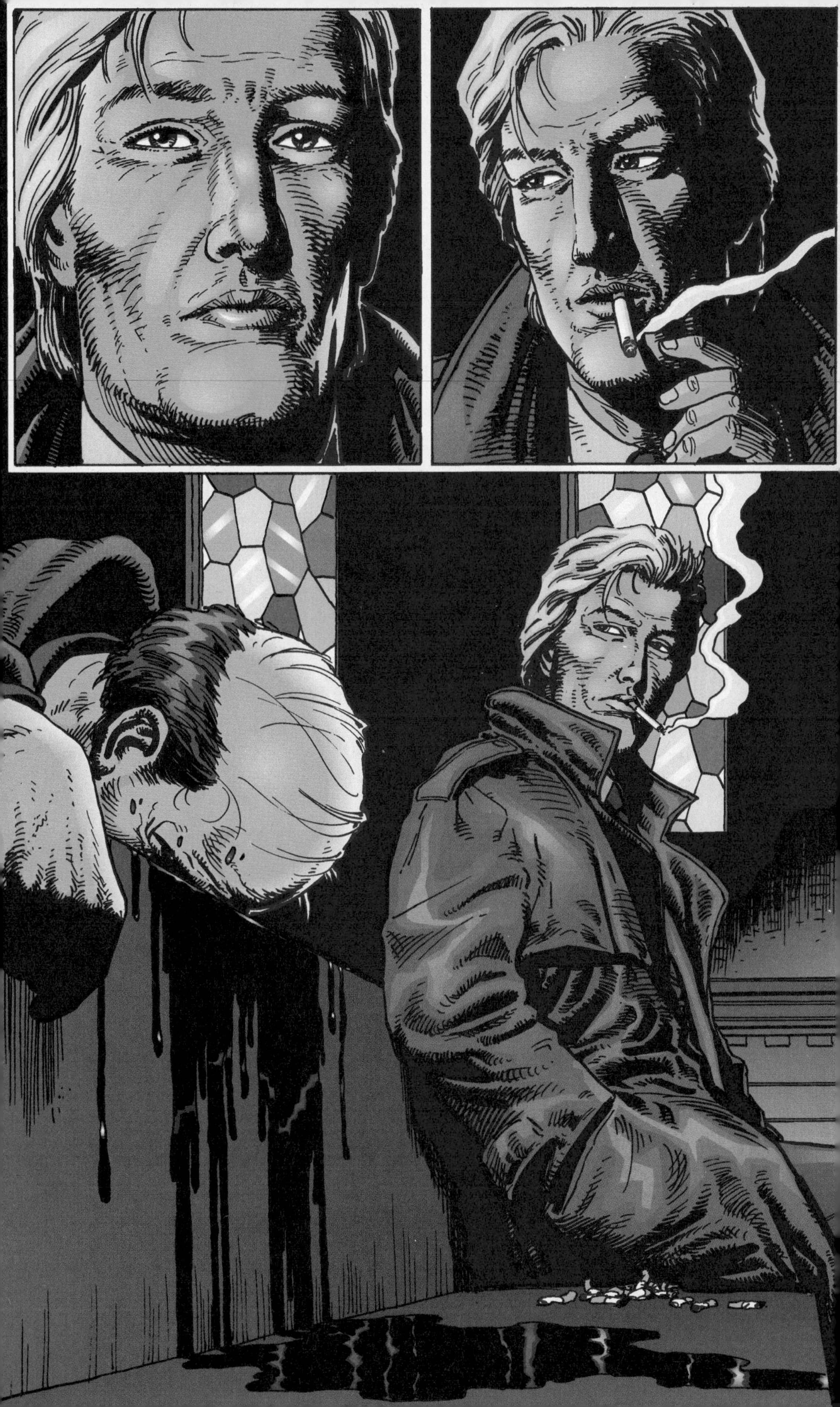

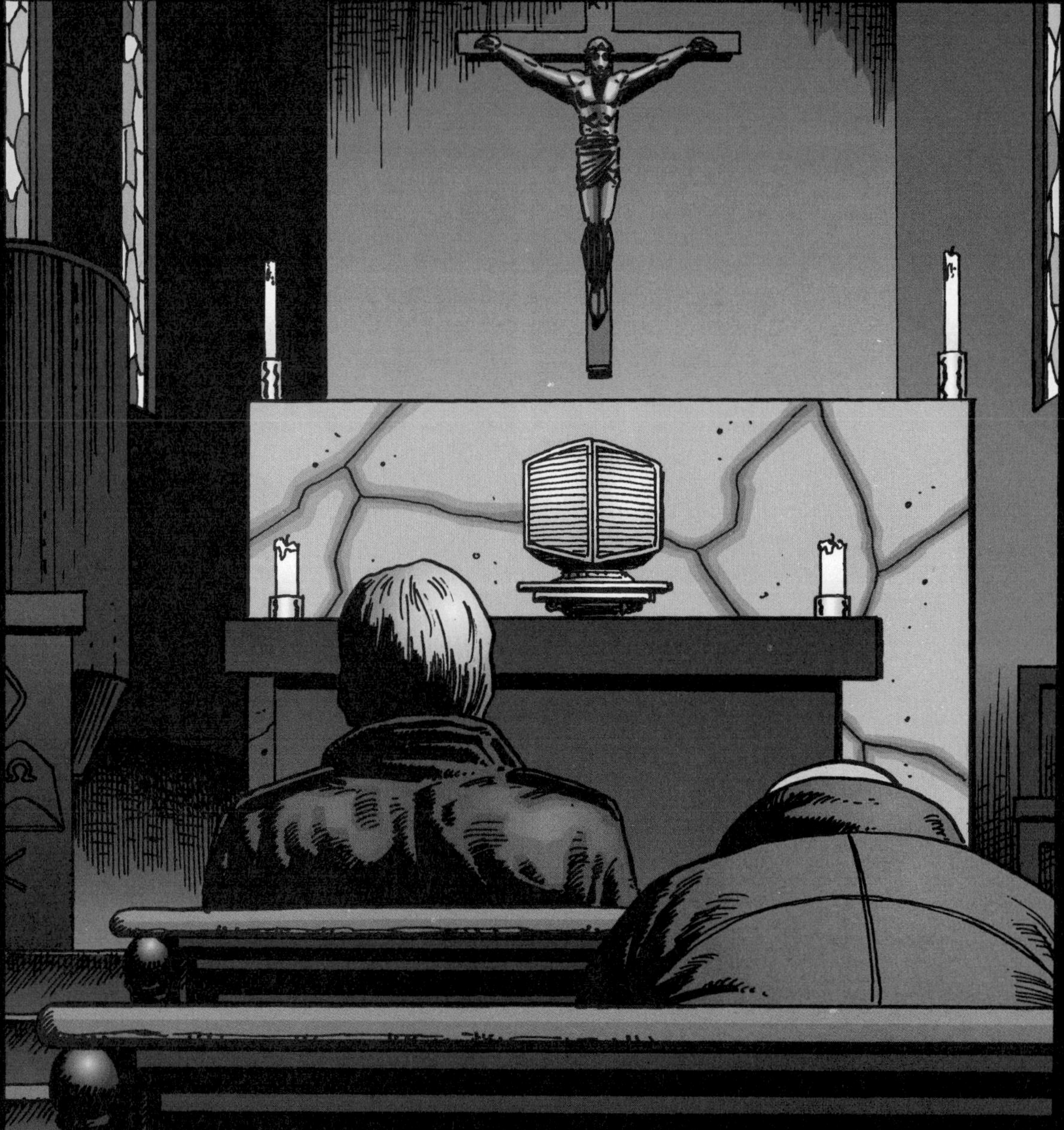

CONFESSIONAL

GARTH ENNIS • *writer* **STEVE DILLON** • *artist* **TOM ZIUKO** • *colors*
GASPAR • *letters* **JULIE ROTTENBERG** • *assistant editor* **STUART MOORE** • *editor*
For Mal Coney, with thanks

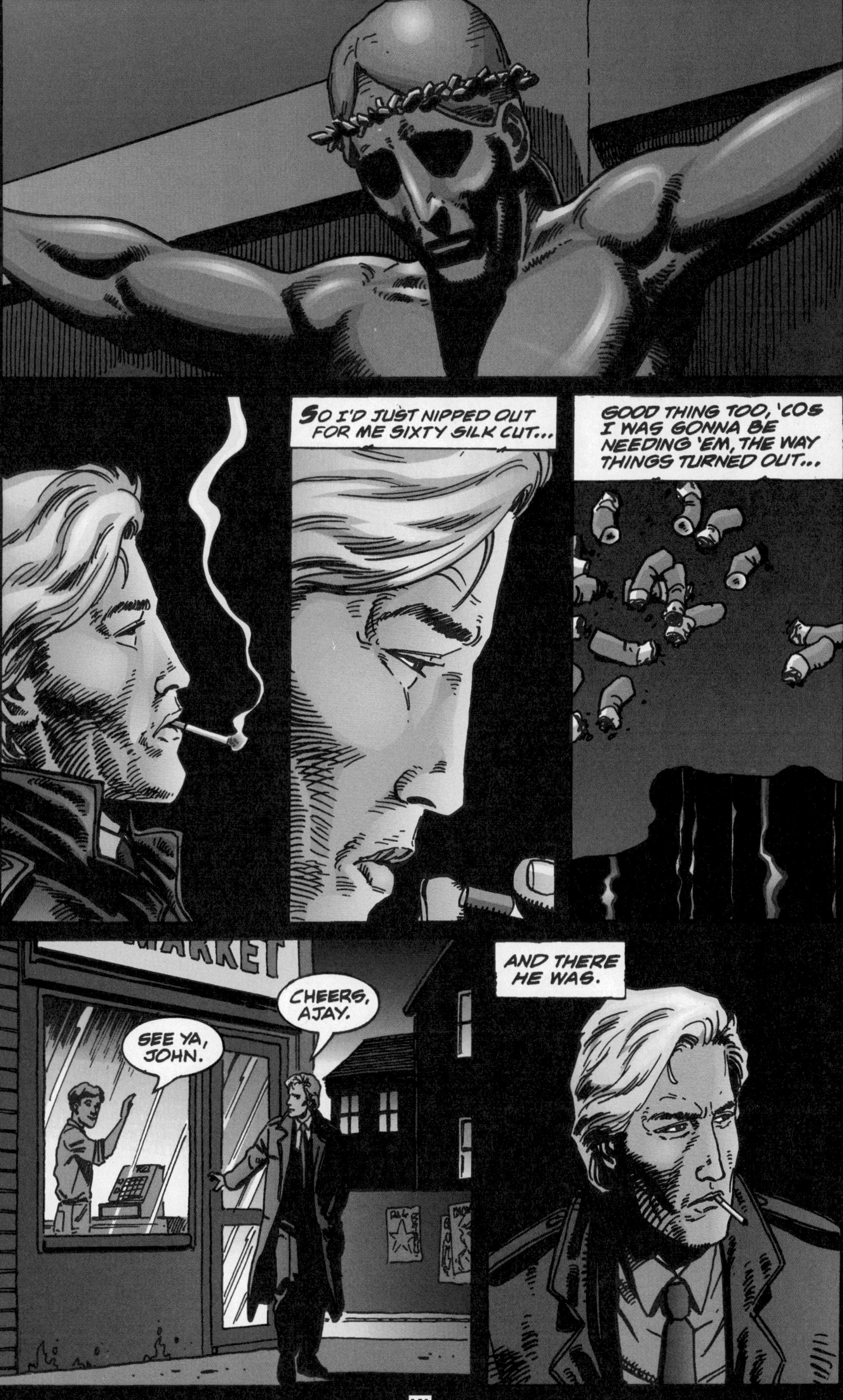

SO I'D JUST NIPPED OUT FOR ME SIXTY SILK CUT...
GOOD THING TOO, 'COS I WAS GONNA BE NEEDING 'EM, THE WAY THINGS TURNED OUT...
MARKET
SEE YA, JOHN.
CHEERS, AJAY.
AND THERE HE WAS.

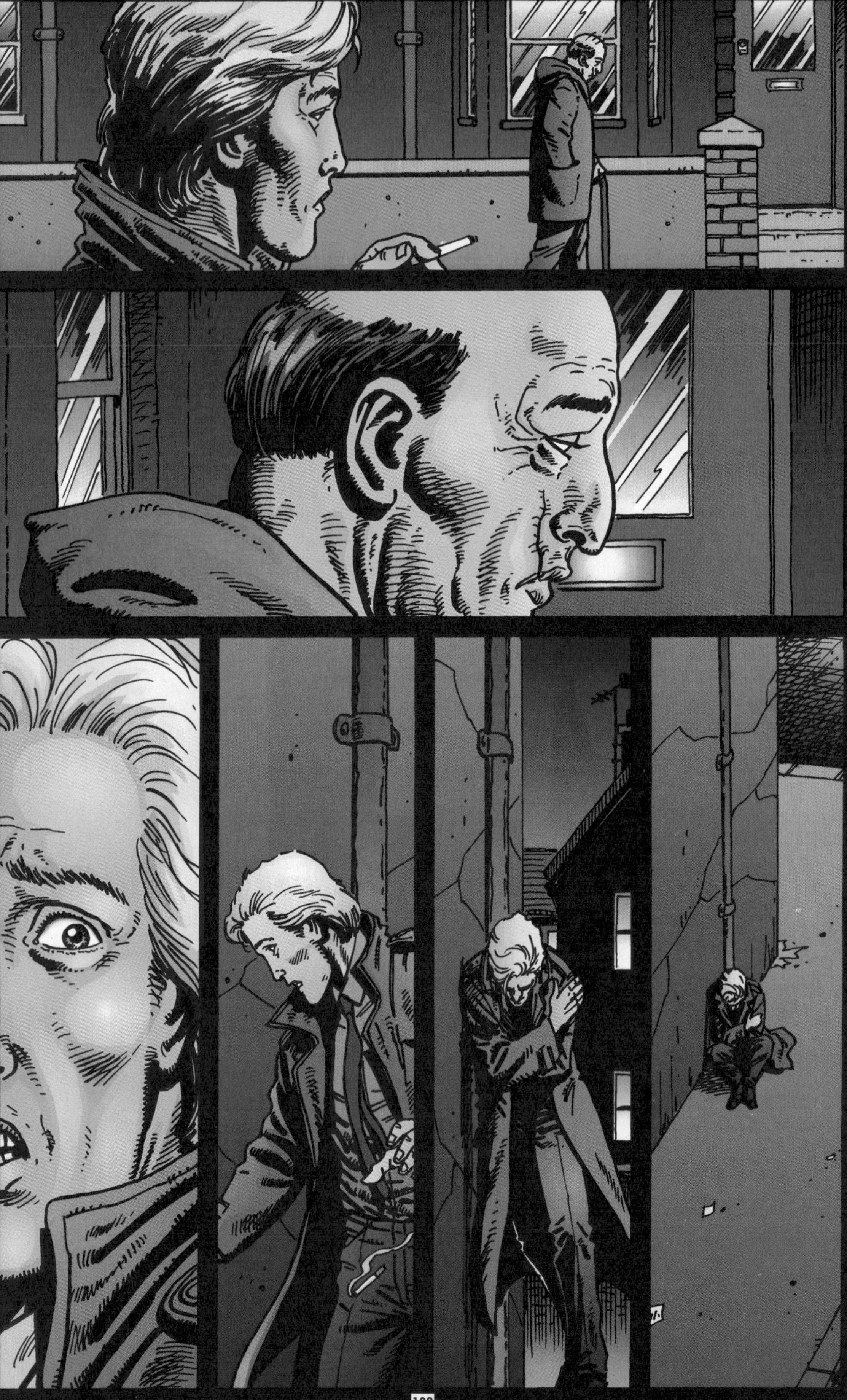

BASTARD--

I'LL **GET** YOU, YOU BASTARD--

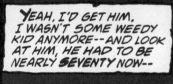

YEAH, I'D GET HIM. I WASN'T SOME WEEDY KID ANYMORE--AND LOOK AT HIM, HE HAD TO BE NEARLY **SEVENTY** NOW--

OH YEAH.

THIS TIME IT WAS GONNA BE DIFFERENT.

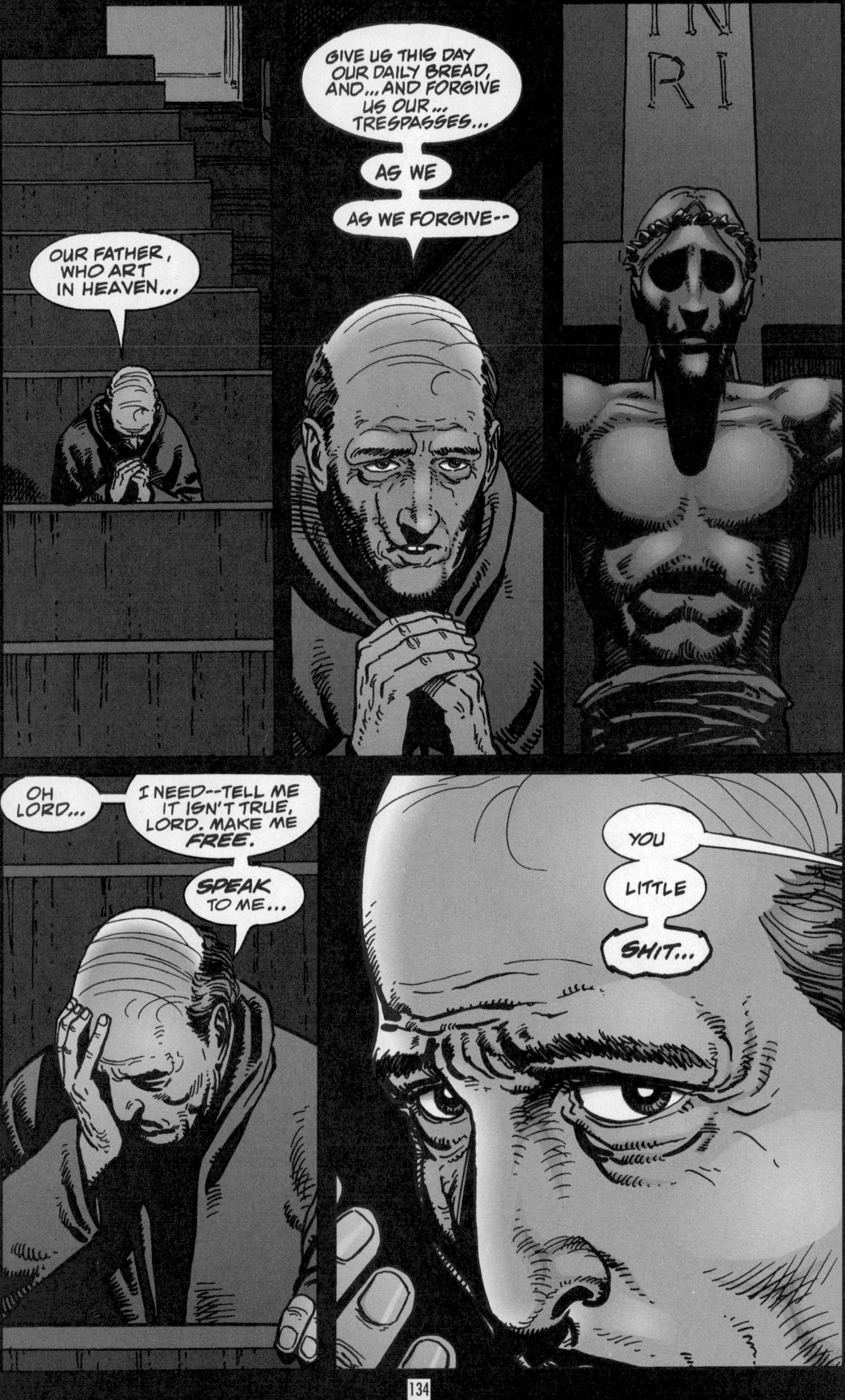
IN
RI
OUR FATHER, WHO ART IN HEAVEN...
GIVE US THIS DAY OUR DAILY BREAD, AND... AND FORGIVE US OUR... TRESPASSES...
AS WE
AS WE FORGIVE--
OH LORD...
I NEED--TELL ME IT ISN'T TRUE, LORD. MAKE ME FREE.
SPEAK TO ME...
YOU
LITTLE
SHIT...

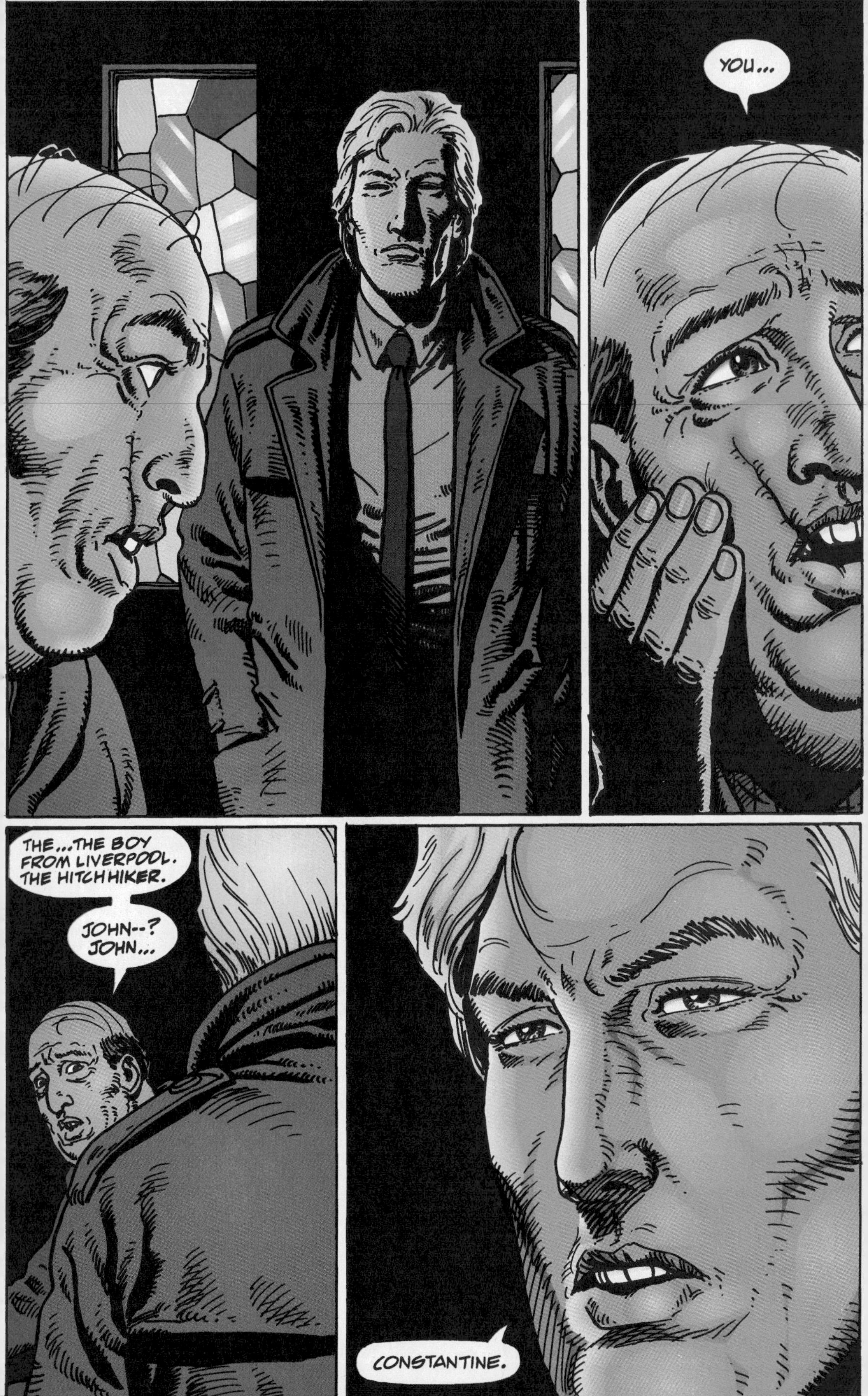
YOU...
THE...THE BOY FROM LIVERPOOL. THE HITCHHIKER.
JOHN--? JOHN...
CONSTANTINE.

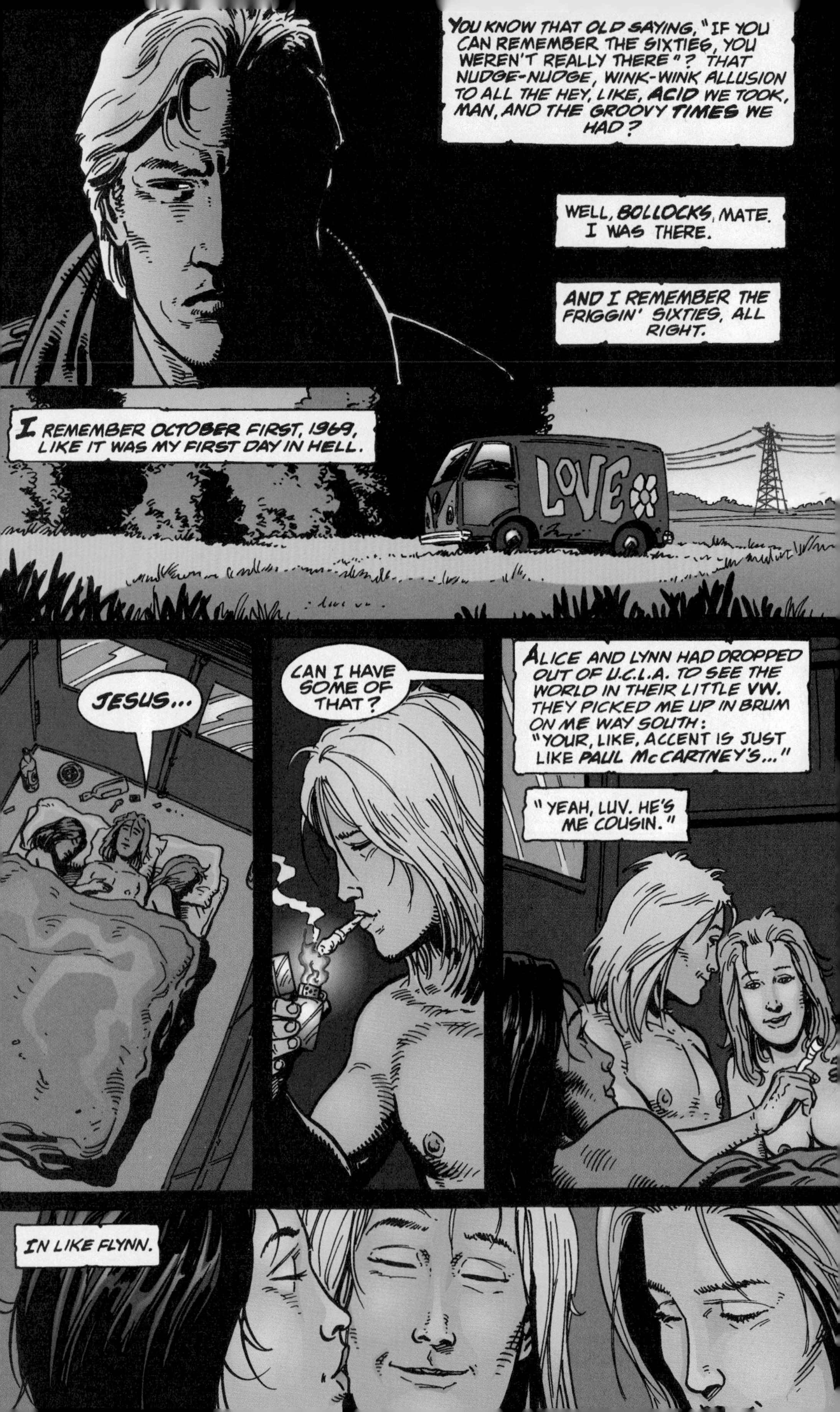

YOU KNOW THAT OLD SAYING, "IF YOU CAN REMEMBER THE SIXTIES, YOU WEREN'T REALLY THERE"? THAT NUDGE-NUDGE, WINK-WINK ALLUSION TO ALL THE HEY, LIKE, ACID WE TOOK, MAN, AND THE GROOVY TIMES WE HAD?
WELL, BOLLOCKS, MATE. I WAS THERE.
AND I REMEMBER THE FRIGGIN' SIXTIES, ALL RIGHT.
I REMEMBER OCTOBER FIRST, 1969, LIKE IT WAS MY FIRST DAY IN HELL.
LOVE
JESUS...
CAN I HAVE SOME OF THAT?
ALICE AND LYNN HAD DROPPED OUT OF U.C.L.A. TO SEE THE WORLD IN THEIR LITTLE VW. THEY PICKED ME UP IN BRUM ON ME WAY SOUTH: "YOUR, LIKE, ACCENT IS JUST LIKE PAUL McCARTNEY'S..."
"YEAH, LUV. HE'S ME COUSIN."
IN LIKE FLYNN.

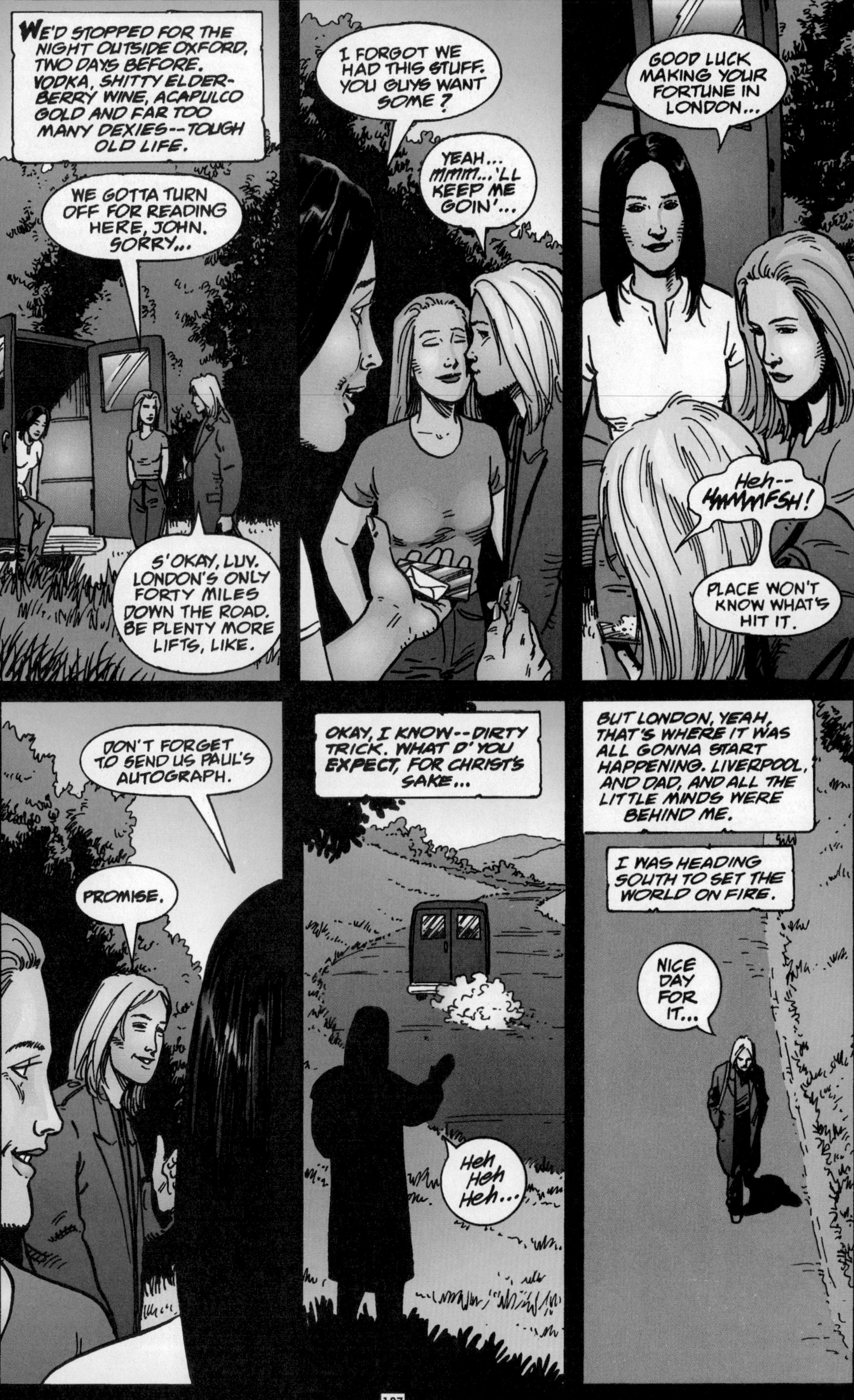
WE'D STOPPED FOR THE NIGHT OUTSIDE OXFORD, TWO DAYS BEFORE. VODKA, SHITTY ELDER-BERRY WINE, ACAPULCO GOLD AND FAR TOO MANY DEXIES--TOUGH OLD LIFE.
WE GOTTA TURN OFF FOR READING HERE, JOHN. SORRY...
S'OKAY, LUV. LONDON'S ONLY FORTY MILES DOWN THE ROAD. BE PLENTY MORE LIFTS, LIKE.
I FORGOT WE HAD THIS STUFF. YOU GUYS WANT SOME?
YEAH... MMMM...'LL KEEP ME GOIN'...
GOOD LUCK MAKING YOUR FORTUNE IN LONDON...
Heh-- HMMMFSH!
PLACE WON'T KNOW WHAT'S HIT IT.
DON'T FORGET TO SEND US PAUL'S AUTOGRAPH.
PROMISE.
OKAY, I KNOW--DIRTY TRICK. WHAT D' YOU EXPECT, FOR CHRIST'S SAKE...
Heh Heh Heh...
BUT LONDON, YEAH, THAT'S WHERE IT WAS ALL GONNA START HAPPENING. LIVERPOOL, AND DAD, AND ALL THE LITTLE MINDS WERE BEHIND ME.
I WAS HEADING SOUTH TO SET THE WORLD ON FIRE.
NICE DAY FOR IT...

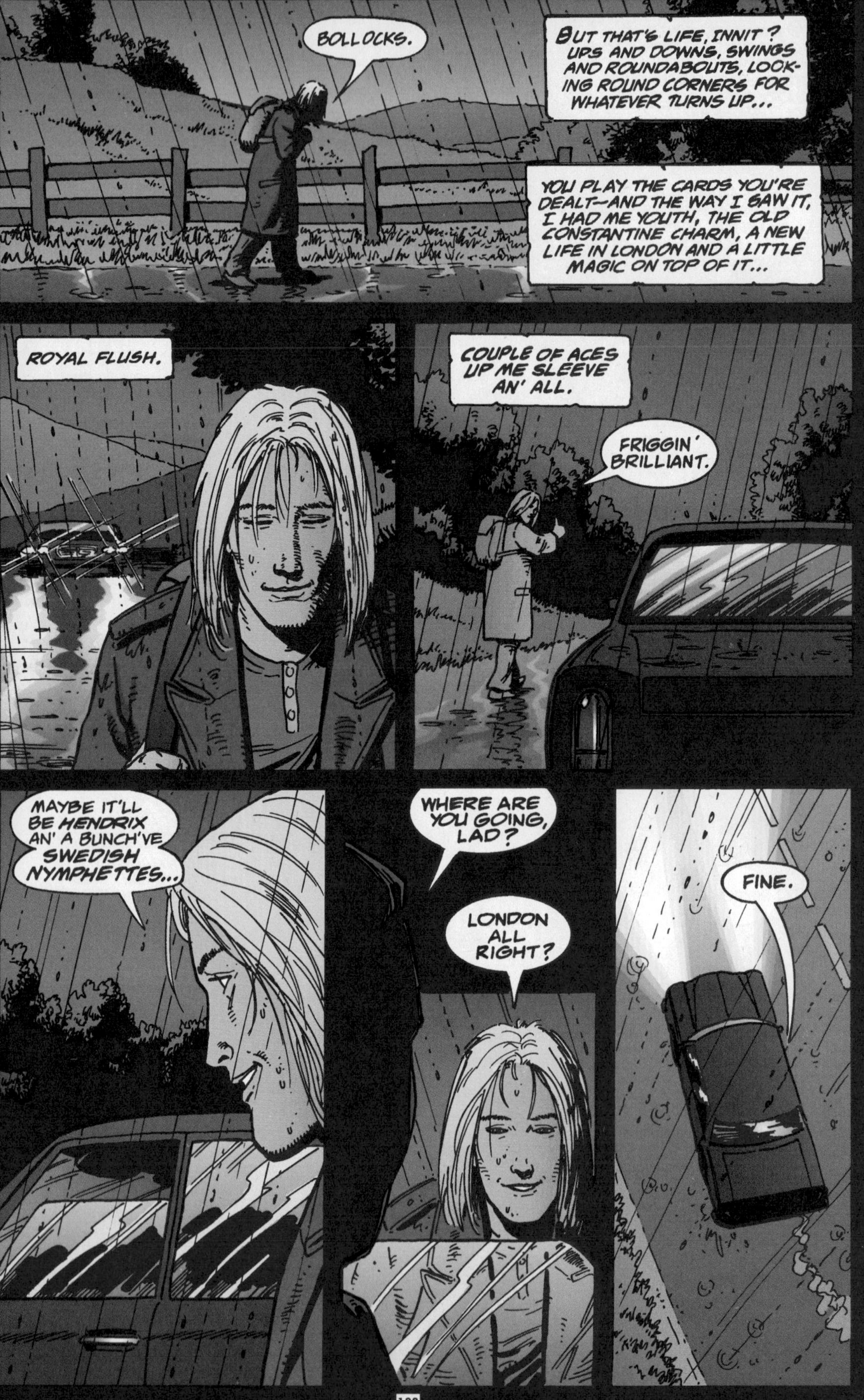
BOLLOCKS.
BUT THAT'S LIFE, INNIT? UPS AND DOWNS, SWINGS AND ROUNDABOUTS, LOOKING ROUND CORNERS FOR WHATEVER TURNS UP...
YOU PLAY THE CARDS YOU'RE DEALT—AND THE WAY I SAW IT, I HAD ME YOUTH, THE OLD CONSTANTINE CHARM, A NEW LIFE IN LONDON AND A LITTLE MAGIC ON TOP OF IT...
ROYAL FLUSH.
COUPLE OF ACES UP ME SLEEVE AN' ALL.
FRIGGIN' BRILLIANT.
MAYBE IT'LL BE HENDRIX AN' A BUNCH'VE SWEDISH NYMPHETTES...
WHERE ARE YOU GOING, LAD?
LONDON ALL RIGHT?
FINE.

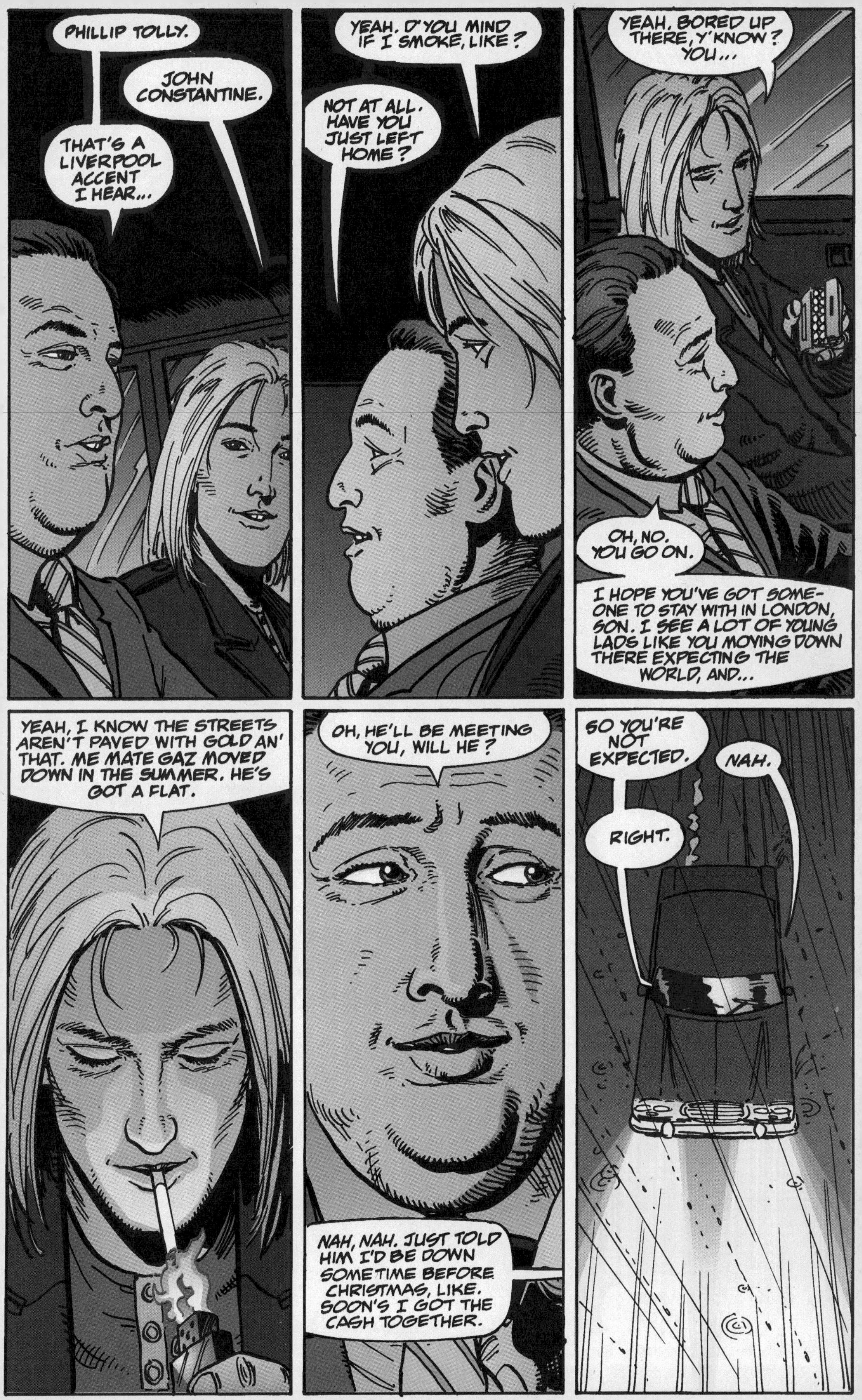
PHILLIP TOLLY.
JOHN CONSTANTINE.
THAT'S A LIVERPOOL ACCENT I HEAR...
YEAH. D'YOU MIND IF I SMOKE, LIKE?
NOT AT ALL. HAVE YOU JUST LEFT HOME?
YEAH, BORED UP THERE, Y'KNOW? YOU...
OH, NO. YOU GO ON.
I HOPE YOU'VE GOT SOME-ONE TO STAY WITH IN LONDON, SON. I SEE A LOT OF YOUNG LADS LIKE YOU MOVING DOWN THERE EXPECTING THE WORLD, AND...
YEAH, I KNOW THE STREETS AREN'T PAVED WITH GOLD AN' THAT. ME MATE GAZ MOVED DOWN IN THE SUMMER. HE'S GOT A FLAT.
OH, HE'LL BE MEETING YOU, WILL HE?
NAH, NAH. JUST TOLD HIM I'D BE DOWN SOMETIME BEFORE CHRISTMAS, LIKE. SOON'S I GOT THE CASH TOGETHER.
SO YOU'RE NOT EXPECTED.
NAH.
RIGHT.

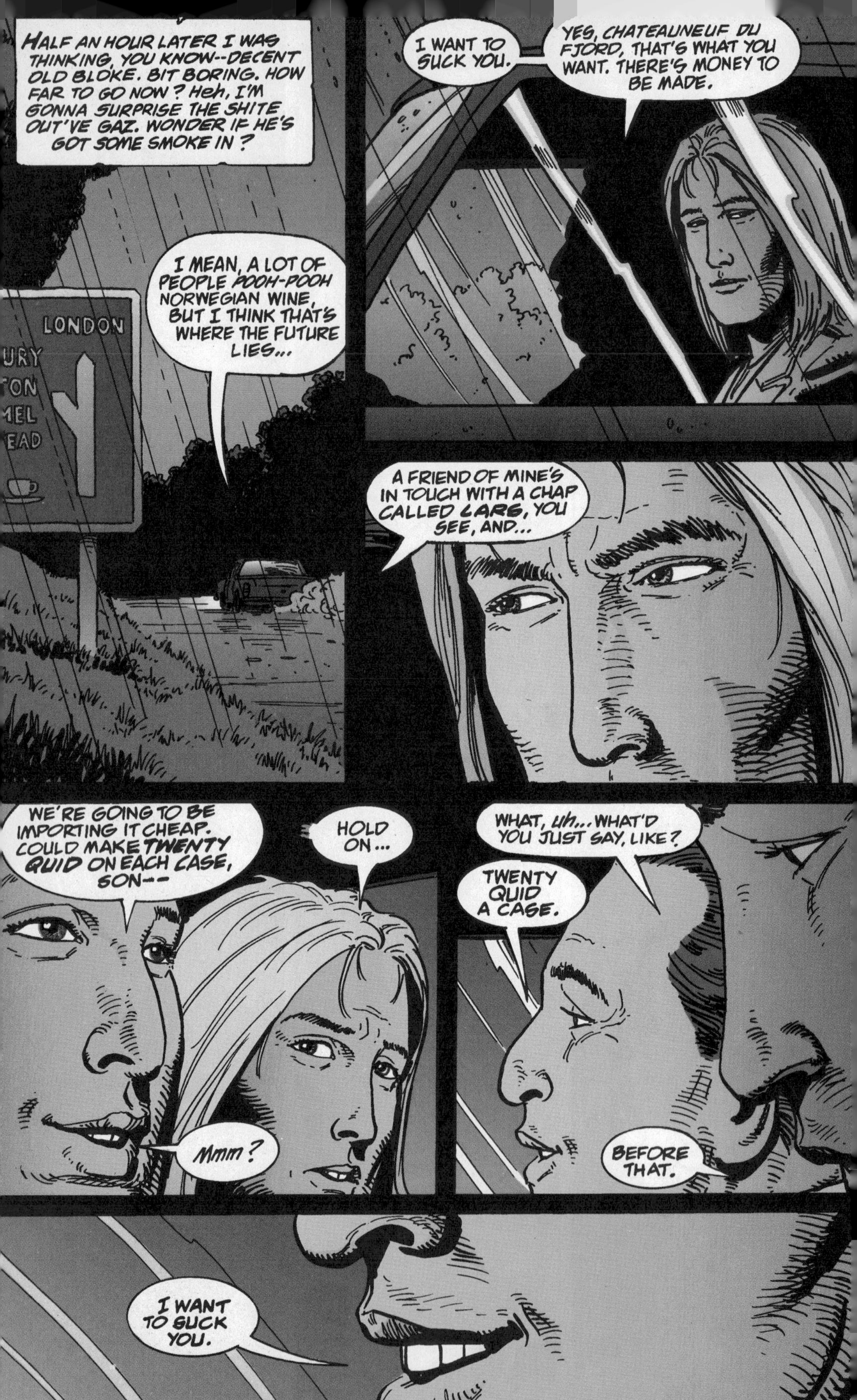

HALF AN HOUR LATER I WAS THINKING, YOU KNOW--DECENT OLD BLOKE. BIT BORING. HOW FAR TO GO NOW? Heh, I'M GONNA SURPRISE THE SHITE OUT'VE GAZ. WONDER IF HE'S GOT SOME SMOKE IN?
I MEAN, A LOT OF PEOPLE POOH-POOH NORWEGIAN WINE, BUT I THINK THAT'S WHERE THE FUTURE LIES...
LONDON
I WANT TO SUCK YOU.
YES, CHATEAUNEUF DU FJORD, THAT'S WHAT YOU WANT. THERE'S MONEY TO BE MADE.
A FRIEND OF MINE'S IN TOUCH WITH A CHAP CALLED LARS, YOU SEE, AND...
WE'RE GOING TO BE IMPORTING IT CHEAP. COULD MAKE TWENTY QUID ON EACH CASE, SON--
HOLD ON...
Mmm?
WHAT, uh... WHAT'D YOU JUST SAY, LIKE?
TWENTY QUID A CASE.
BEFORE THAT.
I WANT TO SUCK YOU.

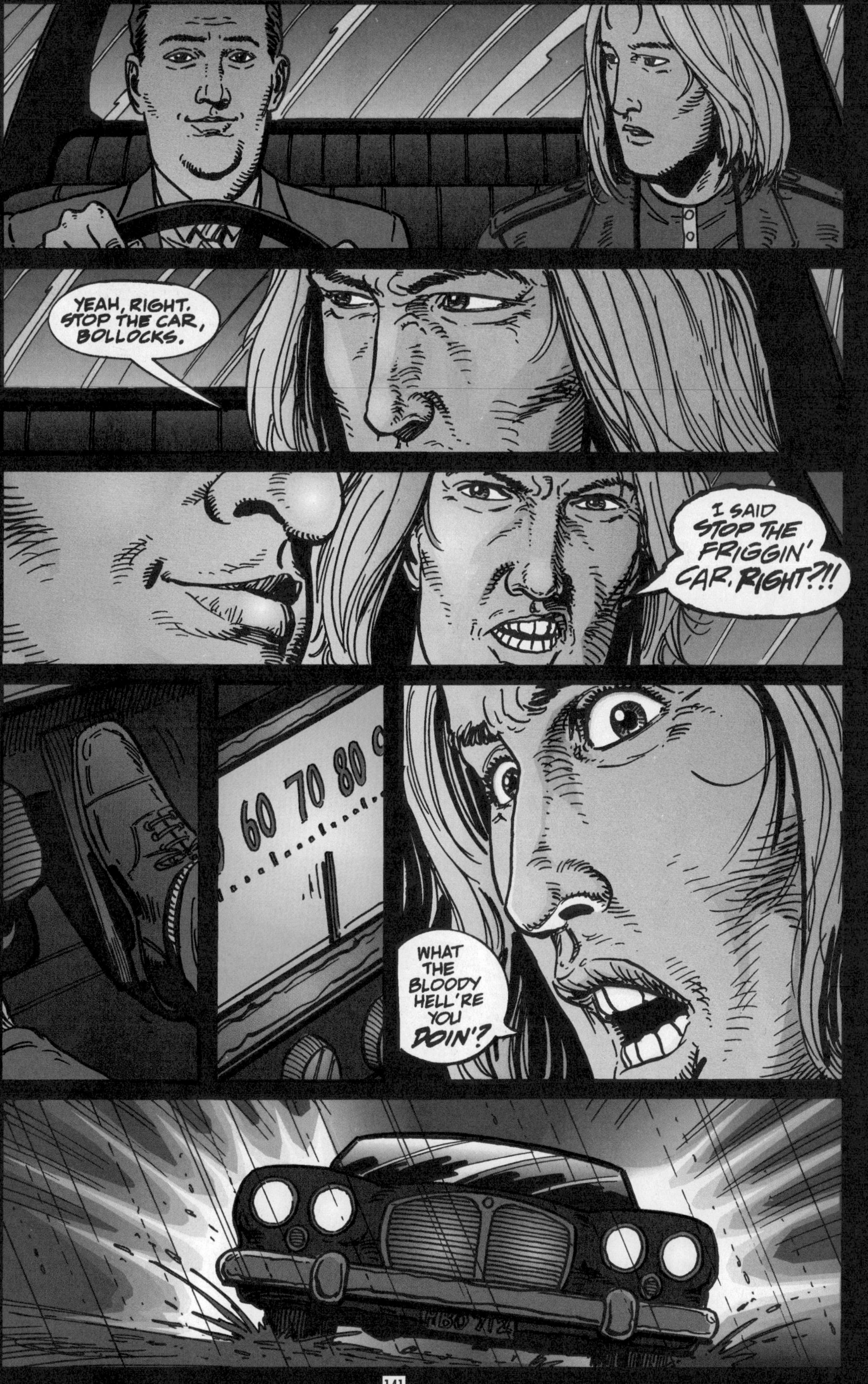
YEAH, RIGHT. STOP THE CAR, BOLLOCKS.
I SAID STOP THE FRIGGIN' CAR, RIGHT?!!
60 70 80
WHAT THE BLOODY HELL'RE YOU DOIN'?

STOP, FOR GOD'S SAKE! YOU'LL KILL US!

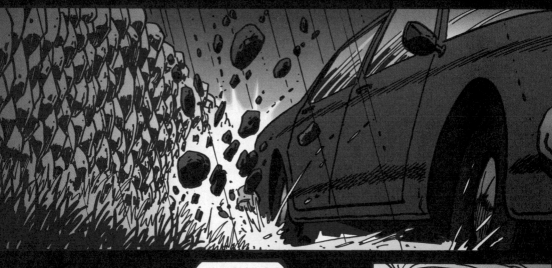

THAT COULD'VE BEEN NASTY.

IT WON'T BE THAT BAD, SON.

OKAY.

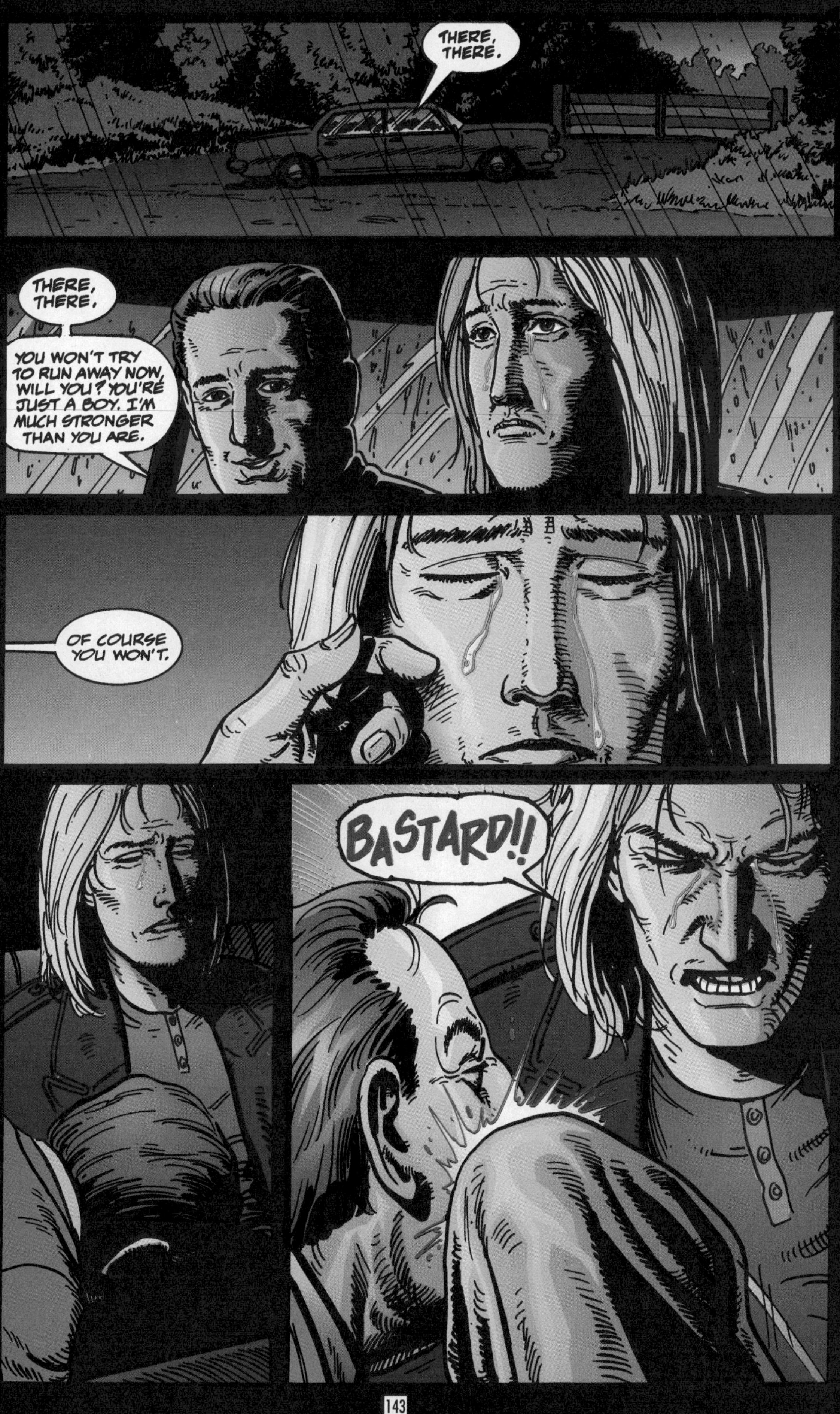
THERE, THERE.
THERE, THERE.
YOU WON'T TRY TO RUN AWAY NOW, WILL YOU? YOU'RE JUST A BOY. I'M MUCH STRONGER THAN YOU ARE.
OF COURSE YOU WON'T.
BASTARD!!

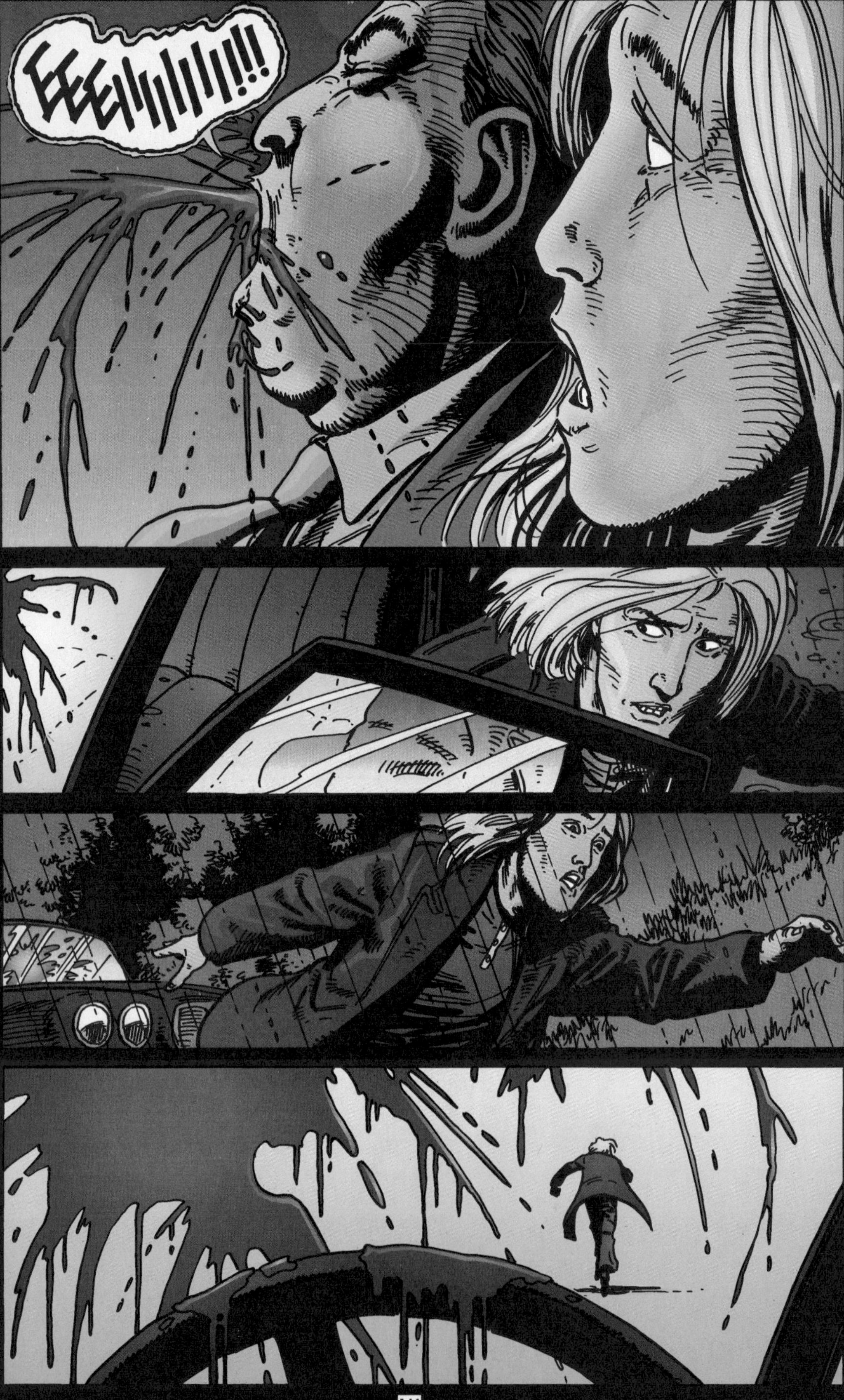
EEEIIIIIIII!!!

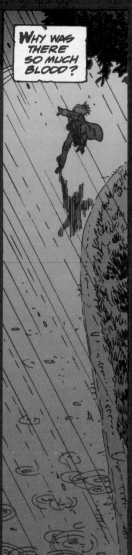

WHY WAS THERE SO MUCH BLOOD?

THAT'S ALL I COULD THINK OF, NOT "SOME WANKER JUST TRIED TO SUCK ME DICK" OR "I'M STRANDED MILES FROM NOWHERE WITHOUT ME GEAR"--

WHY SO MUCH BLOOD?

YOU DON'T BLEED LIKE THAT WHEN YOU BITE YOUR LIP OR BREAK YOUR NOSE, OR EVEN SEVER YOUR TONGUE--

HUHHHHHH!!

HUHHHH-HUHHHHHH!

SON?

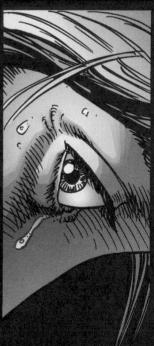

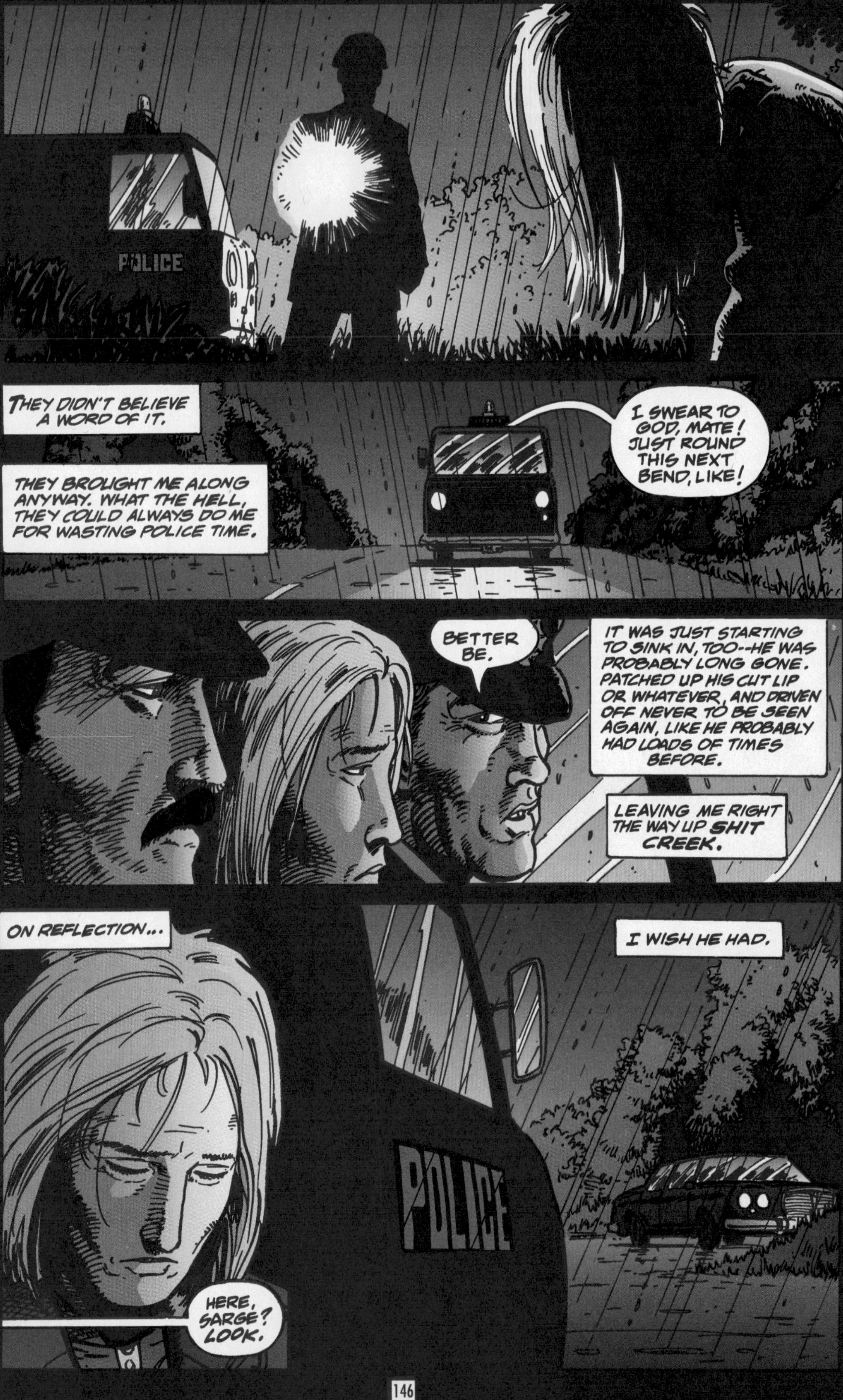
POLICE
THEY DIDN'T BELIEVE A WORD OF IT.
THEY BROUGHT ME ALONG ANYWAY. WHAT THE HELL, THEY COULD ALWAYS DO ME FOR WASTING POLICE TIME.
I SWEAR TO GOD, MATE! JUST ROUND THIS NEXT BEND, LIKE!
BETTER BE.
IT WAS JUST STARTING TO SINK IN, TOO--HE WAS PROBABLY LONG GONE. PATCHED UP HIS CUT LIP OR WHATEVER, AND DRIVEN OFF NEVER TO BE SEEN AGAIN, LIKE HE PROBABLY HAD LOADS OF TIMES BEFORE.
LEAVING ME RIGHT THE WAY UP SHIT CREEK.
ON REFLECTION...
I WISH HE HAD.
POLICE
HERE, SARGE? LOOK.

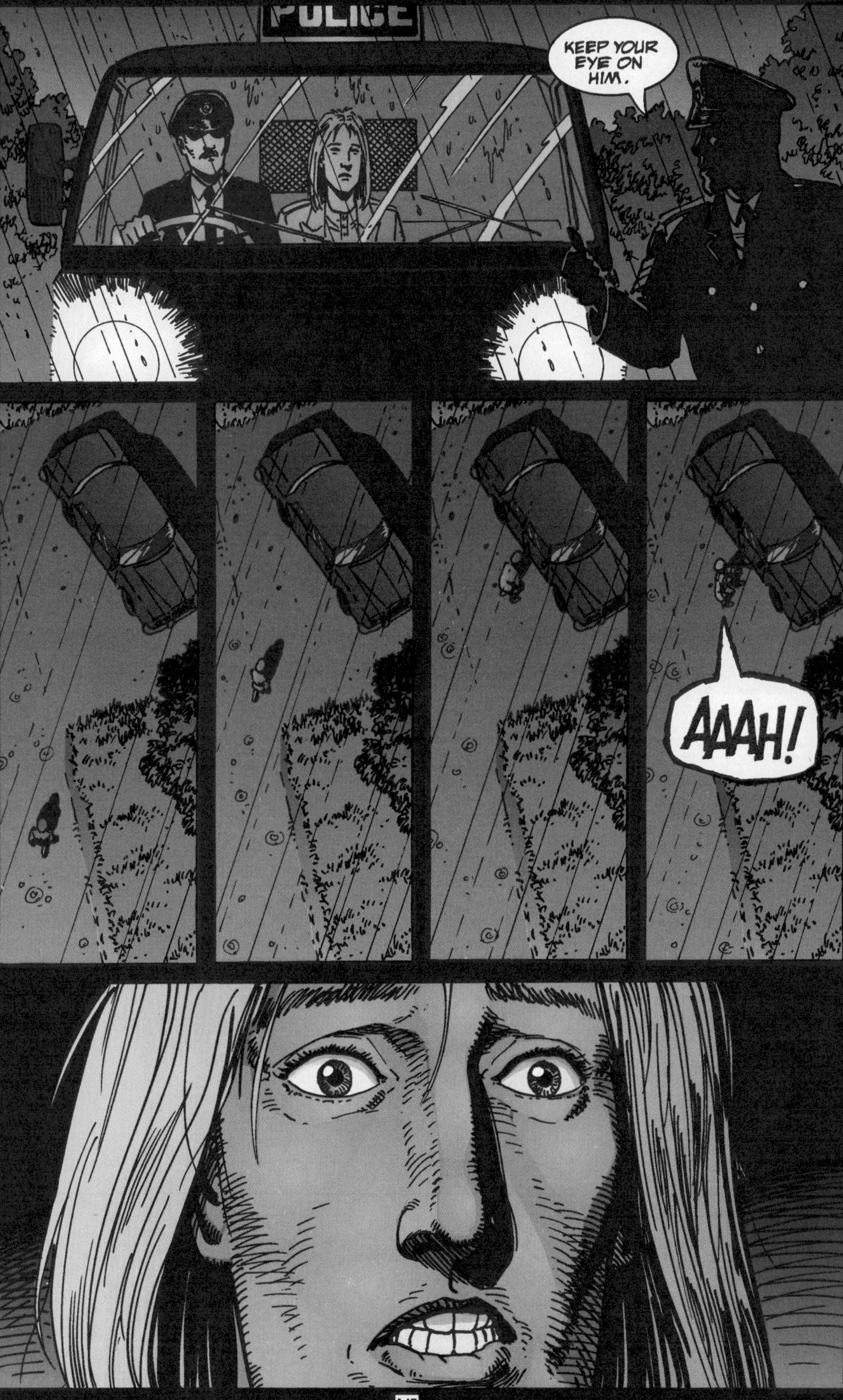
POLICE
KEEP YOUR EYE ON HIM.
AAAH!

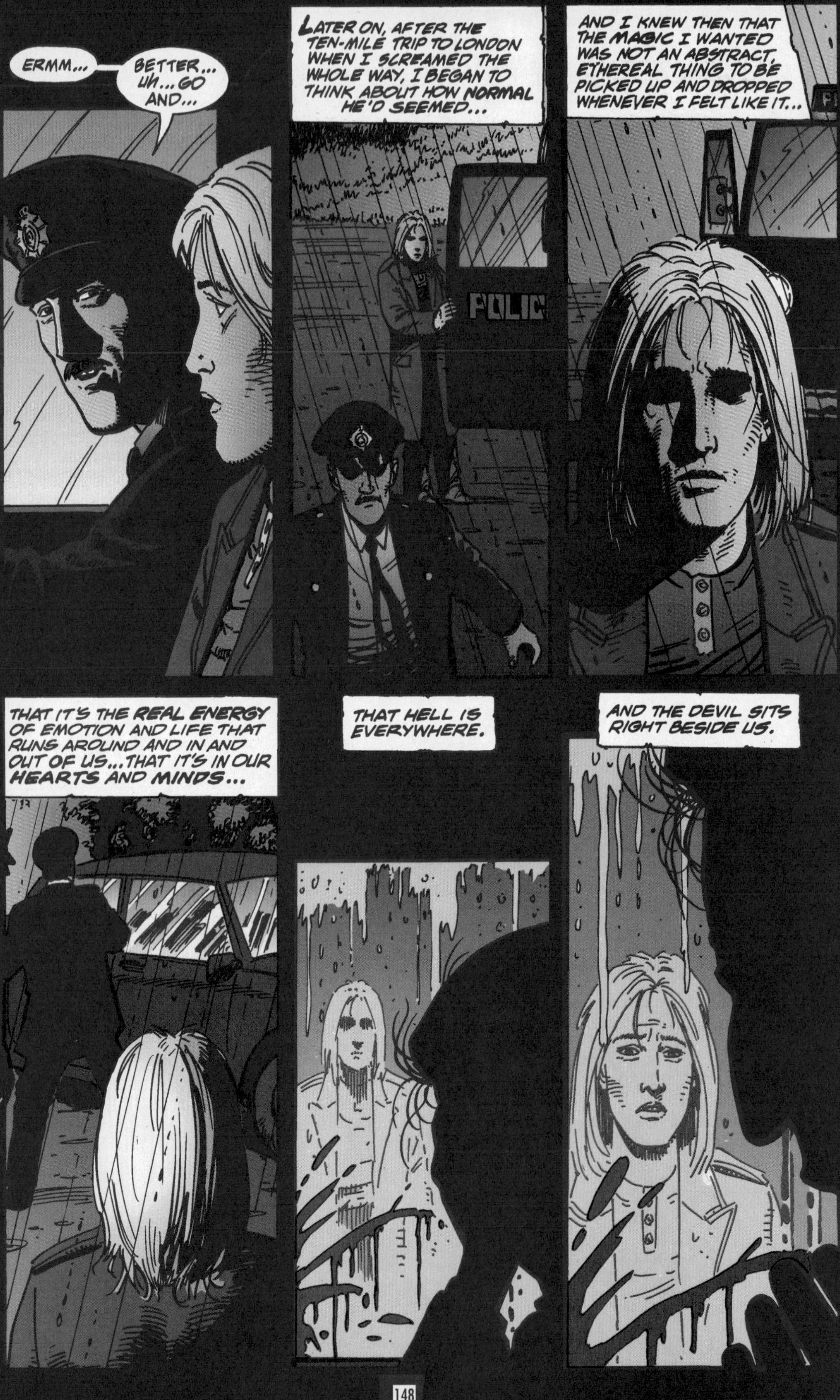
ERMM...
BETTER... UH... GO AND...
LATER ON, AFTER THE TEN-MILE TRIP TO LONDON WHEN I SCREAMED THE WHOLE WAY, I BEGAN TO THINK ABOUT HOW NORMAL HE'D SEEMED...
POLIC
AND I KNEW THEN THAT THE MAGIC I WANTED WAS NOT AN ABSTRACT, ETHEREAL THING TO BE PICKED UP AND DROPPED WHENEVER I FELT LIKE IT...
THAT IT'S THE REAL ENERGY OF EMOTION AND LIFE THAT RUNS AROUND AND IN AND OUT OF US...THAT IT'S IN OUR HEARTS AND MINDS...
THAT HELL IS EVERYWHERE.
AND THE DEVIL SITS RIGHT BESIDE US.

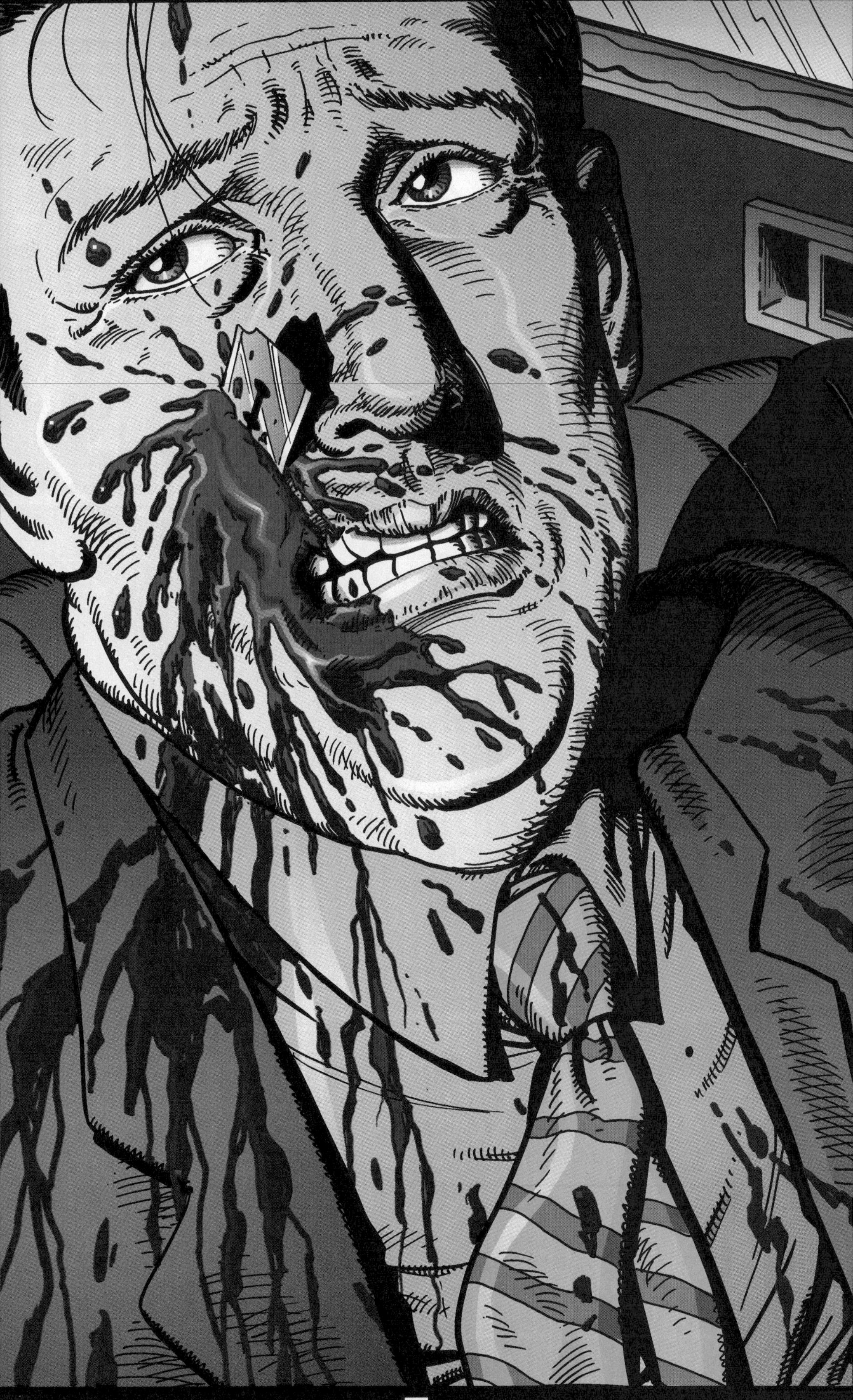

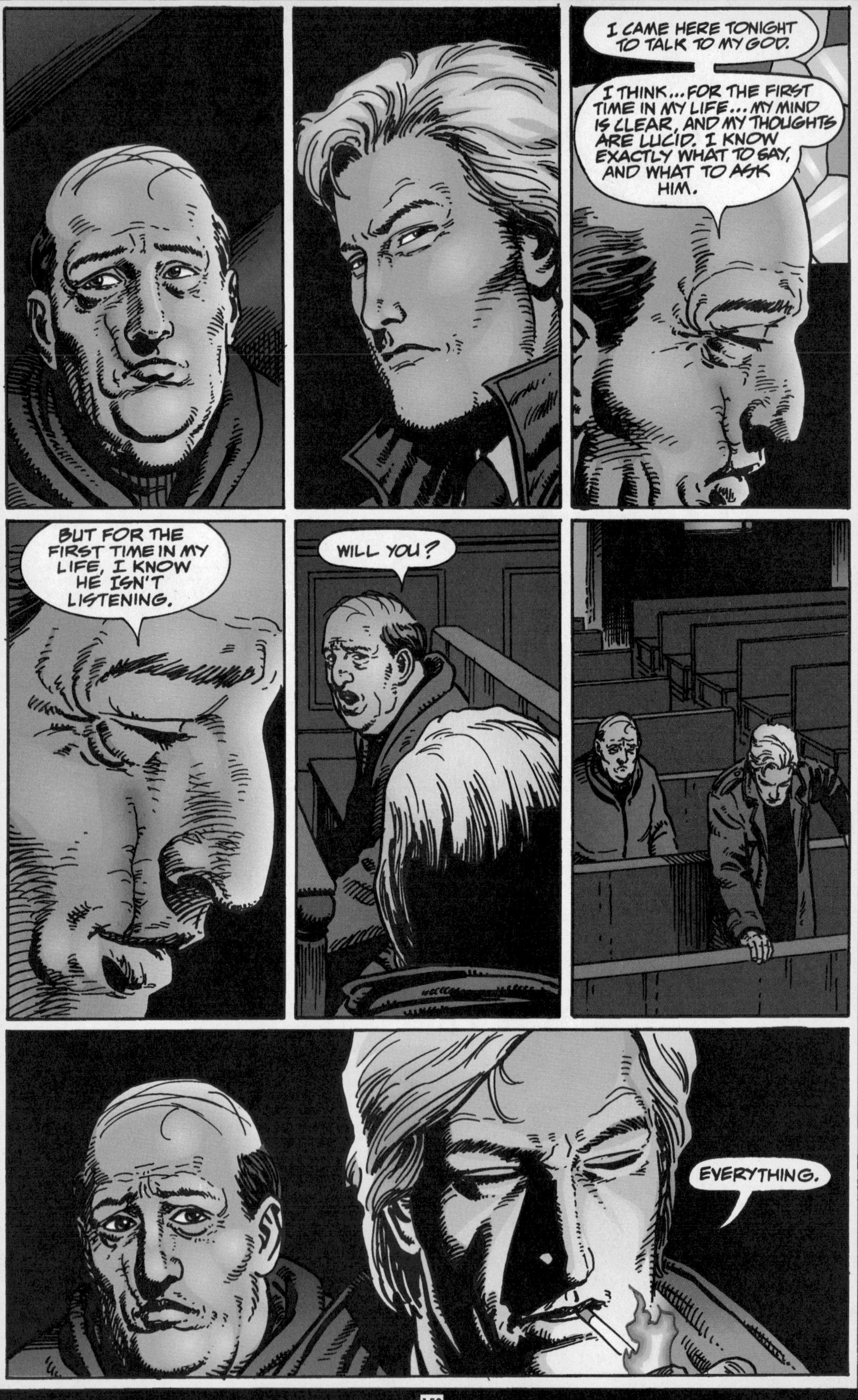
I CAME HERE TONIGHT TO TALK TO MY GOD.
I THINK... FOR THE FIRST TIME IN MY LIFE... MY MIND IS CLEAR, AND MY THOUGHTS ARE LUCID. I KNOW EXACTLY WHAT TO SAY, AND WHAT TO ASK HIM.
BUT FOR THE FIRST TIME IN MY LIFE, I KNOW HE ISN'T LISTENING.
WILL YOU?
EVERYTHING.

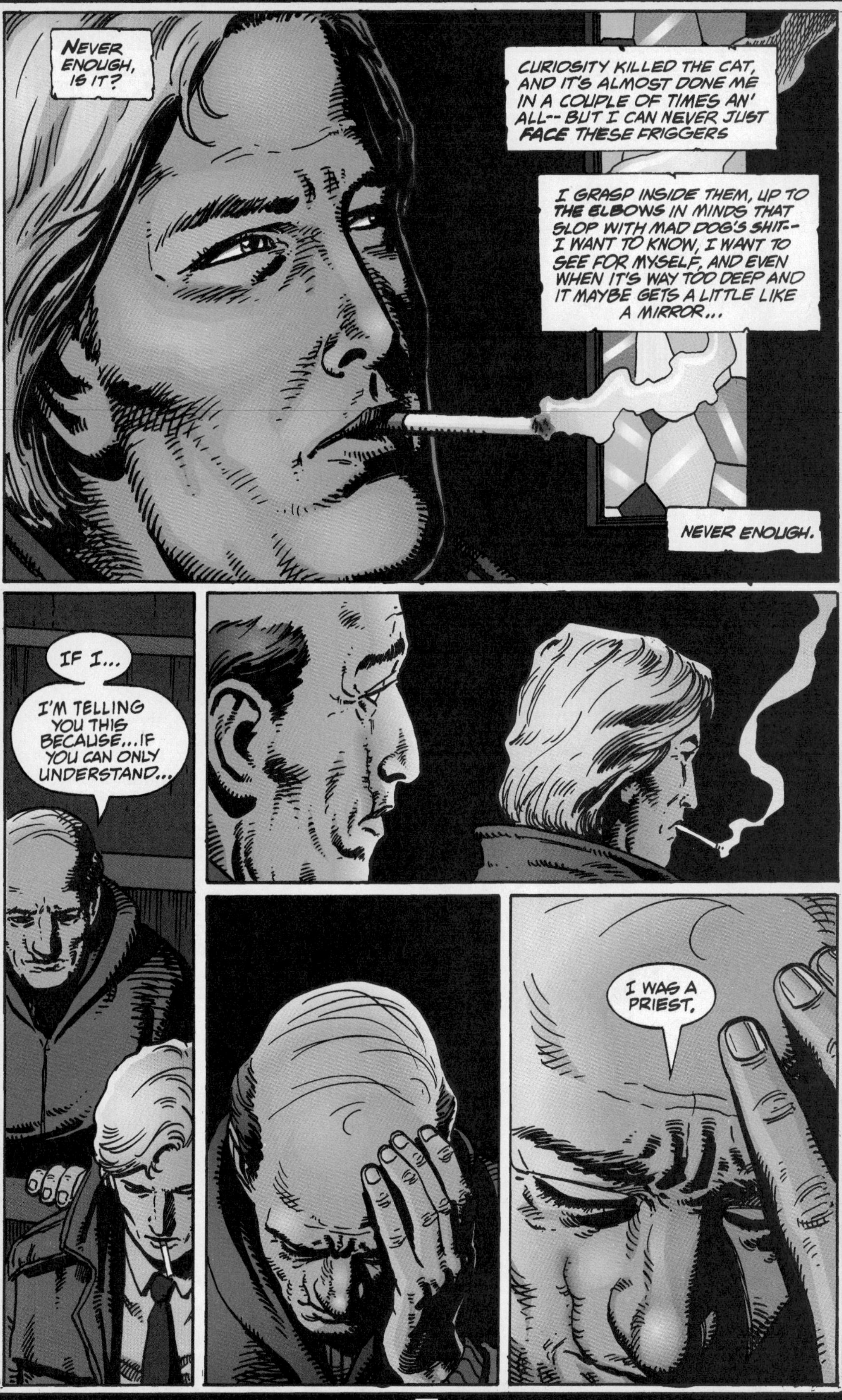

NEVER ENOUGH, IS IT?
CURIOSITY KILLED THE CAT, AND IT'S ALMOST DONE ME IN A COUPLE OF TIMES AN' ALL-- BUT I CAN NEVER JUST FACE THESE FRIGGERS
I GRASP INSIDE THEM, UP TO THE ELBOWS IN MINDS THAT SLOP WITH MAD DOG'S SHIT-- I WANT TO KNOW, I WANT TO SEE FOR MYSELF, AND EVEN WHEN IT'S WAY TOO DEEP AND IT MAYBE GETS A LITTLE LIKE A MIRROR...
NEVER ENOUGH.
IF I...
I'M TELLING YOU THIS BECAUSE...IF YOU CAN ONLY UNDERSTAND...
I WAS A PRIEST.

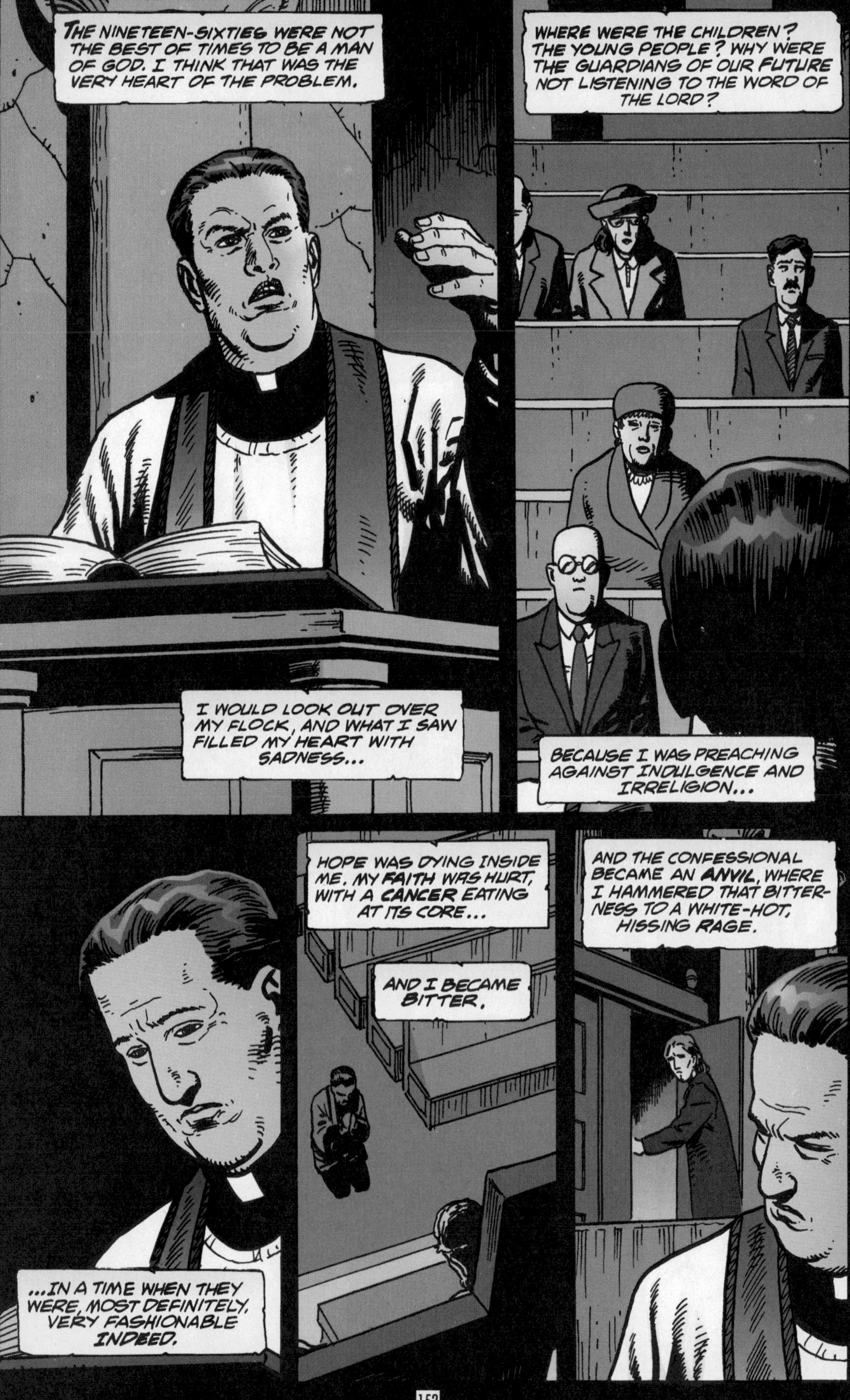
THE NINETEEN-SIXTIES WERE NOT THE BEST OF TIMES TO BE A MAN OF GOD. I THINK THAT WAS THE VERY HEART OF THE PROBLEM.
I WOULD LOOK OUT OVER MY FLOCK, AND WHAT I SAW FILLED MY HEART WITH SADNESS...
WHERE WERE THE CHILDREN? THE YOUNG PEOPLE? WHY WERE THE GUARDIANS OF OUR FUTURE NOT LISTENING TO THE WORD OF THE LORD?
BECAUSE I WAS PREACHING AGAINST INDULGENCE AND IRRELIGION...
...IN A TIME WHEN THEY WERE, MOST DEFINITELY, VERY FASHIONABLE INDEED.
HOPE WAS DYING INSIDE ME. MY FAITH WAS HURT, WITH A CANCER EATING AT ITS CORE...
AND I BECAME BITTER.
AND THE CONFESSIONAL BECAME AN ANVIL, WHERE I HAMMERED THAT BITTER-NESS TO A WHITE-HOT, HISSING RAGE.

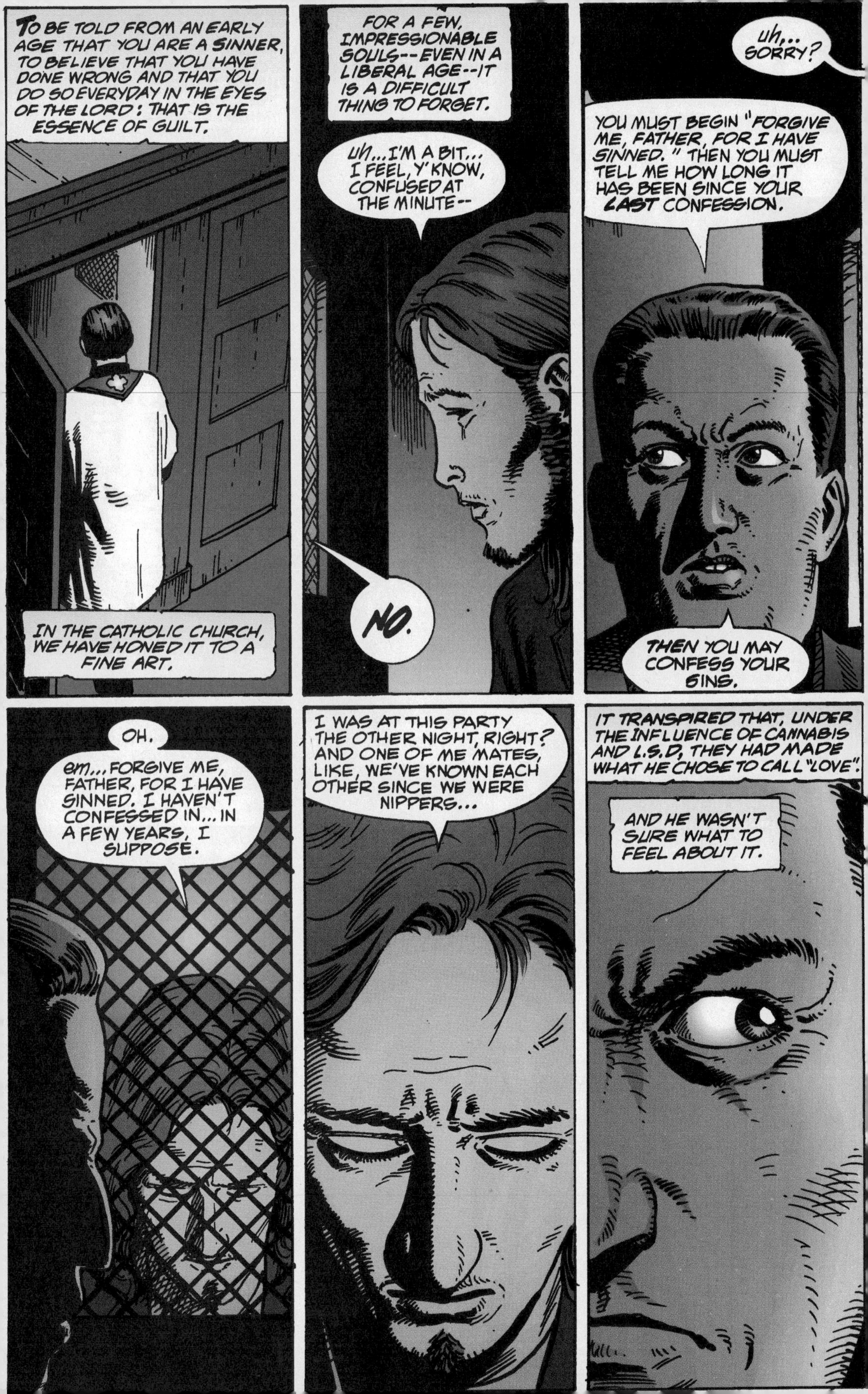
TO BE TOLD FROM AN EARLY AGE THAT YOU ARE A SINNER, TO BELIEVE THAT YOU HAVE DONE WRONG AND THAT YOU DO SO EVERYDAY IN THE EYES OF THE LORD: THAT IS THE ESSENCE OF GUILT.
IN THE CATHOLIC CHURCH, WE HAVE HONED IT TO A FINE ART.
FOR A FEW, IMPRESSIONABLE SOULS-- EVEN IN A LIBERAL AGE--IT IS A DIFFICULT THING TO FORGET.
uh... I'M A BIT... I FEEL, Y'KNOW, CONFUSED AT THE MINUTE--
NO.
uh,... SORRY?
YOU MUST BEGIN "FORGIVE ME, FATHER, FOR I HAVE SINNED." THEN YOU MUST TELL ME HOW LONG IT HAS BEEN SINCE YOUR LAST CONFESSION.
THEN YOU MAY CONFESS YOUR SINS.
OH.
em... FORGIVE ME, FATHER, FOR I HAVE SINNED. I HAVEN'T CONFESSED IN... IN A FEW YEARS, I SUPPOSE.
I WAS AT THIS PARTY THE OTHER NIGHT, RIGHT? AND ONE OF ME MATES, LIKE, WE'VE KNOWN EACH OTHER SINCE WE WERE NIPPERS...
IT TRANSPIRED THAT, UNDER THE INFLUENCE OF CANNABIS AND L.S.D, THEY HAD MADE WHAT HE CHOSE TO CALL "LOVE".
AND HE WASN'T SURE WHAT TO FEEL ABOUT IT.

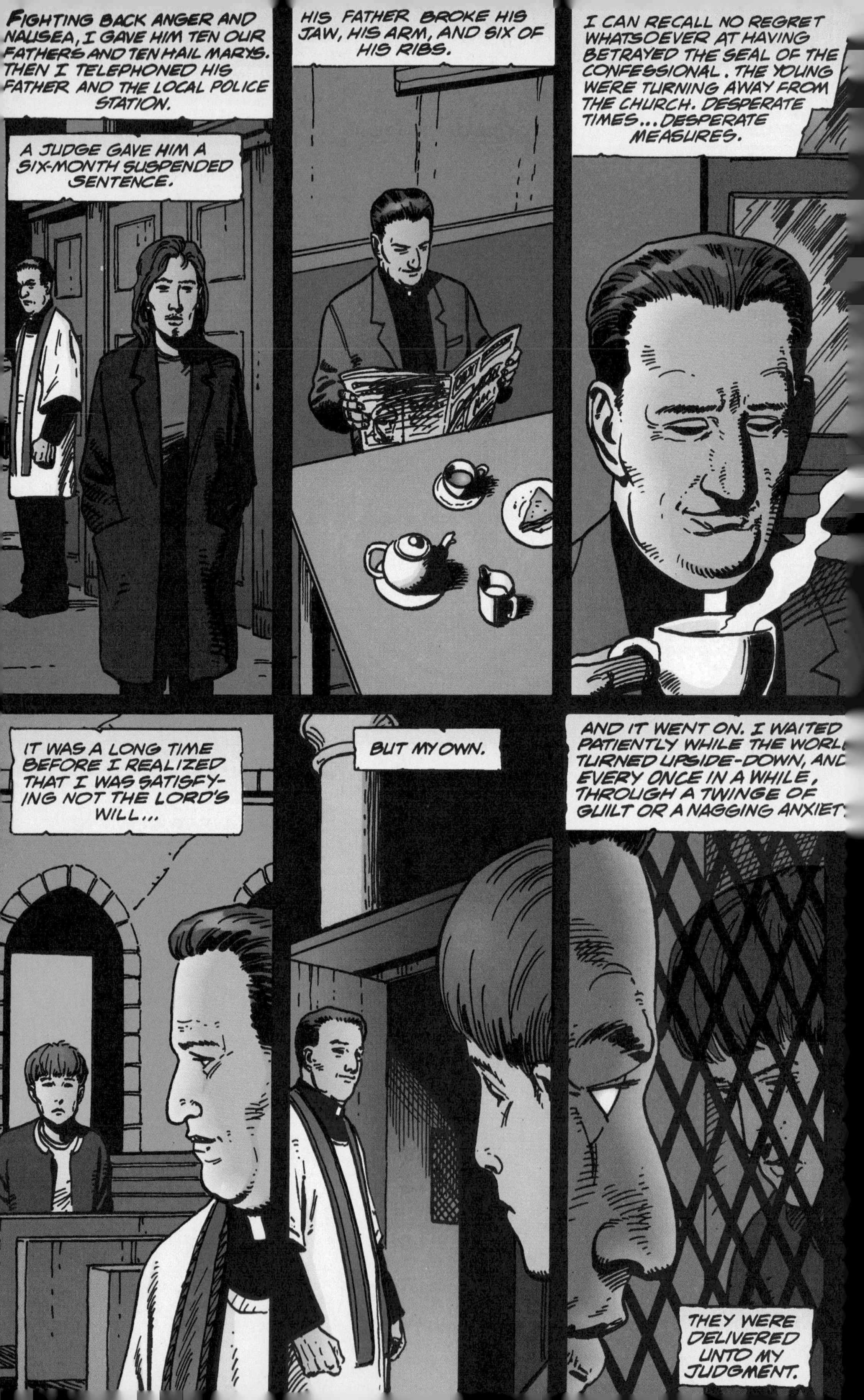
FIGHTING BACK ANGER AND NAUSEA, I GAVE HIM TEN OUR FATHERS AND TEN HAIL MARYS. THEN I TELEPHONED HIS FATHER AND THE LOCAL POLICE STATION.
A JUDGE GAVE HIM A SIX-MONTH SUSPENDED SENTENCE.
HIS FATHER BROKE HIS JAW, HIS ARM, AND SIX OF HIS RIBS.
I CAN RECALL NO REGRET WHATSOEVER AT HAVING BETRAYED THE SEAL OF THE CONFESSIONAL. THE YOUNG WERE TURNING AWAY FROM THE CHURCH. DESPERATE TIMES... DESPERATE MEASURES.
IT WAS A LONG TIME BEFORE I REALIZED THAT I WAS SATISFY-ING NOT THE LORD'S WILL...
BUT MY OWN.
AND IT WENT ON. I WAITED PATIENTLY WHILE THE WORL TURNED UPSIDE-DOWN, AND EVERY ONCE IN A WHILE, THROUGH A TWINGE OF GUILT OR A NAGGING ANXIET
THEY WERE DELIVERED UNTO MY JUDGMENT.

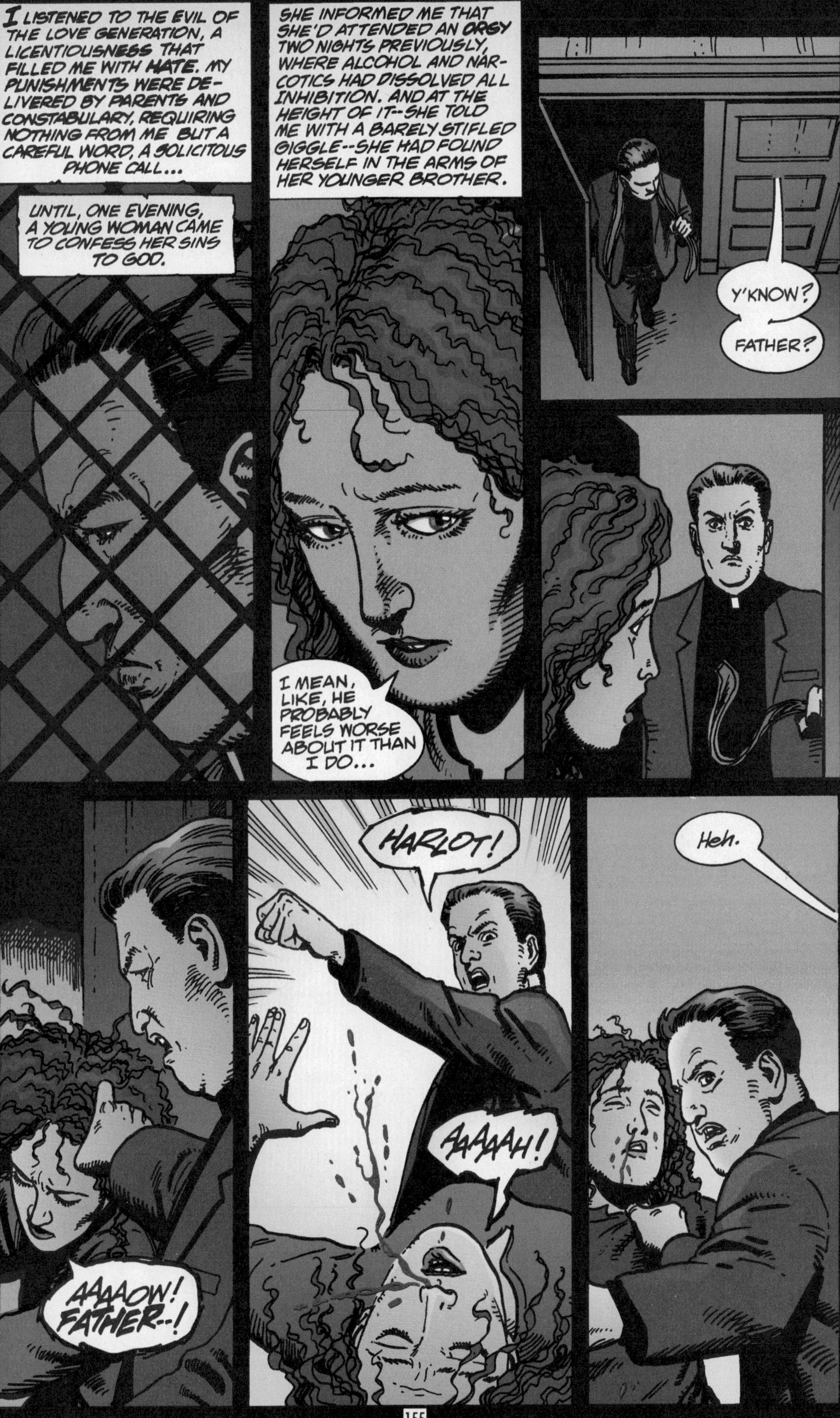
I LISTENED TO THE EVIL OF THE LOVE GENERATION, A LICENTIOUSNESS THAT FILLED ME WITH HATE. MY PUNISHMENTS WERE DELIVERED BY PARENTS AND CONSTABULARY, REQUIRING NOTHING FROM ME BUT A CAREFUL WORD, A SOLICITOUS PHONE CALL...
UNTIL, ONE EVENING, A YOUNG WOMAN CAME TO CONFESS HER SINS TO GOD.
SHE INFORMED ME THAT SHE'D ATTENDED AN ORGY TWO NIGHTS PREVIOUSLY, WHERE ALCOHOL AND NARCOTICS HAD DISSOLVED ALL INHIBITION. AND AT THE HEIGHT OF IT--SHE TOLD ME WITH A BARELY STIFLED GIGGLE--SHE HAD FOUND HERSELF IN THE ARMS OF HER YOUNGER BROTHER.
I MEAN, LIKE, HE PROBABLY FEELS WORSE ABOUT IT THAN I DO...
Y'KNOW?
FATHER?
AAAAOW! FATHER--!
HARLOT!
AAAAAH!
Heh.

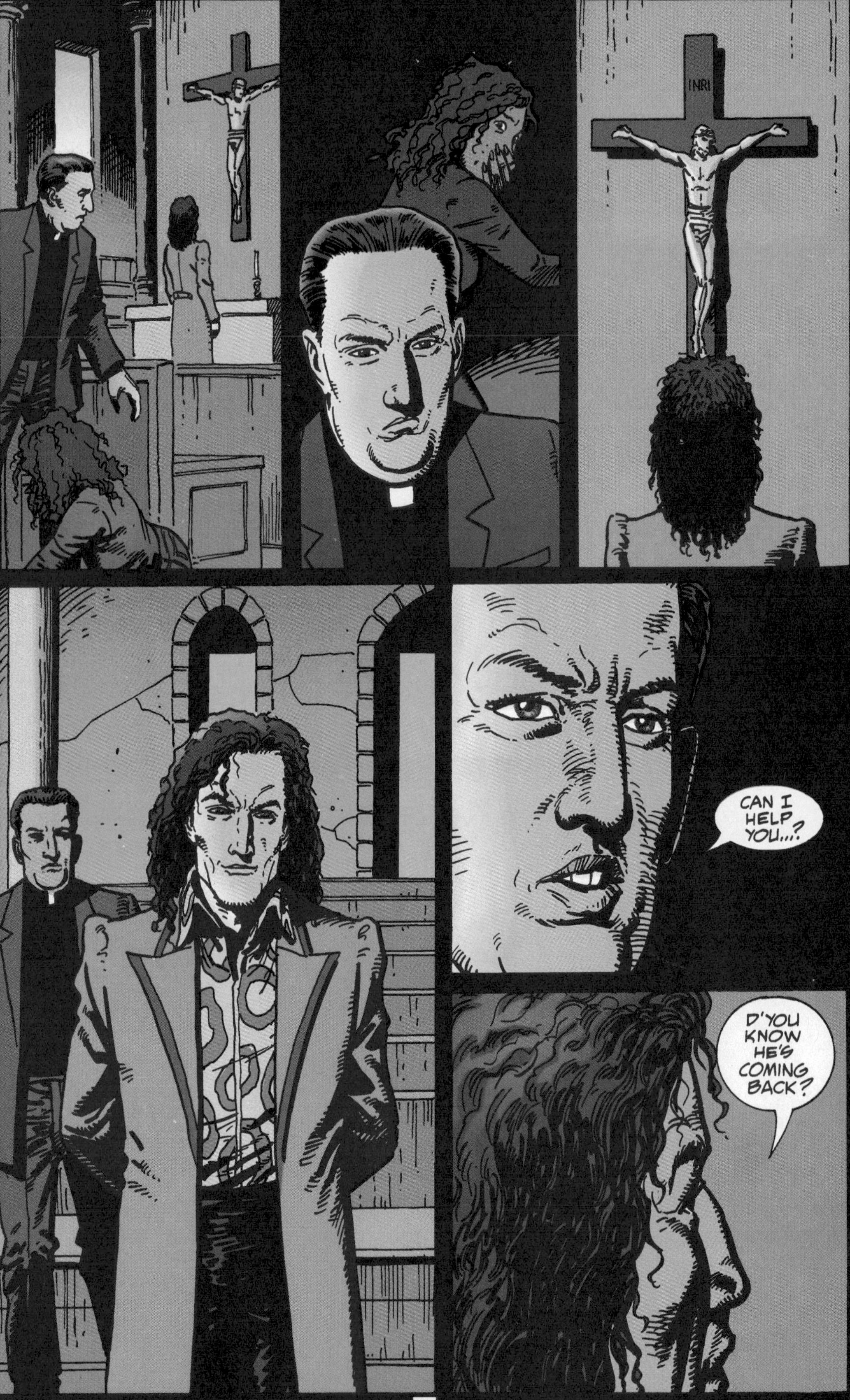

INRI
CAN I HELP YOU...?
D'YOU KNOW HE'S COMING BACK?

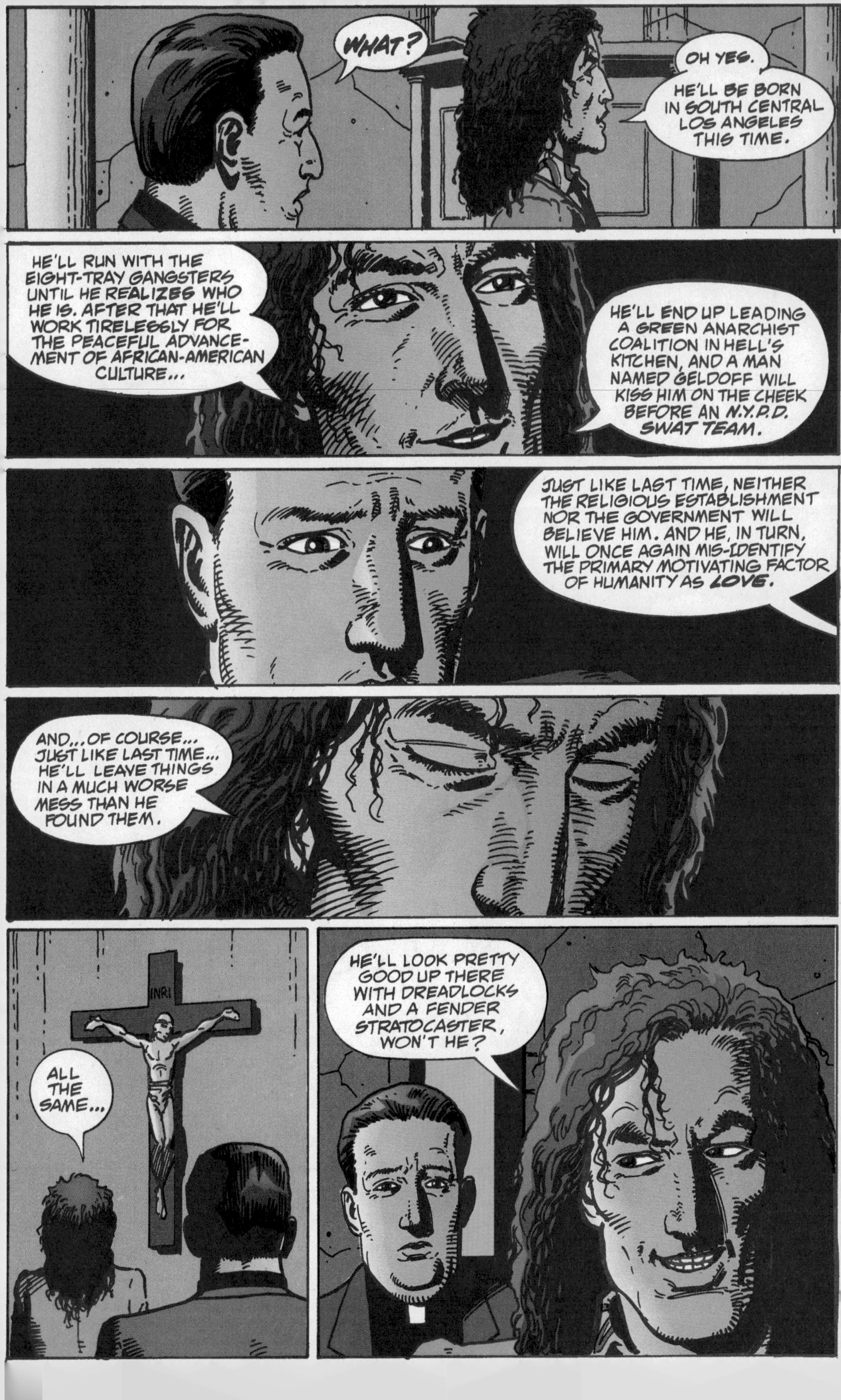
WHAT?
OH YES.
HE'LL BE BORN IN SOUTH CENTRAL LOS ANGELES THIS TIME.
HE'LL RUN WITH THE EIGHT-TRAY GANGSTERS UNTIL HE REALIZES WHO HE IS. AFTER THAT HE'LL WORK TIRELESSLY FOR THE PEACEFUL ADVANCEMENT OF AFRICAN-AMERICAN CULTURE...
HE'LL END UP LEADING A GREEN ANARCHIST COALITION IN HELL'S KITCHEN, AND A MAN NAMED GELDOFF WILL KISS HIM ON THE CHEEK BEFORE AN N.Y.P.D. SWAT TEAM.
JUST LIKE LAST TIME, NEITHER THE RELIGIOUS ESTABLISHMENT NOR THE GOVERNMENT WILL BELIEVE HIM. AND HE, IN TURN, WILL ONCE AGAIN MIS-IDENTIFY THE PRIMARY MOTIVATING FACTOR OF HUMANITY AS LOVE.
AND... OF COURSE... JUST LIKE LAST TIME... HE'LL LEAVE THINGS IN A MUCH WORSE MESS THAN HE FOUND THEM.
INRI
ALL THE SAME...
HE'LL LOOK PRETTY GOOD UP THERE WITH DREADLOCKS AND A FENDER STRATOCASTER, WON'T HE?

WHAT... WHAT ARE YOU TALKING ABOUT...?

WHO ARE YOU?

YOU DON'T KNOW?

YOUR FRIEND THERE WAS FOND OF TELLING ME TO GET BEHIND HIM.

INRI

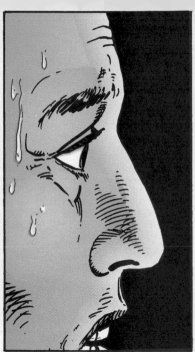

YOU KNOW WHO I AM, FATHER TOLLY.

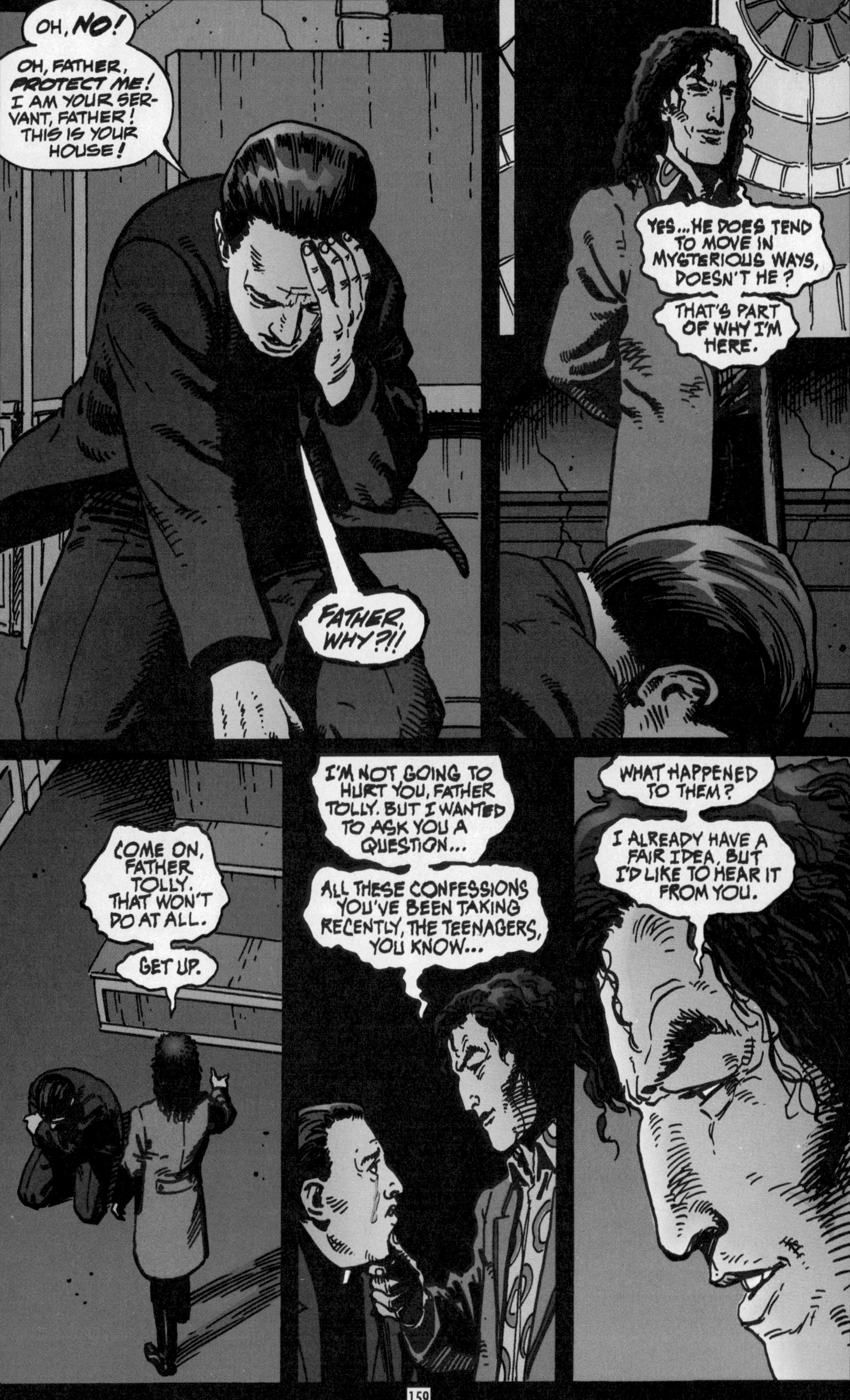
OH, NO!
OH, FATHER, PROTECT ME! I AM YOUR SERVANT, FATHER! THIS IS YOUR HOUSE!
FATHER, WHY?!!
YES...HE DOES TEND TO MOVE IN MYSTERIOUS WAYS, DOESN'T HE?
THAT'S PART OF WHY I'M HERE.
COME ON, FATHER TOLLY. THAT WON'T DO AT ALL.
GET UP.
I'M NOT GOING TO HURT YOU, FATHER TOLLY. BUT I WANTED TO ASK YOU A QUESTION...
ALL THESE CONFESSIONS YOU'VE BEEN TAKING RECENTLY, THE TEENAGERS, YOU KNOW...
WHAT HAPPENED TO THEM?
I ALREADY HAVE A FAIR IDEA, BUT I'D LIKE TO HEAR IT FROM YOU.

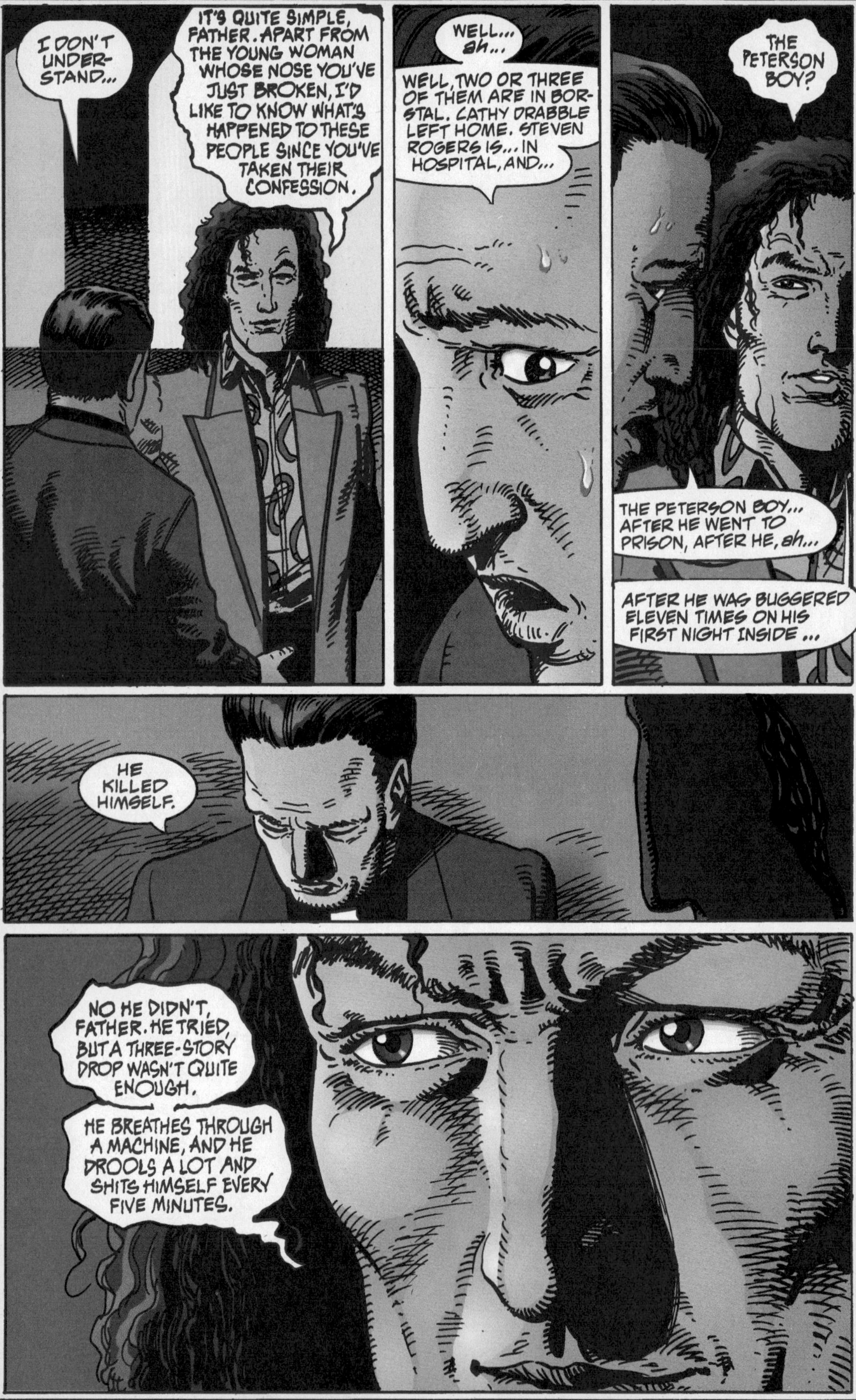
I DON'T UNDER-STAND...
IT'S QUITE SIMPLE, FATHER. APART FROM THE YOUNG WOMAN WHOSE NOSE YOU'VE JUST BROKEN, I'D LIKE TO KNOW WHAT'S HAPPENED TO THESE PEOPLE SINCE YOU'VE TAKEN THEIR CONFESSION.
WELL... ah...
WELL, TWO OR THREE OF THEM ARE IN BOR-STAL. CATHY DRABBLE LEFT HOME. STEVEN ROGERS IS... IN HOSPITAL, AND...
THE PETERSON BOY?
THE PETERSON BOY... AFTER HE WENT TO PRISON, AFTER HE, ah...
AFTER HE WAS BUGGERED ELEVEN TIMES ON HIS FIRST NIGHT INSIDE...
HE KILLED HIMSELF.
NO HE DIDN'T, FATHER. HE TRIED, BUT A THREE-STORY DROP WASN'T QUITE ENOUGH.
HE BREATHES THROUGH A MACHINE, AND HE DROOLS A LOT AND SHITS HIMSELF EVERY FIVE MINUTES.

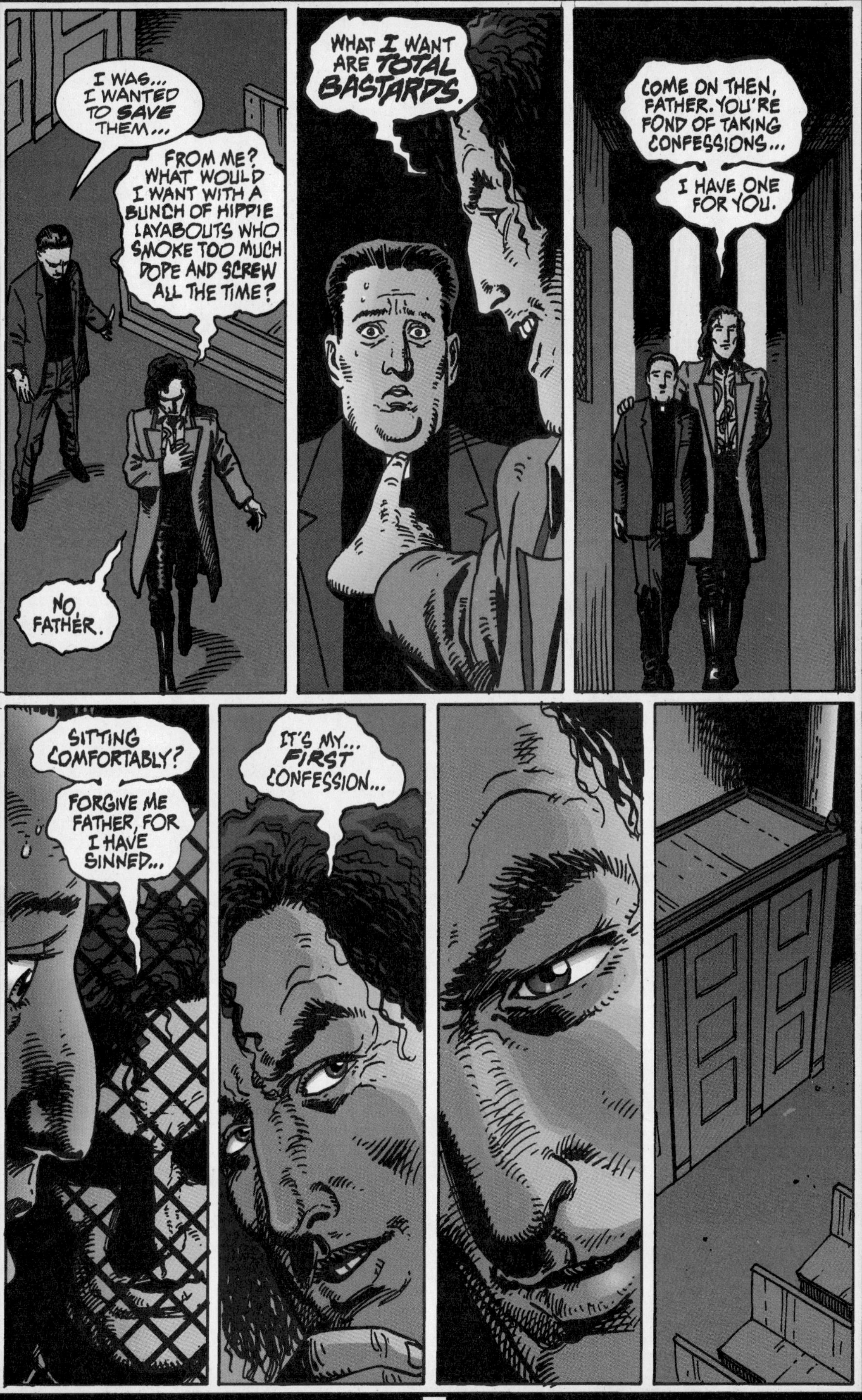
I WAS... I WANTED TO SAVE THEM...
FROM ME? WHAT WOULD I WANT WITH A BUNCH OF HIPPIE LAYABOUTS WHO SMOKE TOO MUCH DOPE AND SCREW ALL THE TIME?
NO, FATHER.
WHAT I WANT ARE TOTAL BASTARDS.
COME ON THEN, FATHER. YOU'RE FOND OF TAKING CONFESSIONS...
I HAVE ONE FOR YOU.
SITTING COMFORTABLY?
FORGIVE ME FATHER, FOR I HAVE SINNED...
IT'S MY... FIRST CONFESSION...

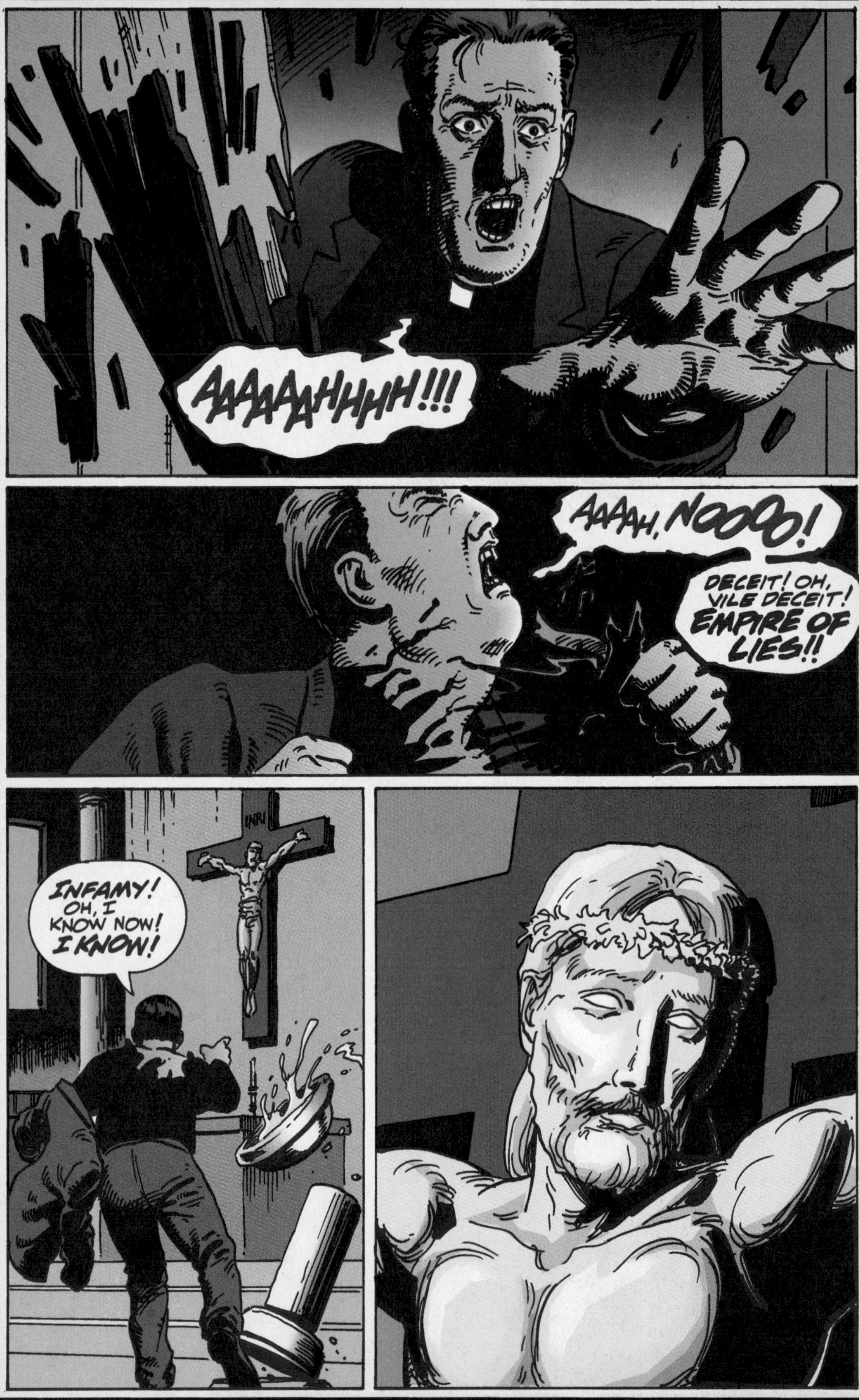
AAAAAAHHHH!!!
AAAAH, NOOOO!
DECEIT! OH, VILE DECEIT! EMPIRE OF LIES!!
INFAMY! OH, I KNOW NOW! I KNOW!
INRI

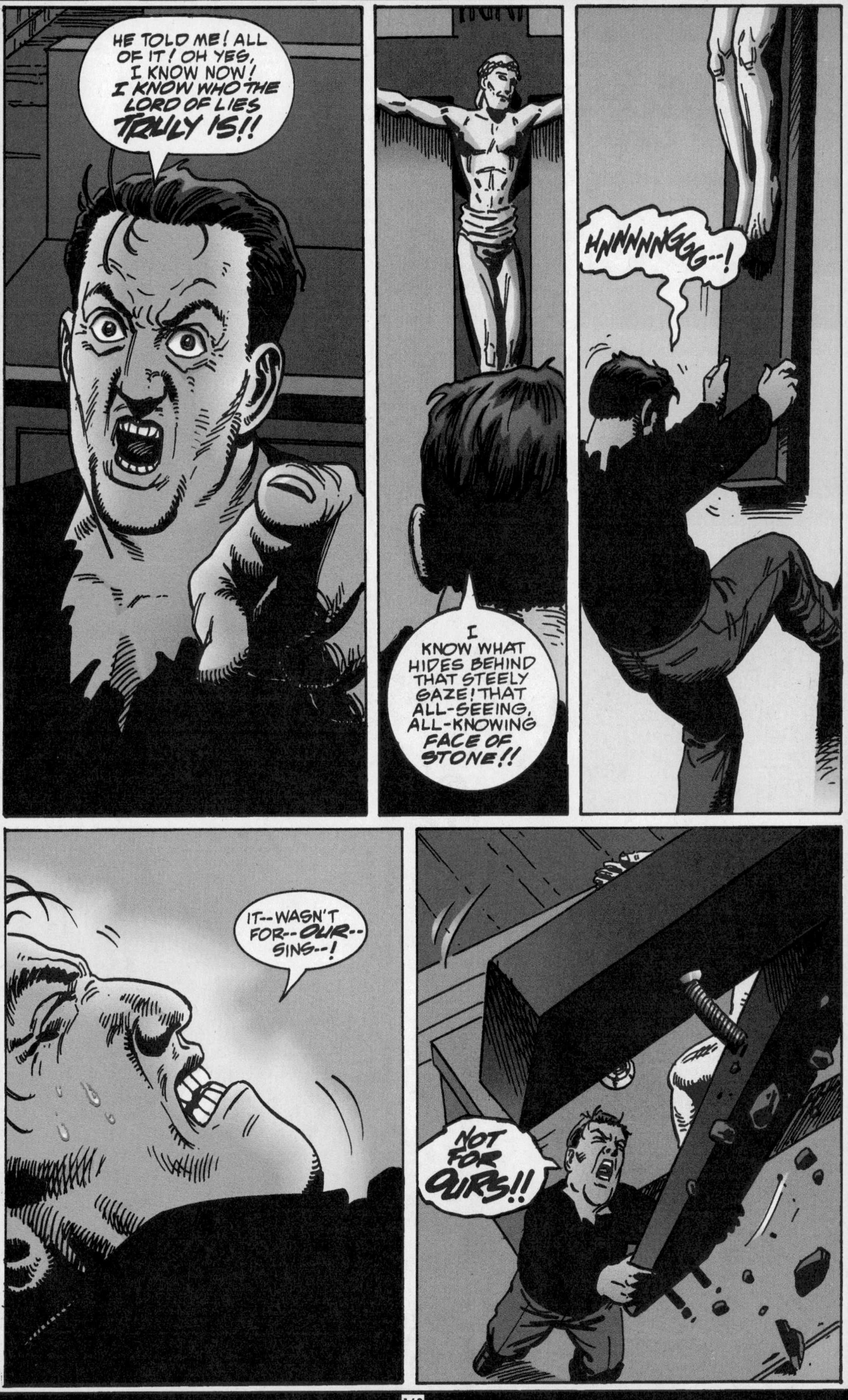
HE TOLD ME! ALL OF IT! OH YES, I KNOW NOW! I KNOW WHO THE LORD OF LIES TRULY IS!!
I KNOW WHAT HIDES BEHIND THAT STEELY GAZE! THAT ALL-SEEING, ALL-KNOWING FACE OF STONE!!
HNNNNNGGG--!
IT--WASN'T FOR--OUR--SINS--!
NOT FOR OURS!!

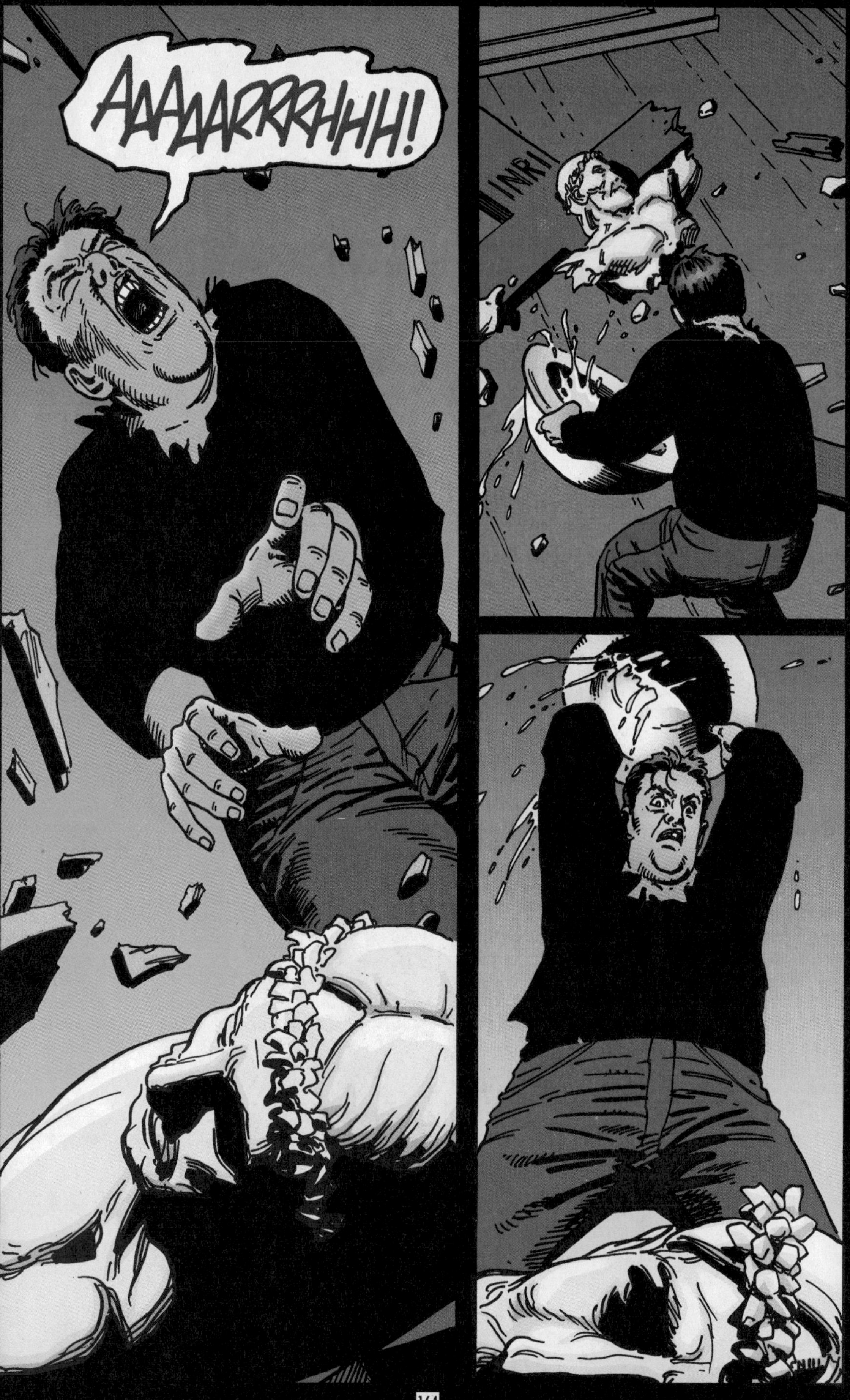
AAAAARRRHHH!
INRI

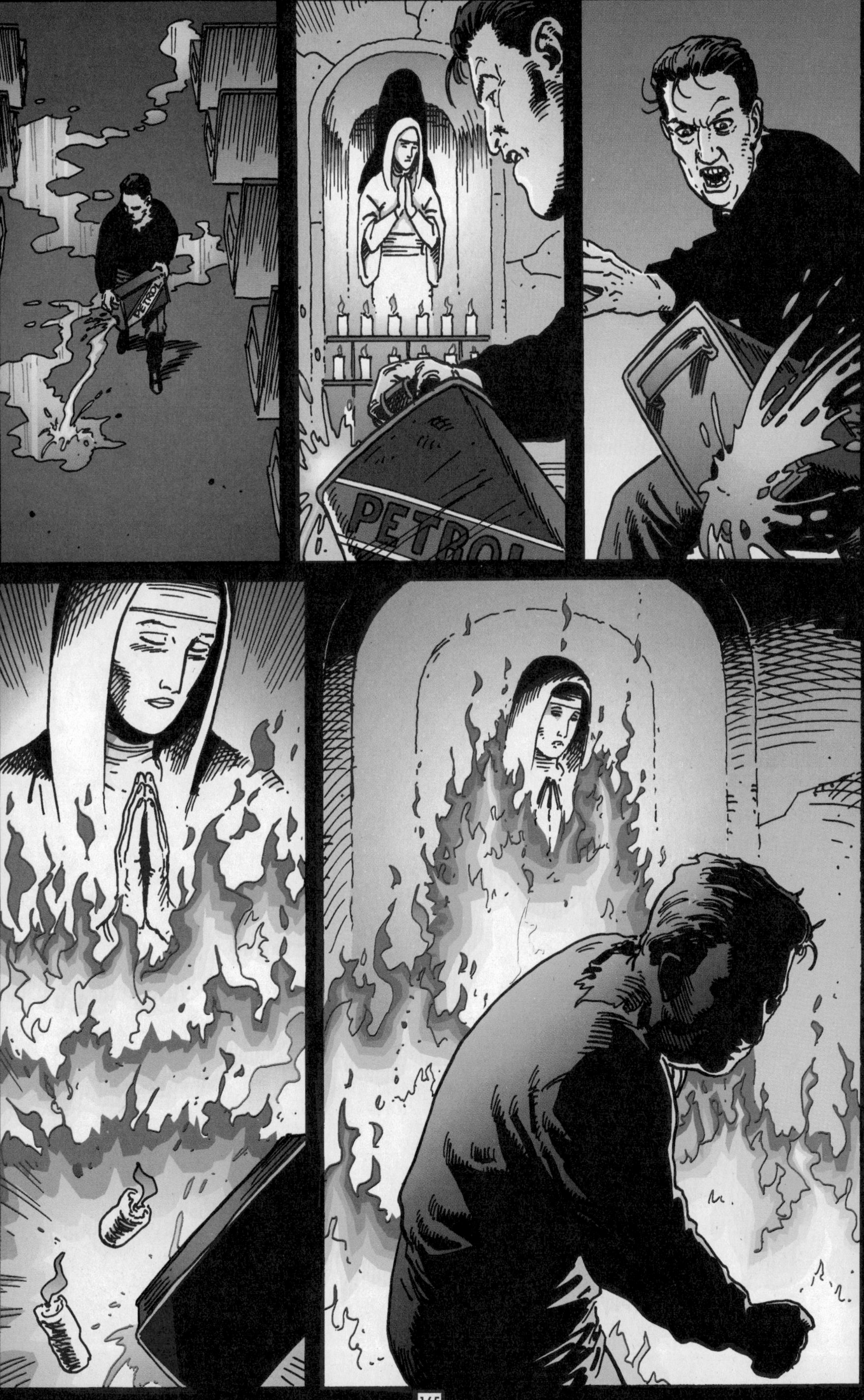
PETROL
PETROL

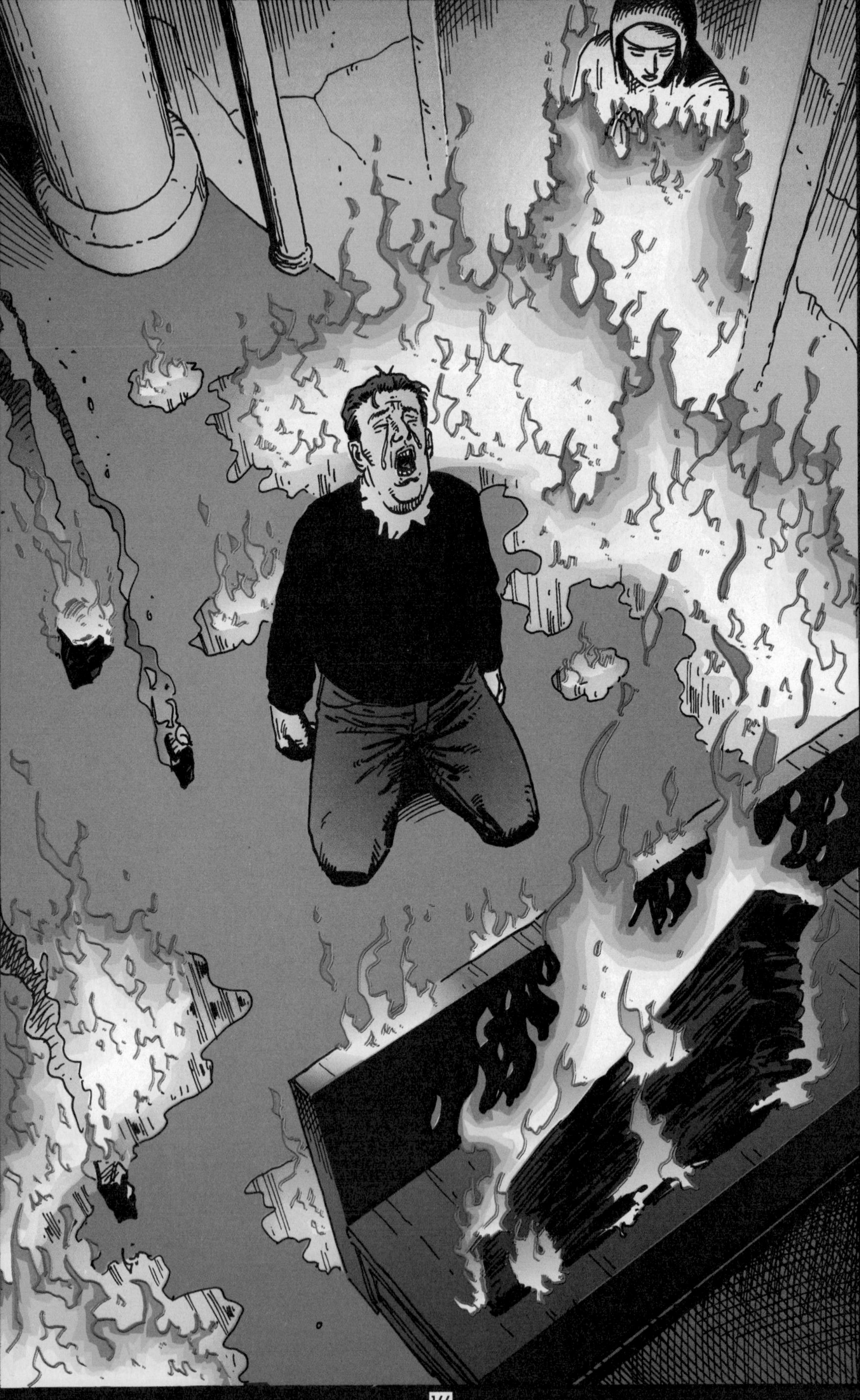

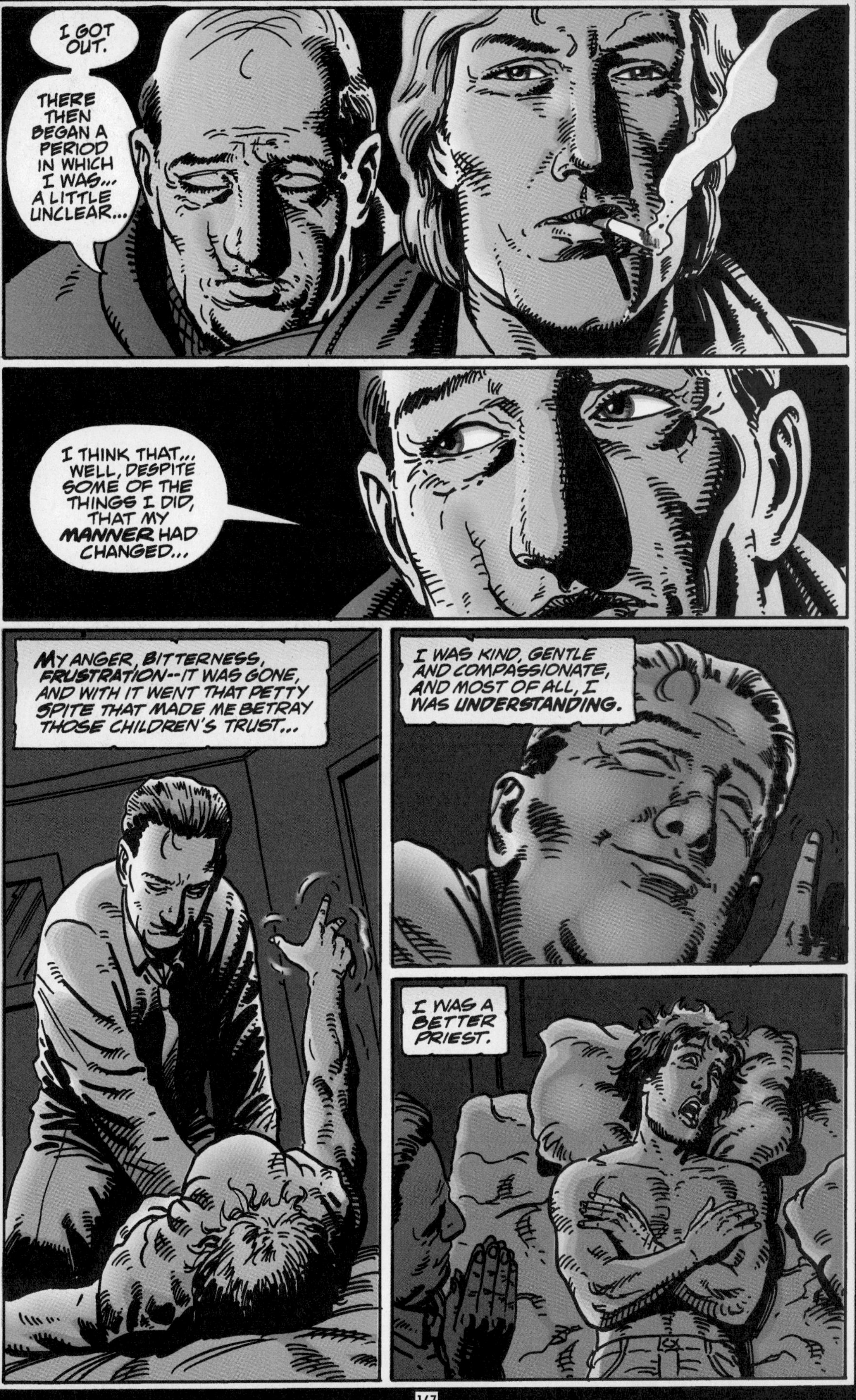
I GOT OUT.
THERE THEN BEGAN A PERIOD IN WHICH I WAS... A LITTLE UNCLEAR...
I THINK THAT... WELL, DESPITE SOME OF THE THINGS I DID, THAT MY **MANNER** HAD CHANGED...
MY ANGER, BITTERNESS, FRUSTRATION--IT WAS GONE, AND WITH IT WENT THAT PETTY SPITE THAT MADE ME BETRAY THOSE CHILDREN'S TRUST...
I WAS KIND, GENTLE AND COMPASSIONATE, AND MOST OF ALL, I WAS UNDERSTANDING.
I WAS A BETTER PRIEST.

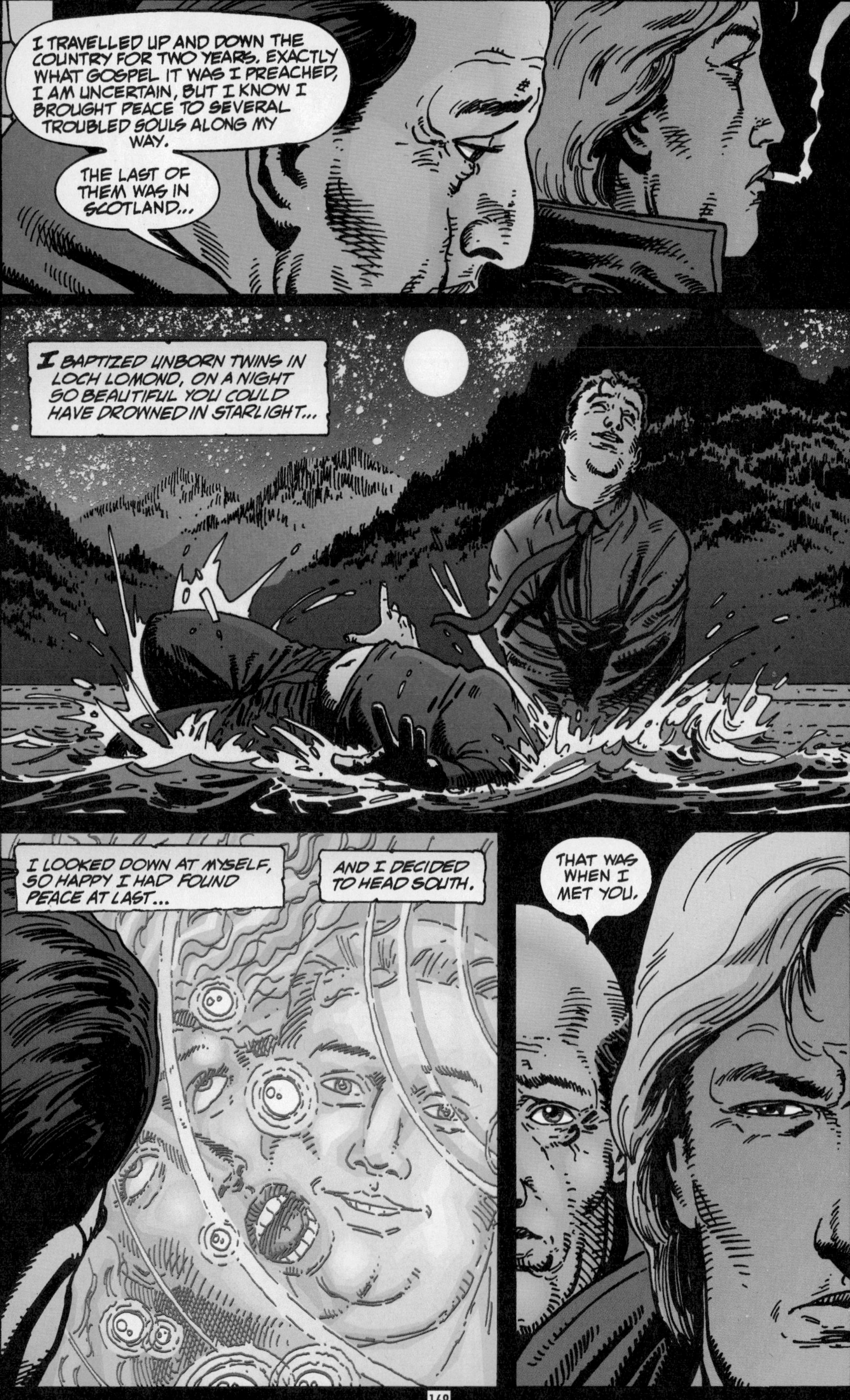
I TRAVELLED UP AND DOWN THE COUNTRY FOR TWO YEARS. EXACTLY WHAT GOSPEL IT WAS I PREACHED, I AM UNCERTAIN, BUT I KNOW I BROUGHT PEACE TO SEVERAL TROUBLED SOULS ALONG MY WAY.
THE LAST OF THEM WAS IN SCOTLAND...
I BAPTIZED UNBORN TWINS IN LOCH LOMOND, ON A NIGHT SO BEAUTIFUL YOU COULD HAVE DROWNED IN STARLIGHT...
I LOOKED DOWN AT MYSELF, SO HAPPY I HAD FOUND PEACE AT LAST...
AND I DECIDED TO HEAD SOUTH.
THAT WAS WHEN I MET YOU.

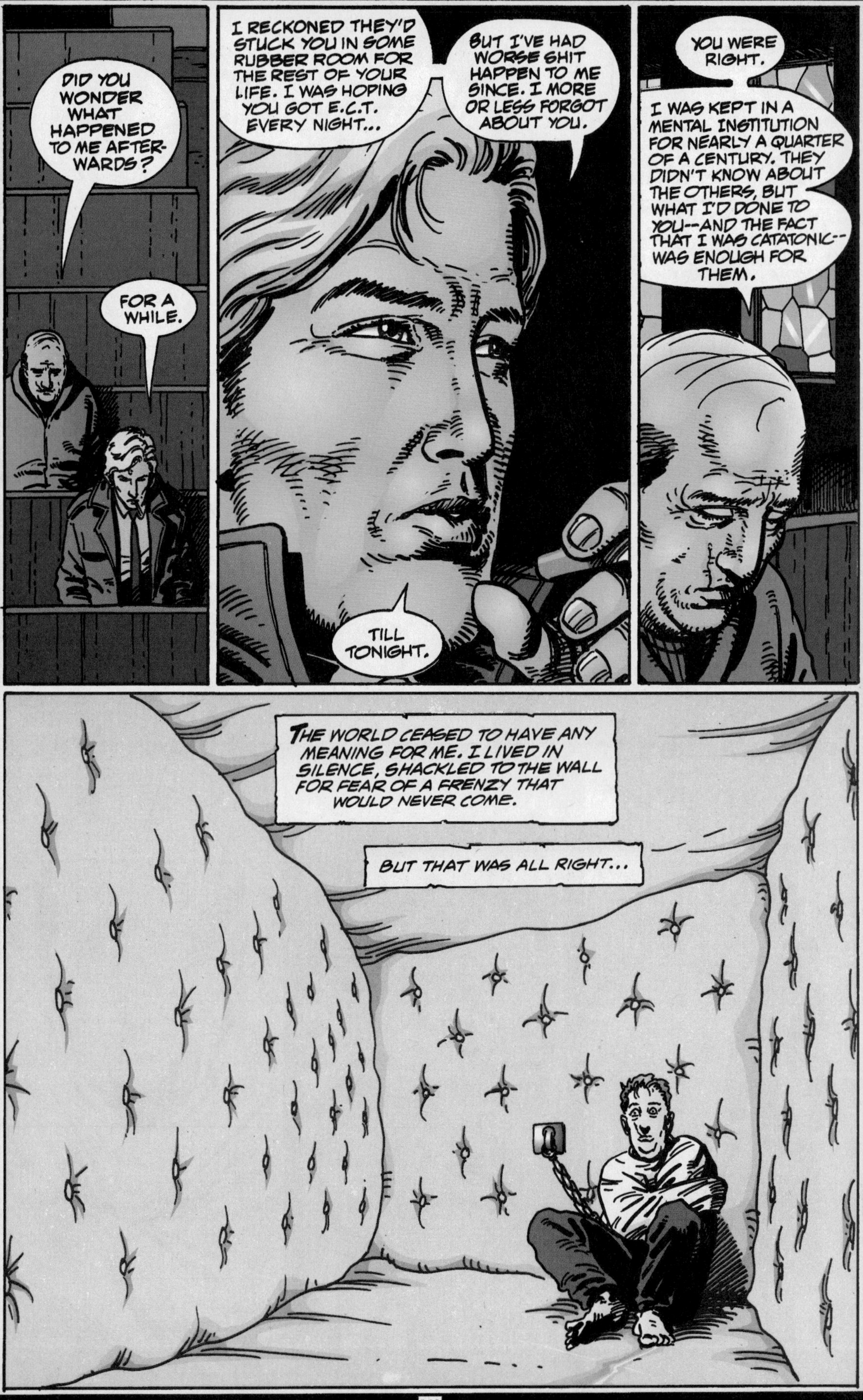
DID YOU WONDER WHAT HAPPENED TO ME AFTER-WARDS?
FOR A WHILE.
I RECKONED THEY'D STUCK YOU IN SOME RUBBER ROOM FOR THE REST OF YOUR LIFE. I WAS HOPING YOU GOT E.C.T. EVERY NIGHT...
BUT I'VE HAD WORSE SHIT HAPPEN TO ME SINCE. I MORE OR LESS FORGOT ABOUT YOU.
TILL TONIGHT.
YOU WERE RIGHT.
I WAS KEPT IN A MENTAL INSTITUTION FOR NEARLY A QUARTER OF A CENTURY. THEY DIDN'T KNOW ABOUT THE OTHERS, BUT WHAT I'D DONE TO YOU--AND THE FACT THAT I WAS CATATONIC--WAS ENOUGH FOR THEM.
THE WORLD CEASED TO HAVE ANY MEANING FOR ME. I LIVED IN SILENCE, SHACKLED TO THE WALL FOR FEAR OF A FRENZY THAT WOULD NEVER COME.
BUT THAT WAS ALL RIGHT...

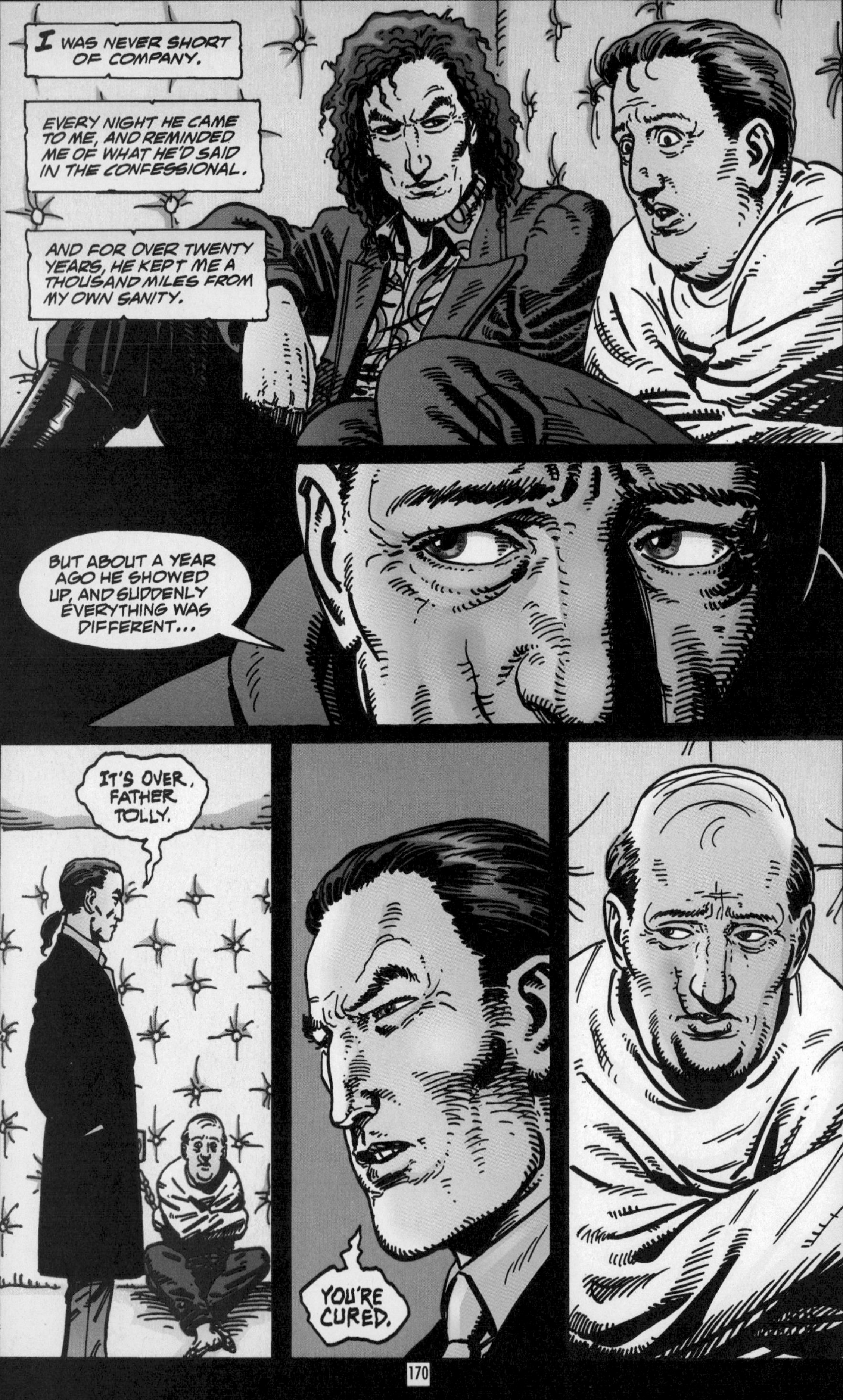
I WAS NEVER SHORT OF COMPANY.
EVERY NIGHT HE CAME TO ME, AND REMINDED ME OF WHAT HE'D SAID IN THE CONFESSIONAL.
AND FOR OVER TWENTY YEARS, HE KEPT ME A THOUSAND MILES FROM MY OWN SANITY.
BUT ABOUT A YEAR AGO HE SHOWED UP, AND SUDDENLY EVERYTHING WAS DIFFERENT...
IT'S OVER, FATHER TOLLY.
YOU'RE CURED.

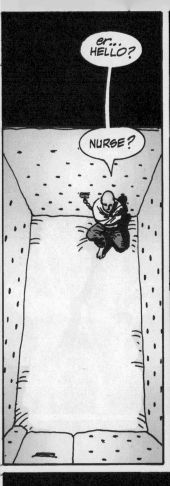

er... HELLO?

NURSE?

AND I *WAS* CURED. ENOUGH FOR THE DOCTORS, ANYWAY.

OH, IT TOOK A YEAR FOR THEM TO BE SURE, BUT THEY'D NO MONEY LEFT TO SPEND ON ME. MENTAL HEALTH IS NOT THE PRIORITY IT ONCE WAS.

I WAS RELEASED THIS AFTER-NOON.

I... I DON'T KNOW WHY HE LET ME GO. I HAVEN'T FORGOTTEN HIS CONFESSION, OR WHAT IT MADE ME DO, BUT... SOMEHOW THE PERSPECTIVE HAS CHANGED...

THAT'S WHY I CAME HERE, TO... TO...

TO ASK...

WHICH REALLY JUST LEAVES ONE QUESTION, DOESN'T IT?

WHAT *WAS* HIS CONFESSION?

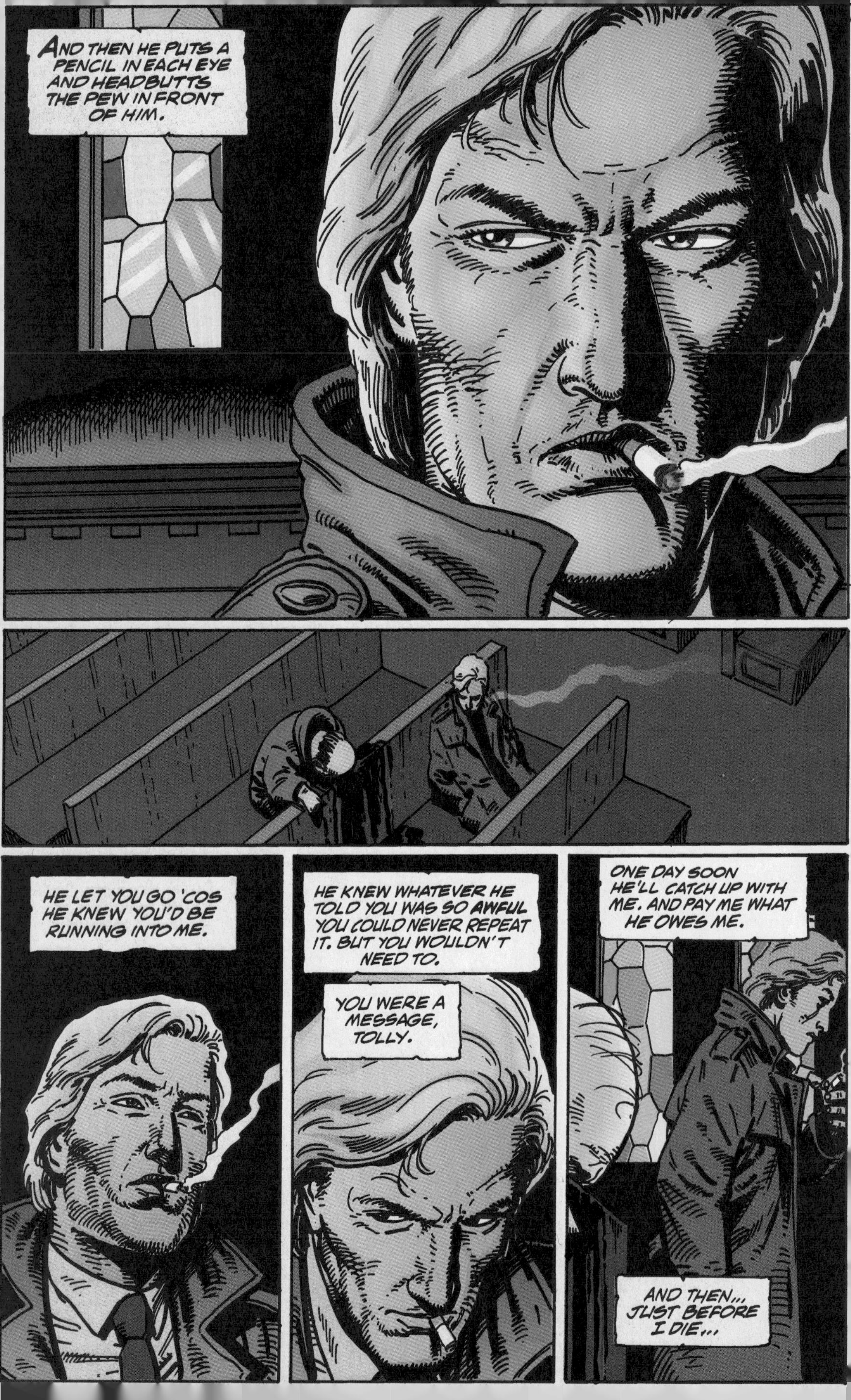
AND THEN HE PUTS A PENCIL IN EACH EYE AND HEADBUTTS THE PEW IN FRONT OF HIM.
HE LET YOU GO 'COS HE KNEW YOU'D BE RUNNING INTO ME.
HE KNEW WHATEVER HE TOLD YOU WAS SO AWFUL YOU COULD NEVER REPEAT IT. BUT YOU WOULDN'T NEED TO.
YOU WERE A MESSAGE, TOLLY.
ONE DAY SOON HE'LL CATCH UP WITH ME. AND PAY ME WHAT HE OWES ME.
AND THEN... JUST BEFORE I DIE...

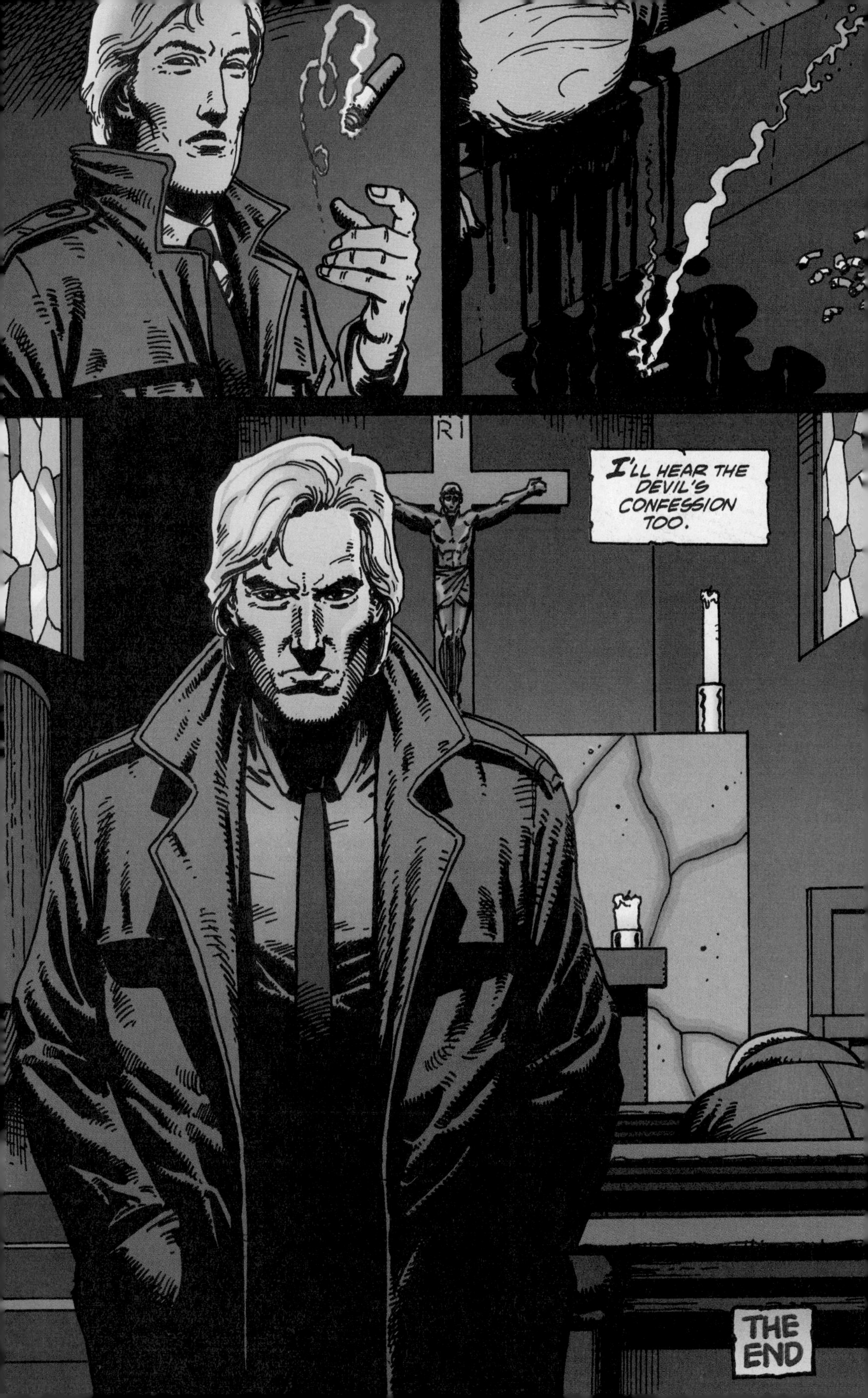

I'LL HEAR THE DEVIL'S CONFESSION TOO.
THE END

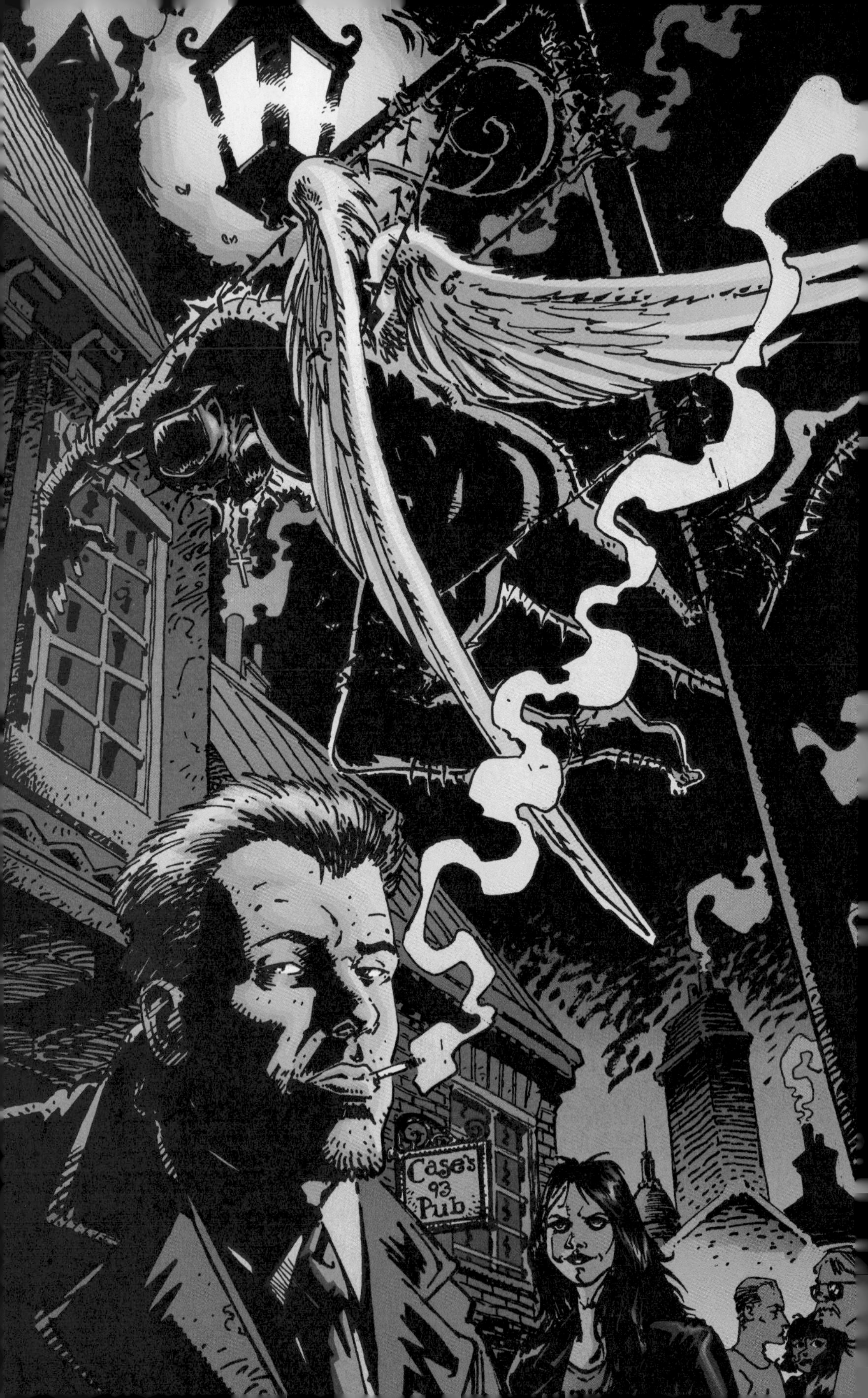
Case's
93
Pub

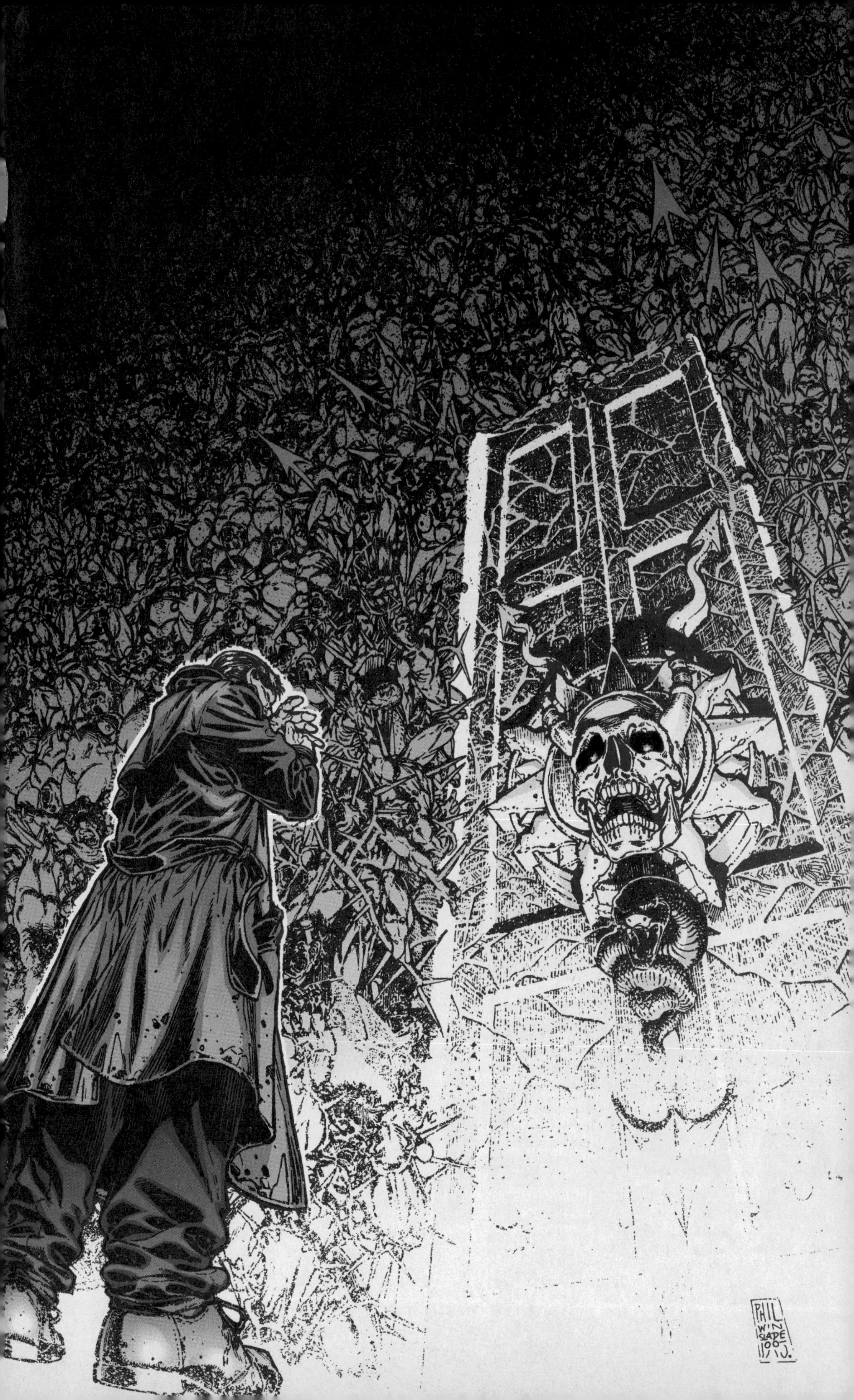
PHIL
WIN
SLADE
'00